Washington County Virginia

BIRTHS AND DEATHS

1853–1892

(incomplete)

↜↝

Deborah Campbell Moore
and
Doris Galliher Stephens

Heritage Books
2024

HERITAGE BOOKS

AN IMPRINT OF HERITAGE BOOKS, INC.

Books, CDs, and more—Worldwide

For our listing of thousands of titles see our website
at
www.HeritageBooks.com

A Facsimile Reprint
Published 2024 by
HERITAGE BOOKS, INC.
Publishing Division
5810 Ruatan Street
Berwyn Heights, MD 20740

Originally published 1984
Sponsored by Holston Territory Genealogical Society
in Conjuncton with Bristol Public Library

International Standard Book Number
Paperbound: 978-0-7884-7781-2

INTRODUCTION

Prior to the initiation of statewide record keeping in 1913, birth and death records were not kept consistently in Virginia. Washington County appears to have kept these vital records fairly meticulously from 1853-1859, and sketchily during 1870, 1871 and 1892.

It is necessary to make clear to the researcher that, while this index includes all of those birth and death records which are to be found in the courthouse in Abingdon, it does not include all records which were kept. Apparently, the county authorities did not always retain a local copy of the records when reporting to the state; thus, the Archives Division, Virginia State Library, has microfilmed records in addition to those found in the county courthouse. Since these additional records, microfilmed from the originals held by the Virginia Bureau of Vital Records, cannot be borrowed on inter-library loan or purchased on microfilm they are not available to the compilers and could not be included in this index. The Archives Division of the State Library of Virginia indicates that incomplete records for the following years may be consulted at the State Library, or, providing the year of birth or death is known, may be obtained for a fee from BUREAU OF VITAL RECORDS AND HEALTH STATISTICS, James Madison Building, P.O. Box 1000; Richmond, Virginia 23208. These years include:

1860-61	1881 (births only)
1865-66	1882-1894
1872-79	1896
1880	

There are no records for the years 1897-1912. The records herein indexed include 1853-1859, 1870-71, and 1892. The compilers have, to the best of their ability, transcribed all pertinent information. Allowances must be made for the difficulty encountered in deciphering the handwritten records which are, in some cases, virtually illegible. All entries have been copied exactly as originally entered, and the researcher must be aware that names often were misspelled.

The original record lacked page numbers. To facilitate locating names in the original record, page numbers have been assigned, and a key to locating each page is provided.

The following abbreviations are used in the text:

y =	years	S =	slave
m =	months	M =	male
d =	days	F =	female
W =	Caucasian	A =	born alive
C =	free Black before Civil War;	D =	born death
	all Blacks after the War.	n.n. =	no name (child not named)

In the interest of space, occupations also are abbreviated, and a table of the abbreviations is included.

All entries are alphabetical by surname, except for slaves entered by given name.

Birth are listed as follows: The first column gives the name of the childre, with the date of birth immediately below. Column 2 lists on the first line the child's race and sex and whether or not it was a live birth. The page number in the original record is then given, then the abbreviation for the father's occupation, and the specific town or district in Washington County where the child was born, if known. In the case of slave children, the mother's name is given if it was listed; also the name of the owner. In most cases, births were reported by one of the parents; however, in some cases a neighbor or relative reported the birth, and in these cases, the name of the person reporting the birth is given on the third line. An index of these names is provided. The following example is given for clarification:

> CLARK, SARAH JANE   WFA   Page 3   F
>   Sept, 1853   Parents: Andw. & Margaret Clark
>   Reported by Jacob Clark, father of father

Sarah Jane Clark was born in September of 1853. The exact day of her birth was not recorded. She was Caucasian, female, and born alive (WFA). Her father's occupation was farmer (F). Her parents were Andrew and Margaret Clark, and Jacob Clark, her paternal grandfather, reported the birth.

Deaths are alphabetized in the same way as births. Entries are as follows: In the first column, the name of the deceased is given. Indented immediately underneath is the date and cause of death. In the second column will be found an abbreviation indicating race and sex of the deceased, followed by the page in the original where the entry can be found and by an abbreviation for the deceased's occupation if given. The town or district in the county where the deceased resided, if available, is also on this line. Underneath is, if available, the names of the deceased's parents or the owner's name in the case of a slave. Also listed is the name of the individual's spouse, if given, and the name and relationship of the person who reported the death, if other than a parent or spouse. An example:

> CRABTREE, JAS. S. (60y)   WM   Page 23   F   Kinderhook Twp.
>   24 July 1871 - unknown: reported by Zackariah Crabtree, son

James S. Crabtree, aged 60, Caucasian, male, farmer, resident of Kinderhook Township. Date of death: 24 July 1871. Cause of death - unknown. Death reported by son Zackariah. Names of deceased's parents not given.

Included is an index to surnames other than those of the main entries. These include, for example, the parents of married women and the names of slaveowners.

Doris Galliher Stephens
Deborah Campbell Moore
Bristol, Virginia   March 1984

OCCUPATIONS

Attorney at law - A
Baptist minister - BP
Barber - BA
Blacksmith - B
Bookkeeper - BO
Bookman - BK
Brakeman - BN
Brickmason - BR
Butcher - BU
Cabinet maker - CM
Carpenter - C
Cigar maker - CI
Clerk - CL
Com'r of revenue - CR
Constable - CN
Cook - CO
Cooper - CP
Dentist - D
Depot agent - DA
Deputy collector - EC
Doctor - DO
Druggist - DG
Drummer - DM
Editor - E
Electrician - EL
Engineer - EN
Farmer - F
Hatter - H
House carpenter - HC
Housekeeper - HK
Innkeeper - I
Ironmonger - IR
Janitor - J
Keeps livery stable - KL
Labourer - L

Lawyer - LW
Mason - M
Mechanic - MC
Merchant - MR
Miller - ML
Millwright - MW
Minister - MN
Ordinary - O
Overseer - OV
Painter - PA
Parson - P
Physician - PH
Porter - PO
Potter - PR
Printer - PT
Professor - PF
R.R. employee - R
Saddler - S
Sawyer - SW
Section boss - SB
Sheriff - SF
Shoemaker - SH
Stone engraver - SE
Stone mason - SM
Student - ST
Tailor - T
Tanner - TR
Teacher - TC
Teamster - TM
Tinker - TK
Undertaker - U
Wagoner or wagonmaker - W
Weaver - WE
Wheelwright - WH

NAME AT TOP OF PAGE - BIRTHS

Page	Name	Date of Birth
1	McCready, Elizabeth M.	2 Oct. 1853
2	Hill, Lucinda Berton	20 May 1853
3	Watson, Margaret Eliz.	6 May 1853
4	Edmundson, Rachel C.	10 Dec. 1853
5	Tilson, Nancy Catharine	2 Jan. 1853
6	Baugh, Milly Vance C.	7 Jan. 1853
7	Marsh, Martha A.	Sept. 1853
8	Berry, Sarah E	20 Jan. 1853
9	Charles	15 Dec. 1853
10	Smith, Elizabeth	30 March 1854
11	Davis, Sarah	6 July 1854
12	McDaniel, Nancy Margaret	10 June 1854
13	Hill, Newton J.	5 Aug. 1854
14	Campbell, Rhoda Ann	26 Aug. 1854
15	Wohlford, Harriet S.	4 April 1854
16	Porterfield, Wilson Graham	15 Oct. 1855
17	Milner, Josephine	5 March 1855
18	McQuown, Wm. Parker	12 March 1855
19	Anderson	7 March 1855
20	Susan	14 July 1855
21	Lowrey	25 Feb. 1855
22	Fickle, Isabella C.	25 Nov. 1855
23	Clark, Isaac W.	3 Nov. 1855
24	Carter, Rosanna C.	7 Oct. 1856
25	White, Frank C	8 April 1856
26	Hurt, Elizabeth	10 or 18 Aug. 1856
27	Hagy, Martha A.	15 June 1856
28	Debusk, Jenette A.	21 Feb. 1856
29	Jones, Franklin J.	6 May 1856
30	Andrew	12 Sept. 1856
31	McClelland, S.W.	25 or 27 March 1856
32	Cunningham, Mary E.	20 Dec. 1857
33	Lukin, Sarah F.	5 Jan. 1857
34	Rose, Jane	12 May 1857
35	Akers, Jos. M.	26 Nov. 1857
36	Howard, Marthy C.	20 Nov. 1857
37	McCormack, Ed. H.	27 Oct. 1857
38	Widener, And. W.	20 July 1857
39	Carmack, H.	19 Dec. 1858
40	Hickman, B.S.	15 March 1858
41	Potter, Reuben	14 May 1858
42	Whicker, Saml.	4 Oct. 1858
43	Frank	15 March 1858
44	Noland, W. King N.	24 Sept. 1858
45	Thomas, S.V.C.	17 July 1858
46	Clark, Fountain B.	8 Aug. 1859
47	Heniger, George R.	5 Dec. 1859
48	Nunley	16 May 1859
49	Thompson, John T.	20 March 1859
50	Fleenor	27 March 1859

51	Moore, A.B.	14 May 1859
52	Weathers, M.A.E.	19 April 1859
53	Rumbly, James	14 Aug. 1871
54	Dickson	20 April 1871
55	Braudy, Joseph	1 April 1870
56	Debusk, Maggie Matilda	1870
57	Sheets, Willie Josephine	1870
58	Hughes, Alfred	25 Oct. 1870
59	Doss, Monroe	4 Sept. 1892
60	Casey, Rachel	20 Jan. 1892
61	Farnsworth, Carl R.	2 May 1892
62	Jackson, Julia	15 June 1892
63	McThenia, Lucy A.	10 April 1892
64	Smith, Mamie A.	25 June 1892
65	Vannoy, Frank	11 Nov. 1892
66	Barb, James	10 Jan. 1892
67	Ingle, C.E.	10 July 1892
68	Smith, Minnie	27 Dec. 1892
69	Collings, Jane	5 March 1892
70	Singleton	16 Nov. 1892
71	Cox, Loyd	20 June 1892
72	Mumpower, Laura J.	3 Oct. 1892
73	Hines	18 Dec. 1892
74	Johnson, George E.	4 Feb. 1892

WASHINGTON COUNTY, VIRGINIA

DEATHS

* Name at top of page

Page	Name	Date of Death
1	Logan, John S.	4 November 1853
2	George	February 1853
3	Wright, John J.	13 July 1854
4	Larimer, Hetty K	6 August 1854
5	Burk, Martha	March 1854
6	Lock, Mary A.	15 December 1854
7	Patsey	4 May 1854
8	Garnes, Elizabeth	11 September 1855
9	Motern, E.C.T.	31 July 1855
10	Reuben	August 1855
11	Price, Elisha	15 March 1856
12	Wooten, Elizabeth	18 June 1856
13	Howell, W.T.	26 February 1856
14	McCloud, [n.n.]	7 June 1857
15	Edwards, Rachel	20 November 1857
16	Spurrier, Sallie	20 November 1857
17	Fleenor, W.J.L.	3 July 1858
18	Shankle, Lafayette M.	14 June 1858
19	Larimore, David	9 January 1858
20	Fanny	15 September 1859
21	Vanhuss, Benjamin	26 December 1859
22	McConnall, Abram	26 March 1859
23	Bumbgardner, [n.n.]	5 April 1871
24	Debusk, Dorcas Almeda	1871
25	Authenwreath, Mary	5 June 1892
26	Keller, Eva J.	28 October 1892
27	Scott, Sarah	15 [March] 1892
28	Allen, Sarah E.	6 January 1892
29	Worley, Jno. W.	12 May 1892
30	Brice, Robt. M.	8 August 1892

* Original pages are un-numbered. Page numbers were assigned by indexers. This list showing the first entry at the top of each page is provided as a finding aid for those who wixh to consult the original record at Abingdon or the microfilm at the Virginia State Library.

Washington County, Va.

Established 1776-77
County Seat: Abingdon

APPROX. SCALE:
1/4" : 1 MILE

VIRGINIA

TENNESSEE

SMYTH COUNTY

RUSSELL COUNTY

SCOTT COUNTY

GRAYSON COUNTY

JOHNSON COUNTY

SULLIVAN COUNTY

NORTH FORK MAGISTERIAL DISTRICT

SALTVILLE MAGISTERIAL DISTRICT

HOLSTON MAGISTERIAL DISTRICT

KINDERHOOK MAGISTERIAL DISTRICT

GOODSON MAGISTERIAL DISTRICT

RICH VALLEY

POOR 802 VALLEY

Holston River

North Fork

Middle Fork

South Fork Holston River

Holston River

South Holston Reservoir

SALTVILLE

MENDOTA

HOLSTON

ABINGDON

BRISTOL

DAMASCUS

Drawn by
Shelby F. Edwards
February 12, 1944

UNNAMED SLAVES

SMA   Page 3
Date: June 1853
Mother: Rachel
Owner: Jno. H. Coleman

SFA   Page 3
Date: July 1853
Mother: Eliza
Owner: Jno. H. Coleman

SFA (twin) Page 6
Date: 1 December 1853
Mother: Dolly
Owner: Jonas Smyth, farmer

SFD (twin) Page 6
Date: 1 December 1853
Mother: Dolly
Owner: Jonas Smyth, farmer

SFA   Page 1
Date: 13 December 1853
Mother: Jenette
Owner: Wm. M. Morison

SMA   Page 11
Date: 31 May 1854
Mother: Amanda
Owner: John Maiden

SFD   Page 13
Date: 23 August 1854
Mother: Mariah
Owner: Jacob Tool
Place: North Fork

SFA   Page 13
Date: October 1854
Mother: Mariah
Master: Whitley Fullen
Place: Poor Valley

SFD   Page 15
Date: 24 December 1854
Master: John Gibson

S_A   Page: 18
Date: 3 January 1855
Mother: Hannah
Owner: Isaac McQuown

SFA   Page 32
Date: 19 January 1855
Owner: Hugh A. McChesney

SFA   Page 23
Date: 4 March 1855
Owner: Jno. F. Preston

SMA   Page 23
Date: 19 March 1855
Owner: E. Lathem

SFA   Page 23
Date: 19 April 1855
Owner: S.W. Montgomery

SFA (twins) Page 23
Date: 20 June 1855
Owner: Jno. Corry

S_D   Page 20
Date: August 1855
Mother: Mary
Owner: James Kelly
Reported by James Kelly, owner

SFA   Page 16
Date: September 1855
Mother: Fanny
Owner: Wm. M. Morison

SFD   Page 23
Date: 29 October 1855
Owner: Jacob Merchant
Remarks: 'stillborn'

SFA   Page 16
Date: November 1855
Mother: Jane
Owner: Wm. M. Morison

SFA (twin to Ellen) Page 27
Date: 13 June 1856
Owner: Elizabeth Lathim

SMA   Page 27
Date: July 1856
Owner: S.E. Goodson

UNNAMED SLAVES, (CONT'D)

SFA   Page 27
Date: 21 September 1856
Owner: W.B. Campbell

SFA   Page 27
Date: 29 November 1856
Owner: Thos. Brown

SFA   Page: 39
Date: 1 January 1858
Owner: J.M. Hamilton

SFA   Page 42
Date: 1 May 1858
Owner: W.B. Dickenson

SMA   Page 41
Date: 8 September 1858
Owner: John Preston

SMA   Page 41
Date: 20 September 1858
Owner: Jas. Vance

SM_   Page 40
Date: 4 November 1858
Owner: S.W. Montgomery

SFA   Page 47
Date: 14 August 1859
Master: Henry Mock

SMA   Page 49
Date: 13 December 1859
Owner: Wm. B. Campbell

ABLE, ELIZABETH
7 Dec. 1871
WFA   Page 53   F   Abingdon Tw
Parents: Joseph & Nancy Able

ABLE, REBECCA S
16 Nov. 1892
WFA   Page 68   F   North Fork
Parents: Valentine & Lucy A. Able

ADAMS, CINTHA A
15 April 1892
WFA   Page 68   North Fork
Parents: James M. & Kate Adams

ADELINE
17 May 1853
SFA   Page 9
Owner: M.R. White

ADISON
17 May 1853
SMA   Page 45
Master: Samuel Dunn

AGGA
15 July 1859
SFA   Page 51
Owner: Wm. A. Preston

AKERS, [n.n.]
21 June 1892
WMA   Page 59   MC
Parents: W.C. & Amanda Akers

AKERS, JOS. M.
26 Nov. 1857
WMA   Page 35   F
Parents: Oscar & E.J. Akers

AKERS, VIVIAN V
9 April 1892
WFA   Page 59   F
Parents: E.W. & Bettie Akers

ALDERSON, GEORGE C
5 Feb. 1857
WMA   Page 35   F
Parents: Geo. W. & Liddy Alderson

ALDERSON, LYDIA
1 Sept. 1859
WFA   Page 45   F
Parents: George W. & Lydia Aldersor

ALDERSON, MARY ANN
5 Jan. 1855
WFA   Page 17   F
Parents: Geo. W. & Lydia Alderson

ALDERSON, MARY ANN M.M.
14 Jan. 1854
WFA   Page 13   F   Middle Fork
Parents: George W. & Lydia Aldersor

ALDERSON, VIRGINIA C
14 Feb. 1853
WFA   Page 3   F
Parents: Geo. W. & Lydia Alderson

ALEX'R
22 Sept. 1855
SMA   Page 17
Mother: Betsey
Owner: Wm. S. Wisely

ALFRED
15 Sept. 1853
SMA   Page 8
Owner: Milton White

ALFRED, ISAAC T
8 Jan. 1858
WMA   Page 38   B
Parents: Isaac & Mary J. ALFREDS

ALFRED, M.R.
25 Nov. 1853
WFA   Page 8   F
Parents: Isaac & Mary J. Alfred

ALFRED, SARAH JANE
31 May 1853
WFA   Page 1
Parents: William & Amanda Alfred

ALFRED, SUSAN F
8 Nov. 1854
WFA   Page 10   F
Parents: William & Amanda Jane Alf

ALICE
12 Oct. 1855
SFA   Page 23
Owner: Peter S. Hanby

ALICE
    19 March 1857
WFA   Page 34
Owner: J.A. Teeter

ALLEN
    15 Oct. 1857
SMA   Page 34
Owner: A.R. Preston

ALLEN, MILLARD F
    26 Nov. 1856
WMA   Page 28   F
Parents: Jeremiah & Charlotte Allen

ALLEN, STERLING W
    17 Aug. 1856
WMA   Page 30   F
Parents: McCay & Martha Allen

ALLISON, WM. E.
    30 April 1892
WMA   Page 59
Parents: James & Virg. Allen

ALMAROAD, BERRY I.
    5 March 1856
WMA   Page 24   B
Parents: Jno. & Amanda Almaroad

ALMARODE, WM. W.
    31 July 1854
WMA   Page 14   F
Parents: Jno. & Amanda Almarode

AMANDA
    29 Oct. 1859
SFA   Page 51
Owner: S.W. Montgomery
    Reported by A.C. Cummings, admr. of owner

ANDERSON, [n.n.]
    7 March 1855
CMA   Page 19   L
Parents: Thomas & Aaline Anderson
    Born in Smyth Co., Va.; father's residence in Washington Co., Va.

ANDIS, CORA
    20 April 1892
WFA   Page 68   F   North Fork Dist.
Parents: Newton & Marg. Andis

ANDIS, ELIZA A.
    20 Sept. 1856
WFA   Page 25   F
Parents: Peter & Harriet Andis

ANDREW
    29 April 1855
SMA   Page 23
Owner: R.T. Legard

ANDREW
    20 June 1855
SMA   Page 17
Mother: Mariah
Owner: Margret Hawthorn

ANDREW
    30 June 1856
SMA   Page 29
Owner: Arthur Hutton

ANDREW
    12 Sept. 1856
SMA   Page 30
Owner: Isaac Horne

ANN
    19 March 1855
SFA   Page 23
Owner: S.A. Teeter

ANN
    1 May 1856
SFA   Page 27
Owner: Jas. L. Davis

ANN
    13 June 1856
SFA   Page 27
Owner: E.E. Lathim

ANN
    3 April 1859
SFA   Page 45
Master: Absalom Beatie

ANNET
    15 Sept. 1853
SFA   Page 1   Saltville
Mistress: Louisa P. King

ANOREN
8 Nov. 1857
SMA   Page 35
Owner: Elizabeth Alderson

ARCHER, WM. M.
22 March 1892
WMA   Page 59   F
Parents: B.F. & Susan E. Archer

ARDEN, ABRAHAM
22 Sept. 1855
WMA   Page 16   CP   Saltville
Parents: Abraham & Kisiah Arden

ARDEN, RACHEL BRANCH
23 May 1853
WFA   Page 1   CP   Saltville
Parents: Abram & Kizeah Arden

AREN, CARSON M
19 June 1857
WMA   Page 31   F
Parents: Wm. [S.] & Ruthan Aren

ARNETT, LEWIS F
1 Oct. 1892
WMA   Page 59   F
Parents: W.F. & Kate Arnett

ARNETT, MARY
2 March 1859
WFA   Page 45   F
Parents: James & Elizabeth Arnett

ARNETT, SARAH
9 May 1859
WFA   Page 45   F
Parents: William & Rebecca Arnett

ARNETT, WILLIAM PAINES
July 1854
WMA   Page 10   F
Parents: William & Rebecca J. Arnett

ARNOLD, JACOB W
23 August 1856
WMA   Page 24   F
Parents: Wm. & Eliz. Arnold

ARNOLD, JAMES
27 Nov. 1892
WMA   Page 72   F   Abingdon
Parents: Wm. & Nannie Arnold

ARNOLD, LOUIS
24 July 1892
WMA   Page 68   F   North Fork Dist.
Parents: Gabe & Ann Arnold

ARNOLD, M.A.
16 Oct. 1859
WFA   Page 49   F
Parents: James & Lucretia Arnold

ARNOLD, MARTHA E
24 Aug. 1858
WFA   Page 38   C
Parents: Wm. & Elizabeth Arnold

ARNOLD, SAMUEL B
April 1853
WMA   Page 5   F
Parents: Samuel & Ellen Arnold

ARNOLD, SUSAN A
13 March 1892
WFA   Page 58   F   North Fork Dist.
Parents: Gabe & Margaret Arnold

ARTHUR
6 March 1855
SMA   Page 16
Mother: Dorcas
Owner: Wm. C. Edmondson

ASTRAP, JESSIE
14 Dec. 1853
WMA   Page 2   TR   Poor Valley
Parents: Andrew J. & Melinda Astrap

ASTRAP, NANCY
10 May 1853
WFA   Page 2   TR
Parents: Oliver & Mary Astrap

ASTRAP, OLIVER
15 July 1855
WMA   Page 20   F
Parents: Oliver & Frances Astrap

AUTHENWREATH, MARY
1 July 1892
WFA   Page 59   TM
Parents: Frank & Mary Authenwreath

AYERS, RACHEL
     1 Aug. 1856
WFA   Page 30   F
Parents: Jno. I. & Mary Ayers

AYRES, JOSEPH
     15 May 1859
WMA   Page 45   F
Parents: John & Mary Ayres

BAILEY, [n.n.]
     19 Sept. 1892
WFD   Page 59   F
Parents: G.M.D. & Sallie L. Bailey

BAILEY, FLORENCE B
     27 Sept. 1856
WFA   Page 31   F
Parents: Robt. & Delphia Bailey

BAILEY, FRANK
     18 June 1855
WMA   Page 16   F
Parents: James A. & Harriet Bailey

BAILEY, MARY JANE
     13 March 1855
WFA   Page 17   F
Parents: Robert & Delila Bailey

BAILEY, MILTON
     30 Nov. 1853
WMA   Page 4   F
Parents: Jas. A. & Harriet Bailey

BAILEY, SAMPSON T
     22 Jan. 1853
WMA   Page 1   F
Parents: Robert & Delila Bailey

BAILY, DAVID H
     8 April 1870
     Reported by J.A. Baily, Jr.
WMA   Page 57   MC   Kinderhook
Parents: Jas. A. & Isabella Baily

BAKER, ANN L
     26 Aug. 1854
WFA   Page 15   PT
Parents: Henry W. & M.S.F. Baker

BAKER, EMMA J
     23 Dec. 1856
WFA   Page 26   PT
Parents: H.W. & M.F. Baker

BAKER, S.A.
     16 Feb. 1853
WFA   Page 8   S
Parents: Isaac & Virginia Baker

BAKER, SALLIE
     29 Nov. 1871
CFA   Page 53   F   Abingdon Twp.
Parents: Walker & Ellen Baker

BAKER, WILLIAM F
     24 Dec. 1858
SMA   Page 42   F
Parents: William & Ellen Baker

BALDWIN, [n.n.]
     25 Aug. 1892
WMA   Page 72   F   Abingdon
Parents: W.T. & A.C. Baldwin

BARB, JAMES
     10 Jan. 1892
WMA   Page 56   F   Kinderhook
Parents: John & Susan Barb

BARB, LAFAYETTE G
     27 Aug. 1859
WFA   Page 49   F
Parents: Gid. & Ellen Barb

BARBARY, [n.n.]
     March 1853
WFD   Page 4   F
Parents: Smittie & Rebecca Barbary

BARBARY, HANNAH JANE
     11 Feb. 1853
WFA   Page 5   F
Parents: Jumbo & Sally Barbary

BARBARY, JAMES S.B.
     1870
WMA   Page 55   F   Glade Spring Twp.
Parents: Peter J. & Mary Ann Barbary

BARBERY, MARTHA W
     2 March 1857
WFA   Page 35   B
Parents: Jno. & Eliza BARBARY

BARE, WM. R.
15 March 1892
WMA   Page 59   F
Parents: Mathew & Ellen Bare

BARKER, A.F., JR.
20 Jan. 1892
WMA   Page 66   F   Kinderhook
Parents: A.F. & Mattie Barker

BARKER, CHARLES F
1870
WMA   Page 55   MC   Glade Spring
Parents: John H. & Rachel C. Barker

BARKER, [CLEUT]
June 1892
WMA   Page 66   F   Kinderhook
Parents: E.C. & Martha Barker

BARKER, EMMA C. (twin)
11 April 1870
WFA   Page 57   Kinderhook
Parents: Daniel S. & Rhoda A. Barker

BARKER, F.W.
18 July 1853
WMA   Page 6   F
Father: Sherwood M. Barker

BARKER, FRANCIS M
2 March 1855
WMA   Page 22   F
Parents: Wm. B. & Lucinda Barker

BARKER, JNO. B.T.
22 March 1857
WMA   Page 31   F
Parents: Geo. & Mary Barker

BARKER, LILLY Y
5 Oct. 1892
WFA   Page 66   F
Parents: D.S. & Rhoda Barker

BARKER, LOUISA V. (twin)
11 April 1870
WFA   Page 57   Kinderhook
Parents: Daniel S. & Rhoda A. Barker

BARKER, LUCY A
5 January 1857
WFA   Page 57   Kinderhook
Parents: Jno. & Mary Barker

BARKER, MARGRET E
29 Dec. 1857
WFA   Page 51   F
Parents: Joel L. & Louisa Barker

BARKER, MARTHA S
1870
WFA   Page 57   Kinderhook
Parents: Solomon & Nancy Barker

BARKER, MARY
Feb. 1892
WFA   Page 66   F   Kinderhook
Parents: C.C. & Yelina Barker

BARKER, MARY
24 July 1870
WFA   Page 57   Kinderhook
Parents: Martin & Matilda Barker

BARKER, NANCY
13 Feb. 1856
WFA   Page 26   F
Parents: Edward & Sarah Barker

BARKER, O.C.
7 Sept. 1853
WMA   Page 6   F
Father: Joel S. Barker

BARKER, OLIVER
1870
WMA   Page 57   Kinderhook
Parents: Edwd. & Hannah Barker

BARKER, RACHEL
19 July 1854
WFA   Page 14   F
Parents: Edward & Sarah Barker

BARKER, RACHEL E
23 March 1856
WFA   Page 26   F
Parents: Jos. & Isabella Barker

BARKER, RHODA
10 August 1853
WFA   Page 6   F
Father: Geo. Barker

BARKER, THOS. H.
9 Oct. 1856
WMA   Page 25   F
Parents: Granville & E. Barker

BARKER, W.K.
    17 Nov. 1859
WMA   Page 49   F
Parents: Henry & Ellen Barker

BARKER, WM.
    4 Feb. 1858
WMA   Page 38   F
Parents: Geo. & Mary Barker

BARLE, DAVID R
    15 Aug. 1858
WMA   Page 42   F
Parents: Jacob & Sarah Barle

BARLO, W.C.
    1 Aug. 1858
WMA   Page 42   F
Parents: Joseph & Sarah Barlo

BARLOW, [n.n.]
    24 March 1856
WFA   Page 28   F
Parents: Jacob & Sarah Barlow

BARLOW, CHS. J.
    16 Feb. 1856
WMA   Page 29
Parents: Jos. & Sarah Barlow

BARLOW, GEORGE W
    13 Sept. 1855
WMA   Page 19   F
Parents: Jonathan & Nancy Barlow

BARLOW, JACOB
    20 Aug. 1854
WFA   Page 11   F
Parents: Jacob & Sally Barlow

BARLOW, JAMES
    24 July 1854
WMA   Page 13   Rush Creek
Mother: Rachel Barlow

BARLOW, MARG. L.
    25 July 1892
WFA   Page 59   F
Parents: David & Hannah Barlow

BARLOW, MARIAN ALICE
    4 April 1853
WFA   Page 5   F
Parents: Joseph & Sally Barlow

BARLOW, REBECCA see [PIERCE], FRANCIS

BARLOW, SAMUEL DUNN
    29 Sept. 1855
WMA   Page 19   F
Parents: John & Member Barlow

BARLOW, SUSAN C
    19 May 1854
WFA   Page 9   F
Parents: Jonathan & Nancy Barlow

BARNETT, MIN. M.
    10 Oct. 1892
WFA   Page 59   F
Parents: A.G. & Cassie Barnett

BARB, MARION W
    12 Nov. 1856
WMA   Page 26   F
Parents: Lacy I. & Eliza'th Barb

BARR, DOUGLAS S
    25 Aug. 1854
WMA   Page 15   DO
Parents: Wm. F. & M.E.P. Barr

BARRISTER, ISAAC
    22 Aug.1853
WMA   Page 5
Mother: Julia Barrister

BARRISTER, ISAAC ALLEN
    3 Feb. 1853
WMA   Page 5   F
Parents: Jas. W. & Lydia Barrister

BARROW, CLARRA L
    1870
WFA   Page 55   F   Glade Spring Twp.
Parents: Jas. W. & Lydia Barrister

BARROW, ISABEL
    12 Sept. 1871
WFA   Page 42   F
Parents: A. Ferd. & Emma Barrow

BAUGH, MILLY VANCE C
    7 Jan. 1853
WFA   Page 6   F
Parents: Caleb & Nancy Baugh

BEAM, JAMES | WMA Page 59
15 Oct. 1892 | Parents: P.M. & Mary Beam

BEATIE, MARY | WFA Page 4 F
18 June 1853 | Parents: Madison & Martha Beatie

BEATTIE, REBECCA J | WFA Page 45 B
10 Jan. 1859 | Parents: Nelson J.M. & Elizabeth Beat

BEATY, [n.n.] | WMD Page 5 B
Aug. 1853 | Parents: Nelson J.M. & Elizabeth Beat

BEATY, THOS. M.P. | WMA Page 27 B
22 June 1856 | Parents: N.J.M. & E.H. Beaty

BECKLEY, REBECCA | WFA Page 42
10 Oct. 1858 | Mother: Ellen BUCKLEY
Reported by Ellen BECKLEY, mother

BELL, JUS. L. | WMA Page 38 F
1 Feb. 1858 | Parents: Wm. & M.E. Bell

BELLAMY, JOHN | WMA Page 66 F Kinderhook
April 1892 | Parents: William & Nancy Bellamy

BELLAMY, JOHN H | WMA Page 66 F Kinderhook
10 Aug. 1892 | Parents: Wm. J. & Hanah Bellamy

BELOMY, JAS. M. | WMA Page 25 F
15 Aug. 1856 | Parents: Thos. & M.E. Belomy

BERRY, [illegible] B | WMA Page 24 F
7 Nov. 1856 | Parents: Jas. S. & Dorcas Berry

BERRY, DOLLY | WFA Page 59 F
17 Dec. 1892 | Parents: Thos. & Sarah J. Berry

BERRY, GEORGE K | WMA Page 15 F
22 Oct. 1854 | Parents: Nathaniel & Isabella Berry

BERRY, HERBERT | WMA Page 59 F
2 Oct. 1892 | Parents: Jessie & Mattie Berry

BERRY, HULDAH F | WFA Page 7 F
19 Sept. 1853 | Parents: Rob't L. & Huldah Berry

BERRY, ROBT. S. | WMA Page 45 F
10 Nov. 1859 | Parents: Robt. S. & Huldah Berry

BERRY, SARAH E | WFA Page 8 F
20 Jan. 1853 | Parents: Jas. S. & Dorcas Berry

BERRY, THOMAS JESSEE | WMA Page 18 F
May 1855 | Parents: John D. & Lucinda Berry

BETSY | SFA Page 34
30 Dec. 1857 | Owner: S.W. Montgomery

BETTERTON, CHAS. | WMA Page 38 MR
31 Oct. 1858 | Parents: W.J. & S.L. Betterton

BETTY | SFA Page 4
Nov. 1853 | Owner: Geo. V. Litchfield

BILL   SFA   Page 34
        8 Nov. 1857   Owner: Margret Moore

BIRCHWELL, EDMUND   WMA   Page 7   F
        30 June 1853   Father: Jno. Birchwell

BIRREL   SMA   Page 23
        1 Oct. 1855   Owner: Rob't F. Preston

BISHOP, GEO. W.H.   WMA   Page 29   F
        3 Sept. 1856   Parents: W.I. & Jane Bishop

BISHOP, JOHN   WMA   Page 13   F   Near Mill Creek
        4 May 1854   Parents: Madison & Emma Bishop

BISHOP, LEVI C   WMA   Page 42   F
        13 Oct. 1858   Parents: Madison & Unis Bishop

BISHOP, MARTHA CORDELIA   WFA   Page 55   F   Glade Spring Twp.
        1870   Parents: Siberius & Margaret Bishop

BISHOP, NANCY V   WFA   Page 42   F
        5 June 1858   Parents: Washington J. & Jane Bishop

BISHOP, RACHEL MARGARET   WFA   Page 19   F
        24 Oct. 1855   Parents: Madison J. & Unice Bishop

BISHOP, SAMUEL   WMA   Page 13   F   Near Mill Creek
        22 Feb. 1854   Parents: Jefferson & Elizabeth Bishop

BLACK, ANNIE   WFA   Page 31   F
        12 Sept. 1857   Parents: Wm. T. & Nannie Black

BLACK, JOHN B   WMA   Page 31   F
        13 July 1857   Parents: John & Susan Black

BLACK, JOHN H   WMA   Page 21   F
        27 June 1855   Parents: Wm. H. & E.C. Black

BLACK, LEWIS   SMA   Page 2
        5 June 1853   Mother: Molly Black
                                        Owner: Thos. Davenport

BLACK, WM. A.   WMA   Page 31   F
        6 April 1856   Parents: Wm. & Mary E. Black

BLACKBURN, BET. M.   WFA   Page 59
        29 April 1892   Parents: D.W. & Amanda Blackburn

BLACKFORD, LIZZI [K]   WFA   Page 27   F
        28 Oct. 1856   Parents: Wm. W. & Mary R. Blackford
        Born in Richmond, Va.; father's residence in 'Richmon'

BLACKFORD, SAMUEL JACKSON   WMA   Page 9   F
        31 Aug. 1854   Parents: Charles & Phoebe Blackford

BLACKLEY, REUBEN L   WMA   Page 24   L
        1 Sept. 1856   Parents: George & Margret Blackley

BLACKWELL, ALEXR. RYBURN   WMA   Page 18   B
        12 May 1854   Parents: Matthew & Elizabeth Blackwell

BLACKWELL, AMANDA   WF_   Page 55   B   Saltville Dist
     13 May 1870   Parents: William & Jane Blackwell

BLACKWELL, C.F.   WMA   Page 72   Abingdon
     26 July 1892   Parents: A.R. & Nancy Blackwell

BLACKWELL, D.C.   WMA   Page 35   B
     6 April 1857   Parents: Matthew & E. Blackwell

BLACKWELL, EL. E.   WFA   Page 59   F
     8 March 1892   Parents: J.A. & Jose Blackwell

BLACKWELL, JOHN D   WMA   Page 9   F
     13 Nov. 1854   Parents: John D. & Elizabeth Blackwel

BLACKWELL, MARTHA   WFA   Page 45   F
     9 June 1858   Parents: Matthew & Rebecca Blackwell

BLACKWELL, MILLIE F   WFA   Page 59   F
     29 Nov. 1892   Parents: D.W. & Mary E. Blackwell

BLACKWELL, SARAH C   WFA   Page 45
     10 July 1859   Parents: John D. & Elizabeth Blackwel

BLAIR, [n.n.]   WF_   Page 57   Kinderhook
     1870   Parents: Pemberton & Mary Blair

BLAIR, ERNEST   CMA   Page 59   L
     15 Sept. 1892   Parents: Henry & Louisa Blair

BLESSING, NANCY E   WFA   Page 25   F
     9 July 1856   Parents: John W. & Cath. Blessing

BLEVINS, A.N.A.   WFA   Page 59   F
     2 January 1892   Parents: Felix & Marth. E. Blevins

BLEVINS, FLORA B   WFA   Page 59   F
     29 March 1892   Parents: Aras & Marth. A. Blevins

BLEVINS, FLORENCE   WFA   Page 70   F   Abingdon Dist
     7 May 1892   Parents: Elcana & Rebecca Blevins

BLEVINS, JAMES M   WMA   Page 35   F
     15 Nov. 1857   Parents: James & Ann Blevins

BLEVINS, JOHN C   WMA   Page 70   F   Goodson Dist.
     28 Oct. 1892   Parents: Preston & Jane Blevins

BLEVINS, THOMAS   WMA   Page 55   F   Glade Spring
     1870   Parents: James & Harriett Blevins

BLEVINS, WILEY S   WMA   Page 59   F
     23 Oct. 1892   Parents: Elisha & Althea Blevins

BLOUNT, NANCY W   WFA   Page 42   F
     30 April 1858   Parents: William & M.A. Blount

BOB   SMA   Page 15
     15 Nov. 1854   Master: T.P. Clapp

BOB   SMA   Page 17
     3 Nov. 1855   Mother: Nancy
                       Owner: P. Carpenter

BOLING, ANDREW   WMA   Page 70   F   Goodson Dist.
   8 June 1892   Parents: Andrew & Sally Boling

BONDURANT, EMILY F   WFA   Page 8   F
   21 Nov. 1853   Parents: J.J. & Catharine Bondurant

BOOHER, [n.n.]   WMD   Page 14   F
   7 July 1854   Parents: F.D. & Ann Booher

BOOHER, ALICE L   WFA   Page 24   F
   4 June 1856   Parents: F.D. & Barbary Booher

BOOHER, AUGUSTUS H   WMA   Page 6   B
   2 Aug. 1853   Parents: Saml. G. & Mary Booher

BOOHER, BENJ.   WMA   Page 38
   8 Feb. 1858   Mother: Margaret Booher

BOOHER, CHARLES (twin)   WMA   Page 49   F
   2 July 1859   Parents: John S. & Mary Booher

BOOHER, CLARACY (twin)   WFA   Page 49   F
   2 July 1859   Parents: John S. & Mary Booher

BOOHER, ERNEST   WMA   Page 70   F   Goodson Dist.
   13 June 1892   Parents: J.W. & Alice Booher

BOOHER, F.D.   WMA   Page 38   F
   8 Jan. 1858   Parents: F.D. & Barbary Booher

BOOHER, JAMES H.W.   WMA   Page 21   F
   25 Oct. 1855   Parents: Leander A. & Sarah Booher

BOOHER, NATHAN E   WMA   Page 31   F
   7 March 1857   Parents: Jno. S. & Mary Booher

BOOHER, POLLY A   WFA   Page 31   F
   9 Jan. 1857   Parents: L.A. & Sarah Booher

BOOHER, SARAH   WFA   Page 49   B
   17 Sept. 1859   Parents: Samuel G. & Mary Booher

BOOHER, STEVEN   WMA   Page 66   ML   Kinderhook
   5 March 1892   Parents: C.S. & Allida Booher

BOOHER, SUSAN C   WFA   Page 6   F
   5 Oct. 1853   Parents: Leander A. & Sarah Booher

BOOHER, TEXANNA A   WFA   Page 31   B
   31 Aug. 1857   Parents: Saml. G. & Mary S. Booher

BOOHER, WALTER   WMA   Page 21   F
   16 Jan. 1855   Parents: John S. & Mary E. Booher

BOOHER, WALTER L   WMA   Page 70   F   Goodson Dist.
   1 Jan. 1892   Father: J.F. Booher
                     Mother: Elizabeth BOOKER

BOOHER, WM. CLEVELAND   WMA   Page 70   F   Goodson Dist.
   7 July 1892   Parents: David & A.E. Booher

BOOKER, CARRIE P   WFA   Page 59   F
   5 July 1892   Parents: Wm. D. & Carrie P. Booker

BOOKER, FRANCIS JANE   WF_   Page 57   Kinderhook
    10 Sept. 1870   Parents: Jas. S. & Rebecca Booker

BOOTH, [n.n.]   WFD   Page 59   F
    1 March 1892   Parents: W.M. & Alice Booth

BOTT, GEO. W,   WMA   Page 25   F
    20 Dec. 1856   Parents: W. & Nancy Bott

BOTT, IRBY   WMA   Page 68   F   North Fork D
    3 March 1892   Parents: William & Elizabeth Bott

BOTT, JAMES G   WMA   Page 54   F   Northfork Tw
    29 July 1871   Parents: John T. & Nancy C. Bott

BOWEN, THEOPHILUS   CMA   Page 73   L   Abingdon
    10 Sept. 1892   Parents: Hensten & Mary Bowen

BOWERS, JAS. C   WMA   Page 38   F
    15 Dec. 1858   Parents: Wm. & Temperance Bowers

BOWERS, JAMES T   WMA   Page 54   Northfork Tw
    8 Feb. 1871   Mother: Martha Bowers
      Reported by Philip Bowers, uncle

BOWERS, JNO. (twin)   WMA   Page 59   F
    24 June 1892   Parents: Henry & Martha Bowers

BOWERS, RACHEL   WFA   Page 8   BU
    13 Oct. 1853   Father: S. Bowers

BOWERS, ROBT. (twin)   WMA   Page 59   F
    24 June 1892   Parents: Henry & Martha Bowers

BOWLS, JOHN P.M.   WMA   Page 53   F   Abingdon Twp
    1 April 1871   Parents: George W. & Martha BOWLES

BOWMAN, AND. H.   WMA   Page 49   F
    14 July 1859   Parents: Peter & M.C. Bowman

BOWMAN, ANN CATHERINE   WFA   Page 2   L
    15 Feb. 1853   Parents: Alexander & Lucinda Bowman

BOWMAN, E.W.   WMA   Page 66   F   Kinderhook
    Aug. 1892   Parents: W.K. & Laura Bowman

BOWMAN, NANNIE   WFA   Page 42   F
    2 Dec. 1858   Parents: Alexander & Lucinda Bowman

BOWMAN, WASHINGTON   WMA   Page 68   F   North Fork [
    10 June 1892   Parents: John & Nannie Bowman

BOWYER, MAMIE J   WFA   Page 59   PH
    2 Dec. 1892   Parents: H.L. & M.K. Bowyer

BOYD, GEO. H.   WMA   Page 15   M
    8 Feb. 1854   Parents: Wm. & Susan Boyd

BOYD, L.H.   WMA   Page 38   BR
    Feb. 1858   Parents: Wm. & Susan Boyd

BOYD, LOUISA   CFA   Page 73   L   Abingdon
    10 Dec. 1892   Parents: J.K. & Katy Boyd

BOYD, MAY DAY
10 May 1892
CFA   Page 73   L   Abingdon
Parents: Wash. & Dell Boyd

BOYD, SARAH
8 Feb. 1856
WFA   Page 24   BR
Parents: Wm. & Susan Boyd

BOYD, W.M.
23 Feb. 1871
WMA   Page 54   BR   Northfork Twp.
Parents: William & Sousan Boyd

BRACKENRIDGE
13 July 1854
SMA   Page 12
Mother: Ann
Owner: John Roe

BRADLEY, [n.n.] (twins)
27 Dec. 1858
WFA   Page 38   F
Parents: Jas. H. & S.J. Bradley

BRADLEY, CHS. S.B.
16 Jan. 1857
WMA   Page 31   F
Parents: Abram F. & Mary E. Bradley

BRADLEY, JNO. B.
21 April 1858
WMD   Page 38   F
Parents: J.L. & S.R. Bradley

BRADLEY, LEVINIA J
5 Nov. 1854
WFA   Page 14   F
Parents: A.F. & Mary E. Bradley

BRADLEY, LUCY E
23 July 1857
WFA   Page 31   F
Parents: Archa. & Sophronie Bradley

BRADLEY, SAMUEL
17 FEb. 1856
WMA   Page 26   F
Parents: Jno. L. & S.R. Bradley

BRADLEY, THOS. G.
27 March 1854
WMA   Page 15   F
Parents: Jno. L. & S.R. Bradley

BRAMSON, ISAAC
18 June 1855
WMA   Page 42
Parents: Moses & Amanda BRANSON

BRANCH, PERTEY LEE
8 Sept. 1892
WFA   Page 68   F   North Fork Dist.
Parents: H.L. & Effie Branch

BRANNEN, JAMES M
18 Aug. 1855
WMA   Page 16   F   Clarksville
Parents: John & Sarah Brannen

BRANNEN, SARAH CATHERINE
14 July 1853
WFA   Page 3   F
Parents: John & Sarah Brannen

BRANSON, CHARLES
8 Feb. 1892
WMA   Page 70   F   Goodson Dist.
Parents: Worley & Ella Branson

BRANSON, CHARLES E
19 Nov. 1870
WMA   Page 57   F   Kinderhook
Parents: Wm. & Tempa Branson

BRANSON, ROBT. C.
18 Dec. 1892
WMA   Page 70   Goodson Dist.
Parents: Tom & Laura Branson

BRAUDY, [n.n.]
7 March 1870
W__   Page 55   F   Saltville Twp.
Parents: John & Elizabeth Braudy

BRAUDY, JOSEPH
1 April 1870
WMA   Page 55   F   Saltville Twp.
Parents: David & Nancy Braudy

BREWER, JOHN (twin)
9 June 1858
WMA   Page 45   F
Parents: Jesse & Elizabeth Brewer

BREWER, MARY J   WFA   Page 54   F   Northfork Twp.
    27 June 1871   Parents: Wm. G. & Margaret A. Brewer

BREWER, MINNIE   WFA   Page 66   F   Kinderhook
    8 Dec. 1892   Parents: Grant & Mattie Brewer

BREWER, ROBERT S. (twin)   WMA   Page 45   F
    9 June 1858   Parents: Jesse & Elizabeth Brewer

BRIDGEMAN, [n.n.]   WMA   Page 68   F   North Fork Dis
    2 Jan. 1892   Parents: Wm. & Sarah Bridgeman

BRIDGEMAN, ELIZ.   WFA   Page 38   F
    4 Oct. 1858   Parents: D.M. & Cath. Bridgeman

BRIDGEMAN, ISAAC   WMA   Page 21
    9 Dec. 1855   Parents: D.M. & C. Bridgeman

BRIDGMAN, PHEBE   WFA   Page 7   F
    27 Dec. 1853   Father: Dan'l Bridgman

BRIGGS, [n.n.]   WFA   Page 10   F
    Oct. 1854   Parents: Wm. J. & Nancy Briggs

BRIGGS, VIRGINIA   WFA   Page 26   F
    20 Nov. 1856   Parents: Fred & Mary Briggs

BRIGHT, BERNARD K   WMA   Page 72   MR   Abingdon
    17 June 1892   Parents: Geo. M. & W.J. Bright

[BRIM], MARTHA S   WFA   Page 12   F
    11 Dec. 1854   Parents: James & Martha [Brim]

BRISCO, JOHN H   WMA   Page 70   F   Abingdon Dist.
    10 Feb. 1892   Father: Chas. BRISCOE
       Mother: Molly Brisco

BROOKS, MOSES M   WMA   Page 53   F   Abingdon Twp.
    14 Nov. 1871   Parents: Solomon & Deborah A. Brooks

BROOKS, NANCY   WFA   Page 38   F
    31 Aug. 1858   Parents: J.A.G. & Sarah Brooks

BROWN, ADA P   WFA   Page 49   F
    17 Feb. 1859   Parents: Edard & Susan Brown

BROWN, ANN E   WFA   Page 31   F
    6 Jan. 1857   Parents: And'w & Mahala Brown

BROWN, CORATIO   CMA   Page 53   F   Abingdon Twp.
    2 June 1871   Parents: Stephen & Susan Brown

BROWN, DOBIE   WMA   Page 38   F
    6 Oct. 1858   Parents: A. & Mahaly Brown

BROWN, MARGRET   WFA   Page 35   F
    1 Feb. 1857   Parents: [Linzy] & Sarah Brown

BROWN, PATON   WMA   Page 45   F
    20 March 1859   Parents: George & Sarah Brown

BROWN, SARAH G   CFA   Page 53   F   Abingdon Twp.
    30 July 1871   Parents: Mark & Hettie Brown

BROWN, SHEFFEY
   21 April 1892

WMA   Page 59   F
Parents: J.T.S. & Eunice C. Brown

BROWN, WILLIAM
   6 Dec. 1853

SMA   Page 3   Cedarville
Mother: Amanda
Owner: James Orr

BROWN, WILLIE
   14 Dec. 1892

CMA   Page 59
Mother: Martha Brown

BROWNING, FRAN.
   29 March 1892

WMA   Page 59   F
Parents: G.W. & N.V. Browning

BROWNLOW, [n.n.]
   26 Oct. 1892
   Remarks: 'stillborn'

WFA   Page 72   MC   Abingdon
Parents: F.B. & E.V. Brownlow

BROWNLOW, FRANKLIN
   31 Aug. 1853

WMA   Page 9   C
Father: Joseph A. Brownlow

BRUMET, ALONZO W
   3 Jan. 1853

WMA   Page 8   E
Parents: J.M.H. & Catharine Brumet

BRYANT, SARAH A
   8 Sept. 1859

WFA   Page 45   F
Parents: James A. & Missouri Bryant

BRYANT, W.C.
   15 Aug. 1858

WMA   Page 42   F
Parents: Jno. A. & M.W. Bryant

BUCHANAN, ADALINE
   15 April 1858

WFA   Page 42   F
Parents: B.K. & Rachel Buchanan

BUCHANAN, BENJ. D.D.
   13 Aug. 1857

WMA   Page 31   F
Parents: Jas. & R. Buchanan

BUCHANAN, BETTIE
   13 Jan. 1853

WFA   Page 8   SF
Parents: Matthew F. & E. Buchanan

BUCHANAN, EDNA
   1870

WFA   Page 55   F   Glade Spring Twp.
Parents: Wm. R. & Martha A. Buchanan

BUCHANAN, JOHN K
   3 March 1855

WMA   Page 23   SF   Abingdon
Parents: M.H. & E. Buchanan

BUCHANAN, JOS. R. (twin)
   26 Sept. 1856

WMA   Page 28   F
Parents: Wm. & Mary A. Buchanan

BUCHANAN, M.S. (twin)
   26 Sept. 1856

WMA   Page 28   F
Parents: Wm. & Mary A. Buchanan

BUCHANAN, MARY E.H.
   1 May 1855

WMA   Page 19   F
Parents: Jno. D. & Sarah Buchanan

BUCHANAN, MARY J
   27 Aug. 1855

WFA   Page 21   F
Parents: Jno. P. & E. Buchanan

BUCHANAN, ROBT.
   [21] Sept. 1857

WMA   Page 35   F
Parents: M.H. & E. Buchanan

BUCHANAN, ROBT. E.
   25 April 1856

WMA   Page 30   MR
Parents: Jas. S. & Margret B. Buchanan

BUCHANAN, ROBT. HENDERSON
   16 Feb. 1855

WMA   Page 17   F
Parents: James & Rebecca Buchanan

BUCHANAN, THOMAS   WMA   Page 9   CL   Near Saltville
    1 April 1854   Parents: Benj'n K. & Rachel Buchanan

BUCK, JOSEPHINE   WFA   Page 31   F
    2 Nov. 1857   Parents: David M. & Mary E. Buck

BUCK, MONTGOMERY   WMA   Page 59   F
    11 July 1892   Parents: A.M. & Mary E. Buck

BUCKLEY, HERBERT   WMA   Page 72   MC   Abingdon
    5 May 1892   Parents: Joseph & M.M. Buckley

BULLOCK, [n.n.]   WM_   Page 57   F   Kinderhook
    4 Oct. 1870   Parents: John A. & Lettie I. Bullock

BUMBGARDNER, [n.n.]   WMD   Page 53   F   Abingdon Twp.
    5 April 1871   Parents: Franklin & Emeline Bumbgardne

BUMGARDNER, G.C.   WMA   Page 70   F   Abingdon Dist.
    10 April 1892   Parents: J.M. & Eliza Bumgardner

BUMGARNER, JNO. M.   WMA   Page 35   F
    4 FEb. 1857   Parents: Adison & Cath. Bumgarner

BURCHNELL, ELIZA I   WFA   Page 31   F
    19 May 1857   Parents: Joseph & Susan Burchnell

BURDINE, ANNIE   WFA   Page 70   F   Goodson Dist.
    10 Feb. 1892   Parents: Charles & Alice Burdine

BURNOP, JAS. R.   WMA   Page 42   F
    29 Aug. 1858   Parents: Richard & Margaret Burnop

BUSH, MARTIN H   WMA   Page 13   F
    22 Feb. 1854   Parents: Thos. M. & Martha Bush
    Father's residence in Allegheny Co., Va.

BUTT, M.T.L.   WFA   Page 7   H
    27 Sept. 1853   Parents: Thos. & Mary Butt

BUTT, SARAH J   WFA   Page 21   H
    21 May 1855   Parents: James H. & Mary E. Butt

BYARS, AGLEEN   WFA   Page 55   F   Glade Spring T
    1870   Parents: James M. & Virginia C. Byars

BYARS, ARMINTA   WFA   Page 45   F
    13 Jan. 1859   Parents: William & Susan Byars

BYARS, JOHN TRIGG   WMA   Page 55   F   Glade Spring T
    1870   Parents: Samuel A. & Virginia E. Byars

CALDWELL, [n.n.]   WMA   Page 42   F
    7 Nov. 1858   Parents: Jas. S. & Patsy Caldwell

CALDWELL, JAMES W   WMA   Page 18   F
    11 May 1855   Parents: Jesse H. & Margaret Caldwell

CALDWELL, JAS. R.   WMA   Page 27   F
    11 Sept. 1856   Parents: James S. & Ellen Caldwell

CALDWELL, LAURA   WFA   Page 42   F
    17 July 1858   Parents: J.H. & Margaret Caldwell

CALDWELL, MARGRET J   WFA   Page 35
    9 Oct. 1857   Parents: Wm. S. & J.A. Caldwell

CALDWELL, ROBERT   WMA   Page 55   F   Glade Spring Twp.
    1870   Parents: Samuel T. & Margaret Caldwell

CALDWELL, THOS. F.   WMA   Page 18   F
    26 March 1855   Parents: John S. & Martha Caldwell

CALIVER, MINNIE J   CFA   Page 60   L
    23 May 1892   Parents: Ambrose & Clara Caliver

CALLAWAY, WILLIE M   CFA   Page 60   L
    9 Sept. 1892   Parents: Laze & Serena Callaway

CALLIHAN, E.M.C.   WFA   Page 29   F
    1 Oct. 1856   Father: Jessee CALLAHAN
    Reported by E. CALLAHAN, mother   Mother: Emaline Callihan

CALLIHAN, WILLIAM   WMA   Page 6
    5 May 1853   Mother: Malinda CALLAHAN
    Reported by Wm. CALAHAN, father of mother

CAMPBELL, [n.n.]   WMA   Page 20   F
    6 Jan. 1855   Parents: Jacob & Ann Campbell

CAMPBELL, DAN T   WM_   Page 38   PH
    18 Oct. 1858   Parents: E.M. & E.S. Campbell

CAMPBELL, DAVID   WMA   Page 28   F
    23 Sept. 1856   Parents: John & Drucilla Campbell

CAMPBELL, ELIZA B   WFA   Page 70   F   Goodson Dist.
    1 Jan. 1892   Parents: D.A.F. & [Anner] Campbell

CAMPBELL, GIFFORD   WMA   Page 60   F
    16 July 1892   Parents: J.V. & Maha Campbell

CAMPBELL, JACOB T   WMA   Page 49   F
    19 Oct. 1859   Parents: Wm. B. & Margaret E. Campbell

CAMPBELL, JAMES W   WMA   Page 49
    25 June 1859   Parents: E.M. & Ellen S. Campbell

CAMPBELL, JOHN W   WMA   Page 26   F
    17 Oct. 1856   Parents: Wm. B. & Margret E. Campbell

CAMPBELL, JULIA J   WFA   Page 12   F
    14 March 1854   Parents: John & Drusilla Campbell

CAMPBELL, MARY K   WFA   Page 32   F
    6 Jan. 1857   Parents: Jas. C. & Ellen B. Campbell

CAMPBELL, NANCY   WFA   Page 15   F
    16 Jan. 1854   Parents: Jacob & Minerva Campbell
    Reported by Jno. S. Bradley, neighbor

CAMPBELL, NANCY J   WFA   Page 53   F   Abingdon Twp.
    21 May 1871   Parents: John H. & Martha E. Campbell

CAMPBELL, PAUL   WMA   Page 11   F
    28 March 1854   Parents: Hugh M. & Jemima Campbell

CAMPBELL, RHODA ANN　　　　　　WFA　　Page 14　　　CR
　　　26 Aug. 1854　　　　　　　Parents: Jas. S.F. & Rosanna E. Campbel

CAMPBELL, RHODA M　　　　　　　WFA　　Page 14　　　F
　　　11 Oct. 1854　　　　　　　Parents: Jas. C. & Ellen Campbell

CAMPBELL, SARAH　　　　　　　　WFA　　Page 8　　　F
　　　9 March 1853　　　　　　　Father: Jacob Campbell

CAMPBELL, SUSAN B　　　　　　　WFA　　Page 31　　　F
　　　8 Aug. 1857　　　　　　　Parents: Jacob & T.M. Campbell

CAMPBELL, SUSAN E　　　　　　　WFA　　Page 31　　　F
　　　9 Nov. 1857　　　　　　　Parents: Jas. L.F. & Rosanah E. Campbe

CAMPBELL, WM. B.　　　　　　　WMA　　Page 8　　　F
　　　16 Dec. 1853　　　　　　　Parents: Wm. B. & M.E. Campbell

CAMPER, ELIZABETH (twin)　　　WF_　　Page 57　　　　　Kinderhook
　　　15 Oct. 1870　　　　　　　Parents: David W. & Mary A. Camper

CAMPER, SAML. P. (twin)　　　　WM_　　Page 57　　　　　Kinderhook
　　　15 Oct. 1870　　　　　　　Parents: David W. & Mary A. Camper

CANTER, ALFRED　　　　　　　　WMA　　Page 20　　　F
　　　1 Aug. 1855　　　　　　　Parents: Wm. & Elizabeth Canter

CANTER, E. [L.]　　　　　　　WFA　　Page 38　　　F
　　　31 Oct. 1858　　　　　　　Parents: Jas. & Mary Canter

CANTER, S.A.F.　　　　　　　　WFA　　Page 6　　　F
　　　26 Sept. 1853　　　　　　Parents: Wm. & Mary Canter

CANTER, WILLIAM C　　　　　　　WM_　　Page 57　　　　　Kinderhook
　　　Oct. 1870　　　　　　　　Parents: W.H. & Mary Canter

CARLTON, JOHN H　　　　　　　WMA　　Page 11　　　F
　　　26 March 1854　　　　　　Parents: Leander L. & Rebecca Carlton

CARMARK, AUGUSTUS P　　　　　　WMA　　Page 23　　　F
　　　19 Oct. 1855　　　　　　　Parents: Wiley & Eliza Carmack

CARMACK, CHARLES C　　　　　　WMA　　Page 15　　　F
　　　12 Feb. 1854　　　　　　　Parents: Wiley & H.E. Carmack

CARMACK, H　　　　　　　　　WFA　　Page 39　　　F
　　　19 December 1858　　　　　Parents: Wiley & Eliza Carmack

CARMACK, JAS. T.　　　　　　　WMA　　Page 32　　　F
　　　27 Dec. 1854　　　　　　　Parents: Isaac & Jane H. Carmack

CARMACK, LAVINIA　　　　　　　WFA　　Page 6　　　F
　　　6 May 1853　　　　　　　Parents: Isaac & Jane Carmack
　　　Reported by Ann Campbell, grandmother

CARMACK, ROBERT　　　　　　　WMA　　Page 70　　　F　　Goodson Dist.
　　　10 March 1892　　　　　　Parents: James & Mary Carmack

CARMACK, VIRGINIA　　　　　　WFA　　Page 31　　　F
　　　25 June 1857　　　　　　　Parents: Wiley & H.E. Carmack

CARNER, F.C.
    20 Feb. 1858
WMA   Page 38   C
Parents: John C. & Mary C. Carner

CAROLINE
    11 Feb. 1854
SFA   Page 9
Mother: Cary
Owner: Philip B. Snapp

CAROLINE
    30 Nov. 1854
SFA   Page 15
Master: Jeremiah Rush

CAROLINE
    April 1855
SFA   Page 16
Mother: Minerva
Owner: Jas. P. Strother

CAROLINE
    26 June 1856
SFA   Page 30
Owner: Whitley Fullen

CARPENTER, ELIZA C
    8 Aug. 1856
WFA   Page 29   F
Parents: James & Margret A. Carpenter

CARPENTER, J.R.
    2 Nov. 1858
WMA   Page 42   C
Parents: James & Margaret Carpenter

CARPENTER, PAMELIA JANE
    13 Feb. 1855
WFA   Page 16   F
Parents: James & Margt. A. Carpenter

CARPENTER, WM. PATRICK
    27 Oct. 1853
WMA   Page 4   F
Father: James Carpenter

CARR, [n.n.]
    26 Aug. 1892
WMA   Page 70   F   Goodson Dist.
Parents: William & Marg. Carr

CARRICO, ALBERT W
    18 Nov. 1871
WMA   Page 54   F   Northfork Twp.
Parents: H.H. & Mary K. Carrico

CARROL, NORA
    5 June 1892
CFA   Page 73   F
Father: George CARROLL
Mother: Mary Carrol

CARSON, JANE
    19 March 1859
WFA   Page 45   F
Parents: William & Mary A. Carson

CARSON, JOHN M
    6 April 1855
WMA   Page 19   F
Parents: William & Marg't Ann Carson

CARSON, MARGRET A
    15 Dec. 1856
WFA   Page 29   F
Parents: Wm. & Margret A. Carson

CARTER, CHESTER B
    15 Aug. 1892
CMA   Page 60   L
Parents: Ned & Lizzie Carter

CARTER, FRANK
    4 June 1892
CMA   Page 60   L
Parents: Wm. & Mary Carter

CARTER, ROSANNA C
    7 Oct. 1856
    Reported by James CANTER, father
WFA   Page 24   F
Father: James Carter
Mother: Mary CANTER

CASEY, DONNIE
    20 July 1892
WMA   Page 50   F
Parents: Sam'l & Elizabeth Casey

CASEY, MARGARET JANE
    25 April 1853
WFA   Page 3   F
Parents: Wm. & Mariah Casey

CASSELL, ADAM MITCHELL
20 March 1853
WMA   Page 3   F   Cedarville
Parents: Saml. & Jane Cassell

CASSELL, EWING J
4 Aug. 1892
WMA   Page 60   CL
Parents: Robt. C. & Sarah E. Cassell

CASSELL, GEO. W.
12 Feb. 1855
WMA   Page 20   F
Parents: Sam'l A. & Eva Jane Cassell

CASSELL, JAS. O.
10 June 1858
WMA   Page 42   F
Parents: Samuel A. & Jane Cassell

CASSELL, LILLY KATE
1870
WFA   Page 55   F   Glade Spring Tw
Parents: Alex S. & Mary F. Cassell

CASSELL, SARAH VIRGINIA
29 July 1854
WFA   Page 10   F
Parents: Saml. A. & Jane E. Cassell

CASTLE, BETTY J
15 Aug. 1892
WFA   Page 66   F   Kinderhook
Parents: Ralph & Rachel Castle

CATO, [n.n.]
14 March 1853
C_A   Page 1   W
Parents: Andrew & Susan Cato

CATREN, MARY ANN
10 Nov. 1854
WFA   Page 12   F
Parents: Francis & Nancy Catren

CATRON, C.E.
21 Sept. 1857
WFA   Page 35   F
Parents: Francis & Nancy M. Catron

CATRON, JAMES
16 Nov. 1855
WMA   Page 19   F
Parents: Philip W. & Delila Catron

CATRON, JOHN
11 June 1854
WMA   Page 10   F
Parents: Philip & Sarah J. Catron

CATRON, ROBT. K.
15 March 1859
WMA   Page 45   F
Parents: Philip & Jane Catron

CATRON, S.Z.
15 Nov. 1857
WFA   Page 35   F
Parents: Thos. J. & N.E. Catron

CATRON, SARAH M.C.
20 Nov. 1856
WFA   Page 30   F
Parents: Leander & Rebecca C. Catron

CATRON, THOMAS J
15 Aug. 1859
WMA   Page 45   F
Parents: Francis & Nancy Catron

CATRON, W.F.
4 or 11 May 1857
WFA   Page 35   F
Parents: Philip & Sarah J. Catron

CATRON, WALTER JOHNSON
November 1853
WMA   Page 5   F
Parents: Philip W. & Delila Catron

CAULDWELL, JOSEPH M
11 April 1859
WMA   Page 45   F
Parents: James & Ellen Cauldwell

CAWOOD, CASINE
9 Sept. 1858
WFA   Page 42   F
Parents: B.B. & Mary Cawood

CAWOOD, CONNALLY
22 March 1853
WMA   Page 1
Parents: John, Jr., & Minerva Cawood

CAWOOD, HARRIET
8 June 1855
WFA   Page 21   F
Parents: John & Minerva Cawood

CAWOOD, MOSES   WMA   Page 1
        March 1853   Parents: John M. & Lucy Cawood

CAYLOR, ELISHA W   WMA   Page 25   F
        Reported by David KAYLOR, uncle   Father: Thos. Caylor
                                       Mother: Sarah KAYLOR

CHAPMAN, BRUCE L   WMA   Page 60   F
        3 July 1892   Parents: W.M. & At. E. Chapman

CHAPMAN, GEO. W.   WMA   Page 38   F
        7 May 1858   Parents: Jos. C. & M.A. Chapman

CHAPMAN, JAMES   WMA   Page 6   SW
        1 Jan. 1853   Father: Joseph Chapman

CHAPMAN, JAS. H.   WMA   Page 68   F   North Fork Dist.
        21 Oct. 1892   Parents: J.H. & Alcy Chapman

CHAPMAN, JOHN   WMA   Page 68   F   North Fork Dist.
        20 Oct. 1892   Parents: John & Ellen Chapman

CHAPMAN, JNO. W.   WMA   Page 32   F
        1 Oct. 1857   Parents: Geo. & Ellen Chapman

CHAPMAN, JOS. W.   WMA   Page 49   F
        6 Aug. 1859   Parents: Theoph & J.E. Chapman

CHAPMAN, MARY A   WFA   Page 31   F
        23 Aug. 1856   Parents: Jas. & Margret Chapman

CHAPMAN, MILTON W   WMA   Page 13   F   North Fork
        21 June 1854   Parents: James & Margaret Chapman

CHAPMAN, NANCY L   WFA   Page 66   F   Kinderhook
        4 Nov. 1892   Parents: C.C. & Nancy A. Chapman

CHAPPEL, SARAH   CFA   Page 53   F   Abingdon Twp.
        22 Nov. 1871   Father: Wyatt CHAPPLE
                                       Mother: Frances CHAPPELL

CHAPPLE, PAUL (twin)   CMA   Page 73   L   Near Abingdon
        8 Feb. 1892   Parents: Wyatt & Francis Chapple

CHAPPLE, SILAS (twin)   CMA   Page 73   L   Near Abingdon
        8 Feb. 1892   Parents: Wyatt & Francis Chapple

CHARLES   SMA   Page 8
        Oct. 1853   Owner: Jas. C. Campbell

CHARLES   SMA   Page 9
        15 Dec. 1853   Owner: William Rodafer

CHARLES   SMA   Page 12
        Dec. 1854   Mother: Sarah
        Reported by Mary C. Sugart, mistress   Owner: Claiborne S. SHUGART

CHARLES   SMA   Page 16
        2 April 1855   Mother: Ann
                                       Owner: Arthur D. Hutton

CHARLES 2 April 1855	SMA Page 16 Mother: Harriet Owner: Rob't B. Edmondson
CHARLES 31 May 1856	SMA Page 34 Owner: J. Rush
CHARLES 7 or 9 Jan. 1857	SMA Page 35 Owner: Absolem Beaty
CHARLES 8 Sept. 1857	SMA Page 34 Owner: W.H. Medley
CHARLES 19 May 1858	SMA Page 39 Owner: Jno. Fleenor
CHARLOTTE 15 Sept. 1857	SFA Page 34 Owner: R.B. Rogers
CHILDERS, JAS. FRANKLIN 11 May 1855	WMA Page 18 B Parents: James J. & Marg't J. Childers
CHILES, HENRY 19 Feb. 1856	WMA Page 26 Parents: E. & Margret Chiles
CISCO, FRANCIS 20 March 1892	SFA Page 73 L Abingdon Parents: Henry & Stella Cisco
CLABURN 12 July 1859	SMA Page 46 Master: Ballard P. Smith
CLAIBORNE, [n.n.] 21 Nov. 1858	WFA Page 38 L Parents: J.H. & Virginia Claiborne
CLAPP, ANNIE B 27 July 1892	WFA Page 70 F Abingdon Dist. Parents: Jerry & Mary B. Clapp
CLAPP, GROVER CLE. 11 Dec. 1892	WMA Page 70 F Abingdon Dist. Parents: John M. & Mary J. Clapp
CLARK, [n.n.] 15 Sept. 1858	WFA Page 38 F Parents: W. & Cath. Clark
CLARK, [n.n.] 1870	WMA Page 55 F Glade Spring Parents: John H. & Mariam R. Clark
CLARK, BEVERLEY R.J. 4 July 1854	WMA Page 11 F Parents: Job & Lucinda Clark
CLARK, C.B. 9 Feb. 1853	WMA Page 8 F Parents: Jno. P. & Martha A. Clark
CLARK, CHAS A. 4 Dec. 1892	WMA Page 59 TM Parents: John F. & Mattie Clark
CLARK, CHAS. ALFRED 16 May 1854	WMA Page 13 F Near Glade Sp Parents: James A. & Mary Clark
CLARK, D.C. 21 Feb. 1859	WMA Page 49 F Parents: James & Ann E.C. Clark
CLARK, DAVID 14 Nov. 1854	WMA Page 14 F Parents: James & Elizabeth Clark

CLARK, DAVID D   WMA   Page 59   F
        15 June 1892   Parents: T.C. & Mary J. Clark

CLARK, E.M.C. (twin)   WMA   Page 35   F
        5 Jan. 1857   Parents: Job. & L.F.C. Clark

CLARK, EDWD. F.   WMA   Page 69   North Fork Dist.
        12 Jan. 1892   Mother: Hattie Clark

CLARK, ELB. M.   WMA   Page 59   F
        5 Aug. 1892   Parents: Robt. E. & Caledo. Clark

CLARK, ELLEN ANN   WFA   Page 11
        15 Dec. 1854   Parents: John S. & Isabella Clark

CLARK, ELLEN E   WFA   Page 32
        18 Oct. 1857   Parents: Jno. P. & Martha A. Clark

CLARK, ELLEN L.C. (twin)   WFA   Page 35   F
        5 Jan. 1857   Parents: Job. & L.F.C. Clark

CLARK, FOUNTAIN B   WMA   Page 46   F
        8 Aug. 1859   Parents: Matthew R. & Isabella Clark

CLARK, GEORGE W   WFA   Page 17   F
        24 Oct. 1855   Parents: John B. & Mary Clark

CLARK, HATTIE   WFA   Page 66   F   Kinderhook
        10 Nov. 1892   Parents: David & Amanda Clark

CLARK, ISAAC W   WMA   Page 23   F
        3 Nov. 1855   Father: Jas. G. Clark

CLARK, JOHN   WMA   Page 55   F
        1870   Parents: John B. & D.M. Clark

CLARK, JNO. A.M.   WMA   Page 59   F
        1 Aug. 1892   Parents: T.W. & Geneva Clark

CLARK, JOS. N.   WMA   Page 68   F   North Fork Dist.
        10 Sept. 1892   Parents: J.C. & Julia S. Clark

CLARK, LAURA L   WFA   Page 59   R
        22 May 1892   Parents: F.B. & M.E. Clark

CLARK, LAURIA M.M.   WFA   Page 55   MC   Glade Spring Twp.
        1870   Parents: Francis S. & Catharine Clark

CLARK, MARTHA (twin)   WFA   Page 59   F
        23 Feb. 1892   Parents: John H. & Miriam Clark

CLARK, MARTHA I.E.   WFA   Page 30   F
        7 Feb. 1856   Parents: Frs. S. & Catherine Clark

CLARK, MARY (twin)   WFA   Page 59   F
        23 Feb. 1892   Parents: John H. & Miriam Clark

CLARK, MARY V   WFA   Page 45   F
        7 Nov. 1859   Parents: Francis & Cathrine Clark

CLARK, REBECCA J   WFA   Page 29   F
        3 Dec. 1856   Parents: Rob't & Margret Clark

CLARK, RHODA E   WFA   Page 70   F   Abingdon Dist.
      14 Dec. 1892   Parents: Trigg & Eva Clark

CLARK, ROBERT   WMA   Page 10   F
      6 March 1854   Parents: Robert & Margret Clark

CLARK, ROBERT   WMA   Page 35   F
      10 Feb. 1857   Parents: Jas. A. & M.E. Clark

CLARK, ROB'T W   WMA   Page 29   F
      7 Feb. 1856   Parents: Jas. A. & Mary E. Clark

CLARK, RUTH C   WFA   Page 59   F
      5 Oct. 1892   Parents: W.B. & Martha Clark

CLARK, SARAH JANE   WFA   Page 3   F
      Sept. 1853   Parents: Andw. & Margaret Clark
      Reported by Jacob Clark, father of father

CLARK, SARAH M   WFA   Page 42   F
      4 March 1858   Parents: Job & Lucinda T. Clark

CLARK, SUSAN MARGARET   WFA   Page 11   F
      26 Feb. 1854   Parents: John J. & Susan Clark

CLARK, THOMAS A   WMA   Page 35   F
      11 Aug. 1857   Parents: W.T. & Lavinia Clark

CLARK, THOMAS A   WMA   Page 57   Kinderhook
      30 ---- 1870   Parents: Jno. & Martha Clark

CLARK, THOS. B.   WMA   Page 32   F
      15 Sept. 1857   Parents: Wm. B. & Martha A. Clark

CLARK, W.R.   WMA   Page 6   B
      29 Nov. 1853   Parents: Jas. & Elizabeth Clark

CLARK, WALTON L   WMA   Page 66   F   Kinderhook
      5 Jan. 1892   Parents: Sandy & Mollie Clark

CLARK, WM. CAMPBELL   WMA   Page 3   F
      11 July 1853   Parents: Jno. B. & Mary Clark

CLARK, WM. F.   WMA   Page 23   F
      3 Feb. 1855   Parents: Wm. B. & M.A. Clark

CLARK, WM. H.   WMA   Page 6   F
      1 Jan. 1853   Parents: Jos. & R. KAYLOR

CLARK, WM. JAMES   WMA   Page 9   L   Near Saltville
      1 Feb. 1854   Parents: Matthew & Mary Clark

CLARK, WYNDHAM   WMA   Page 14   F
      29 Nov. 1854   Parents: Jas. G. & Edney R. Clark

CLARK, WYNDHAM R   WMA   Page 3   F
      20 Sept. 1853   Parents: Andw. & Margaret Clark

CLARK, Y.W.   WMA   Page 66   F   Kinderhook
      8 Sept. 1892   Parents: James C. & Julia Clark

CLAYMAN, [n.n.]   WMA   Page 32   F
      25 Jan. 1857   Parents: Jacob L. & R. Clayman

CLAYMAN, ELIZA   WFA   Page 70   F   Goodson Dist.
    21 April 1892   Parents: Joseph & Amanda Clayman

CLAYMAN, ROBERT F   WMA   Page 70   F   Goodson Dist.
    19 July 1892   Parents: W.F. & Bettie Clayman

CLIFTON, ARTHUR   WMA   Page 68   F   North Fork Dist.
    10 Aug. 1892   Parents: Jas. E. & Susan Clifton

CLIFTON, ROBT. J.   WMA   Page 68   F   North Fork Dist.
    10 Jan. 1892   Parents: Thomas & Sarah Clifton

COALE, SAMPSON   WMA   Page 38   F
    4 March 1858   Parents: L.D. & Pheby Coale

COCHRAN, ELDRIDGE   WMA   Page 23   F
    10 June 1855   Parents: Robert B. & Mary Cochran

COFFIN, LAURA J.E.   WFA   Page 24   F
    13 Oct. 1856   Parents: Clarkson & Susan R. Coffin

COLE, [n.n.]   WMA   Page 5   F
    8 March 1853   Parents: Andw. & Mary Cole

COLE, [n.n.]   WFD   Page 12   F
    29 Oct. 1854   Parents: Jas. S. & Elizabeth Cole

COLE, ANDREW C   WMA   Page 42   F
    23 April 1858   Parents: Andrew C. & Eliza Cole

COLE, BRAN. B.   WMA   Page 59   DM
    22 June 1892   Parents: H.C. & Sallie C. Cole

COLE, C.J.   WFA   Page 7   F
    21 April 1853   Father: Joshua Cole

COLE, CHARLES G   WMA   Page 55   F   Glade Spring Twp.
    1870   Parents: James L. & Eliza Cole

COLE, CHLOE E   WFA   Page 59   F
    9 May 1892   Parents: E.H. & Media Cole

COLE, ELEANOR   WFA   Page 19   F
    30 Dec. 1855   Parents: And'w C. & Eliza Cole

COLE, ESTHER M   WFA   Page 30   F
    17 Nov. 1856   Parents: Wm. & Christina Cole

COLE, GEO. W.   WMA   Page 29   F
    20 Oct. 1856   Parents: Peleg & Martha Cole

COLE, ISAAC C   WMA   Page 21   F
    1 Oct. 1855   Parents: Lorenzo D. & Phoebe Cole

COLE, JAMES B   WMA   Page 29   F
    12 March 1856   Parents: Jas. L. & Eliz'th Cole

COLE, JAMES J   WMA   Page 11   F
    12 Sept. 1854   Parents: Andrew & Mary Cole

COLE, JOHN C   WMA   Page 42   F
    18 May 1858   Parents: Andrew & Mary Cole

COLE, JOS. S.   WMA   Page 69   F   North Fork Dist.
    6 June 1892   Parents: D.F. & Susan J. Cole

COLE, MARTHA J
15 July 1859
WFA   Page 45   F
Parents: Andrew & Mary Cole

COLE, NANNIE B
25 Dec. 1892
CFA   Page 60   L
Parents: Eli & Julia Cole

COLE, PRISCILLA CATHARINE
30 Oct. 1855
WFA   Page 19   F
Parents: Andrew & Mary Cole

COLE, SARAH E
20 Jan. 1857
WFA   Page 35   F
Parents: Andrew & Mary Cole

COLE, WILLIAM R
29 SEpt. 1858
WMA   Page 42   F
Parents: Jas. L. & Elizabeth Cole

COLEGATE, MARGARET ELLEN
26 Feb. 1854
WFA   Page 12   L
Parents: John F. & Nancy N. Colegate

COLEMAN, ARCHEY
5 Nov. 1855
WMA   Page 20   F
Parents: Jno. H. & Mary S. Coleman

COLGATE, CATH. A.
12 June 1856
WFA   Page 28   F
Parents: Jno. F. & Nancy A. Colegate

COLLINS, JNO. H.
19 June 1857
WMA   Page 31   F
Parents: Jno. D. & Nancy Collins

COLLAY, GEORGE
8 Feb. 1855
WMA   Page 20   F
Parents: David L. & Spicey Collay

COLLEY, CATHERINE
29 April 1853
WFA   Page 2   L   North Fork
Parents: David L. & Spicey Colley

COLLEY, DAVID C
18 Oct. 1892
WMA   Page 59   F
Parents: T.W. & Ann E. Colley

COLLEY, SARAH M.S.
20 July 1856
WFA   Page 30   F
Parents: C.M. & Mary Colley

COLLIN (twin of Thornton)
15 Aug. 1854
SMA   Page 15
Master: John Preston

COLLINGS, [n.n.]
Sept. 1853
WMD   Page 1   Saltville
Parents: David A. & Mary Collings

COLLINGS, DICA
March 1892
WFA   Page 66   F   Kinderhook
Parents: G.W. & Dica Collings

COLLINGS, HATTIE J
7 Oct. 1892
WFA   Page 60   F
Parents: J.K. & Pris. Collings

COLLINGS, JANE
5 March 1892
WFA   Page 69   F   North Fork Di
Parents: Thomas & Mary Collings

COLLINGS, M.C.
1 Dec. 1892
WMA   Page 66   F   Kinderhook
Parents: J.H.W. & Mary Collings

COLLINGS, MABEL
3 Dec. 1892
WFA   Page 66   F   Kinderhook
Parents: E.J. & [Dona] Collings

COLLINGS, THOS. F.
8 March 1856
WFA   Page 28   F
Parents: Jno. & Catherine Collings

COLLINS, [n.n.]   WMA   Page 32   F
    3 June 1857   Parents: Henry & Margret Collins

COLLINS, FLORENCE J   WFA   Page 38   F
    16 March 1858   Parents: N.W. & M.J. Collins

COLLINS, MAGGIE J   WF_   Page 57   Kinderhook
    22 July 1870   Parents: Geo. W. & Barbara H. Collins

COLLINS, MARTHA M   WFA   Page 49   F
    15 Dec. 1859   Parents: Jerry & Nancy Collins

COLLINS, R.D.   WFA   Page 49   F
    21 Dec. 1859   Parents: N.W. & M.J. Collins

COMANN, HENRY   WMA   Page 26   T
    10 March 1856   Father: J.C. Comann
                     Mother: Lucy COMAN

COMANN, THOS.   WMA   Page 32   F
    15 Oct. 1857   Parents: J.C. & Lucy COMAN

COMBS, M.J.   WFA   Page 38   F
    21 Dec. 1858   Parents: Thos. & Elizabeth Combs

COMBS, NETTIE G   WFA   Page 69   F   North Fork Dist.
    18 Jan. 1892   Parents: W.H. & M.J. Combs

CONAN, ANDREW J   WMA   Page 42   F
    3 May 1858   Parents: Hiram & Lida Conan

COOK, CHRISTENIA   WFA   Page 53   F   Abingdon Twp.
    18 July 1871   Parents: James & Elizabeth Cook

COOK, F.A.A.   WFA   Page 35   F
    1 April 1857   Parents: William & Margret S. Cook

COOK, LOWREY E   WMA   Page 46   F
    10 April 1859   Parents: William & Elizabeth Cook

COOK, MARY ANN   WFA   Page 6
    6 Dec. 1853   Mother: Lucy Cook

COOK, MARY JANE   WFA   Page 11   F
    8 May 1854   Parents: William & Margaret Cook

COOK, MARY S   WFA   Page 72   MC   Abingdon
    8 Dec. 1892   Parents: John F. & Dora Cook

COOK, WM. K.   WMA   Page 60   F
    19 March 1892   Parents: S.A. & Eliza Cook

COOPER, BASIL   WMA   Page 13   S   Glade Spring
    24 Jan. 1854   Parents: Alex'r & Emeline Cooper

COOPER, JAMES   WMA   Page 22   F
    2 June 1855   Parents: Aglister & Amanda Cooper
    Reported by A. Stewart, neighbor

COOPER, JNO. CROTON   WMA   Page 19   S
    19 Dec. 1855   Parents: Alex'r C. & Emeline Cooper

COOPER, LEWIS   WMA   Page 31   F
    15 June 1857   Parents: Aglister & A. Cooper
    Reported by AYLESTON Cooper, father

COPENHAVER, AUGUSTU   WMA   Page 42   F
   24 Aug. 1858   Parents: James & Jane Copenhaver

COPENHAVER, CHAS. C.   WMA   Page 19   F
   24 July 1855   Parents: Valentine & Rebecca J. Copenl

COPENHAVER, CORDELIA   WFA   Page 55   F   Glade Spring
   1870   Parents: Hugh & [ill.] Ann Copenhaver

COPENHAVER, F.B.   WMA   Page 35   F
   5 Jan. 1857   Parents: Valentine & R.J. Copenhaver

COPENHAVER, JOHN B   WMA   Page 45   F
   10 Nov. 1859   Parents: Valentine & Rebecca Copenhav

COPENHAVER, MARY E   WFA   Page 11   F
   14 April 1854   Parents: James & Nancy Jane Copenhave

CORNELIUS, GEO. W.   WMA   Page 72   SB   Abingdon
   27 June 1892   Parents: Geo. P. & Mary R. Cornelius

COTTEN, CATHARINE   CFA   Page 73   L   Abingdon
   4 Nov. 1892   Parents: Henry & Martha Cotten

COTTON, ELIZA A   CFA   Page 54   F   Northfork Twp
   10 June 1871   Parents: Wesley & Clara Cotton

COTTON, THOS. J.   WMA   Page 42   F
   6 Dec. 1855   Parents: L.L. & R.C. Cotton

COUCH, JOHN C   WMA   Page 11   F
   Oct. 1854   Parents: David & Margaret Couch

COUCH, MARY B.A.   WFA   Page 35   SM
   14 Feb. 1857   Parents: David & Margret Couch

COUNTESS, DICA   WFA   Page 66   F   Kinderhook
   20 March 1892   Parents: John & Eliza Countess

COUNTS, [n.n.] (twin)   WFA   Page 60   F
   15 Oct. 1892   Parents: Wm. E. & M.E. Counts

COUNTS, [n.n.] (twin)   WFD   Page 60   F
   15 Oct. 1892   Parents: Wm. E. & M.E. Counts

COUNTS, FLOYD R   WMA   Page 60   F
   21 Oct. 1892   Parents: W.H. & Maggie Counts

COUNTS, JAMES C   WMA   Page 14   F
   26 Oct. 1854   Parents: Geo. & Mary Counts

COUNTS, JOSEPH D   WMA   Page 54   F   Northfork Tw
   13 Aug. 1871   Parents: Joseph S. & Elizabeth Count

COUNTS, MARY FRANCES   WFA   Page 13   F   Poor Valley
   8 Sept. 1854   Parents: Linic & Mary Counts

COUNTS, MAUD V   WFA   Page 68   F   North Fork D
   17 Feb. 1892   Parents: Gilbert & Sally Counts

COUNTS, WM.   WMA   Page 31   F
   18 Oct. 1856   Parents: Lenox & Mary Counts

COWAN, [n.n.]   W_D   Page 31   F
    27 June 1856   Parents: And. I. & Mariah Cowan

COWAN, [n.n.]   WMD   Page 17   F
    22 Sept. 1855   Parents: Hiram & Sabina Cowan

COWAN, MARG'T FRANKLIN   WFA   Page 3   F
    11 Aug. 1853   Father: And'w J. Cowan

COWAN, NORA J   WFA   Page 60   F
    15 Aug. 1892   Parents: Jasper & Mary Cowan

COWAN, WM. N.   WM_   Page 57   Kinderhook
    2 July 1870   Parents: Rich'd W. & Rhoda Cowan

COWAN, WM. P.   WMA   Page 60   F
    17 Aug. 1892   Parents: T.H. & Marth. W. Cowan

COWIN, L.F.   WFA   Page 35   F
    22 March 1857   Parents: J.G. & E. COWAN

COX, LOYD   WMA   Page 71   F   Goodson Twp.
    20 June 1892   Parents: Joseph & Alice Cox

COX, MARY ELIZABETH   WFA   Page 9   F
    1 Aug. 1854   Parents: Michael & Isabella J. Cox

COX, NANCY C   WFA   Page 35   F
    22 Oct. 1857   Parents: W.C. & E.C. Cox

CRABTREE, [n.n.]   WMA   Page 38   F
    23 March 1858   Parents: Zach & Caroline Crabtree

CRABTREE, A.C.   WFA   Page 8   S
    19 Dec. 1853   Parents: R.H. & Mary Crabtree

CRABTREE, JASPER   WMA   Page 1   C
    17 July 1853   Parents: Joseph & Mary Crabtree

CRABTREE, JOHN F   WMA   Page 22   F
    6 Oct. 1855   Parents: Zach & Caroline Crabtree

CRABTREE, MARGARET A   WFA   Page 49   F
    16 May 1859   Parents: Zach & Caroline Crabtree

CRANE, ROY L   WMA   Page 60   F
    3 June 1892   Parents: Nath'l & Amanda Crane

CRAWFORD, W.I.   WMA   Page 25   F
    26 Sept. 1856   Parents: John & Mary Crawford
    Reported by Mrs. Fleenor, neighbor

CRENSY, BENJ. H.   WMA   Page 59   F
    29 June 1892   Parents: Geo. W. & Lucy Crensy

CRESS, FRANCIS E   WFA   Page 31   F
    18 June 1857   Parents: Benj. & Margret E. CRISS

CRIGGER, FANNIE   WFA   Page 60   F
    1 Sept. 1892   Parents: J.W. & N.A. Crigger

CRISS, THOMAS J   WMA   Page 21   F
    5 Aug. 1855   Parents: Benj'n & M.E. Criss

CRISSA
    6 Oct. 1859   SFA   Page 50
           Owner: John M. Hamilton

CROSS, [n.n.]   WMA   Page 71   F   Goodson Twp.
    20 Feb. 1892   Parents: Andrew & Alice Cross

CROSS, ANDREW D   WM_   Page 57   Kinderhook
    8 June 1870   Parents: Jas. A. & Lydia Cross

CROSSWHITE, DIXIE   WFA   Page 60   F
    7 Nov. 1892   Parents: A.J. & Jennie Crosswhite

CROSSWHITE, NANCY JANE   WFA   Page 10   F
    15 June 1854   Parents: Jacob & Elizabeth Crosswhite

CROUEL, [n.n.]   WMD   Page 24   F
    1 June 1856   Father: Jno. M.C. CROUELL
    Reported by J.M.C. Crouel, father   Mother: Margret A. Crouel

CROUEL, JOS. B.   WMA   Page 24   F
    8 March 1856   Father: W.T. CROUELL
           Mother: Mary I. Crouel

CROUELL, ISAAC C   WMA   Page 31   F
    30 June 1857   Parents: Jno. M.C. & Mary A. Crouell

CROUELL, SAM'L A.   WMA   Page 24   F
    9 Dec. 1856   Parents: Jos. & Mary Crouell

CROW, AMANDA C   WFA   Page 42   F
    29 June 1858   Parents: W.R. & Elizabeth Crow

CROW, AND. W.   WMA   Page 35   F
    7 May 1857   Parents: James & Eliza A. Crow

CROW, JAMES   WMA   Page 5   F
    23 March 1853   Parents: William & Eliza M. Crow

CROW, MARTHA W   WFA   Page 29   F & MR
    16 March 1856   Parents: Wm. & E.M. Crow

CROW, MARY ELIZABETH   WFA   Page 19   F
    28 March 1855   Parents: William & Eliza M. Crow

CROWELL, SARAH   WFA   Page 49   F
    17 Sept. 1859   Parents: M.T. & Mary J. Crowell

CUBINE, RALPH   WMA   Page 24   F   Goodson
    27 Nov. 1892   Parents: George & Mary Cubine

CUDDY, [n.n.]   WMA   Page 8   F
    15 June 1853   Father: A. Cuddy

CUDDY, [n.n.]   WMA   Page 21   F
    14 Sept. 1855   Parents: John & Judith Cuddy
    Reported by A.C. Maxwell, physician

CUDDY, GEO.   WMA   Page 39   MW
    20 Aug. 1858   Parents: John & Judith Cuddy

CUDDY, LEANDER   WMA   Page 46   F
    15 July 1859   Parents: David & Mary Cuddy

CUDDY, WM. FRANKLIN   WMA   Page 13   F   North Fork
    13 March 1854   Parents: David & Mary Cuddy

CUDY, LEANAN   WFA   Page 49   F
    15 July 1859   Parents: David & Mary Cudy

CULLOP, [n.n.]   WMD   Page 59   F
    1 Aug. 1892   Parents: Ed. & Maggie Cullop

CULLOP, B. GROVER C.   WMA   Page 59   F
    4 Nov. 1892   Parents: J.R. & Mallie C. Cullop

CULLOP, JNO. A.B.   WMA   Page 60   F
    25 May 1892   Parents: L.C. & Berlin Cullop

CULLER, LOUISA   WFA   Page 22   F
    15 Sept. 1855   Parents: Martin A. & E. Culler

CUMMINGS, ELLEN W   WFA   Page 15   LW
    27 April 1854   Parents: Arthur C. & Elizabeth E. Cummings

CUMMINGS, JAMES W   WMA   Page 23   MR   Abingdon
    19 Sept. 1855   Parents: David C. & E.W. Cummings

CUMMINGS, JNO. M.P.   WMA   Page 26   LW
    29 June 1856   Parents: A.C. & E.E. Cummings

CUNNINGHAM, [n.n.]   WF_   Page 57   Kinderhook
    1870   Parents: Jo. & Lucinda Cunningham

CUNNINGHAM, [n.n.]   WF_   Page 57   Kinderhook
    1 Oct. 1870   Parents: Elijah & Lou Cunningham

CUNNINGHAM, ABRAM   WMA   Page 25   F
    1 Feb. 1856   Parents: Thos. B. & M. Cunningham

CUNNINGHAM, CAMPBELL J   WMA   Page 14   F
    23 Aug. 1854   Parents: Wm. B. & Catharine Cunningham

CUNNINGHAM, CHARLES N   WMA   Page 54   F   Northfork Twp.
    4 July 1871   Parents: Wm. B. & Catherine Cunningham

CUNNINGHAM, JAS. E.   WMA   Page 49   F
    10 April 1859   Parents: Jno. W. & J.A. Cunningham

CUNNINGHAM, JOSEPH   WMA   Page 22   F
    17 Feb. 1855   Parents: Robert & M. Cunningham

CUNNINGHAM, JOSEPH   WMA   Page 69   F   North Fork Dist.
    10 March 1892   Parents: Robt. & Julia Cunningham

CUNNINGHAM, MARTH. E.   WFA   Page 31   F
    20 Oct. 1857   Parents: Elijah & Lucinda Cunningham

CUNNINGHAM, MARY E   WFA   Page 32   F
    20 Dec. 1857   Parents: Wm. B. & Cath. Cunningham

CUNNINGHAM, MARY I   WFA   Page 32   F
    3 Oct. 1857   Parents: Geo. F. & Unity Cunningham

CUNNINGHAM, R.C. (twin)   WM_   Page 57   Kinderhook
    20 Sept. 1870   Parents: Washington & Mary Cunningham

CUNNINGHAM, R.E.
    22 Dec. 1892
    WMA   Page 71   F   Goodson
    Parents: J.E. & E.A. Cunningham

CUNNINGHAM, RUFUS
    5 Nov. 1859
    WMA   Page 49   F
    Parents: A.J. & Lucinda Cunningham

CUNNINGHAM, WILLIAM (twin)
    20 Sept. 1870
    WMA   Page 57   Kinderhook
    Parents: Washington & Mary Cunningham

CYNTHIA
    6 Dec. 1856
    SFA   Page 27
    Owner: A.F. Bradley

DABNEY, SUSAN H
    22 Aug. 1892
    WFA   Page 59

DABNEY, SUSAN H
    22 Aug. 1892
    WFA   Page 60   BO
    Parents: Jno. C. & Florence Dabney

DANIEL
    31 Aug. 1854
    SMA   Page 15
    Master: C.F. Trigg

DANIEL
    19 June 1855
    WMA   Page 23
    Owner: S.W. Montgomery

DANIEL
    Aug. 1855
    SMA   Page 28
    Mother: Eliza
    Owner: Thos. Davenport

DANIEL A
    20 Oct. 1855
    SMA   Page 23
    Owner: Jno. H. Clark

DANIEL W
    1 Aug. 1854
    SMA   Page 15
    Master: R.E. Cummings

DAUGHERTY, ALICE
    1 July 1859
    WFA   Page 46   F
    Parents: John & Rutha Daugherty

[DAUN], ROBT. P.
    19 Aug. 1854
    WMA   Page 14   F   Brook Hall
    Parents: John & Mariah [Daun]

DAVENPORT, [n.n.]
    Nov. 1854
    WFA   Page 11   F
    Parents: James M. & Lydia Davenport

DAVENPORT, [n.n.]
    23 Dec. 1855
    WFA   Page 17
    Mother: Emily Davenport

DAVENPORT, [n.n.]
    29 May 1858
    WMA   Page 42   F
    Parents: Henry & E. Davenport

DAVENPORT, [n.n.]
    10 April 1859
    WMD   Page 49   F
    Parents: Jas. N. & Lydia Davenport

DAVENPORT, A.C.
    25 March 1892
    WMA   Page 60   F
    Parents: R.H. & Mary M. Davenport

DAVENPORT, A.E.
    1 Sept. 1853
    WMA   Page 8   F
    Parents: E.L. & Mary Davenport

DAVENPORT, FRANKLIN PIERCE
    16 April 1853
    WMA   Page 3   F
    Father: Jas. N. Davenport

DAVENPORT, G.G.
    6 May 1857
    WMA   Page 35   F
    Parents: Jas. M. & Liddy Davenport

DAVENPORT, J.W.   WMA   Page 39   F
    18 Oct. 1858   Parents: David & M.A. Davenport

DAVENPORT, [JULIN] T.   WMA   Page 35   F
    1 July 1857   Parents: J.F. & J.F. Davenport

DAVENPORT, L.T.   WMA   Page 60   F
    10 March 1892   Parents: R.S. & N.A. Davenport

DAVENPORT, MARTHA   WFA   Page 46
    3 Nov. 1859   Parents: Julias T. & Sarah Davenport

DAVENPORT, W.H.   WMA   Page 60   F
    29 Nov. 1892   Parents: D.T. & Sarah E. Davenport

DAVENPORT, WILLIAM   WMA   Page 55   Saltville Dist.
    23 March 1870   Parents: J.T. & Sally Davenport

DAVID   SMA   Page 8
    18 Oct. 1853   Owner: Jno. F. Preston

DAVID   SMA   Page 15
    27 Jan. 1854   Master: Abram M. Connell

DAVID   SMA   Page 42
    17 March 1855   Owner: B. Carpenter

DAVID   SMA   Page 27
    15 Aug. 1856   Owner: Wm. Fields

DAVIDSON, DOROTHY L   WFA   Page 32   F
    28 Jan. 1857   Parents: Jn. B.R. & Mary Davidson

DAVIDSON, GEORGE   WMA   Page 1   L   Saltville
    July 1853   Parents: Jesse & Rebecca Davidson

DAVIDSON, JAMES   WMA   Page 16   F
    25 March 1855   Parents: Jesse & Rebecca Davidson

DAVIDSON, MITTY H   WMA   Page 39   F
    13 May 1858   Parents: T.C. & A.C. Davidson

DAVIS, [n.n.]   WMA   Page 21   LW
    13 May 1858   Parents: A. & Mary Davis

DAVIS, [n.n.]   WMA   Page 32   F
    4 Aug. 1857   Parents: W.L. & Susan Davis

DAVIS, [n.n.]   WFA   Page 69   North Fork Dist.
    5 Jan. 1892   Mother: Alice Davis

DAVIS, [n.n.]   WFA   Page 69   F   North Fork Dist.
    5 Jan. 1892   Parents: W.S.N. & V.B. Davis

DAVIS, ANNA L   WFA   Page 39   F
    4 Aug. 1858   Parents: W.L. & Susan Davis

DAVIS, ARTHUR C   WMA   Page 22   LW
    20 Nov. 1855   Parents: A. & Mary V. Davis

DAVIS, E.B.   WFA   Page 26   L
    15 April 1856   Parents: Chs. E. & Jane F. Davis

DAVIS, FAROLINE C   WFA   Page 60   F
21 Oct. 1892   Parents: Eli & Sarah J. Davis

DAVIS, JAMES FRANKLIN   WMA   Page 17   F
18 Jan. 1855   Parents: Thos. J. & Mary Davis

DAVIS, JAMES L   WMA   Page 21   F
6 April 1855   Parents: Jas. L. & E.J. Davis

DAVIS, JOSEPH   WMA   Page 42   F
20 Sept. 1858   Parents: W.R. & E.J. Davis

DAVIS, MARY ELDRIDGE   WFA   Page 3   PF   E&H College
24 July 1853   Parents: James A. & Sarah Jane Davis

DAVIS, ROLAND L   WMA   Page 70   F   Abingdon Dist
11 Dec. 1892   Parents: R.V. & M.L. Davis

DAVIS, SARAH   WFA   Page 11   F
6 July 1854   Parents: William & Mary Ann Davis

DAVIS, THURSA   SFA   Page 42
4 April 1858   Owner: R. Buchanan

DAVIS, WALTER W   WMA   Page 49   F
25 Dec. 1859   Parents: John M. & Elizabeth W. Davis

DAVIS, WILLIAM L   WMA   Page 16   PF   E&H College
16 Oct. 1855   Parents: James A. & Sarah Jane Davis

DAVISON, L.E.   WFA   Page 66   F   Kinderhook
10 Feb. 1892   Parents: S.W. & Martha DAVIDSON

DEBORD, MAUD   WFA   Page 60   F
18 April 1892   Parents: J.K. & Nancy E. Debord

DEBOSE, POWELL   CMA   Page 73   L   Near Abingdon
10 June 1892   Parents: Frank & Alice Debose

DEBUSK, [n.n.]   WMD   Page 55   F   Glade Spring
1870   Parents: Thomas & Catharine Debusk

DEBUSK, WLBERT O   WMA   Page 35   F
22 May 1857   Parents: Isaac & Fras. Debusk

DEBUSK, ELIZABETH   WFA   Page 9   WH
4 July 1854   Parents: Elisha & Abigail Debusk

DEBUSK, GEORGE W   WMA   Page 46   F
20 May 1859   Parents: Samuel & Eliza Debusk

DEBUSK, ISAAC N   WMA   Page 19   F
1 July 1855   Parents: Christo. & Lydia Debusk

DEBUSK, JACOB   WMA   Page 29   F
15 Sept. 1856   Parents: Ira & Unice Debusk

DEBUSK, JAMES   WMA   Page 13   F   Widner Valley
28 June 1854   Parents: Elijah & Elizabeth Debusk

DEBUSK, JAMES M   WMA   Page 17   F
8 Sept. 1855   Parents: Samuel & Dorcas Debusk

DEBUSK, JEANNETTE   WFA   Page 18   F
  12 Nov. 1855   Parents: Elijah & Elizabeth Debusk

DEBUSK, JENETTE A   WFA   Page 28   F
  21 Feb. 1856   Parents: Isaac & Frs. Debusk

DEBUSK, JOHN   WMA   Page 13   F   Widner Valley
  28 June 1854   Parents: Ira & Eunice Debusk

DEBUSK, MAGGIE MATILDA   WFA   Page 56   MC   Glade Spring Twp.
  1870   Parents: David & Eliza Debusk

DEBUSK, ROBT.   WMA   Page 46   F
  11 Jan. 1859   Parents: Ira & Dorcas Debusk

DEBUSK, SALLY   WFA   Page 5   F
  1 March 1853   Parents: Jacob & Elinder Debusk

DEBUSK, SETIN   WMA   Page 46   F
  8 Sept. 1859   Parents: Isaac & Frances Debusk

DEBUSK, UNAS CATHARINE   WFA   Page 55   Glade Spring Twp.
  1870   Parents: Isaac E. & Martha Jane Debusk

DEBUSK, WILLIAM   WMA   Page 46   F
  20 May 1859   Parents: David & Dorcas Debusk

DEBUSK, WM. R.   WMA   Page 35   F
  3 May 1857   Parents: Christ. & L. Debusk

DEBUSK, WM. SAMUEL   WMA   Page 55   F   Glade Spring Twp.
  1870   Parents: David & Sallie J. Debusk

DECK, HERBERT   WMA   Page 66   F   Kinderhook
  8 Oct. 1892   Parents: J.S. & Martha Deck

DECK, JAS. L.F.   WMA   Page 39   F
  6 Jan. 1858   Parents: Jas. & Susan Deck

DECK, SARAH C   WFA   Page 14   F
  7 Feb. 1854   Parents: Joseph & Susan Deck

DEFRIES, VIRGINIA ELLEN   WFA   Page 12   F
  20 Nov. 1854   Parents: Aquilla & Mary Defries

DENNY, HARRIET   WFA   Page 23   F
  30 March 1855   Parents: George & R. Denny

DENTON, ANN E.B.   WFA   Page 7   F
  20 Dec. 1853   Parents: Rob't & Eliza Denton

DENTON, D.B. (twin)   WMA   Page 7   F
  28 June 1853   Parents: Thos. A. & Mary Denton

DENTON, D.P.T.   WMA   Page 42   F
  30 Dec. 1858   Parents: James D. & B.J. Denton

DENTON, DAVID M.C.W.   WMA   Page 26   F
  14 March 1856   Parents: Rob't & S.J. Denton

DENTON, DEBLE ANN ELIZA   WFA   Page 18   F
  15 Sept. 1855   Parents: David, Jr., & Margaret Denton

DENTON, FRANKLIN   WMA   Page 72   D   Abingdon
    7 Dec. 1892   Parents: W.W. & L.G. Denton

DENTON, GEO. W.   WMA   Page 7   F
    20 Oct. 1853   Father: Jacob Denton
                            Mother: Rebecca RAMSEY

DENTON, KINDRICK HEISKELL   WMA   Page 18
    24 Nov. 1855   Parents: David C. & Elizabeth Denton

DENTON, L.R.F.   WMA   Page 39   F
    15 Aug. 1858   Parents: Robt. & S.J. Denton

DENTON, MARTHA M   WFA   Page 26
    20 Sept. 1856   Parents: William & M.E. Denton

DENTON, OSCAR H   WMA   Page 60   F
    12 April 1892   Parents: D.A. & Martha A. Denton

DENTON, V.C.   WFA   Page 39
    17 March 1858   Parents: D.C. & Eliza Denton

DENTON, WM. C. (twin)   WMA   Page 7   F
    28 June 1853   Parents: Thos. A. & Mary Denton

DERRY, [n.n.]   WFA   Page 71   F   Goodson
    Oct. 1892   Parents: William & Ellen Derry

DICKENSON, MARY M   WFA   Page 60   F
    21 Feb. 1892   Parents: Jas. F. & Callie Dickenson

DICKENSON, ROBT. M.C.   WMA   Page 60   F
    16 Dec. 1892   Parents: J.T. & Mary Dickenson

DICKENSON, T.L.G.   WMA   Page 39   F
    23 March 1858   Parents: Mongle & Sarah Dickenson

DICKERSON, ALBERT   CMA   Page 73   L   Near Abingdon
    1 Sept. 1892   Parents: J.A. & Caroline Dickerson

DICKERSON, ELLEN   WFA   Page 46   F
    27 April 1859   Parents: D.C. & Ema Dickerson

DICKERSON, NORAH   WFA   Page 71   F   Goodson
    12 Feb. 1892   Parents: Powell & Mariah Dickerson

DICKSON, [n.n.]   WFA   Page 54   F   Abingdon Twp.
    20 April 1871   Parents: John & Mary Dickson

DINKINS, JOHN   WMA   Page 46   F
    10 July 1859   Parents: William & Margaret DINKIN

DINSMOORE, [n.n.]   WMA   Page 49   F
    24 May 1859   Parents: G.L. & S.C. Dinsmoore

DINSMORE, FRANCES   WFA   Page 10   F
    5 June 1854   Parents: Samuel & Rebecca Dinsmore

DINSMORE, GEO. W.   WMA   Page 28   F
    1 June 1856   Parents: Saml. & Rebecca Dinsmore

DINSMORE, SAML. (twin)   WMA   Page 11   F
    8 May 1854   Parents: James & Nancy Dinsmore

DINSMORE, WM. A. (twin)   WMA   Page 11   F
    8 May 1854   Parents: James & Nancy Dinsmore

DISHMAN, JAMES C   WMA   Page 7   F
    24 Aug. 1853   Father: Jno. D. Dishman

DISHMAN, JULIA A   WFA   Page 22   F
    20 April 1855   Parents: Jno. D. & Eliza Dishman

DISHNER, [n.n.]   WMD   Page 24   F
    20 Oct. 1856   Parents: Christ. & Mary Dishner

DISHNER, CHRISTOPHER   WMA   Page 6   F
    20 Dec. 1853   Parents: Martin & Matilda Dishner

DISHNER, EDWARD   WMA   Page 24   F
    26 Oct. 1856   Parents: Jno. & Martha Dishner

DISHNER, GEO. F.   WMA   Page 32   F
    10 Dec. 1857   Parents: Christ. & Mary Dishner

DISHNER, JOHN   WMA   Page 25   F
    28 Sept. 1856   Parents: Martin & Matilda Dishner

DISHNER, MARGRET J   WFA   Page 14   F
    30 Oct. 1854   Parents: Christ. & Mary Dishner

DISHNER, S.E.   WMA   Page 39   F
    15 Sept. 1858   Parents: Samul & Ann Dishner

DISHNER, WILLIAM   WMA   Page 25   F
    1 May 1856   Parents: Saml. & Ann Dishner

DIXON, [n.n.]   WFA   Page 49   F
    6 Nov. 1859   Parents: Isaac W. & Rachel Dixon

DIXON, C.E.   WFA   Page 39   F
    6 Oct. 1858   Parents: Isaac W. & Rachel Dixon

DIXON, CHARITY   WFA   Page 32   F
    17 Nov. 1857   Parents: Oliver & Louisa Dixon

DIXON, ELBERT C   WMA   Page 21
    1 Sept. 1855   Parents: Oliver & Louisa Dixon

DIXON, FRANK   CMA   Page 73   L   Near Abingdon
    30 May 1892   Parents: Frank & Edna Dixon

DIXON, ISAAC P   WMA   Page 7   F
    Oct. 1853   Parents: Oliver & Eliza Dixon

DIXON, JAMES C   WMA   Page 54   F   Northfork Twp.
    28 Dec. 1871   Parents: Charles B. & Lucinda Dixon

DIXON, JOHN C   WMA   Page 39   F
    30 Oct. 1858   Parents: Ed. & Margaret Dixon

DIXON, L.C.   WFA   Page 69   North Fork Dist.
    28 Feb. 1892   Parents: C.B. & Loucinda Dixon

DIXON, MARTHA E   WFA   Page 25   F
    4 April 1856   Parents: Edward & Margret Dixon

DOBBINS, AND. J.   WMA   Page 25   F
    1 Nov. 1856   Parents: Geo. W. & E.J. Dobbins
    Reported by Jas. Crabtree, grandfather

DOBYNS, JAMES W   WMA   Page 22   F
    22 June 1855   Parents: Geo. W. & E. Dobyns

DOLINGER, BEATY R   WMA   Page 29   F
    5 Nov. 1856   Parents: Wm. & Lydia Dolinger

DONAPHIN, ALEXANDER   CMA   Page 55   F   Saltville Dist.
    20 Dec. 1870   Parents: Robert & Mary Donaphin

DOLLY ANN   SFA   Page 17
    15 July 1855   Mother: Tempe Ann
    Reported by Rob't F. Wilkerson, ex'r of owner   Owner: Thos. Wilke?

DOSS, HENRY   WMA   Page 60   F
    22 Aug. 1892   Parents: Henry & Mary Doss

DOSS, MONROE   WMA   Page 59 & 60 F
    4 Sept. 1892   Parents: E.D. & Clarinda Doss

DOSS, THOMAS   WMA   Page 19   L
    9 Nov. 1855   Parents: Henry & Nancy Doss

DOSS, WILLARD G   WMA   Page 60   F
    18 March 1892   Parents: T.P. & Margaret Doss

DOWELL, [n.n.]   WMD   Page 59 & 60 F
    9 March 1892   Parents: J.C. & Belle Dowell

DOWELL, [GILLIS] M   WF_   Page 57   Kinderhook
    21 Dec. 1870   Parents: James & Elizabeth Dowell

DROKE, JOSEPH N.D.   WMA   Page 14   F
    1 Sept. 1854   Parents: Job. K. & Elizabeth Droke

DROKE, JOHN   WMA   Page 39   B
    15 March 1858   Parents: Job K. & E. Droke

DROKE, MARIAH A   WFA   Page 24   B
    13 June 1856   Parents: Job D. & E.B. Droke

DUFF, [n.n.]   WMA   Page 3   F
    8 Jan. 1853   Father: Stephen B. Duff

DUFF, [n.n.]   WFA   Page 18
    22 June 1855   Mother: Rebecca Duff
    Reported by Jno. N. Duff, father to mother

DUFF, AMANDA FLORENCE   WFA   Page 5   F
    31 Aug. 1853   Parents: Thos. J. & Elizabeth Duff

DUFF, CAMPBELL W   WMA   Page 54   F   Abingdon Twp.
    4 March 1871   Parents: John S.B. & Maria Duff

DUFF, DICY A   WFA   Page 28   F
    27 July 1856   Parents: Wm. K. & Martha A. Duff

DUFF, HANNAH P   WFA   Page 29   F
    20 Sept. 1856   Parents: S.B. & Sarah Duff

DUFF, JOHN   WMA   Page 11   F
      14 Sept. 1854   Parents: Samuel H. & Deborah Duff

DUFF, MARTHA ANN FARRIS (twin)   WFA   Page 4   F
      13 June 1853   Parents: John A. & Lucretia Duff

DUFF, MARY HOPKINS   WFA   Page 4   F
      17 Sept. 1853   Parents: Wm. K. & Martha Duff

DUFF, SAML. FRANK BARR (twin)   WMA   Page 4   F
      13 June 1853   Parents: John A. & Lucretia Duff

DUKES, WALTER   WMA   Page 60   F
      12 Jan. 1892   Parents: Jas. L. & Mary Dukes

DUNCAN   SMA   Page 16
      17 Feb. 1855   Mother: Dicey
      Reported by Mrs. S.P. King, mother of the heirs   Owner: Wm. King's heirs

DUNCAN, ACENETH   WFA   Page 13   F   Poor Valley
      10 May 1854   Parents: Henry & Margaret Duncan

DUNCAN, JOHN HENRY   WMA   Page 10   F
      11 Dec. 1854   Parents: John & Susan Duncan

DUNCAN, LELIA Y   WFA   Page 60   F
      7 Dec. 1892   Parents: Wm. L. & Mollie J. Duncan

DUNCAN, SUSAN DORCAS   WFA   Page 2   F
      18 Feb. 1853   Parents: John & Susan Duncan

DUNGAN, THOMAS J   WMA   Page 12   L
      12 Oct. 1854   Parents: Absalom H. & Ann E. Dungan

DUNKIN, EMORY   WMA   Page 46   F
      10 July 1859   Parents: Henry & Amanda Dunkin

DUNKIN, LUCINDA   WFA   Page 46   F
      10 Sept. 1859   Parents: John & Susannah Dunkin

DUNN, ABNER M   WMA   Page 32   MR
      6 July 1857   Parents: A.J. & Eliza J. Dunn

DUNN, CHESTER   WMA   Page 59 & 60 F
      10 March 1892   Parents: John F. & Martha Dunn

DUNN, CONNALLY   WMA   Page 8   I
      15 Sept. 1853   Parents: D.C. & H.N. Dunn

DUNN, ELIZABETH   WFA   Page 27   O
      10 June 1856   Parents: D.C. & H.A. Dunn

DUNN, JNO. O.   WMA   Page 60   BO
      10 Dec. 1892   Parents: H.B. & E.G. Dunn

DUNN, MARY   SFA   Page 9
      15 Dec. 1853   Owner: D.C. Dunn

DUNN, WILLIE F   WMA   Page 60
      16 Oct. 1892   Mother: Catherine Dunn

DUTTON, CHARLES   WMA   Page 60   MC
      1 Sept. 1892   Parents: D.H. & Mary E. Dutton

DUTTON, DAVID HENRY
13 March 1853
WMA   Page 2   B
Parents: John J. & Louisa Dutton

DUTTON, JAMES
10 Sept. 1859
WMA   Page 46   F
Parents: John & Louisa Dutton

DUTTON, JNO. EVERETT
1 April 1854
WMA   Page 10   F
Parents: Peter & Mary E. Dutton

DUTTON, MARGARET ELIZABETH
15 Oct. 1855
WFA   Page 17   B
Parents: John J. & Louisa Dutton

DUTTON, MARY K
26 June 1857
WFA   Page 35   F
Parents: Jn. J. & L.S. Dutton

DUTTON, SARAH ELIZA
1870
WFA   Page 55   F   Glade Spring Twp
Parents: James & Martha Jane Dutton

DUWALL, ALVIN
10 Oct. 1892
WMA   Page 60   F
Father: Wm. DUVALL
Mother: Mary DUVAL

DYE, ANDREW
16 June 1854
WMA   Page 11
Mother: Letitia Dye

DYE, CATHARINE
Oct. 1870
WF_   Page 57   Kinderhook
Parents: Archibald & Mary A. Dye

DYE, OLIVIA MAY
8 Nov. 1892
WFA   Page 66   F   Kinderhook
Parents: Branson & Sallie Dye

DYE, SARAH L.J.
23 Oct. 1892
WFA   Page 59 & 60 F
Parents: C.G. & Angeline Dye

EADS, J.T.
June 1892
WMA   Page 66   F   Kinderhook
Parents: W.K. & S.F. Eads

EADS, MARY
4 Oct. 1858
WFA   Page 39   B
Parents: Jno. & Sarah Eads

EADS, MARY C
2 Sept. 1859
WFA   Page 49   F
Parents: William & Nancy Eads

EADY
20 Sept. 1856
SFA   Page 17
Owner: Wm. Spurrier

EAKIN, ALEXANDER
26 Sept. 1859
WMA   Page 46   F
Parents: William & Semantha Eakin

EAKIN, ARTHUR
7 Dec. 1859
WMA   Page 46   F
Parents: John & Rebecca Eakin

EAKIN, JAMES
10 Aug. 1857
WMA   Page 35   F
Parents: John & Rebecca Eakin

EAKIN, JOHN LAFAYETTE M
1 Aug. 1855
WMA   Page 17
Parents: James M. & Emily Eakin

EAKIN, JOHN M
18 March 1854
WMA   Page 10   F
Parents: William A. & Mary E. Eakin

EAKIN, MARY E
16 May 1857
WFA   Page 35   F
Parents: Jas. M. & Emily Eakin

EAKIN, SARAH
    26 Dec. 1855
WFA   Page 17   F
Parents: John & Rebecca Eakin

EAKIN, THOS. M.
    15 March 1858
WMA   Page 42   F
Father: W.A. Eakin

EAKIN, WM. A.
    5 March 1856
WMA   Page 28   F
Parents: Jas. G. & Sarah A. Eakin

EAKIN, WM. J.
    10 March 1856
WMA   Page 28   TC
Parents: Wm. A. & Mary E. Eakin

EARLES, ALICE A
    26 Nov. 1892
WFA   Page 60   F
Parents: L.D. & Martha Earles

EARLS, EDMUND L
    21 April 1854
WMA   Page 11   L
Parents: Jesse & Ann Earls

EASTRAGE, ELIZABETH ANN
    1 July 1853
WFA   Page 2
Mother: Drusilla Eastrage

EASTRAGE, MARY
    12 April 1853
WFA   Page 2
Mother: Abbey Eastrage

EASTRIDGE, HENRY
    30 May 1857
WMA   Page 35   F
Parents: E. & M. Eastridge

EASTRIDGE, MARTHA (twin)
    18 Aug. 1892
WFA   Page 69   F   North Fork Dist.
Father: David ESTRIDGE
Mother: Lucinda Eastridge

EASTRIDGE, MARY (twin)
    18 Aug. 1892
WFA   Page 69   F   North Fork Dist.
Father: David ESTRIDGE
Mother: Lucinda Eastridge

EASTRIDGE, MATTHEW
    26 May 1856
WMA   Page 30   F
Parents: Wm. & Abigal Eastridge

EASTRIDGE, NANCY E
    24 June 1856
WFA   Page 30   F
Father: Cal Whitaker
Mother: Drucilla Eastridge

EATON, MARY E
    22 Feb. 1858
WFA   Page 42   F
Parents: Wm. & M. Eaton

EAVENS, NANCY
    16 Aug. 1859
WFA   Page 36   F
Parents: William & Ruth EVENS

EDITH
    20 Sept. 1853
SFA   Page 8
Owner: Jas. L. Davis

EDMONDSEN, MARGARET SHEFFEY
    7 Oct. 1853
WFA   Page 3   F
Parents: Wm. C. & Susan Edmondsen

EDMONDSON, [n.n.]
    15 July 1855
WMA   Page 19   F
Parents: William & Elizabeth Edmondson

EDMONDSON, [n.n.]
    8 March 1892
WMD   Page 60   MC
Parents: J.A. & Sarah Edmondson

EDMONDSON, ABEDNEGO W
    1 Feb. 1855
WMA   Page 17   F
Parents: Wm. M. & Matilda Edmondson

EDMONDSON, ANDREW C   WMA   Page 19   F
      30 Aug. 1855   Parents: James & Eleanor Edmondson

EDMONDSON, ANDREW RUSSELL   WMA   Page 56   F   Glade Spring
      1870   Parents: John B. & Mary J. Edmondson

EDMONDSON, ESTHER A.A.   WFA   Page 28   F
      21 May 1856   Parents: Rob't, Jr., & Eliz. J. Edmon(

EDMONDSON, FRS. N.   WFA   Page 28   F
      12 Jan. 1856   Parents: Jno. D. & Margret Edmondson

[EDMONDSON], HENRY WALKER   WMA   Page 56   F   Glade Spring
      1870   Parents: Thomas & Rachel Edmondson
         Child is listed as Henry Walker; however, Thomas & Rachel Edmondson
         are clearly indicated as the parents.

EDMONDSON, JAS. A.   WMA   Page 31   F
      21 Dec. 1856   Parents: Jno. L.G. & Margret Edmondso

EDMONDSON, MARY E.H.   WFA   Page 46   F
      22 Oct. 1859   Parents: Robt. & Jane Edmondson

EDMONDSON, NICKERSON SNEAD   WMA   Page 19   F
      1855   Parents: David & Mary Edmondson

EDMONDSON, S   WFA   Page 42   F
      24 July 1858   Parents: Isaac & Martha Edmondson

EDMONDSON, SUSAN   WFA   Page 35   F
      16 April 1857   Parents: Wm. & E. Edmondson

EDMONDSON, VIRGINIA F   WFA   Page 46   F
      15 June 1859   Parents: John L.G. & Margaret J. Edmo

EDMONDSON, W.B.   WMA   Page 42   F
      23 June 1858   Parents: Jas. & Ellen Edmondson

EDMUND   SMA   Page 23
      5 Dec. 1855   Owner: Rob't F. Preston

EDMUNDSON, ANN   WFA   Page 4   F
      5 May 1853   Parents: Wm. & Eliz. Edmundson

EDMUNDSON, ARCHIBALD   WMA   Page 4   F
      4 April 1853   Parents: Andrew & Nancy Edmundson

EDMUNDSON, RACHEL C   WFA   Page 4   F
      10 Dec. 1853   Parents: John D. & Margaret Edmundson

EDWARD   SMA   Page 8
      28 Feb. 1853   Owner: Peter S. Hanby

EDWARD   SMA   Page 8
      5 Sept. 1853   Owner: Wm. R. Rhea

EDWARD   SMA   Page 34
      20 Nov. 1857   Owner: A. Edwards

EDWARDS, FRANK   WMA   Page 66   F   Kinderhook
      8 June 1892   Parents: Peter & Polly Edwards

ELDRETH, CHAS. O.   WMA   Page 60   F
      24 Nov. 1892   Parents: Wash. & Nancy Eldreth

ELDROD, SOPH. A. WFA Page 60 F
  21 June 1892 Parents: S.H. & V.C. ELROD

ELIAS SMA Page 8
  15 Nov. 1853 Owner: Francis Preston

ELIZA SFA Page 34
  8 Oct. 1857 Owner: R.T. Legard

ELIZA SFA Page 39
  14 March 1858 Owner: Rachel Fickle

ELIZABETH SFA Page 30
  1 May 1856 Owner: Wm. Byars

ELIZABETH SFA Page 46
  9 April 1859 Master: Caleb Logan

ELIZABETH SFA Page 51
  20 Sept. 1859 Owner: Richard Nuckols

ELLEN SFA Page 4
  1 Oct. 1853 Owner: Jas. A. Bailey

ELLEN SFA Page 12
  15 April 1854 Mother: Ann
    Owner: Joseph Snodgrass

ELLEN SFA Page 13
  30 April 1854 Mother: Mariah
    Owner: Jas. M. Crockett

ELLEN (twin; sister unnamed) SFA Page 27
  13 June 1856 Owner: Elizabeth Lathim

ELLEN SFA Page 27
  11 Aug. 1857 Owner: Jas. C. Campbell

ELLEN SFA Page 38
  4 Sept. 1858 Owner: Mary Bondurant

ELLEN SFA Page 46
  10 April 1859 Owner: Richard Montgomery

ELROD, JOSEPH EMORY WMA Page 56 F Glade Spring Twp.
  1870 Parents: Wiley & Delilah Elrod

ERNEST, WM. BYARS WMA Page 4 A
  29 April 1853 Parents: John H. & Amanda Jane Ernest

EVANS, MARTHA WFA Page 12 F
  24 April 1854 Parents: William S. & Ruth Evans

EVERSOLE, GEO. W. WMA Page 49 F
  8 May 1859 Parents: Robert & Mary D. Eversole

EWING, MARTHA J WFA Page 69 F North Fork Dist.
  15 April 1892 Parents: Robt. & Alberta Ewing

[FANALRHAY, n.n.] CMA Page 56 F Glade Spring Twp.
  1870 Parents: H. & Elian [Fanahrhay]

FANNIE
11 April 1854

SFA   Page 15
Master: Henry F[illegible]

FANNIE
15 Dec. 1859

SFA   Page 51
Owner: Wallace Maxwell

FANNING, FRS. A.
6 Oct. 1856

WMA   Page 30   P
Parents: Frs. M. & Elmira R. Fanning

FARENSWORTH, WM. G.
27 July 1871

WMA   Page 54   F   Abingdon Twp.
Parents: Joseph S. & Sarah O. Farensworth

FARIS, ANN ELIZA
20 March 1853

WFA   Page 1   L
Parents: Thomas & Mary Faris

FARIS, DANIEL
12 May 1859

WMA   Page 46   F
Parents: David & Elizabeth Faris

FARIS, EFFIE A
2 Jan. 1892

WFA   Page 60   F
Parents: G.W. & Annie Faris

FARIS, FRANCIS
24 July 1856

WFA   Page 30
Mother: Rachel FARRIS

FARIS, LUMAS
4 April 1892

WMA   Page 60   F
Parents: Wm. & Nan. L. Faris

FARIS, MAHALA
1 Nov. 1856

WFA   Page 30   F
Parents: David & Eliz'th FARRIS

FARIS, RACHEL
25 Aug. 1859

WFA   Page 46   F
Parents: Julias & Rachel Faris

FARIS, WILLIAM DAVID
16 Dec. 1853

WMA   Page 1   L
Parents: Julius C. & Rachel Faris

FARNSWORTH, CARL R
2 May 1892

WMA   Page 61   F
Parents: Wm. G. & Nancy Farnsworth

FARRIS, [n.n.]
15 Jan. 1854

WFA   Page 9   W   Saltville
Parents: James & Betsy Jane Farris

FARRIS, BALLARD
6 Nov. 1854

WMA   Page 9   F   Saltville
Parents: David & Elizabeth Farris

FARRIS, JAS. W.
4 July 1857

WMA   Page 35   F
Parents: Jacob M. & Mary Y. Farris

FARRIS, JOHN H
6 Sept. 1857

WMA   Page 35   F
Parents: David & Eliz'th Farris

FARRIS, MILLY
28 Oct. 1855

WFA   Page 16   L   Saltville
Parents: James & Elizabeth Farris

FARRIS, THOMAS
1 Sept. 1892

WMA   Page 71   F   Goodson
Parents: A.J. & Nettie D. Farris

FARRIS, VIRGINIA
10 Nov. 1858

WFA   Page 43   F
Parents: Jacob M. & M.Y. Farris

FARRIS, WM. R.
4 Nov. 1857

WMA   Page 35   F
Parents: James & E.J. Farris

FEATHERS, WILLIAM
21 July 1892
WMA   Page 71   L   Goodson
Parents: Isaac & Jennie Feathers

FELTA, BETTIE
Nov. 1892
WFA   Page 36   F   Kinderhook
Parents: Joseph & Ann Felta

FELTY, ELIZA J
28 July 1856
WFA   Page 24   F
Parents: H.R. & Abigal Felty

FELTY, ELIZABETH R
9 June 1854
WFA   Page 14   F
Parents: Henry R. & Elizabeth Felty

FELTY, GEORGE
15 Aug. 1859
WMA   Page 46   F
Parents: Michael & Rebecca Felty

FELTY, JAS. H.
25 March 1857
WMA   Page 32   F
Parents: Malon & Deborah Felty

FELTY, JOS. D.
27 Oct. 1857
WMA   Page 32   F
Parents: Geo. W. & Margret Felty

FELTY, MARTIN F
25 March 1858
WMA   Page 39   F
Parents: Frank & Susan Felty

FELTY, MARY E
14 May 1856
WFA   Page 30   F
Parents: Jno. M. & Nancy Felty

FERGERSON, MATTIE
5 March 1892
WFA   Page 66   F   Kinderhook
Parents: G.W. & Alice Fergerson

FERN, ADA
1 June 1892
WFA   Page 61   F
Parents: M.L. & Lou Fern

FERN, MARGARET
25 April 1853
WFA   Page 2   F
Father: William Fern

FERRELL, MARTHA W
17 June 1858
WFA   Page 40   F
Parents: S.O. & Mary Ferrell

FERRELL, WESLEY
8 Oct. 1855
WMA   Page 23   F
Parents: Samuel & Mary Ferrell

FICKLE, ISABELLA C
25 Nov. 1855
WFA   Page 22   F
Parents: Isaac & Louisa Fickle

FICKLE, MALVINA
21 July 1859
WFA   Page 50   F
Parents: Isaac & Louisa Fickle

FICKLE, SARAH J
2 Dec. 1859
WFA   Page 50   F
Parents: A.B. & Ellen Fickle

FICKLE, SARAH J
28 Dec. 1858
WFA   Page 39   F
Parents: A.B. & Ellen Fickle

FIELDS, GEO. H.
30 July 1856
WMA   Page 26   BR
Parents: Jas. & Susan E. Fields

FIELDS, THOS. E.B.
4 Aug. 1855
WMA   Page 20   BR
Parents: Wm. & Eleanor M. Fields

FIELDS, WILLIE
5 Aug. 1892
WMA   Page 66   F   Kinderhook
Parents: Henry & Mary Fields

FINDLAY, THOMAS   WMA   Page 46   F
    5 Dec. 1859   Parents: Alexander & Ann B. FINDLEY

FISHER, GEO. D.   WMA   Page 71   F   Goodson
    20 June 1892   Parents: Joseph & Amanda Fisher

FLANEGAN, MARY JANE   WFA   Page 3   L
    July 1853   Father: John Flanegan

FLANNAGAN, LOUISE   WFA   Page 61   F
    22 April 1892   Parents: J.F. & Nancy J. Flannagan

FLANNAGAN, MARY R   WFA   Page 61   F
    20 July 1892   Parents: Lewis & Alice Flannagan

FLANNAGAN, WILL L   WMA   Page 61   F
    7 March 1892   Parents: Trigg & Mary Flannagan

FLEENOR, [n.n.]   WFD   Page 39   F
    6 July 1858   Parents: Jasper & Margaret Fleenor

FLEENOR, [n.n.]   WFD   Page 50   F
    27 March 1859   Parents: Jasper & Margaret Fleenor

FLEENOR, [n.n.]   WMA   Page 50   F
    9 Oct. 1859   Parents: David & Matilda Fleenor

FLEENOR, [n.n.]   WF_   Page 57   Kinderhook
    29 Feb. 1870   Parents: E.H. & Francis R.V. Fleenor

FLEENOR, A.L.   WMA   Page 49   F
    14 July 1859   Parents: Frank & Sarah A. Fleenor

FLEENOR, AMANDA   WFA   Page 66   F   Kinderhook
    8 Aug. 1892   Parents: Joseph & Mary Fleenor

FLEENOR, ANDREW R   WMA   Page 14   F
    28 July 1854   Parents: Elisha M. & R.C. Fleenor

FLEENOR, ANN E   WFA   Page 50   F
    7 Sept. 1859   Parents: John H. & Sarah A. Fleenor

FLEENOR, CHARLES   WM_   Page 57   Kinderhook
    1870   Parents: Moses & Rachel Fleenor

FLEENOR, CHARLES   WM_   Page 57   Kinderhook
    15 Sept. 1870   Parents: Alfred P. & Virginia Fleenor

FLEENOR, CYNTHIA A.S.E.   WFA   Page 26   F
    25 March 1856   Parents: Drury & Latitia Fleenor

FLEENOR, DELLA FRANCIS   WF_   Page 57   Kinderhook
    15 June 1870   Parents: John R. & Elizabeth Fleenor

FLEENOR, ELIZA   WFA   Page 50   F
    1 Aug. 1859   Parents: John B. & Eliza D. Fleenor

FLEENOR, ELIZA B   WFA   Page 25   F
    9 July 1859   Parents: Isaac & Jane Fleenor

FLEENOR, ELIZABETH A   WFA   Page 21   F
    8 Oct. 1855   Parents: Peter H. & Elizabeth Fleenor

48

FLEENOR, LAFAYETTE Mc
6 May 1854
WMA   Page 14   F
Parents: Robert & Elizabeth Fleenor

FLEENOR, HAMSON
1870
WM_   Page 57   Kinderhook
Parents: Geo. & Delilah Fleenor

FLEENOR, HANSON
15 Dec. 1856
WMA   Page 26   F
Parents: David & Matilda Fleenor

FLEENOR, HARRY I.B.
10 Jan. 1857
WMA   Page 32   F
Parents: Joel & Mary A. Fleenor

FLEENOR, ISAAC E
1 Aug. 1856
WMA   Page 24   F
Parents: Daniel & Cath Fleenor

FLEENOR, JEFFERSON
12 March 1855
WMA   Page 21   F
Parents: Jeremiah & E. Fleenor

FLEENOR, JETTIE
10 Nov. 1892
WFA   Page 71   F   Goodson
Parents: Jeff & Mary C. Fleenor

FLEENOR, JOHN
10 Aug. 1892
WMA   Page 66   F   Kinderhook
Parents: Jacob & Sallie Fleenor

FLEENOR, JNO. D.E.
25 July 1859
WMA   Page 50   F
Parents: Joel & Ann Fleenor

FLEENOR, JOHN J
30 June 1859
WMA   Page 50   F
Parents: Rufus & Sarah Fleenor

FLEENOR, JNO. R.
21 Nov. 1857
WMA   Page 32   F
Parents: Levi & Mary Fleenor

FLEENOR, JOHN R
1 March 1858
WMA   Page 39
Parents: Levi & Mary Fleenor

FLEENOR, JOHN W
20 Nov. 1870
WM_   Page 57   Kinderhook
Parents: Robt. & Julia A. Fleenor

FLEENOR, KATIE
1 July 1892
WFA   Page 66   F   Kinderhook
Parents: H.S. & Hart Fleenor

FLEENOR, LEVI C
29 Oct. 1857
WMA   Page 21   F
Parents: Gasper & Margaret Fleenor

FLEENOR, M.J.
3 Sept. 1853
WFA   Page 7   F
Father: Thos. D. Fleenor

FLEENOR, MAMIE
10 Aug. 1892
WFA   Page 66   F   Kinderhook
Parents: J.G. & Nannie Fleenor

FLEENOR, MARGARET E
1 June 1858
WFA   Page 39   F
Parents: W.G. & E.A. Fleenor

FLEENOR, MARTHA
1 Dec. 1892
WFA   Page 66   F   Kinderhook
Father: J.R. Fleenor

FLEENOR, MARTHA D
4 June 1854
WFA   Page 14   F
Parents: Thos. W. & Deida Fleenor

FLEENOR, MARTHA M
5 March 1858
WFA   Page 39   F
Parents: Martin & M.A.M. Fleenor

FLEENOR, MARY A 7 Oct. 1859	WFA Page 50 F Parents: John & Sarah Fleenor
FLEENOR, MARY A 8 April 1853	WFA Page 7 F Parents: Elisha P. & Ellen Fleenor
FLEENOR, MARY V 5 Nov. 1858	WFA Page 39 F Parents: Daniel & Cath Fleenor
FLEENOR, MILTON W 19 Aug. 1857	WMA Page 32 F Parents: Elisha P. & Ellen Fleenor
FLEENOR, NANCY C 24 Aug. 1853	WFA Page 7 F Parents: Jno. Q. & Julia A. Fleenor
FLEENOR, NANCY C 25 May 1857	WFA Page 32 F Parents: Jas. A. & R.I. Fleenor
FLEENOR, NELSON Aug. 1892	WMA Page 66 F Kinderhook Parents: E.O. & [Dicee] Fleenor
FLEENOR, NICHOLAS 16 Oct. 1855	WMA Page 22 F Parents: Elijah & Rebecca Fleenor
FLEENOR, RHODA 26 March 1853	WFA Page 6 F Father: David Fleenor
FLEENOR, ROB'T E 17 Nov. 1858	WMA Page 39 F Parents: David & M.E. Fleenor
FLEENOR, SADIE 10 June 1892	WFA Page 66 Kinderhook Mother: Dell Fleenor
FLEENOR, SARAH E 2 Sept. 1855	WFA Page 22 F Parents: Thos. W.D. & Lucinda Fleenor
FLEENOR, SARAH E 20 Sept. 1855	WFA Page 22 F Parents: Adam & M.J. Fleenor
FLEENOR, SARAH E 14 June 1892	WFA Page 69 F North Fork Di Paarents: Geo. L. & Cintha Fleenor
FLEENOR, SIDNEY J 30 June 1853	WMA Page 7 F Parents: Drury & Letitia Fleenor
FLEENOR, THOS. W 21 Aug. 1857	WMA Page 32 F Parents: T.W. & Deida Fleenor
FLEENOR, THOS. W.D. 6 Dec. 1859	WMA Page 50 F Parents: Wm. P. & Minerva Fleenor
FLEENOR, W.M. 31 Sept. 1892	WMA Page 66 F Kinderhook Parents: Robert & Sallie Fleenor
FLEENOR, W.W. 31 Dec. 1857	WMA Page 32 F Parents: Rufus & Sarah Fleenor
FLEENOR, WM. 30 Sept. 1858	WMA Page 39 F Parents: David & Matilda Fleenor
FLEENOR, WM. F. 31 Oct. 1855	WMA Page 22 F Parents: E.P. & Nancy E. Fleenor

FLEENOR, WM. L.
    10 May 1855
WMA   Page 21   F
Parents: Joel & M.A. Fleenor

FLEENOR, ZACH
    28 Oct. 1856
WMA   Page 26   F
Parents: Robt. & E. Fleenor

FLEENOR, ZACHARIAH
    17 April 1870
WM_   Page 57   Kinderhook
Parents: Milton & Sarah Fleenor

FLORANCE
    15 Sept. 1859
SFA   Page 46
Master: Absalom Beattie

FLORENCE
    10 Oct. 1856
SFA   Page 30
Owner: W.T. Fulcher

FLOYD
    15 Feb. 1859
SMA   Page 46
Master: Samuel Dunn

FORAN, HENRY P
    1871
WMA   Page 54   F   Northfork Twp.
Parents: Hesekiah & Catharine Foran

FORISTER, MARTHA JANE
    8 Oct. 1855
WFA   Page 18   SM
Parents: Joseph & Dorcas Forister

FORISTER, WILLIAM
    9 Sept. 1853
WMA   Page 6   SM
Father: Joseph Forister

FORTNER, EDDIE BENTLEY
    1870
WMA   Page 56   F   Glade Spring Twp.
Parents: S.G. & Millie Fortner

FOSTER, [n.n.]
    25 June 1892
WMA   Page 51   F
Parents: R.C. & Sarah M. Foster

FOSTER, FRANK
    6 April 1892
CMA   Page 73   L   Goodson
Parents: Henry & Celia Foster

FRANCES
    25 Aug. 1854
SFA   Page 15
Master: Sam'l E. Goodson

FRANCIS
    6 April 1856
SFA   Page 30
Owner: Madison Beaty

FRANCIS
    15 Aug. 1856
SFA   Page 30
Owner: Jacob Morell

FRANCIS A
    10 Nov. 1853
SMA   Page 18
Owner: Jno. F. Preston

FRANCISCO, SEYTON A
    2 July 1892
WMA   Page 61   F
Parents: J.C. & Mary Francisco

FRANK
    15 March 1858
SMA   Page 43
Owner: Martin Hagy

FRANK
    14 May 1859
SMA   Page 46
Master: John Clark

FRESHOUR, VICTORIA B
    23 May 1857
WFA   Page 32   F
Parents: A.J. & Elizabeth Freshour

FRY, FRS. F.
    4 March 1856
WFA   Page 30   F
Parents: Geo. & Mary Fry

FRY, JOHN R   WMA   Page 35   F
  15 Dec. 1857   Father: Geo. W. Fry

FRY, NANCY   WFA   Page 43   F
  20 Sept. 1858   Parents: Robert & Nancy Fry

FRY, RACHEL L   WFA   Page 12   CP
  27 June 1854   Parents: George N. & Sally Fry

FRY, SARAH ANN   WFA   Page 9   CP
  20 Aug. 1854   Parents: Robert M. & Nancy Fry

FULCHER, VIRGINIA   WFA   Page 4   B
  3 Dec. 1853   Parents: James & Sally Fulcher

FULLEN, HIRAM G   WMA   Page 32   F
  6 June 1857   Parents: Hiram & Rebecca Fullen

FULLEN, LEVI   CMA   Page 61   F
  28 May 1892   Parents: Baren & Mary A. Fullen

FULLEN, MARGARET   WFA   Page 39   F
  10 Oct. 1858   Parents: [Frank] & A.J. Fullen

FULLER, DANIEL T.G. WMA   Page 54   MC   Abingdon Twp.
  3 Oct. 1871   Parents: Thomas J. & Adaline R. Fuller

FULLER, DAVID G   WMA   Page 26   W
  6 May 1856   Parents: Thos. & A.R.M.C. Fuller

FULTON, WM. B   WMA   Page 69   F   North Fork Dist
  20 July 1892   Parents: G.W. & Nannie Fulton

FURGERSON, JOEL   WMA   Page 46   F
  21 Aug. 1859   Parents: William & Martha Furgerson

GAINES, HARVEY   SMA   Page 13   Poor Valley
  20 Sept. 1854   Mother: Rebecca Gaines
                     Master: Moses Whitaker

GAINES, M.M.   WMA   Page 43   F
  30 June 1858   Father: Benj. F. Gaines

GAITHER, NANCY J   WFA   Page 35   F
  1 Jan. 1857   Father: Wm. Gaither
                     Mother: Margret GATHER

GALIHER, CHARLES   WMA   Page 71   F   Goodson
  24 May 1892   Parents: John & Jennie Galiher

GALLIHER, [n.n.]   WFA   Page 9   F   Near Saltville
  26 Dec. 1854   Parents: William & Nancy Galliher

GALLIHER, [n.n.]   WMA   Page 61   F
  14 Feb. 1892   Parents: Jn. J. & Nannie Galliher

GALLIHER, A.B.   WMA   Page 6   B
  2 Dec. 1853   Parents: C. & Marg't Galliher

GALLIHER, ANN ELIZA WFA   Page 2   L   Near Saltville
  27 Jan. 1853   Parents: William & Nancy Galliher

GALLIHER, DOLLY A   WFA   Page 29   F
    7 Dec. 1856   Parents: Henry & Alice GALIHER

GALLIHER, WILLIAM   WMA   Page 46   F
    23 May 1859   Parents: William & Nancy Galliher

GALLOWAY, JAMES   WM_   Page 57   MC   Kinderhook
    1870   Parents: G.W. & Catharine B. Galloway

GARDNER, C.F.   SMA   Page 9
    12 Sept. 1853   Owner: Jacob Lynch

GARLAND, FRACTION   CMA   Page 73   L   Near Abingdon
    15 July 1892   Parents: Alfred & Dora Garland

GARNES, [n.n.]   WFA   Page 23   B   Abingdon
    30 Oct. 1855   Parents: Wm. & Sarah Garnes

GARNES, [n.n.]   WMA   Page 39   B
    29 Nov. 1858   Parents: W.G. & S.B. Garnes

GARNES, ELIZABETH   WFA   Page 46   F
    26 Jan. 1859   Parents: Benjamin T. & Martha Garnes

GARNES, WALTER P   WMA   Page 32   B
    15 June 1857   Parents: Wm. G. & Sarah B. Garnes

GARNETT, ED M.C.   WMA   Page 54   F   Northfork Twp.
    1 Oct. 1871   Parents: Samuel B. & Elizabeth GARRETT
    Reported by S.B. GARNETT, father

GARRET, [n.n.]   WMD   Page 35   F
    24 Oct. 1857   Father: Henry C. Garret
    Reported by Henry C. GARRETT, father   Mother: Nancy J. GARRETT

GARRET, JACOB C   CMA   Page 73   F   Goodson
    15 Dec. 1892   Parents: Ruben & Lillie Garret

GARRETT, CHARLES H   WMA   Page 69   F   North Fork Dist.
    25 July 1892   Parents: A.J. & Nancy J. Garrett

GARRETT, EDWARD C   WMA   Page 3   F
    28 Dec. 1853   Father: Henry C. Garrett

GARRETT, EMILY ELIZ.   WFA   Page 4   F
    18 March 1853   Father: Francis Garrett

GARRETT, GEORGE W   WMA   Page 17   F
    Aug. 1855   Parents: Henry C. & Nancy Jane Garrett

GARRETT, GRAHAM   WMA   Page 61   F
    20 March 1892   Parents: Frank & Lou Garrett

GARRETT, JAMES   WMA   Page 24   F
    5 July 1856   Parents: Nash L. & Susan Garrett

GARRETT, JAS. H.   WMA   Page 26   F
    4 Nov. 1856   Parents: Abram & Catherine Garrett

GARRETT, JUDIA C   WFA   Page 50   F
    10 Sept. 1859   Parents: Abram & Catharine Garrett

GARRETT, NANCY E
   1 Feb. 1853
WFA   Page 7   F
Father: Abram Garrett

GARRETT, SAMUEL B
   21 Aug. 1859
WMA   Page 50   F
Parents: Henry S. & Mary A. Garrett

GARRETT, SARAH E
   23 Dec. 1855
WFA   Page 22   F
Parents: S.B. & E.J. Garrett

GARRISON, WILLIE
   5 March 1892
WMA   Page 66   F   Kinderhook
Parents: Joseph & Lettia Garrison

GEER, JAMES
   22 May 1853
WMA   Page 5   F
Parents: Joshua & Nancy Geer

GENTRY, EDDIE F
   14 June 1892
WMA   Page 61   F
Parents: Wm. M. & Eunice Gentry

GEORGE
   15 Sept. 1853
SMA   Page 9
Owner: William Fields

GEORGE
   Nov. 1853
SMA   Page 4
Owner: Wm. Byars

GEORGE
   30 Nov. 1853
SMA   Page 5
Mother: Martha
Owner: Henry Mock

GEORGE
   15 Sept. 1854
SMA   Page 15
Master: James Vance

GEORGE
   18 June 1855
SMA   Page 16
Mother: Senah
Owner: David B. Clark

GEORGE
   17 Feb. 1856
SMA   Page 30
Owner: Wm. F. Clark

GIBSON, SARAH
   19 July 1856
WFA   Page 12   CL
Parents: Jas. K. & Eliza Gibson

GILES, JOS. M.
   30 Sept. 1856
WMA   Page 26   F
Parents: Jesse F. & Sarah Giles

GILL, DAVID P
   4 April 1854
WMA   Page 12   F
Parents: Thomas & Ellen Gill

GILL, JAS. W.
   28 Feb. 1857
WMA   Page 32   F
Parents: Jacob & Caroline Gill

GILL, ROBT. E.
   27 Jan. 1856
WMA   Page 35   F
Parents: Jno. E. & E'th Gill

GILL, THOS. C.
   8 July 1856
WMA   Page 29   F
Parents: Thos. & Ellen Gill

GILLENWATER, L.C.
   7 Oct. 1853
WFA   Page 7   F
Parents: Geo. S. & Sarah Gillenwater

GILLENWATERS, MARY E
   7 April 1858
WFA   Page 39   F
Parents: Geo. L. & S.F. Gillenwaters

GILLENWATERS, WILLIAM
   17 July 1856
WMA   Page 25   F
Parents: Geo. L. & Sarah F. Gillenwater

GILLILAND, [n.n.]   WMA   Page 21   SH
     29 March 1855   Father: Jno. K. Gilliland
     Reported by A.C. Maxwell, physician

GILLISON, LORENIA   CFA   Page 54   F   Abingdon Twp.
     18 March 1871   Parents: Clarance & Martha Gillison

GILPIN, JOHN   WMA   Page 43   F
     15 Dec. 1858   Parents: Francis & Mary Gilpin

GLENN, SARAH E   WFA   Page 12   F
     23 Feb. 1854   Parents: William & Martha Ann Glenn

GLOVER, JAMES S   WMA   Page 10   B
     9 Sept. 1854   Parents: William J. & Susan E. Glover

GLOVER, JNO. T.   WMA   Page 30   B
     24 Dec. 1856   Parents: Wm. & Susan E. Glover

GLOVER, MARGARET ANN   WFA   Page 18   B
     2 Nov. 1855   Parents: Wm. J. & Martha Ann Glover

GLOVER, NANCY MALVINA   WFA   Page 1   B
     9 Jan. 1853   Parents: William J. & Eveline Glover

GOBBLE, BESSIE   WFA   Page 69   North Fork Dist.
     10 March 1892   Parents: Noah & Sally Gobble

GOBBLE, CHARLES M   WMA   Page 54   F   Northfork Twp.
     20 Nov. 1871   Parents: Samuel & Elizabeth Gobble

GOBBLE, DREWRY   WMA   Page 69   F   North Fork Dist.
     10 May 1892   Parents: John & Alsie Gobble

GOBBLE, EDMONDSON C   WMA   Page 25   F
     1 May 1856   Parents: Jno. & Mahala Gobble

GOBBLE, ELIJAH   WMA   Page 50   F
     15 May 1859   Parents: Elijah & Lucinda Gobble

GOBBLE, EMORY   WMA   Page 8   F
     1 Sept. 1853   Father: Archibald Gobble

GOBBLE, ETHEL   WFA   Page 69   F   North Fork Dist.
     20 Aug. 1892   Parents: C.E.B. & Mary B. Gobble

GOBBLE, GLENNIE   WFA   Page 66   F   Kinderhook
     10 July 1892   Parents: A.D. & Mary Gobble

GOBBLE, LOUISA F   WFA   Page 26   F
     14 Dec. 1856   Parents: Abram & Catherine Gobble

GOBBLE, LOUISA F   WFA   Page 32   F
     19 Oct. 1857   Parents: Abram & Cath Gobble

GOBBLE, LUCRETIA   WFA   Page 7   F
     1 Dec. 1853   Father: Jno. Gobble

GOBBLE, MAHALA   WFA   Page 39   F
     14 Sept. 1858   Parents: Saml. & Elizabeth Gobble

GOBBLE, MARGRET   WFA   Page 25   F
     13 July 1856   Parents: Jonathan & Millie Gobble

GOBBLE, MARGRET L   WFA   Page 25   F
     13 May 1856   Parents: Elijah & Lucinda Gobble

GOBBLE, MARY I   WFA   Page 32   F
     16 Jan. 1856   Parents: B.H. & Eliza Gobble

GOBBLE, MATILDA C   WFA   Page 39   F
     1 March 1858   Parents: Jno. & Mahala Gobble

GOBBLE, ROBT. E.   WMA   Page 46   F
     13 May 1859   Parents: John & Sarah Gobble

GOBBLE, SAMUEL C   WMA   Page 22   F
     22 Dec. 1855   Parents: Sam'l & Elizabeth Gobble

GOBBLE, SAM'L W   WMA   Page 22   F
     15 Oct. 1855   Parents: Abram & Catharine Gobble

GOBBLE, SARAH   WFA   Page 25   F
     1 April 1856   Parents: Martin & Margret Gobble

GOBBLE, SARAH ANN   WFA   Page 2   F
     11 Dec. 1852   Father: John Gobble

GOBBLE, SARAH F   WF_   Page 57   Kinderhook
     27 Dec. 1870   Parents: Wm. & Margaret Gobble

GOBBLE, VIRGIE G   WFA   Page 61   F
     2 Oct. 1892   Parents: M.P. & Cynthia J. Gobble

GOBBLE, W.E.   WMA   Page 69   F   North Fork Di
     13 May 1892   Parents: Abner & Clara Gobble

GOFF, DAVID ALEX'R   WMA   Page 13   F   North Fork
     19 June 1854   Parents: Wilson F. & Sarah Goff

GOFF, GEORGE W   WMA   Page 9   L   Near Saltvill
     28 April 1854   Parents: Elijah & Rachel Goff

GOFF, MARGRET   WFA   Page 2   L   North Fork
     17 May 1853   Parents: Wilson F. & Sarah Goff

GOFF, THOMAS   WMA   Page 35   F
     25 Dec. 1856   Parents: Wilson & Sarah Goff

GOINS, MARY JANE   CFA   Page 20
     7 Sept. 1855   Father: Eliza Goins

GOODMAN, [n.n.]   WFA   Page 32   F
     1 Sept. 1857   Parents: Isaac S. & Elizabeth Goodma

GOODMAN, [n.n.]   WFA   Page 39   F
     11 April 1858   Parents: J.B. & Jane Goodman

GOODMAN, ESTEL H   WMA   Page 71   F   Goodson
     29 Aug. 1892   Parents: Ed & Mary E. Goodman

GOODMAN, S   WFA   Page 6   F
     27 April 1853   Parents: Isaac S. & Elizabeth Goodma

GOODSON, JAMES M   WMA   Page 71   F   Goodson
     25 April 1892   Parents: James & Mollie Goodson

GOODSON, [JAMES] P   WM_   Page 57   F   Kinderhook
    28 Feb. 1870   Parents: Marshall D. & Susan C. Goodson

GOODSON, JOHN M.R.   WMA   Page 71   F   Goodson
    11 Sept. 1892   Parents: Wm. & Rebecca Goodson

GOODSON, S.M.   WFA   Page 50   F
    22 April 1859   Parents: Lyons & Eve Goodson

GOTHER, ELIZABETH W   WFA   Page 46   F
    12 Dec. 1859   Parents: William & Mary Gother

GRACE, JULIA C   WFA   Page 54   F   Northfork Twp.
    29 Jan. 1871   Parents: Thomas J. & Cynthia A. Grace

GRACE, MARY   WFA   Page 10   F
    9 March 1854   Parents: James M. & Rosannah Grace

GRACE, MINERVA E   WFA   Page 9   F   Near Saltville
    Sept. 1854   Parents: William & Mary Grace

GRACE, ROBERT   WMA   Page 17   F
    8 Sept. 1855   Parents: James M. & Rosanna Grace

GRADY, JNO. J.   WMA   Page 35   F
    26 July 1857   Parents: Alsom & Alsey Grady

GRADY, THOS. WHITLEY   WMA   Page 20   L
    3 Feb. 1855   Parents: Alsey & Ilsey Grady

GRAHAM, CHARLES   WMA   Page 23   B
    22 April 1855   Parents: Robert & Mary Graham

GRANT, [n.n.]   WMA   Page 35   F
    17 April 1857   Parents: G., Sr., & Mary Grant

GRANT, [n.n.]   WFA   Page 39   D
    12 Feb. 1858   Parents: H.M. & M.E. Grant

GRANT, ALBERT   WMA   Page 32   S
    12 March 1857   Parents: Wm. & Alice A. Grant

GRANT, AMANDA   WFA   Page 11   F
    26 April 1854   Parents: Archibald S. & Margaret Grant

GRANT, ARTHUR Mc   WMA   Page 61   F
    4 Nov. 1892   Parents: Jos. L. & Mollie Grant

GRANT, BETTIE J   WFA   Page 32   D
    12 Feb. 1857   Parents: Hugh M. & Martha G. Grant

GRANT, ELIZABETH   WFA   Page 11   MR
    7 July 1854   Parents: John C. & Theodora Grant
      Reported by Gardner Grant, grandfather

GRANT, F   WMA   Page 46   F
    12 June 1859   Parents: David G. & Permetia Grant

GRANT, HARRY D   WMA   Page 61   F
    10 Nov. 1892   Parents: R.G. & Blanche Grant

GRANT, JAMES L   WMA   Page 35   F
    15 July 1857   Parents: Rob't G. & Mary I. Grant

GRANT, LAY — WFA — Page 66 — F — Kinderhook
Dec. 1892
Parents: J.J. & Mary Grant

GRANT, MARGARET SOPHIA — WFA — Page 19 — D
17 May 1855
Parents: Robert E. & Ann Grant

GRANT, ROBERT S — WMA — Page 46 — F
17 Sept. 1859
Parents: Robt. G. & Mary J. Grant

GRANT, SARAH C — WFA — Page 46 — F
30 April 1859
Parents: Robt. E. & Ann S. Grant

GRAVES, GEORGE — CMA — Page 73 — L — Near Abingdon
1 March 1892
Parents: W.P. & Cornelia Graves

GRAY, [n.n.] — WFD — Page 39 — F
29 Nov. 1856
Parents: Wm. H. & Ann Gray

GRAY, ANNAH — WFA — Page 70 — F — Abingdon Dist
4 April 1892
Parents: Frank & Elizabeth Gray

GRAY, FRANCES — WFA — Page 12 — F
19 Aug. 1854
Parents: John & Margaret Gray

GRAY, JNO. F. — WMA — Page 32 — F
4 April 1857
Parents: Jno. C. & Nancy D. Gray

GRAY, JOHN W — WMA — Page 54 — F — Abingdon Twp.
1 March 1871
Parents: James & Susan Gray

GRAY, MARY E — WFA — Page 54 — F — Abingdon Twp.
15 July 1871
Parents: Charles P. & Cornenia Gray

GRAY, MOLLY E — CFA — Page 73 — L — Near Abingdon
6 July 1892
Parents: John & Milly Gray

GRAY, WILLIAM — WMA — Page 1 — CP
8 June 1853
Parents: John & Margaret Gray

GREENWAY, DANIEL T — WMA — Page 23 — MR — Abingdon
31 Dec. 1855
Parents: Jas. C. & Nannie B. Greenway

GREER, DAVID R — WMA — Page 5 — F
19 June 1853
Parents: Elijah & Nancy Greer

GREER, ISAAC R — WMA — Page 28 — F
17 Oct. 1856
Parents: Elijah & Nancy Greer

GREER, WM — WMA — Page 29 — F
11 Nov. 1856
Parents: Joshua & Nancy Greer

GREGORY, JAMES S — WMA — Page 46 — F
14 Oct. 1859
Parents: Jacob & Elizabeth Gregory

GREGORY, LUMENSY — WFA — Page 11 — SH
17 April 1854
Parents: Philip J. & Rhoda Gregory

GREGORY, PEARL M — WFA — Page 61 — F
26 Aug. 1892
Parents: S. & Cath. Gregory

GREGORY, WALTER — WMA — Page 56 — F — Glade Spring
1870
Parents: Philip & Marietta Gregory

GRIFFIN, WILLIAM H   CMA   Page 54   F   Abingdon Twp.
    18 June 1871   Parents: Robert & Florence Griffin

GRINSTEAD, JOSEPH N   WMA   Page 43
    1 Oct. 1858   Parents: Benj. F. & Cath. Grinstead

GRINSTEAD, MARGARET ANN   WFA   Page 19   F
    23 March 1855   Parents: Benj'n F. & Cath. A. Grinstead

GRINSTEAD, PARKER SMITH   WMA   Page 4   F
    16 April 1853   Parents: Benjamin F. & Catherine Ann Grinstead

GRINSTEAD, WM. M.   WMA   Page 35   ML
    1 Jan. 1857   Parents: Benj. F. & Cath. Grinstead

GROGG, [n.n.]   WFA   Page 71   F   Goodson
    15 May 1892   Parents: John & Louvenia Grogg

GRUBB, ELIZABETH H   WFA   Page 17   F
    20 Oct. 1855   Parents: Martin H. & Prudence Grubb

GRUBB, JACOB W   WMA   Page 61   MR
    16 June 1892   Parents: W.P. & Harriet Grubb

GRUBB, MARY L   WFA   Page 10   F
    20 March 1854   Parents: Martin H. & Prudence Grubb

GRUBB, PATTERSON F   WMA   Page 35   F
    20 Oct. 1857   Parents: M.H. & Prudence Grubb

GRUBB, PEARL MAY   WFA   Page 61   F
    14 Sept. 1892   Parents: Joshua & Grace E. Grubb

GWIN, ELIZABETH   WFA   Page 55   Saltville Dist.
    11 Oct. 1870   Mother: Ann Gwin

GWINN, PRICE H   WMA   Page 61   MN   Albemarle Co., Va.
    4 Aug. 1892   Parents: Ph. H. & Mary W. Gwinn

GWYN, HARRISON   WMA   Page 50
    21 May 1859   Mother: Sarah Gwyn

GWYN, NATHAN   WMA   Page 50   F
    21 Feb. 1859   Parents: Levi & Ann Gwyn

HACKLER, JOS. W.A.   WMA   Page 61   F
    19 Jan. 1892   Parents: J.A. & A.V. Hackler

HADEN, RACHEL   WFA   Page 47   F
    9 Feb. 1859   Parents: Thomas & Rachel Haden

HAGY, [n.n.]   WMA   Page 72   MC   Abingdon
    19 May 1892   Parents: J.L.P. & Roxy Hagy

HAGY, [n.n.]   WFD   Page 72   MC   Abingdon
    1 Dec. 1892   Parents: Jos. E. & Alice Hagy

HAGY, ANDREW (twin)   WMA   Page 10   F
    28 Oct. 1854   Parents: Jacob & Catharine Hagy

HAGY, ANN A   WFA   Page 36   F
    20 Feb. 1857   Parents: Jas. W. & Mary A. Hagy

HAGY, CALADONIA L
13 Oct. 1871
WFA   Page 54   F   Northfork Twp.
Parents: David C. & Mary J. Hagy

HAGY, GEO. W. (twin)
28 Oct. 1854
WMA   Page 10   F
Parents: Jacob & Catharine Hagy

HAGY, GUY
18 July 1892
WMA   Page 61   F
Parents: Elbert & Susan Hagy

HAGY, JANE L.T.
13 May 1858
WFA   Page 39   L
Parents: Jus. A. & Mary Hagy

HAGY, JNO. F.
4 Oct. 1856
WMA   Page 26   PT
Parents: John A. & Emaline Hagy

HAGY, JOHN G
13 Nov. 1871
WMA   Page 54   F   Northfork Twp.
Parents: J.L.H. & Sarah E. Hagy

HAGY, JOHN HORTENSTINE
23 Dec. 1854
WMA   Page 13   F
Parents: William C. & Eliza Ann Hagy

HAGY, LILLIAN MAY
13 May 1892
WFA   Page 72   CI   Abingdon
Parents: Worthey & Lula Hagy

HAGY, MARGARET MINERVA
6 April 1854
WFA   Page 16   T   Cedarville
Parents: James V. & Mary A. Hagy

HAGY, MARIA FRANCES
29 May 1853
WFA   Page 1   T   Stone Castle
Parents: James N. & Ann Hagy

HAGY, MARTHA A
15 June 1856
WFA   Page 27   F
Parents: Jas. A. & Mary A. Hagy

HAGY, MARTHA C
20 June 1859
WFA   Page 46   F
Parents: Jas. & Mary A. Hagy

HAGY, MARY J
4 June 1858
WFA   Page 40   L
Parents: J.A. & Emaline Hagy

HAGY, SARAH ELIZABETH
6 Feb. 1853
WFA   Page 4   F
Father: Wm. C. Hagy

HAGY, WM. Y.
2 Oct. 1892
WMA   Page 61   F
Parents: A.J. & Louisa Hagy

HALL, ELIZABETH
19 March 1857
WFA   Page 36
Mother: [Fanny] Hall

HALL, ELLEN A
22 May 1856
WFA   Page 30   F
Parents: W.M. & Mary Hall

HALLIARD, SARAH ANN
8 Feb. 1854
WFA   Page 11   F
Parents: William & Mary Halliard

HAM, LESSIE A
1 May 1892
WFA   Page 61   F
Parents: Monroe & Millie E. Ham

HAMER, [n.n.]
5 Feb. 1892
CMD   Page 61   F
Parents: Sam'l & Carrie Hamer

HAMILTON
17 June 1857
SMA   Page 36

HAMILTON, ABRAM   WMA   Page 7   F
    22 May 1853   Parents: Rob't B. & Matilda Hamilton

HAMILTON, CHARLES K   WMA   Page 2   L
    25 Jan. 1853   Parents: Adam & Mary Hamilton

HAMILTON, ROBT. C.   WMA   Page 32   F
    4 April 1857   Parents: Jno. H. & Sarah Hamilton

HAMMENS, [TAYMER] [TORETTA]   WFA   Page 16   L
    8 April 1855   Father: Alfred HAMMONS
    Mother: Mary Hammens

HAMMONDS, MAY L   WFA   Page 61   F
    11 Oct. 1892   Parents: Tob. & Lil. Hammonds

HAMMONS, SAMUEL   CMA   Page 53   F   Abingdon Twp.
    14 Nov. 1871   Parents: Jeremiah & Lerina Hammons

HAMNER, [n.n.]   WMD   Page 24   PH
    20 Sept. 1856   Father: Jno. P. Hamner
    Mother: Margret HAMMER

HAMONS, [n.n.]   WMD   Page 47   F
    5 Oct. 1859   Parents: Godfrey & Mary Hamons

HAMPTON, ANNIS   WFA   Page 39   F
    24 Nov. 1858   Parents: S.J. & Martha Hampton

HANBY, JONATHAN L   WMA   Page 50   F
    9 May 1859   Parents: A.T.F. & Susan E. Hanby

HAND, [n.n.]   CMD   Page 61   F
    24 Oct. 1892   Parents: Wm. T. & Laura Hand

HAND, CHARLES C   WMA   Page 56   F   Glade Spring Twp.
    1870   Parents: Wm. A. & Araminta Hand

HAND, DAVID WM.   WMA   Page 56   F   Glade Spring Twp.
    1870   Parents: James & Eliza Hand

HAND, ELIZA J   WFA   Page 36   F
    24 Oct. 1857   Parents: Thomas & M.C. Hand

HAND, HOPE W   CMA   Page 61   F
    22 March 1892   Parents: Wm. T.S. & Marg. E. Hand

HAND, LIDDY   CFA   Page 36
    2 May 1857   Mother: Mary Hand

HAND, JOHN   WMA   Page 46   F
    12 May 1859   Parents: Thomas & Nancy Hand

HAND, MARY   WFA   Page 12   F
    1854   Parents: Thomas & Margaret Hand

HAND, WILLIE   WFA   Page 61   F
    19 Feb. 1892   Parents: H.F. & Cora Hand

HANES, RACHEL   WFA   Page 55   F   Saltville Twp.
    30 Feb. 1870   Parents: Thomas & Louisa Hands

HANEY, E.S.
31 March 1892

WMA   Page 72   DA   Abingdon
Parents: E.S. & Eliz. Haney

HANK, SARAH J
31 Nov. 1858

WFA   Page 39   SH
Father: A.J. Hank
Mother: Susan HAWK

HANKET, J.M.
12 Aug. 1858

WMA   Page 43   F
Parents: John & M.I. Hanket

HANKLEY, ANN ELIZA (twin)
11 Feb. 1855

WFA   Page 17   SH
Parents: James H. & Mary Ann Hankley

HANKLEY, GRANVILLE SCOTT
7 Sept. 1853

WMA   Page 1   SH
Parents: James H. & Ann Hankley

HANKLEY, MARY ANN (twin)
11 Feb. 1855

WFA   Page 17   SH
Parents: James H. & Mary Ann Hankley

HANKLEY, WILLIAM
1870

WMA   Page 56   F   Glade Spring
Parents: James H. & Caroline HANKLA

HANN, SARAH ANN
27 Sept. 1855

WFA   Page 18   F
Parents: Tho's & Margaret Hann

HANNAH
24 Oct. 1858

SFA   Page 38
Owner: A.M. Appling

HARDIN, GEO. W.
10 Nov. 1892

WMA   Page 71   F   Goodson
Parents: John M. & Amanda Hardin

HARRISON FREEMONT
20 Sept. 1856

SMA   Page 30
Owner: Jas. Kelly

HARLESS, CORDELIA
17 June 1892

WFA   Page 69   F   North Fork Di
Parents: Isham & Rebecca Harless

HARLESS, MARY A
15 Oct. 1858

WFA   Page 39   L
Parents: E. & Jerusha Harless

HARLESS, NANCY E
20 Sept. 1892

WFA   Page 69   F   North Fork Di
Parents: Wm. & Elizabeth Harless

HARLESS, SAMUEL M
Nov. 1871

WFA   Page 54   F   North Fork Tw
Parents: Elisha & [Jerutha] Harless

HARLEY, MAUD
8 Feb. 1892

WFA   Page 66   F   Kinderhook
Parents: W.D. & Ellen Harley

HARLOW, JOHN W
22 July 1855

WMA   Page 22   F
Parents: John & Harriet Harlow

HARLOW, LILLIE
5 May 1892

WFA   Page 66   F   Kinderhook
Parents: J.W. & Lou Harlow

HARLOW, MATILDA
7 Feb. 1859

WFA   Page 50   F
Parents: Thomas & Margaret Harlow

HARLOW, ROBT. H.
10 July 1858

WMA   Page 39   F
Parents: Jno. & Harriet Harlow

HARLOW, SARAH
6 Nov. 1870

WF_   Page 58
Parents: Jno. & Harriet Harlow

HARLOW, W.H.   WMA   Page 39   F
        16 May 1858   Parents: Jos. & Lar. Harlow

HARLY, NANCY V   WFA   Page 54   F   North Fork Twp.
        1871   Parents: Alex & Mahaly HARLEY

HAROLD, [n.n.]   W_D   Page 7   F
        17 May 1853   Parents: Geo. W. & Mary Harold

HARR, A.H.   WMA   Page 7   F
        June 1853   Parents: Adam L. & Malinda Harr

HARREY   SMA   Page 29
        1 July 1856   Owner: Jas. P. Strother

HARRIET   SFA   Page 36
        6 May 1856   Owner: Thos. W. Preston

HARRIET   SFA   Page 50
        26 March 1859   Owner: Isaac Fleenor

HARRIETT   SFA   Page 27
        15 May 1856   Owner: F.P. Clapp

HARRIETT   SFA   Page 50
        2 Jan. 1859   Owner: Samuel H. Millard

HARRINGTON, M.A.   WFA   Page 50
        6 April 1859   Parents: Moses & Alice Harrington

HARRIS, R.J.   WFA   Page 36   F
        18 Oct. 1857   Parents: Alexander & Nancy M. Harris

HARRIS, SAML. J.   WMA   Page 3   L
        8 May 1853   Father: Alex'r Harris

HARRIS, SAML. J.   WMA   Page 12   F
        2 Sept. 1854   Parents: John M. & Alcey J. Harris

HARRIS, SOPHIA C   WFA   Page 18   F
        20 May 1855   Parents: Alex'r & Nancy J. Harris

HARROLD, [n.n.]   WMD   Page 14   F
        29 Nov. 1854   Father: Geo. W. Harrold
        Reported by Geo. W. HAROLD, father   Mother: Susanna HAROLD

HART, WM. R.   WMA   Page 61   F
        22 May 1892   Parents: A.J. & Rebecca Hart

HAWTHORN, JAMES   WMA   Page 19   F
        4 April 1855   Parents: James & Ann Hawthorn

HAWTHORN, MARY B   WFA   Page 36   F
        23 May 1856   Parents: James & Mary Hawthorn

HAWTHORN, MARY E   WFA   Page 27   F
        1 Dec. 1856   Father: B.D. Hawthorn
                              Mother: E.H. HATHHORN

HAWTHORN, NOE   WMA   Page 46   F
        5 July 1859   Parents: Bracken D. & Elizabeth HAWTHORNE

HAWTHORN, REBECCA JANE
12 June 1854
WFA   Page 12   F
Parents: Horatio T. & Margaret Hawthorn

HAWTHORN, SARAH MARGARET
16 Dec. 1855
WFA   Page 17   F
Parents: William & Martha HAWTHORNE

HAWTHORN, WALTER
10 April 1859
WMA   Page 46   F
Parents: William & Margaret Hawthorn

HAWTHORNE, [n.n.]
15 Nov. 1892
WFD   Page 61   F
Parents: Walter & M.E. Hawthorne

HAWTHORNE, BRACK. D.
11 Nov. 1892
WMA   Page 61   F
Parents: W.J. & Nan. H. Hawthorne

HAYNES, BENJ'N WORTHEY
29 Sept. 1855
WMA   Page 18   F
Parents: Peter & Alty Haynes

HAYNES, DAVID COLLINGS
12 Nov. 1853
WMA   Page 4   F
Parents: Peter & Altiza Haynes

HAYNES, JAMES
19 Dec. 1854
WMA   Page 12   F
Parents: Robert & Rosanna Haynes

HAYNES, RACHEL BRANCH
2 January 1853
WFA   Page 1   CP   Near Saltville
Parents: James & Esther Haynes

HAYTER, [n.n.]
Aug. 1854
WFD   Page 11   F
Parents: Isaac & Jane Hayter

HAYTER, [n.n.]
20 Oct. 1892
WFA   Page 69   F   North Fork Dis
Parents: [Litch] & Alice Hayter

HAYTER, AARON WHITLEY
3 Nov. 1853
WMA   Page 4   F
Father: Aaron H. Hayter

HAYTER, ELIZA E.C.
4 Oct. 1857
WFA   Page 36   F
Parents: James E. & L. Hayter

HAYTER, FLOY B
10 March 1892
WFA   Page 72   DC   Abingdon
Parents: Paul E. & Lula R. Hayter

HAYTER, TRIGG
11 April 1892
WMA   Page 61   F
Parents: J.W. & Marg. Hayter

HAYTER, WM. THOMPSON
10 Sept. 1853
WMA   Page 4   F
Parents: James E. & Louisa Hayter

HAYTON, AMANDA C
28 July 1858
WFA   Page 43   F
Parents: W.J. & Mary E. Hayton

HAYTON, CHARLES
19 Nov. 1870
WMA   Page 55   F   Saltville Twp.
Parents: John & Frances Hayton

HAYTON, HARVEY L
22 March 1853
WMA   Page 1   L   Near Saltville
Parents: Champ H. & Hetty Hayton

HAYTON, THOMAS
29 Aug. 1892
WMA   Page 61   F
Parents: Wm. & Ellen Hayton

HEARTMANN, HANNAH
22 March 1859
WFA   Page 50   F
Parents: James R. & M.E. Heartmann

HEATH, ISABELLA
    1 Sept. 1854
WFA   Page 13   F   Near Mill Creek
Parents: John & [Aery] Heath

HEATH, JOHN
    15 March 1859
WMA   Page 46
Mother: Mary Heath

HEATH, LAVINIA
    22 April 1857
WFA   Page 36   F
Parents: Jno. & Ann Heath

HEATH, SAML. T.
    14 March 1854
WMA   Page 13   Rush Creek
Mother: Margaret Heath

HEATH, WILLIAM
    1870
WMA   Page 56   F   Glade Spring Twp.
Parents: Scott & Marthy Heath

HEATH, WILLIE B
    25 Nov. 1892
WMA   Page 61   ML
Parents: John & Eliz. Heath

HEBERLAND, MARGARET C
    8 Oct. 1855
WFA   Page 18   F
Parents: Joel & Lucinda Heberland

HEDGEPATH, VIRGINIA FRANCES
    30 Oct. 1854
WFA   Page 11   HC
Parents: William & Cornelia Hedgepath

HEISKELL, C.K.
    5 Aug. 1859
WMA   Page 50   PH
Parents: M.Y. & Caroline Heiskell

HELBERT, GEORGE
    25 Dec. 1892
WMA   Page 71   F   Goodson
Parents: George & M[illegible] Helbert

HELTON, ARCHER B
    16 May 1856
WMA   Page 30   F
Parents: Bryant & Nancy Helton

HELTON, CAROLINE M
    3 June 1855
WFA   Page 20   F
Parents: Samuel & Caroline Helton

HELTON, HENRY M
    30 June 1858
WMA   Page 43   F
Parents: W. & Nancy Helton

HELTON, JAMES
    20 Oct. 1855
WMA   Page 20   F
Parents: Ewel & Nancy Helton

HELTON, MAHALA C
    17 May 1853
WFA   Page 5   F
Parents: Wm. B. & Rachel Helton

HELTON, MAHALA FRANCES
    29 Aug. 1853
WFA   Page 2   F   Tumbling Cove
Parents: Ewel & Nancy Helton

HELTON, REUBEN
    2 Feb. 1853
WMA   Page 2   F
Parents: Bryant A. & Nancy Helton

HELTON, RICHARD A
    4 Sept. 1892
WMA   Page 61   F
Parents: J.R. & Rosan. Helton

HELTON, THOMAS
    10 June 1858
WMA   Page 43   F
Parents: Bryant & Nancy Helton

HENDERSON, BAR. L.
    16 Sept. 1892
WMA   Page 61   F
Parents: R.L. & S.A. Henderson

HENDERSON, DAVID M
    11 Nov. 1856
WMA   Page 30   F
Parents: Rob't & Mary Henderson

HENDERSON, FRANK WMA Page 61 F
2 Oct. 1892 Parents: J.M. & Lula Henderson

HENDERSON, HIRAM WMA Page 36 F
4 May 1856 Parents: Whitley & M.W. Henderson

HENDERSON, JASPER WMA Page 55 CP Saltville Twp
23 March 1870 Parents: William & Adelia Henderson

HENDERSON, JULIUS CONNER WMA Page 1 CP
26 Aug. 1853 Parents: William & Parthenia Henderso

HENDERSON, MARGRET WFA Page 36 F
1 Sept. 1857 Father: William Henderson

HENDERSON, MARTHA WFA Page 55 F Saltville Twp
25 July 1870 Parents: Robert & Mary Henderson

HENDERSON, MARY WFA Page 61 F
30 April 1892 Parents: Sam'l & Eliz. Henderson

HENDERSON, MARY E WFA Page 43 F
1 Aug. 1858 Parents: Robt. & Mary Henderson

HENDERSON, MARY L WFA Page 69 MN North Fork D
20 April 1892 Parents: W.H. & Laura Henderson

HENDERSON, NANCY WFA Page 9 CP Near Saltvil
31 July 1854 Parents: Robert & Mary Henderson

HENDERSON, RYBURN WMA Page 16 CP
9 June 1855 Parents: William & Parthenia Henders

HENDERSON, SARAH WFA Page 46 F
27 Nov. 1859 Parents: James & Sarah J. Henderson

HENDERSON, SARAH E WFA Page 20 F
23 Jan. 1855 Parents: Whitley & Mary Henderson

HENDERSON, THOS. M. WMA Page 36 F
7 Sept. 1856 Parents: Ro. H. & Mary L. Henderson

HENDERSON, WILLIAM WMA Page 9 F Near Saltvil
15 Jan. 1854 Parents: James & Jane Henderson

HENDERSON, WM. B. WMA Page 61 F
15 April 1892 Parents: A.J. & Callie Henderson

HENDERSON, WILLIE S WMA Page 61 F
4 Aug. 1892 Parents: Jasper & Mary C. Henderson

HENDRICK, ISABELLA WFA Page 14 F
30 May 1854 Parents: Jno. W. & Frances HENDRICK

HENDRICKS, MARY E WFA Page 32 F
25 Feb. 1857 Parents: Thos. P. & Cath. Hendricks
Reported by Thos. P. HENDRIX, father

HENEGAR, SARAH WFA Page 13 Near Saltvi
Sept. 1854 Mother: Margaret Henegar
Reported by Mrs. Jno. Moore, neighbor

HENIGER, GEORGE R   WMA   Page 47   F
     5 Dec. 1859   Parents: James H. & Rebecca Heniger

HENLY, JOHN W   WMA   Page 2   L
     26 Feb. 1853   Father: Stephen Henly

HENRITZE, [n.n.]   WFD   Page 8   PA
     6 March 1853   Parents: Sam'l & Catharine Henritze

HENRITZE, [n.n.]   WFA   Page 26   CN
     29 Dec. 1856   Parents: James & Eliza Henritze

HENRITZE, THEONA   WFA   Page 50   MR
     20 Sept. 1859   Parents: P.E.B.C. & Anna J. Henritze

HENRY   SMA   Page 8
     April 1853   Owner: Sophia Teeter

HENRY   SMA   Page 15
     13 Oct. 1854   Master: Sam'l E. Goodson

HENRY   SMA   Page 23
     26 May 1855   Owner: Jno. H. Wallace

HENRY   SMA   Page 36
     27 May 1856   Owner: Jno. Byars

HENRY H.A.   SMA   Page 8
     4 Feb. 1853   Owner: Jonathan Hanby

HENRY, JAMES B   WMA   Page 26   F
     28 Sept. 1856   Parents: Jas. Y. & Jenett Henry

HENSLEY, ETTA   WFA   Page 66   F   Kinderhook
     22 June 1892   Parents: R.M. & Mary Hensley

HENSLEY, J.K.R.   WMA   Page 39   L
     10 May 1858   Parents: J.B. & Cath. Hensley

HERNDON, SARAH   WFA   Page 10
     1854   Mother: Elizab. Herndon
     Reported by Elliot Herndon, uncle

HERNEN, THOMAS   WMA   Page 55   F   Saltville Twp.
     19 Dec. 1870   Parents: Jessee & Rachel Hernen

HERRON, MARTHA   WFA   Page 4   F
     1 Sept. 1853   Father: Levi Herron

HICKEY, MARY E   WFA   Page 50   F
     5 March 1859   Parents: John A.W. & M.E. Hickey

HICKMAN, B.S.   WMA   Page 40   DG
     15 March 1858   Parents: R.H. & R.R. Hickman

HICKMAN, BETTIE C   WMA   Page 26   F
     8 March 1856   Parents: Rob't M. & M.B. Hickman

HICKMAN, GEO. L.   WMA   Page 50   MR
     20 Feb. 1859   Parents: Robt. M. & R.B. Hickman

HICKMAN, SARAH V   WFA   Page 8   S
     13 July 1853   Parents: H.H. & Louisa H. Hickman

HICKMAN, SUSAN J   WFA   Page 23   F
    3 March 1855   Parents: H.H. & Louisa Hickman

HICKOCK, LAURA L   WFA   Page 53   C   Abingdon Twp
    21 Dec. 1871   Parents: Charles H. & Martha E. Hick

HICKOK, [n.n.]   WMA   Page 21   F
    3 Aug. 1855   Parents: Charles & Eveline Hickok
    Reported by A.C. Maxwell, physician

HICKOK, M.E.   WFA   Page 8   C
    9 Feb. 1853   Parents: Chas. & E.M. Hickok

HICKOK, MARY E   WFA   Page 50   F
    12 May 1859   Parents: C.H. & E.M. Hickok

HIGGINS, ELLIS L   CMA   Page 61   PO
    8 Nov. 1892   Parents: Ellis & Belle Higgins

HILL, DAVID B   WMA   Page 43   F
    15 June 1858   Parents: Noah & Nancy Hill

HILL, EMELINE   WFA   Page 14   F
    19 Feb. 1854   Parents: Felix & Sarah Hill

HILL, GEORGE   WMA   Page 55   F   Saltville Tw
    23 July 1870   Parents: Noah & Nancy Hill

HILL, LUCINDA BERTON   WFA   Page 2   L   Near Saltvil
    20 May 1853   Parents: Washington & Lucinda Hill

HILL, NEWTON J   WMA   Page 13   F
    5 Aug. 1854   Parents: Washington & Lucinda Hill

HILL, NOAH M   WMA   Page 10   F
    21 Jan. 1854   Parents: Noah & Nancy Hill

HILLENBERY, [n.n.]   WMD   Page 61   TC
    6 March 1892   Parents: C.G. & Mar. Hillenbery

HILLIARD, [n.n.]   WMA   Page 17   F
    18 Sept. 1855   Parents: William & Mary Hilliard

HILLIARD, GEO. C.   WMA   Page 36   F
    15 Oct. o856   Parents: Wm. & Mary [W.] Hilliard

HINES, [n.n.]   WMA   Page 73   MR   Abingdon
    18 Dec. 1892   Parents: R.A. & Mary B. Hines

HITE, JOHN N   WMA   Page 54   F   Northfork Tw
    29 Oct. 1871   Parents: Nickolas & Eve Hite

HITE, MARY FRANCES   WMA   Page 2   F   River Hills
    19 Feb. 1853   Parents: Nicholas & Martha S. Hite

HOBBS, ANN E   WFA   Page 39   F
    12 Jan. 1858   Parents: H.B. & Mary A. Hobbs

HOBBS, MARGRET   WFA   Page 32   F
    6 Oct. 1856   Parents: Elsana & N.J. Hobbs

HOBBS, MARTHA C   WFA   Page 26   F
    16 Nov. 1856   Parents: Nash & Catherine Hobbs

HOBBS, MARY H.C.   WF_   Page 58
    3 Aug. 1870   Parents: Jefferson & Martha J. Hobbs

HOBBS, [MAY] F   WFA   Page 39   F
    11 April 1858   Parents: P. & Elizabeth Hobbs

HOBBS, MATILDA   WFA   Page 14   F
    1 Sept. 1854   Parents: Henry B. & Mary A. Hobbs

HOBBS, RENO   WFA   Page 66   F   Kinderhook
    10 June 1892   Parents: Sanford & Sallie Hobbs

HOBBS, WILLIAM   WMA   Page 66   Kinderhook
    7 Aug. 1892   Mother: Martha Hobbs

HOBBS, WILLIAM H   WM_   Page 58
    May 1870   Parents: Elkana & Nancy J. Hobbs

HOBBS, WILLIAM J   WM_   Page 58
    1870   Parents: Craig & Marg. E. Hobbs

HOCKET, MARTHA W   WFA   Page 30   F
    25 Dec. 1856   Parents: Jno. & Mary Hocket

HOCKETT, JNO. C.   WMA   Page 10   F
    26 Nov. 1854   Parents: John & Mary Jane Hockett

HOCKETT, SARAH JANE   WFA   Page 10   F
    15 March 1854   Parents: Isaac & Eliza Hockett

HOGSDEN, AARON L   WMA   Page 13   CP   Near Saltville
    12 April 1854   Parents: Francis & Ann Hogsden

HOGSHEAD, DAVID A   WMA   Page 32   MN
    20 Sept. 1857   Parents: A.L. & Mary E. Hogshead

HOGSHEAD, NANNIE M   WFA   Page 24   MN
    19 May 1856   Parents: A.L. & Mary E. Hogshead
    Born in Montgomery Co., Va.

HOLAWAY, SERENA   WFA   Page 46   F
    23 Aug. 1859   Parents: Wills & Rachel Holaway

HOLMES, [n.n.]   W_D   Page 30   F
    1 Jan. 1856   Father: Alfd. Holmes
                          Mother: Mary HOLMS

HOLMES, BENJ. H.   WMA   Page 61   F
    7 Sept. 1892   Parents: Basil & Fran. Holmes

HOLMES, JAMES   WMA   Page 30   F
    6 Aug. 1856   Parents: [Fulins] & Francis HOLMS

HOLMES, NOAH   WMA   Page 20   F
    13 Nov. 1855   Parents: Geo. W. & Susannah P. Holmes

HOLMES, R. [H.]   WMA   Page 39   L
    25 May 1858   Parents: Geo. W. & S.P. Holmes

HOLT, [n.n.]   WMD   Page 24   BR
    1 Nov. 1856   Parents: Wm. & Mary A. Holt

HOLT, P.K.
1 Dec. 1853
WMA   Page 6   L
Parents: Bird & [Lela] Holt

HOLT, WM. R.J.
17 Aug. 1854
WMA   Page 14   F
Parents: C.B. & Elizabeth Holt

HOOFNAGLE, ALICE
2 March 1859
WFA   Page 50   MR
Parents: Thos. P. & S.J. Hoofnagle

HOPE, JAMES W
30 Sept. 1871
WMA   Page 53   F   Abingdon Twp
Parents: Peter J. & Margaret Hope

HOPE, THOS. A.
20 May 1853
WMA   Page 7   F
Parents: Jas. W. & Sarah Hope

HOPE, VIRGINIA LEE
1870
WFA   Page 56   F   Glade Spring
Parents: James & Mary E. Hope

HORN, AND. F.
14 Nov. 1856
WMA   Page 30   F
Father: Jno. E. HORNE
Mother: Mary B. Horn

HORN, CLAUD
5 June 1892
WMA   Page 66   F   Kinderhook
Parents: B.F. & Susan Horn

HORN, JOHN
23 July 1853
WMA   Page 7   F
Parents: Augustus & Hannah Horn

HORN, JOHN
April 1892
WMA   Page 66   Kinderhook
Mother: Mary Horn

HORN, JOHN W
21 June 1859
WMA   Page 46   F
Parents: John E. & Mary Horn

HORNE, ELBERT S
19 Feb. 1856
WMA   Page 26   F
Parents: Joel & Malvina Horne

HORNE, EMMET M
3 Oct. 1856
Reported by A. Horne, grandfather
WMA   Page 26
Mother: Eliza'th Horne

HORNE, LOUISA
1 April 1859
WMA   Page 50   F
Parents: Joel & Malvina Horne

HORNE, MARY ELIZABETH
21 Aug. 1854
WFA   Page 10   F
Parents: John E. & Mary Horne

HORNE, ROBERT E.L.
28 Nov. 1870
WM_   Page 57   Kinderhook
Parents: Jas. & Malvina Horne

HOUSTON, JAMES M
13 July 1853
WMA   Page 6   F
Parents: James & Mary Houston

HOUSTON, JAS. MADISON
13 July 1853
WMA   Page 5   F
Parents: Jas. & Mary Houston

HOWELL, LEANDER JANE
22 Sept. 1853
WFA   Page 1   F
Parents: William & Eliza Howell

HOWELL, W.E.
4 Jan. 1857
WFA   Page 36   F
Parents: Wm. D. & Mary J. Howell

HOWARD, ALICE
    1 Feb. 1892

CFA   Page 73   Near Abingdon
Mother: Alice Howard

HOWARD, JAMES T
    12 March 1871

WMA   Page 53   F   Abingdon Twp.
Parents: Thomas H. & Margaret E. Howard

HOWARD, MARTHY C
    20 Nov. 1857

WFA   Page 36   F
Parents: Edward & D. Howard

HOWARD, WILLIAM T
    26 Oct. 1855

WMA   Page 18   F
Parents: William & Mary Jane Howard

HOWINGTON, NEWTON C
    20 Jan. 1857

WMA   Page 36   F
Parents: Jabez & A.L. Howington

HOWSER, MARY E
    30 March 1892

WFA   Page 71   F   Goodson
Father: Alex HOWSOR
Mother: Sarah HOUSER

HUBERLIN, NANCY
    5 April 1854

WMFA   Page 11   F
Parents: Joel & Lucinda Huberlin

HUDSON, MARY V
    15 March 1858

WFA   Page 39   F
Parents: Hiram & Nancy Hudson

HUGHES, ALFRED
    25 Oct. 1870

WM_   Page 58   MC   Kinderhook Twp.
Parents: Wm. F. & Malvina Hughes

HUGHES, M.J.
    30 Aug. 1859

WFA   Page 50   F
Parents: William A. & M.J. Hughes

HUGHES, MARY ANN
    8 Aug. 1854

WFA   Page 9   F
Parents: John & Ellen Hughes

HUGHES, RACHEL E
    8 Dec. 1857

WFA   Page 32   L
Parents: Wm. F. & Hariet Hughes

HUGHS, MARY A
    15 Oct. 1856

WFA   Page 32   F
Parents: Wm. & Eady HUGHES

HUGHS, SARAH G
    12 May 1859

WFA   Page 50   F
Parents: James & Edith Hughs

HUMPHREY, GAR. D.
    28 Feb. 1892

WMA   Page 61   F
Parents: H.H. & Mil. O. Humphrey

HUMPHREYS, C.E.C.
    23 July 1853

WMA   Page 7   F
Father: Able H. Humphreys

HUMPHREYS, ELLEN W
    7 April 1858

WFA   Page 39   F
Parents: A.H. & M.A. Humphreys

HUMPHREYS, MARY C
    17 May 1856

WFA   Page 26   F
Parents: A.H. & Mary A. Humphreys

HUMPHRIES, WILLIAM
    1870

WMA   Page 57   F   Glade Spring Twp.
Parents: John & Margaret Humphries

HUMPHRY, JAS. E.
    4 July 1856
    Reported by Geo. W. Humphry, father

WMA   Page 31   F
Parents: Geo. W. & Eliz'th HUMPHRYS

HUNSUCKER, [HAMILTON] F
    23 Sept. 1856
    WMA   Page 25   F
    Parents: Jas. J. & M.E. Hunsucker

HURLEY, LADY J
    28 May 1892
    WFA   Page 61   F
    Parents: W.R. & Nancy Hurley

HURT, ALICE C
    1 Dec. 1858
    WFA   Page 39   F
    Parents: Geo. W. & Rebecca Hurt

HURT, ELIZABETH
    10 or 18 Aug. 1856
    WFA   Page 26   F
    Parents: Geo. W. & Rebecca Hurt

HURT, GROVER CLEVELAND
    24 Feb. 1892
    WMA   Page 69   F   North Fork Dis
    Parents: L.C. & Ann Hurt

HUTTON, ALLISON
    11 Feb. 1856
    WMA   Page 29   F
    Parents: Rob't S.C. & E.S. Hutton

HUTTON, AMANDA FRANCES
    8 Sept. 1854
    WFA   Page 11   F
    Parents: John & Jane Hutton

HUTTON, AMANDA LAVINIA
    3 Aug. 1855
    WFA   Page 16   PH   Cedarville
    Parents: Arthur D. & Sarah Jane Hutton

HUTTON, BESSIE E
    12 June 1892
    WFA   Page 61   F
    Parents: Wm. E. & Sallie R. Hutton

HUTTON, J
    13 Dec. 1857
    WFA   Page 36   F
    Parents: Lilburn L. & C. Hutton

HUTTON, MARTHA L
    19 Nov. 1870
    WF_   Page 58   F
    Parents: W.L. & Dorcas Hutton

HUTTON, MARY C
    1 Jan. 1859
    WFA   Page 50   F
    Parents: L.L. & Mary C. Hutton

HUTTON, MATILDA
    13 March 1859
    WFA   Page 46   F
    Parents: Robt. & Steel Hutton

HUTTON, SAML. O.
    3 Sept. 1856
    WMA   Page 30   F
    Parents: Jno. & Ann J. Hutton

HUTTON, SARAH JANE
    6 Oct. 1853
    WFA   Page 3   PH   Cedarville
    Parents: Arthur D. & Sarah Jane Hutto

HUTTON, WM.
    24 March 1892
    WMA   Page 61   F
    Parents: E.J. & M.E. Hutton

HUTTON, WM. E.
    2 May 1857
    WMA   Page 36   F
    Parents: Ro. S.C. & E.C. Hutton

HUTTON, WILLIE
    Jan. 1892
    WMA   Page 66   F   Kinderhook
    Parents: W.L. & Bell Hutton

HYLER, SARAH
    9 Feb. 1859
    WFA   Page 50   F
    Parents: George W. & Sarah A. Hyler

INGLE, C.E.
    10 July 1892
    WMA   Page 67   F   Kinderhook
    Parents: William & Malinda Ingle

INGLE, [EMIE]
    10 July 1892
    WFA   Page 67   F   Kinderhook
    Parents: M.C. & Eliza Ingle

INGLE, GRACE
    5 May 1892
    WFA   Page 66   F   Kinderhook
    Parents: A.H. & Mary E. Ingle

INGLE, MARTHA J
    4 Oct. 1870
    WF_   Page 58
    Parents: Anthony H. & Mary E. Ingle

INGLE, MINERVA C
    3 June 1856
    WFA   Page 25   F
    Parents: Jos. & M.J. Ingle

INGRAM, JACOB W
    7 April 1858
    WMA   Page 43   F
    Parents: Jacob & Sarah A. Ingram

INGRAM, JOHN
    3 Sept. 1853
    WMA   Page 6   F
    Parents: Jacob & Sarah Ann Ingram

IRESON, AB. S.
    9 Nov. 1858
    WMA   Page 43   F
    Parents: Robt. C. & Martha Ireson

IRESON, EDWARD M
    26 June 1856
    WMA   Page 26   L
    Parents: Jas. L. & Nancy Ireson

IRESON, EDWARD McDANIEL
    21 Feb. 1855
    WMA   Page 17   MW
    Parents: James C. & Ellen Ireson

IRESON, ELIZA JANE
    20 April 1853
    WFA   Page 2   MW
    Parents: James C. & Eleanor Ireson

IRESON, JAS. C.
    15 Dec. 1858
    WMA   Page 40   F
    Parents: Jas. & A.O.S. Ireson

IRESON, JNO. C.
    11 Dec. 1857
    WMA   Page 36   C
    Parents: James & Elinder Ireson

IRESON, R.V.
    15 Dec. 1858
    WMA   Page 40   MW
    Parents: Jas. C. & Ellen Ireson

IRESON, WM. DAVID
    13 Feb. 1853
    WMA   Page 4   F
    Parents: Jas. L. & Nancy Ireson

IRVING, SARAH FRANCIS
    27 Oct. 1854
    WFA   Page 9   F
    Parents: John W. & Mary Irving

ISA
    April 1856
    SFA   Page 27
    Owner: John Preston

JACK
    28 Sept. 1856
    SMA   Page 27
    Owner: Thos. G. McConnell

JACKSON, [n.n.]
    4 April 1858
    WMD   Page 40   F
    Parents: Jno. & Matilda Jackson

JACKSON, BRYANT (twin)
    15 June 1892
    WMA   Page 62   F
    Parents: A.W. & Sarah E. Jackson

JACKSON, CHAS. R. (twin)
    15 June 1892
    WMA   Page 62   F
    Parents: A.W. & Sarah E. Jackson

JACKSON, EZEKIEL
    10 Nov. 1892
    WMA   Page 62   F
    Parents: G.M. & Alline M. Jackson

JACKSON, JULIA
    15 June 1892
    WFA   Page 62   F
    Parents: F.M. & Sarah E. Jackson

JACKSON, MARTHA   WFA   Page 47   F
    9 June 1859   Parents: T.M. & Rebecca Jackson

JACKSON, ROBB F   WM   Page 58
    7 May 1870   Parents: James & Francis Jackson

JACKSON, STONEWALL J   WMA   Page 62   F
    7 June 1892   Parents: Thomas & Virginia Jackson

JACOB   SMA   Page 13
    Sept. 1854   Mother: Viney
    Reported by W.J. Bishop   Owner: Mary Jones

JACOB   SMA   Page 27
    20 Feb. 1856   Owner: Mosby Davidson

JAMES   SMA   Page 8
    5 July 1853   Owner: Jonathan Hanby

JAMES   SMA   Page 8
    Dec. 1853   Owner: D. Campbell

JAMES   WMA   Page 17
    June 1855   Mother: Amanda
                                    Owner: John Maiden

JAMES   SMA   Page 16
    Oct. 1855   Mother: Hannah
                                    Owner: Rob't Clark

JAS.   SMA   Page 27
    29 April 1856   Owner: Isaac Carmack

JAMES   SMA   Page 27
    10 Aug. 1856   Owner: Benj. Reid

JAMES   SMA   Page 51
    24 Sept. 1858   Owner: Jos. [W.] Rhea

JAMES, [n.n.]   WMA   Page 56   F   Glade Spring 1
    1870   Parents: Andrew & Susan James

JAMES, ELI V   WMA   Page 29   F
    17 Dec. 1856   Parents: James & Ann James

JAMES, MATHEW H   WMA   Page 47   F
    30 March 1859   Parents: James & Ann James

JAMES, NICKERSON   WMA   Page 19   F
    30 May 1855   Parents: James & Ann James

JAMISON, [n.n.]   WFA   Page 40   F
    15 Dec. 1858   Parents: D.P. & L.J. Jamison

JANE   SFA   Page 1
    6 Nov. 1853   Owner: Wm. L. Hunter
    Reported by Elisha McNew

JANE   SFA   Page 9
    March 1854   Mother: Betsey
                                    Owner: Arthur Hutton

JANE
    26 Aug. 1856
    SFA   Page 30
    Owner: Whitley Fullen

JANE
    15 Sept. 1856
    SFA   Page 34
    Owner: John Preston

JANE
    4 Oct. 1856
    SFA   Page 27
    Owner: Jno. M. Hamilton

JANE
    31 July 1857
    SFA   Page 34
    Owner: Elizabeth Lathim

JANE
    15 Jan. 1858
    SFA   Page 43
    Owner: John H. Smyth

JERRY
    1 Nov. 1855
    SMA   Page 18
    Mother: Amanda
    Owner: Capt'n Wm. Duff

JESSEE, GEO. L.
    18 Sept. 1853
    WMA   Page 7   F
    Father: Wm. F. Jessee

JESSEE, MARY E (twin)
    25 Sept. 1855
    WFA   Page 22   F
    Parents: Wm. F. & Mary J. Jessee

JESSEE, WILLIAM E (twin)
    25 Sept. 1855
    WMA   Page 22   F
    Parents: Wm. F. & Mary J. Jessee

JIM
    4 Feb. 1858
    SMA   Page 39
    Owner: Henry Forest

JOE
    1 Aug. 1857
    SMA   Page 34
    Owner: A.R. Preston

JOHN
    May 1854
    Reported by W.J. Bishop
    SMA   Page 13
    Owner: Mary Jones

JOHN
    12 Aug. 1854
    SMA   Page 13   Poor Valley
    Mother: Esther
    Master: Whitley Fullen

JOHN
    April 1855
    SMA   Page 23
    Owner: John Preston

JOHN
    4 Oct. 1855
    Reported by Jas. Rambo, son of owner   Owner: David Rambo
    SMA   Page 18
    Mother: Catharine

JOHN
    25 Dec. 1855
    SMA   Page 23
    Owner: Jno. Gibson

JOHN
    7 March 1856
    SMA   Page 27
    Owner: Geo. L. Nunley

JOHN
    1 April 1856
    SMA   Page 27
    Owner: Henry Forest

JOHN
    1 July 1856
    SMA   Page 28
    Mother: Martha Mock
    Owner: Peter Mock

JOHN		SMA	Page 34
15 Aug. 1857		Owner: Alfred Carmack	
JOHN		SMA	Page 36
6 Feb. 1857		Owner: F.M. Preston	
JOHN		SMA	Page 43
24 Aug. 1858		Owner: W.T. Fulcher	
JOHN		SMA	Page 43
20 Dec. 1858		Owner: Jas. C. Hayter	
JOHN N		SMA	Page 15
29 Aug. 1854		Master: Wm. B. Campbell	
JOHN W		SMA	Page 36
10 April 1856		Owner: A.H. Hayter	

JOHNSON, C. ISIAH
   8 Dec. 1892
WMA   Page 62   F
Parents: G.W., Jr., & Sarah Johnso

JOHNSON, CLAUD
   8 Oct. 1892
WMA   Page 71   L   Goodson
Parents: Henry & Mary Johnson

JOHNSON, ELGIN
   18 May 1892
WMA   Page 62   F
Parents: G.W., Sr., & Maggie Johns

JOHNSON, ELLA M
   5 Nov. 1892
CFA   Page 74   F   Goodson
Parents: W.J. & Alcy Johnson

JOHNSON, GEORGE E
   4 Feb. 1892
CMA   Page 73 & 74 F   Goodson
Mother: Emma Johnson

JOHNSON, GROVER F
   29 Aug. 1892
WMA   Page 62   F
Parents: J.H. & Cornelia Johnson

JOHNSON, GUARTEE
   25 Dec. 1892
CMA   Page 73   L   Near Abinç
Parents: Peter & Rachel Johnson

JOHNSON, HENRY V
   29 Dec. 1855
WMA   Page 21   F
Parents: Walter & Mary Johnson

JOHNSON, LEANDER
   6 March 1892
CMA   Page 73   L   Near Abinç
Parents: Bob & Alice Johnson

JOHNSON, MARY
   12 Dec. 1858
WFA   Page 40   F
Parents: W.J. & Susan Johnson

JOHNSON, MARY F
   1 Nov. 1855
WFA   Page 23   F
Parents: John F. & Julia A. Johns:

JOHNSON, MINERVA A.W.
   2 Dec. 1857
WFA   Page 32   L
Parents: Walter & Mary A. Johnson

JOHNSON, MITCHEL
   20 March 1892
CMA   Page 73   L   Near Abin
Parents: Ben & Josephine Johnson

JOHNSON, NANCY
   13 Nov. 1859
WFA   Page 47   F
Parents: John & Lydia Johnson

JOHNSON, OLLIE E
   3 May 1892
WFA   Page 62   F
Parents: Dan'l J. & Mary J. Johns

JOHNSON, S.V.   WFA   Page 6   F
    28 June 1853   Parents: Jno. J. & Julia Johnson

JOHNSON, SARAH JANE   WFA   Page 16   F   Near Saltville
    17 June 1855   Parents: John & Lydia Johnson

JOHNSON, SHADRACK   WMA   Page 20   F
    28 Feb. 1855   Parents: Benj. & Mary Johnson

JOHNSON, SUSAN A   WFA   Page 71   L   Goodson
    24 March 1892   Parents: Melvin & Nancy Johnson

JOHNSON, WALTER   WMA   Page 27   F
    25 July 1856   Parents: Wm. J. & Susan Johnson

JOHNSON, WALTER A   WMA   Page 56   F   Glade Spring Twp.
    1870   Parents: William R. & Sarah N. Johnson

JOHNSTON, MARGARET ANN   WFA   Page 2   L
    1 March 1853   Parents: John & Dorcas Johnston

JONES, [n.n]   WFA   Page 12
    7 July 1854   Parents: Finney & Rebecca Jones

JONES, [n.n.]   WFA   Page 40   F
    13 Sept. 1858   Parents: Jas. M. & M.F. Jones

JONES, [n.n.]   WMA   Page 71   F   Goodson
    16 June 1892   Parents: Sidney & Lucy Jones

JONES, CALVIN   WMA   Page 53   F   Abingdon Twp.
    11 July 1871   Parents: Robert & Martha Jones

JONES, DEXTER T   WMA   Page 62   F
    12 Aug. 1892   Parents: J. Frank & Jennie C. Jones

JONES, [E.] [C.]   WFA   Page 40   F
    27 April 1858   Parents: W.D.L. & M.C. Jones

JONES, FRANKLIN J   WMA   Page 29   F
    6 May 1856   Parents: Wm. B. & Cath Jones

JONES, GEO. LEE   WMA   Page 62   F
    26 Aug. 1892   Parents: T.L. & Virginia Jones

JONES, HANSON ALEXANDER WMA   Page 5   F
    5 June 1853   Parents: Wm. B. & Catharine Jones

JONES, JAMES   WMA   Page 47   F
    17 Aug. 1859   Parents: Andrew & Mary Jones

JONES, JAMES C   WMA   Page 21   F
    8 Sept. 1855   Parents: M.M. & Mary J. Jones
    Reported by A.C. Maxwell, physician

JONES, JAMES E   WMA   Page 53   WH   Abingdon Twp.
    14 May 1871   Parents: Isaac F. & Martha Jones

JONES, JOHN R   WMA   Page 43   F
    4 Sept. 1858   Parents: John & Idithe Jones

JONES, L.H.   WMA   Page 71   F   Goodson
    25 July 1892   Parents: M.D. & Lucy T. Jones

JONES, MAGGIE   WFA   Page 61   F
    2 June 1892   Parents: Robt. & Mary Jones

JONES, MARY   WFA   Page 47   F
    21 July 1859   Parents: Nathan & Bartholime Jones

JONES, [MILUND] F   WFA   Page 25   PH
    19 April 1856   Parents: Jas. M. & W.F. Jones

JONES, NANCY F.V.   WFA   Page 29   F
    24 Oct. 1856   Parents: Andrew M. & Mary Jones

JONES, S.W.   WMA   Page 43   F
    2 Dec. 1858   Parents: William & Catherine Jones

JONES, SARAH ANN   WFA   Page 5
    24 Aug. 1853   Mother: Eliza Jones

JONES, WM. D.   WMA   Page 71   F   Goodson
    26 Nov. 1892   Parents: John & Maggie Jones

JONES, WM. JNO. R.   WMA   Page 9   F
    2 Jan. 1854   Parents: Andrew M. & Mary Jones

JONES, WILLIAM K   WMA   Page 11   B
    22 Feb. 1854   Parents: John & Judith Jones

JOSEPH   SMA   Page 8
    1 April 1853   Owner: Jas. L. Davis

JOSEPH   SMA   Page 8
    23 May 1853   Owner: Jno. H. Wallace

JOSEPH   SMA   Page 29
    6 Jan. 1856   Owner: Micajah McCormick

KAHLE, E.A.   WFA   Page 62   MN
    6 April 1892   Parents: E.F. & Eva Kahle

KATE   SFA   Page 41
    31 Oct. 1858   Owner: Milton White

KAYLOR, ELIZABETH   WFA   Page 32   F
    15 June 1856   Parents: Daniel & Hulda Kaylor

KAYLOR, JAS. R.   WMA   Page 40
    15 Feb. 1858   Parents: Daniel & A. Kaylor

KAYLOR, JOHN   WMA   Page 25   F
    15 Nov. 1856   Parents: Hiram & C. Kaylor

KAYLOR, M.E.   WFA   Page 7   F
    2 April 1853   Father: Daniel Kaylor

KAYLOR, MARY W   WF_   Page 58
    1870   Parents: Joel & Martha Kaylor

KAYLOR, MOLLIE   WFA   Page 67   F   Kinderhook
    8 Nov. 1892   Parents: H.H. & Eliza Kaylor

KAYLOR, W.B.   WMA   Page 67   F   Kinderhook
    8 Nov. 1892   Parents: J.B. & Martha Kaylor

[KAYLOR], WM. H. CLARK see CLARK, WM. H.

KEATH, VINEY   WFA   Page 20   SH
    4 Aug. 1855   Parents: Burwell & Rebecca Keath

KEBLER, FANNIE L   WFA   Page 32   MR
    12 Oct. 1857   Parents: Valentine & M.C. Kebler

KEESSEE, CLARENCE   WMA   Page 71   F
    7 July 1892   Parents: John & Alice Keessee

KEGLEY, GERTIE (twin)   WFA   Page 62   SH
    2 Sept. 1892   Parents: Wm. & Eliz. Kegley
    Born in Grayson Co., Va.

KEGLEY, LUSTER (twin)   WMA   Page 62   SH
    2 Sept. 1892   Parents: Wm. & Eliz. Kegley
    Born in Grayson Co., Va.

KELLER, BEULAH 21 March 1892	WFA	Page 62	F
	Parents: Geo. L.C. & Lucinda Keller		
KELLER, GEO. L.C. 5 April 1857	WMA	Page 36	F
	Parents: George & Ann Keller		
KELLER, JOS. A. 1 May 1856	WMA	Page 29	F
	Parents: Joseph & Dorcus Keller		
KELLER, MARY M 5 October 1859	WFA	Page 50	MR
	Parents: Valentine & Mary C. Keller		
KELLER, NANCY C 22 June 1855	WFA	Page 17	F
	Parents: George & Ann C. Keller		
KELLER, SARAH 3 November 1859	WFA	Page 47	F
	Parents: John & Nancy Keller		
KELLER, THOMAS B 15 September 1859	WMA	Page 47	F
	Parents: Joseph & Dorcas Keller		
KELLER, [TRIG] F.D. 29 May 1856	WFA	Page 29	B
	Parents: James & Susanah Keller		
KELLEY, B 26 July 1857	WMA	Page 36	F
	Parents: John & E. Kelley		
KELLEY, EDGAR 15 May 1892	WMA	Page 62	F
	Parents: J.D. & Mary Kelley		
KELLEY, JONAS S 11 June 1892	WMA	Page 62	F
	Parents: D.A. & Sallie Kelley		
KELLEY, MARY E 1 March 1892	WFA	Page 62	F
	Parents: Chas. R. & Nan V. Kelley		
KELLEY, MINNIE 17 August 1892	WFA	Page 62	F
	Parents: W.H. & Hattie Kelley		
KELLY, MARGARET ALICE 1 October 1855	WFA	Page 20	F
	Parents: James & Mahala Kelly		
KELLY, SARAH 1 August 1853	WFA	Page 4	F
	Parents: James E. & Margaret Kelly		
KELLY, THOMAS JEFFERSON 23 December 1855	WMA	Page 16	F
	Parents: Fulton & Jane Kelly		
KELLY, WM. KEYS 23 March 1855	WMA	Page 18	F
	Parents: John & Elizabeth Kelly		
KENT, EUGENE (twin) 9 June 1892	WMA	Page 62	CL
	Parents: J.C. & Fannie Kent		
KENT, FAN. (twin) 9 June 1892	WFA	Page 62	CL
	Parents: J.C. & Fannie Kent		
KENT, REBECCA C 9 September 1855	WFA	Page 20	CM
	Parents: Jacob B. & Martha A.B. Kent		
KESNER, DAVID H 1 April 1855	WMA	Page 21	F
	Parents: John & Adeline Kesner		
KESNER, JAMES D 18 February 1855	WMA	Page 17	F
	Parents: Jacob H. & Margaret Kesner		

KESNER, JNO. G   WMA   Page 25   F
    7 May 1856   Parents: Jno. & Mary Kesner

KESNER, LOUISA   WFA   Page 50   F
    12 March 1859   Parents: John & Matilda Kesner

KESNER, M.E.   WFA   Page 40   F
    23 November 1858   Parents: Jno. & Sarah A. Kesner

KESNER, MARTHA E.C.   WFA   Page 32   F
    23 November 1857   Father: John Kesner
                        Mother: Adaline KESTNER

KESNER, MARY C   WFA   Page 40   F
    11 June 1858   Parents: Wash. & Sarah A. Kesner

KESNER, SARAH E   WFA   Page 32   F
    12 March 1857   Parents: John & Matilda Kesner

KESNOR, M.H.   WMA   Page 43   F
    1 July 1858   Parents: Philip & Jane R. Kesnor

KESTNER, LAURA A   WFA   Page 54   F   Northfork Twp.
    18 February 1871   Parents: Andrew J. & Mary Jane Kestner

KETCHEM, HATTIE   WFA   Page 62   F
    8 December 1892   Parents: J.L. & Marth Ketchem

KETCHUM, JOSEPH   WMA   Page 36   F
    1 November 1857   Parents: Jacob & Matilda Ketchem

KEYS, GEO. H   WMA   Page 71   CL   Goodson
    10 February 1892   Parents: T.G. & Susan R. Keys

KEYS, JAMES A   WMA   Page 36   PH
    5 April 1857   Parents: Jno. & Mary P. Keys

KEYS, JNO. H   WMA   Page 36   F
    9 May 1857   Parents: Ro., Jr., & J.J. Keys

KEYS, LOISA K   WFA   Page 62   MR
    8 March 1892   Parents: A.E. & Florence Keys

KEYS, MARTHA JANE   WFA   Page 11   F
    11 September 1854   Parents: Robert & Elizabeth Jane Keys

KEYS, MATTHEW B.G.   WMA   Page 18   PH
    29 April 1855   Parents: John & Mary Jane Keys

KID   SMA   Page 27
    30 May 1856   Owner: E.L. Davenport

KILLINGER, MILTON B   WMA   Page 47   F
    10 December 1859   Parents: A.P. & Sarah Killinger

KINDRICK, ANNIE S   WF_   Page 58
    3 June 1870   Parents: Robert & Mary Kindrick

KINDRICK, THOMAS   WMA   Page 55   F   Saltville Twp.
    30 August 1870   Parents: Thomas & Angaline Kindrick

KING, ALEX   CMA   Page 73   L   Near Abingdon
    26 March 1892   Parents: Frank & Cally King

KING, AMANDA
 22 April 1857
WFA Page 32 F
Parents: Jont. S. & Mary King

KING, JAS. A.D.
 15 April 1856
WMA Page 27 F
Parents: Jas. A. & E.M. King

KING, LAURA
 20 March 1858
WFA Page 40 F
Parents: W.D. & Susan E. King

KING, ROENA E
 20 September 1857
WFA Page 32 F
Parents: James A. & Maranda King

KING, WILLIAM G
 15 November 1855
WMA Page 21 F
Parents: S.J. & Mary King

KINGSOLVER, EDITH
 10 September 1892
WFA Page 69 F North Fork Di
Parents: James & Fannie Kingsolver

KINGSOLVER, JAMES
 29 August 1859
WMA Page 50 F
Parents: David & Mary Kingsolver

KINGSOLVER, MARY
 29 March 1870
WFA Page 55 C Saltville Twp
Parents: David & Lucy Kingsolver

KINSOLVER, SARAH C
 13 August 1859
WFA Page 47 F
Parents: Charles & Malinda Kinsolver

KITZEMILLER, EMMA JANE
 1870
WFA Page 56 F Glade Spring
Parents: David & Elizabeth Kitzemille

LAMBERSON, [n.n.]
 10 December 1858
WMA Page 43 F
Parents: John & S.A. Lamberson

LAMBERSON, EDWARD C
 22 September 1855
WMA Page 23 F
Parents: John & Sarah Lamberson

LAMBERSON, R
 26 April 1853
WMFA Page 7 IR
Parents: Jno. & Sarah Lamberson

LANAHAN, [IDA] R
 1 July 1858
WFA Page 40 C
Parents: John L. & S.E. Lanahan

LANDRUM, [n.n.]
 10 February 1855
WMD Page 19 F
Parents: Tho's W. & Mary J. Landrum

LANE, DEWITT
 1 September 1892
WMA Page 62 F
Parents: Robt. & Callie Lane

LANGLEY, ELI S
 20 January 1855
WMA Page 20 F
Parents: James O. & Margaret Langley

LANGLEY, ELLIA L
 October 1855
WFA Page 20 F
Parents: John & Sally Langley

LANGLEY, JNO. WILSON
 15 July 1853
WMA Page 2 L
Parents: John & Sally Langley

LARGE, [n.n.]
 11 December 1857
WFA Page 33 F
Parents: Jas. & Eady Large

LARGE, [n.n.]
 18 December 1892
WMA Page 69 F
Parents: Vincent & Jennie Large

LARGE, EDWARD
 10 July 1892
WMA Page 67 F Kinderhook
Parents: Amos & Julia Large

LARGE, ISAAC
    26 September 1853
WMA   Page 7   F
Father: Isaac Large

LARGE, MATTIE
    5 June 1892
WFA   Page 67   F   Kinderhook
Parents: E.K. & Bettie Large

LARGE, R.W.
    10 November 1892
WMA   Page 67   F   Kinderhook
Parents: J.W. & Elizabeth Large

LARIMER, HENRY T.C.
    23 August 1871
WMA   Page 53   F   Abingdon Twp.
Parents: Jeremiah F. & Susanah M. Larimer

LARIMER, JAMES CAMPBELL
    November 1855
WMA   Page 17   F
Parents: John & Sarah Larimer

LARIMER, JAMES HENRY
    11 October 1854
WMA   Page 11   F
Parents: William & Judy Larimer

LARIMER, JAMES WINTER
    28 August 1855
WMA   Page 19   F
Parents: Robert E. & Mary Larimer

LARIMER, MALISSA A
    July 1853
WFA   Page 3   F
Parents: John & Catharine Larimer

LARIMER, MARIAH L
    12 June 1853
WFA   Page 4   F
Parents: Robt. E. & Mary Larimer

LARIMER, ROBERT A
    10 March 1855
WMA   Page 18   F
Parents: Alex'r W. & Barshaba C. Larimer

LARIMER, SARAH
    July 1854
WFA   Page 12   F
Parents: Robert & Rachel Larimer

LARIMER, THOS. R
    15 September 1858
WMA   Page 43   F
Parents: J.F. & Susan Larimer

LARIMORE, DAVID G.W.
    20 September 1857
WMA   Page 36   F
Parents: Alex & B.C. Larimore

LARIMORE, ELIZABETH E
    21 September 1859
WFA   Page 47   F
Parents: William & Judeath Larimore

LARIMORE, GEO. L.F.
    12 October 1857
WMA   Page 36   F
Parents: Wm. G. & Judy Larimore

LARIMORE, JOHN B.F.
    30 November 1859
WMA   Page 47   F
Parents: Alexr. & Barsheba Larimore

LARIMORE, JULEY E.S.
    1 September 1859
WFA   Page 47   F
Parents: Andrew M. & Jane Larimore

LARIMORE, MARY A.J.R.
    11 November 1856
WFA   Page 28   F
Parents: Jno. & E.I. Larimore

LARIMORE, MARY M.A.
    28 February 1857
WFA   Page 36   F
Parents: And. M. & Jane L. Larimore

LARIMORE, MOSES M
    17 April 1856
WMA   Page 27   F
Parents: Rob't & Rachel Larimore

LARIMORE, [NANCEAN] J
    30 April 1857
WFA   Page 36   F
Parents: Jno., Jr., & Sarah Larimore

LARIMORE, PHEBY JANE   WFA   Page 56   F   Glade Spring
    1870   Parents: Robt. J. & Sarah Larimore

LARIMORE, ROBERT G.D.   WMA   Page 56   F   Glade Spring
    1870   Parents: James & Eliza Larimore

LARIMORE, VIRGINIA A   WFA   Page 36   F
    20 December 1857   Parents: Robt. & Sarah Larimore

LATHEM, FRANCES   WFA   Page 15   F
    17 September 1854   Parents: Jacob H. & Sarah M. Lathem

LATHIM, DANIEL C   WMA   Page 15   F.
    4 April 1854   Parents: M.H. & Ellen Lathim

LATHIM, DANL. H   WMA   Page 33   F
    20 February 1857   Parents: Jacob H. & Sarah A. Lathim

LATHIM, JNO. W   WMA   Page 62
    26 January 1892   Mother: Marg. Lathim

LATHIM, LAURA L   WFA   Page 20   F
    28 November 1855   Parents: M.H. & Ellen Lathim

LAWSON, [n.n.]   WFA   Page 54   F   Northfork Twp
    April 1871   Parents: Wm. M.B. & Sarah Lawson

LAWSON, [n.n.]   WFA   Page 52   L
    14 April 1892   Parents: J.R. & Isabel Lawson

LAYNE, RHODA A   WF_   Page 58
    25 August 1870   Parents: Isaac & Jemima Layne

LEANARD, DAVID C   WMA   Page 25   F
    1 March 1856   Parents: Geo. & Martha Leanard
         Reported by Henry Shaffer, grandfather

LEANARD, DAVID [I]   WMA   Page 25   F
    28 September 1856   Parents: Jno. I. & Ann Leanard

LEANARD, MARY M   WFA   Page 28   F
    20 April 1856   Parents: Wm. M. & Sarah LEONARD

LEE, [n.n.]   WMA   Page 43   F
    25 August 1858   Parents: James & M.J. Lee

LEE, [n.n.]   W_A   Page 54   F   Northfork Twp
    1 September 1871   Parents: James M. & Amanda J. Lee

LEE, HENRY M   WMA   Page 16   B   Saltville
    19 October 1855   Parents: James M. & Amanda Lee

LEE, MARY E   WFA   Page 47   F
    15 August 1859   Parents: Emory H. & Eliza H. Lee

LEE, WILLIAM   WMA   Page 9   F   Near Saltvill
    21 October 1854   Parents: Emory H. & Eliza Lee

LEGARD, ELIZABETH V   WFA   Page 22   F
    29 May 1855   Parents: R.T. & Ann J. Legard

LEGARD, JULIA A   WFA   Page 40   F
    16 January 1858   Parents: R.T. & Ann J. Legard

LEGARD, NANCY J   WFA   Page 33   F
        13 January 1857   Parents: R.T. & Ann J. Legard

LEGARD, SAMUEL P   WMA   Page 14   F
        11 February 1854   Parents: R.T. & Ann J. Legard

LEGG, GERTIE   WFA   Page 53   F
        11 June 1871   Parents: James & Elizabeth Legg
        Place of birth: Tennessee; residence: Abingdon Twp.

LENTICUMB, GEO. W   WMA   Page 29   F
        14 October 1856   Father: Hiram HUGHES
                                   Mother: Martha Lenticumb

LEONARD, [n.n.]   WMA   Page 24   F
        15 November 1856   Parents: Jordon & Viney Leonard

LEONARD, [n.n.]   WFA   Page 71   F   Goodson
        5 March 1892   Parents: Jackson & Mary Leonard

LEONARD, A.F.B.   WMA   Page 50   F
        12 June 1859   Parents: Joseph & Catharine Leonard

LEONARD, AMANDA   WFA   Page 50   B
        10 January 1859   Parents: Peter H. & Susan Leonard

LEONARD, BIRDIE   WFA   Page 71   F   Goodson
        9 January 1892   Parents: Saml. & Mary E. Leonard

LEONARD, ELIZABETH J   WFA   Page 22   F
        4 September 1855   Parents: John & Elizabeth J. Leonard

LEONARD, ELIZABETH J   WFA   Page 40   F
        16 May 1858   Parents: Wm. & Sarah Leonard

LEONARD, FREDERICK   WMA   Page 14   F
        8 September 1854   Parents: Henry & Mary Leonard

LEONARD, HENRY   WM_   Page 58
        1870   Parents: And. & Francis Leonard

LEONARD, ISAAC B   WMA   Page 32   F
        21 June 1857   Parents: Geo. & Martha Leonard

LEONARD, J.C.   WMA   Page 67   F   Kinderhook
        8 December 1892   Parents: M.H. & Rebecca Leonard

LEONARD, JAMES E   WM_   Page 58   F
        13 November 1870   Parents: Franklin & Mary J. Leonard

LEONARD, JOHN   WMA   Page 67   F   Kinderhook
        10 August 1892   Parents: Robert & Nannie Leonard

LEONARD, JOHN A   WMA   Page 22   B
        15 July 1855   Parents: Fred. B. & Elizabeth Leonard

LEONARD, LUCY F   WFA   Page 33   F
        1 September 1857   Parents: Wm. A. & Sarah Leonard

LEONARD, M.J.   WMA   Page 67   F   Kinderhook
        5 August 1892   Parents: Joseph & Maggie Leonard

LEONARD, MARY [C]　　　　　　　　WFA　　Page 40　　　F
　　15 January 1858　　　　　　　Parents:　Peter & [M] C. Leonard

LEONARD, MARY E　　　　　　　　　WFA　　Page 33　　　F
　　13 April 1857　　　　　　　　Parents:　Geo. & M.M. Leonard

LEONARD, MARY E　　　　　　　　　WFA　　Page 71　　　F　　　Goodson
　　9 November 1892　　　　　　　Parents:　Alex. & Mary J. Leonard

LEONARD, NELSON　　　　　　　　　WMA　　Page 67　　　F　　　Kinderhook
　　August 1892　　　　　　　　　Parents:　David & Mary Leonard

LEONARD, P. [S]　　　　　　　　　WMA　　Page 40　　　F
　　15 December 1858　　　　　　Parents:　Jordan & Virginia Leonard

LEONARD, ROBT.　　　　　　　　　WMA　　Page 40　　　F
　　14 February 1858　　　　　　Parents:　Henry & Mary Leonard

LEONARD, S.J.　　　　　　　　　　WFA　　Page 7　　　　C
　　7 January 1853　　　　　　　Father:　Henry Leonard

LEONARD, SARAH J.M.　　　　　　WFA　　Page 14　　　F
　　14 April 1854　　　　　　　　Parents:　Henry & Elizabeth Leonard

LEONARD, WILLIAM　　　　　　　　WM_　　Page 58
　　October 1870　　　　　　　　Parents:　Jno. & Margaret Leonard

LEONARD, WILSON　　　　　　　　WMA　　Page 71　　　MR　　Goodson
　　9 January 1892　　　　　　　Parents:　John & Josephine Leonard

LESTER, ANDREW I　　　　　　　　WMA　　Page 36　　　F
　　8 April 1857　　　　　　　　Parents:　Levi J. & Margret Lester

LESTER, DOCIA　　　　　　　　　　WFA　　Page 36　　　F
　　30 April 1857　　　　　　　　Parents:　David & Esther Lester

LESTER, GEORGE M　　　　　　　　WMA　　Page 12　　　F
　　September 1854　　　　　　　Parents:　David & Esther Lester

LESTER, JOSEPH E　　　　　　　　WMA　　Page 47　　　F
　　15 November 1859　　　　　　Parents:　William & Ann E. Lester

LESTER, MARY J　　　　　　　　　WFA　　Page 47　　　F
　　16 February 1859　　　　　　Parents:　Jesee & Emeline Lester

LETHCO, JNO. H　　　　　　　　　WM_　　Page 58
　　1870　　　　　　　　　　　　Parents:　Henry & Ellen Lethco

LEWIS　　　　　　　　　　　　　　SMA　　Page 1
　　12 December 1853　　　　　　Master:　Moses Cawood

LEWIS　　　　　　　　　　　　　　SMA　　Page 23
　　30 December 1855　　　　　　Owner:　Jno. F. Preston

LEWIS　　　　　　　　　　　　　　SMA　　Page 36
　　12 January 1857　　　　　　Owner:　Wm. Clark

LEWIS　　　　　　　　　　　　　　SMA　　Page 41
　　15 October 1858　　　　　　Owner:　John Preston

LEWIS, [n.n.]　　　　　　　　　WFA　　Page 33　　　F
　　15 March 1857　　　　　　　Parents:　Isaac & Francis Lewis

LEWIS, ANDREW
    20 August 1858
WMA   Page 40   F
Parents: Jno. & Eliza Lewis

LEWIS, ENOCH E
    28 December 1892
WMA   Page 62   F
Parents: J.C. & Eunice E. Lewis

LEWIS, LAURETTA
    26 April 1892
WFA   Page 62   F
Parents: S.E. & Martha Lewis

LEWIS, LOUISA F
    31 August 1858
WFA   Page 40   F
Parents: Wm. & Mary C. Lewis

LEWIS, MALVINA
    29 November 1855
WFA   Page 21   F
Parents: James & M. Lewis

LEWIS, MARTHA
    1870
WF_   Page 58
Parents: Jno. & Eliza Lewis

LEWIS, ROSANAH C
    2 September 1856
WFA   Page 24   F
Parents: Isaac & Mary Lewis

LEWIS, SUSAN E
    2 June 1856
WFA   Page 24   F
Parents: Jno. & Eliza Lewis

LEWIS, VIRGINIA E
    17 July 1859
WFA   Page 47   F
Parents: Philip & Margaret

LEWIS, W.J.
    15 October 1858
SMA   Page 43
Owner: J.F. Glenn

LEWIS, WILEY WINTON
    19 June 1853
WMA   Page 2   L
Father: James Lewis

LIGGIN, DAVID
    17 June 1892
CMA   Page 73   L   Near Abingdon
Parents: Robert & Lucinda Liggin

LILBORNE
    September 1853
SMD   Page 8
Owner: Susannah Baker

LILLY, CALLIE V
    25 October 1892
WFA   Page 52   F
Parents: Jefferson & [Theresa] Lilly

LILLY, JAS. WESLEY
    15 April 1853
WMA   Page 4   F
Father: Henderson W. Lilly

LILLY, JEFFERSON
    26 September 1858
WMA   Page 40   F
Parents: Henry & M.O. Lilly

LILLY, JNO. M
    5 November 1857
WMA   Page 36   F
Parents: John & Mary Lilly

LILLY, LAKE P
    14 October 1892
WFA   Page 69   F   North Fork Dist.
Parents: John H. & Mollie Lilly

LILLY, MARGRET J
    22 July 1857
WFA   Page 33   F
Parents: Wm. & Mary C. Lilly

LINDER, [n.n.]
    5 September 1859
WMA   Page 50   F
Parents: J.D. & Elizabeth Linder

LINDER, CHARLES
    30 September 1870
WM_   Page 58
Parents: Jeriel D. & Isabella Linder

LINDER, CHARLES H   WMA   Page 47   F
    10 January 1859   Parents: Abram & Elizabeth Linder

LINDER, HARMAN J   WMA   Page 33   F
    6 May 1857   Parents: E.G. & Mary Linder

LINDER, MARTHA W   WFA   Page 22   F
    22 December 1855   Parents: Jerial D. & Isabella Linder
    Reported by E.S. Linder, uncle

LINDER, MARY V   WFA   Page 7   F
    22 September 1853   Parents: Jerial D. & Isabella Linder

LINDER, THOS. MILTON   WMA   Page 13   F   North Fork
    16 May 1854   Parents: Abram & Elizabeth Linder

LINDSAY, HARRY   CMA   Page 73   Near Abingdon
    16 December 1892   Mother: Betty Lindsay

LITERAL, [n.n.]   WFA   Page 20   MW
    22 January 1855   Parents: Wm. A. & Mary Literal

LITERAL, WM. RICHARD   WMA   Page 12   F
    15 October 1854   Parents: Jno. M. & Catharine Literal

LITTLE   SMA   Page 51.
    20 February 1859   Parents: Wm. A. Preston

LITTLE, JAS. HENRY   WMA   Page 13   F   Poor Valley
    1 September 1854   Parents: John & Mary Little

LITTLE, TABITHA   WFA   Page 2   L
    24 September 1853   Father: Alexander Little

LITTON, CLOYD H   WMA   Page 62   F
    3 February 1892   Parents: W.B. & M.V. Litton

LITTON, EDDIE   WMA   Page 67   F   Kinderhook
    August 1892   Parents: J.B. & Lizzie Litton

LITTON, SALLIE M   WFA   Page 62   F
    15 April 1892   Parents: L.R. & Emma Litton

LIVINGSTON, N.L.   WMA   Page 8   T
    4 July 1853   Parents: N.L. & Sarah C. Livingston

LIZZIE   SFA   Page 34
    30 July 1857   Owner: D.C. Dunn

LLOYD, BERTHA L   WFA   Page 62   BK
    19 October 1892   Parents: Wm. P. & Frances LOYD

LLOYD, [NATHANIEL]   WMA   Page 36   F
    12 January 1857   Father: Sam'l M. Lloyd
                       Mother: Marthy LOYD

LOCK, CORNELIA E   WFA   Page 14   M
    14 May 1854   Parents: Wm. J. & Caroline Lock
    Reported by A.F. Bradley, neighbor

LOCKE, WILLIAM   WMA   Page 24   M
    [5] October 1856   Father: Wm. J. Locke
                       Mother: Caroline LOCK

LOCKHART, FANNIE A   CFA   Page 62   F
     23 June 1892   Parents: Walter & Easter Lockhart

LOCKHART, ROSCOE C   CMA   Page 62   F
     23 June 1892   Parents: T.A. & Ollie Lockhart

LOGAN, [n.n.]   WFA   Page 43   F
     21 September 1858   Parents: Joseph & M.C. Logan

LOGAN, CALEB J   WMA   Page 43   F
     5 February 1858   Parents: C.J. & B.J. Logan

LOGAN, ELLEN JANE   WFA   Page 1   F
     29 May 1853   Parents: Joseph & Margaret Logan

LOGAN, JOHN   CMA   Page 73   L   Near Abingdon
     12 October 1892   Parents: John & Jennie Logan

LOGAN, JOSEPHINE   WFA   Page 10   F
     27 April 1854   Parents: Caleb J. & Barbara J. Logan

LOGAN, L.T. SMITH   WMA   Page 30   F
     18 or 28 March 1856   Parents: L.T. & Eliza Logan

LOGAN, MARGRET A   WFA   Page 31   F
     20 or 30 July 1856   Parents: Caleb J. & Barbary J. Logan

LOGAN, SARAH L   WFA   Page 16   F
     24 July 1855   Parents: Joseph & Margaret Logan

LOGGANS, MARY L   WFA   Page 19   L
     1 January 1855   Parents: Levi & [Orissa] Loggans

LOGGINS, RACHEL M   WFA   Page 36   F
     2 April 1857   Parents: Levi & Orfa Loggins

LONG, CHARLES   WMA   Page 71   F   Goodson
     25 August 1892   Parents: John W. & Elizabeth Long

LONG, EDGAR   WMA   Page 59   F
     18 June 1892   Parents: J.F. & Nannie Long

LONG, JAMES ELLIS (twin)   CMA   Page 56   F   Glade Spring Twp.
     1870   Parents: John & Charity Long

LONG, WM. MITCHELL (twin)   CMA   Page 56   F   Glade Spring Twp.
     1870   Parents: John & Charity Long

LONGLEY, MARY L   WFA   Page 62   M
     31 January 1892   Parents: E. & Mary L. Longley

LOUISA   SFA   Page 50
     7 March 1859   Owner: Catharine Hanby

LOUREY, DAVID P   WMA   Page 8   F
     16 December 1863   Parents: Jas. K. & Eliza Lourey

LOVE, [n.n.]   WFD   Page 62   F
     20 August 1892   Parents: James R. & Laura G. Love

LOVE, ALICE L   WFA   Page 62   MC
     24 July 1892   Parents: T.W. & Lou C. Love

LOVE, ELIAS J
10 December 1870
WM_ Page 58 MC
Parents: Thos. & Margaret Love

LOVE, JAS. R
8 November 1858
WMA Page 43 F
Parents: Andrew K. & Susan Love

LOVE, JOHN
25 March 1856
WMA Page 29 F
Parents: Jas. C. & Celia Love

LOVE, LEONIDAS (twin)
14 July 1853
WMA Page 4 SH
Father: Oscar Love

LOVE, MARTHA ORLENA
20 March 1855
WFA Page 20 F
Parents: Andrew K. & Susan Love

LOVE, PERLINA
4 July 1854
WFA Page 9 F
Parents: James C. & Sedelia Love

LOVE, SUSAN C
1 December 1856
WFA Page 36 F
Parents: Jas. C. & S. Love

LOVE, SUSANNAH T (twin)
14 July 1853
WFA Page 4 SH
Father: Oscar Love

LOVERN, ELBERT
17 March 1892
WMA Page 62 F
Parents: J.J. & Sarah P. Lovern

LOVERN, JNO. J
31 July 1854
WMA Page 9 F
Parents: Pyrant & Catharine Lovern

LOW, EDWIN L
10 May 1855
WMA Page 21
Mother: Ellen Low

LOWREY, [n.n.]
25 February 1855
WFA Page 21 F
Parents: James K. & Eliza Lowrey

LOWREY, JOHN F
14 October 1854
WMA Page 15 F
Parents: John & Rosanna Lowrey

LOWRY, HARRIET R
16 January 1858
WFA Page 40 F
Parents: Jas. K. & Eliza Lowry

LOYD, [n.n.]
8 February 1853
WMD Page 5 C
Parents: Wm. H. & Elizabeth Loyd

LOYD, [n.n.]
11 January 1859
WMA Page 50 F
Parents: James A. & Martha A. Loyd

LOYD, CYRILDA C
19 October 1857
WFA Page 33 F
Parents: Jas. & Martha Loyd

LOYD, NANCY
15 June 1853
WFA Page 8 F
Father: Wm. C. Loyd

LOYD, NANCY CAROLINE
17 July 1854
WFA Page 11 F
Parents: Samuel & Martha Jane Loyd

LOYD, THOMAS E
20 August 1854
WMA Page 11 C
Parents: William H. & Elizabeth Loyc

LOYD, WALTER P
12 December 1856
WMA Page 30 F
Parents: Saml. & Martha J. Loyd

LUCY
9 February 1853
SFA Page 2
Owner: Jacob Tool

LUKIN, SARAH F
    5 January 1857
WFA   Page 33   F
Parents: F.C. & Elizabeth Lukin

LUNSFORD, THOS. N
    September 1892
WMA   Page 71   F   Goodson
Parents: W.A. & Gilla Lunsford

LYDIA
    26 June 1859
SFA   Page 47
Master: Robt E. Grant

LYNCH, ELLEN H
    24 August 1858
WFA   Page 40   L
Parents: [Con.] H. & [A] J. Lynch

LYEN, JULIA A
    24 April 1855
WFA   Page 21   F
Parents: James & Sarah Lyen

LYON, HENRY
    10 July 1892
WMA   Page 62   PT
Parents: Jno. W. & Heng. Lyon

LYON, SARAH E
    11 August 1857
WFA   Page 33   F
Parents: Jas. S. & Sarah Lyon

LYTZ, J.M.
    6 June 1892
WMA   Page 67   F   Kinderhook
Parents: E.W. & Annie Lytz

McALLISTER, AD. S
    25 April 1892
WMA   Page 52   F
Parents: J.B. & J. McAllister

McCALL, [n.n.]
    3 May 1857
WMD   Page 37   F
Parents: Jno. & R.J. McCall

McCALL, ANDREW
    30 September 1858
WMA   Page 43   F
Parents: James & M. McCall

McCALL, ARTHER
    1870
WMA   Page 56   F   Glade Spring Twp.
Parents: James & Malettia McCall

McCALL, BETTY J
    23 March 1871
WFA   Page 54   F   Northfork Twp.
Parents: John & Margaret McCall

McCALL, EDWIN R
    28 September 1892
WMA   Page 71   M   Goodson
Parents: J.H & S.A. McCall

McCALL, ELIZA
    8 September 1856
WFA   Page 28   F
Parents: James & Charlotte McCall

McCALL, HUGH J.T.
    1870
WMA   Page 56   F   Glade Spring Twp.
Parents: John M. & Margaret McCall

McCALL, JOHN E
    20 December 1859
WMA   Page 47   F
Parents: John & Rebecca McCall

McCALL, NANCY JANE
    17 April 1855
WFA   Page 18   F
Parents: James & Jane McCall

McCALL, NANCY MATILDA
    5 June 1854
WFA   Page 10   F
Parents: John & Rebecca J. McCall

McCALL, WM. J
    16 March 1859
WMA   Page 47   F
Parents: Robt. & Elizabeth McCall

McCANLEY, AMANDA R
    18 April 1856
WFA   Page 29   F
Parents: Frs. J. & M.N. McCanley

McCANLEY, MARY R
    16 June 1854
WFA   Page 15   F
Parents: L.M. & Mary McCanley

McCANN, [n.n.]   WMD   Page 27   F
    28 September 1856   Parents: James & Lydia McCann

McCANN, JOHN   WMA   Page 37   F
    1857   Parents: James & Mary McCann

McCANN, JOHN FLOYD   WMA   Page 56   F   Glade Spring 1
    1870   Parents: Isaac & Margaret McCann

McCANN, MARIAH   WFA   Page 11   MW
    14 July 1854   Parents: James & Lydia McCann

McCARM, [n.n.]   WFA   Page 47   F
    2 January 1859   Parents: James & Lydia McCarm

McCHESNEY, [n.n.]   WMA   Page 21   F
    6 August 1855   Parents: G.C. & Elizabeth C. McChesney
    Reported by A.C. Maxwell, physician

McCHESNEY, ELLEN R   WFA   Page 40   F
    11 February 1858   Parents: T.W. & E.C. McChesney

McCHESNEY, GRAY   WMA   Page 71   F
    11 October 1892   Parents: T.G. & L.J. McChesney

McCHESNEY, JAS. O.K.   WMA   Page 33   F
    12 May 1857   Parents: G.C. & E.M. McChesney

McCHESNEY, L.M.   WMA   Page 25   F
    25 January 1853   Parents: G.C. & E. McChesney

McCHESNEY, MINERVA   WFA   Page 51   F
    18 August 1859   Parents: G.C. & E.M. McChesney

McCHESNEY, SAML. W   WMA   Page 26   F
    22 October 1856   Parents: Thos. W. & E.C. McChesney
    Reported by F. Arent, grandfather

McCLANNAHAN, BERTHA   CFA   Page 63   L
    17 March 1892   Parents: Allen & Jane McClannahan

McCLANNAHAN, H.L.   CFA   Page 63   L
    6 December 1892   Parents: Geo. & El. McClannahan

McCLELLAN, JACOB   WMA   Page 1   F
    19 December 1853   Parents: Robert & Dolly McClellan

McCLELLAND, JOANAH   WFA   Page 10   F
    19 October 1854   Parents: Robert & Dolly McClelland

McCLELLAND, JULIA M   WFA   Page 43
    25 January 1858   Parents: Jas. & Ann E. McClelland

McCLELLAND, LICENIUS   WMA   Page 43   F
    30 September 1858   Parents: Robt. & Dolley McClelland

McCLELLAND, [S.] W.   WMA   Page 31   F
    25 or 27 March 1856   Parents: Saml. & Mary McClelland

McCLELLAND, SAMUEL W   WMA   Page 11   F
    31 March 1854   Parents: Saml. W. & Mary McClelland

McCLELLAND, ZACHARY   WMA   Page 31   F
    17 December 1856   Parents: Jas. & Ann E. McClelland

McCLELLEN, NETTIE   WFA   Page 71   F   Goodson
     5 September 1892   Parents: J.C. & Nannie McClellen

McCLOUD, DAVID O   WMA   Page 24   F
     June 1856   Parents: James & Eliza McCloud

McCONNELL, JOHN T   WMA   Page 71   M   Goodson
     July 1892   Parents: W.T. & R.A. McConnell

McCONNELL, LAURA B   WFA   Page 40   M
     2 May 1858   Parents: T.G. & Bettie R. McConnell

McCONNELL, S.J.R.   WFA   Page 51   F
     9 March 1859   Parents: A.A. & Mary A. McConnell

McCONNELL, WM. F   WMA   Page 26   F
     21 October 1856   Parents: A.A. & Mary A. McConnell
     Reported by Mrs. Hope, grandmother

McCORMACK, [n.n.]   WMA   Page 17
     7 October 1855   Mother: Ellen McCormack
     Reported by Washington McCormack, 'uncle to child'

McCORMACK, ED. H   WMA   Page 37   F
     27 October 1857   Father: P.H. McCORMICK
         Mother: Mary McCormack

McCORMACK, EMMA   WFA   Page 54   PA   Northfork Twp.
     2 August 1871   Parents: Fairmain H. & Nancy McCormack

McCORMACK, JAS. MADISON   WMA   Page 1   F
     20 March 1853   Parents: Micajah & [Malita] McCormack

McCORMACK, LULIA   WFA   Page 53   F   Abingdon Twp.
     12 May 1871   Parents: Richard & Mary McCormack

McCORMACK, SARAH CATHERINE   WFA   Page 20   PT
     29 September 1855   Parents: Fairman H. & Nancy M. McCormack

McCORMACK, WM. CLAYTON   WMA   Page 10   B
     8 October 1854   Parents: Pleasant & Mary McCormack

McCOY, MARTHA JOSEPHINE   WFA   Page 9   F   Near Saltville
     6 June 1854   Parents: Allen P. & Martha McCoy

McCRACKEN, [n.n.]   W A   Page 54   L   Northfork Twp.
     March 1871   Mother: Margaret McCracken

McCRACKEN, AMELIA   WFA   Page 71   F   Goodson
     25 March 1892   Parents: James & Delia McCracken

McCRACKEN, ANDW.   WMA   Page 5   F
     November 1853   Father: Robt. M. McCracken

McCRACKEN, JAS. D   WMA   Page 51   F
     16 July 1859   Parents: Jas. & Huldah McCracken

McCRACKEN, JNO. F   WMA   Page 28   F
     25 May 1856   Parents: Wm. & Mary McCracken

McCRACKEN, JNO. H   WMA   Page 28   F
     5 July 1856   Parents: Madison & Emily P. McCracken

McCRACKEN, SAML. D   WMA   Page 63   F
        15 April 1892   Parents: W.A. & Flor. McCracken

McCRACKEN, SARAH E   WFA   Page 23   F
        1 November 1855   Parents: David & Elizabeth McCracken

McCRACKEN, THOS.   WMA   Page 50   F
        2 October 1859   Parents: David & Elizabeth McCracken

McCREA, ELLEN D   WFA   Page 53   F
        8 May 1871   Parents: J.H. & Sheldenia McCrea
        Born in Richmond, Va.; parents' residence in Abingdon Twp.

McCREADY, ELIZABETH M   WFA   Page 1   F
        2 October 1853   Parents: John J. & Margaret McCready

McCROSKEY, WM. H   WMA   Page 21   F
        10 August 1855   Parents: Jno. R. & M. McCroskey

McCROSKY, J.L.   WMA   Page 67   F   Kinderhook
        12 August 1892   Parents: Jas. & Annie McCrosky

McCROSKY, JAMES M   WMA   Page 33   F
        11 August 1857   Father: Jn. B. McCrosky
                                  Mother: M. McCROSKEY

McCROSKY, LILLIE   WFA   Page 67   F   Kinderhook
        10 June 1892   Parents: Robert & Mary McCrosky

McCULLOCK, JAS. K   WMA   Page 71   F   Goodson
        29 May 1892   Parents: Robert & Amanda McCullock

McCULLOCK, LEWIS   WMA   Page 55   TC   Saltville Twp
        3 July 1870   Parents: James & Rebeca McCullock

McCULLOCK, MAY   WFA   Page 71   F   Goodson
        2 April 1892   Parents: John & Irene McCullock

McDANIEL, [n.n.]   WFA   Page 21   F
        2 May 1855   Parents: Jos. A. & S.J. McDaniel
        Reported by A.C. Maxwell, physician

McDANIEL, ASA   WMA   Page 36   F
        4 May 1857   Parents: Job. H. & E. McDaniel

McDANIEL, ELIZA C   WFA   Page 33   F
        16 September 1857   Parents: Asa & M.E. McDaniel

McDANIEL, GEO. B   WMA   Page 26   F
        20 November 1856   Parents: Alfred & Sara McDaniel
        Reported by Geo. McDaniel, grandfather

McDANIEL, JAS. C   WMA   Page 7   F
        1 December 1853   Father: Asa McDaniel

McDANIEL, JOHN A   WMA   Page 51   F
        17 April 1859   Parents: Asa & Margaret McDaniel

McDANIEL, LAURA ALICE   WFA   Page 18   F
        24 July 1855   Parents: John & Livia McDaniel

McDANIEL, MARGARET S   WFA   Page 23   F
    15 September 1855   Parents: Asa & M. McDaniel

McDANIEL, NANCY MARGARET   WFA   Page 12   F
    10 June 1854   Parents: James & Catharine McDaniel

McDANIEL, REBECCA   WFA   Page 33   F
    1 August 1857   Parents: John & [Larica] McDaniel

McDANIEL, S.D.   WFA   Page 50   F
    2 January 1859   Parents: Alfred & Susan J. McDaniel

McDANIEL, S.J.P.   WFA   Page 37   F
    14 May 1857   Parents: Jas. & Cath. McDaniel

McDANIEL, SARAH VIRGINIA   WFA   Page 3   F
    4 July 1853   Father: John McDaniel

McFADDIN, BARNETT   WMA   Page 63   F
    6 December 1892   Parents: John & Millie McFaddin
    Born in Russell Co., Va.

McGEE, CORAL E   WFA   Page 62   MC
    25 October 1892   Parents: J.L. & Florence McGee

McGHEE, JNO. A   WMA   Page 29   F
    13 August 1856   Parents: Wm. & Susanah McGEE

McGINNIS, THOMPSON   WMA   Page 56   F   Glade Spring Twp.
    1870   Parents: Lewis & Fannie McGinnis

McGLOCKLIN, CATHARINE   WFA   Page 16   L
    22 January 1855   Parents: Henry & Nancy McGlocklin
    Reported by Isabella Clark, neighbor

McGORICK, LITHIE   WFA   Page 53   F   Abingdon Twp.
    15 May 1871   Parents: Thomas & Cornelia McGorick

McGUIRE, GILBERT C   WM_   Page 58
    12 August 1870   Parents: Robt. W. & Elizabeth E. McGuire

McGUIRE, MARY C   WF_   Page 58
    20 August 1870   Parents: Wm. & Alice A. McGuire

McKEE, ANDW. BUCHANAN   WMA   Page 4   F
    26 February 1853   Parents: Andw. J. & Mary Jane McKee

McKEE, LOUISA   WFA   Page 47   F
    10 May 1859   Parents: Andrew & Mary McKee

McKEE, M.F.C.   WFA   Page 43   F
    4 March 1858   Parents: W.T.H. & Jane McKee

McKEE, MARTHA I.A.E.F.   WFA   Page 36   F
    7 September 1857   Parents: Jno. R. & E.A. McKee

McKEE, RACHEL NANCY MARY JANE REBECCA FAYETTA WFA   Page 19   F
    5 May 1855   Parents: John R. & Elizabeth Ann McKee

McKEE, THOS. JEFFERSON   WMA   Page 4   F
    5 January 1853   Parents: Jno. R. & Ann McKee

McKEE, W.R.S.B.   WMFA   Page 36   F
    1 March 1857   Parents: And. J. & Mary J. McKee

McKINZIE, B.K.   WMA   Page 67   F   Kinderhook
    10 July 1892   Parents: J.R. & P.V. McKinzie

McNEAL, E   WMA   Page 37   F
    12 November 1857   Parents: Austin & A. McNeal

McNEEL, ALEMISE   WFA   Page 47   F
    15 September 1859   Parents: Austin & Emily McNeel
    Reported by Austin McNEW, father

McNEW, [n.n.]   WMA   Page 17
    26 November 1855   Mother: Emily McNew

McNEW, [n.n. twins]   W D   Page 55   F   Saltville Twp.
    18 July 1870   Parents: Elisha & Dorcas McNew

McNEW, ADELINE VIRGINIA   WFA   Page 20   F
    5 June 1855   Parents: Julius C. & Sophia McNew

McNEW, ALICE   WFA   Page 47   F
    18 February 1859   Parents: Julias T. & Sophia McNew

McNEW, ALSA   WFA   Page 47   F
    8 March 1859   Parents: Samuel & Huldah McNew

McNEW, BERRY   WMA   Page 1   F
    6 October 1853   Parents: John & Martha McNew

McNEW, CALAFORNIA   WFA   Page 31   F
    15 November 1856   Parents: Julius & Sophia McNew

McNEW, CHARLIS   WMA   Page 47   F
    22 April 1859   Parents: John T. & Mary McNew

McNEW, ELIZ.   WFA   Page 63   F
    23 November 1892   Parents: D.S. & Alcey McNew

McNEW, GEORGE EAKIN   WMFAD Page 1   F   Near E&H Colle
    21 December 1853   Parents: Alexander E. & Nancy McNew

McNEW, GEO. W.H.   WMA   Page 43   F
    10 August 1858   Parents: Elisha & Dorcas McNew

McNEW, JOHN   WMA   Page 47
    27 March 1859   Mother: Emily McNew

McNEW, VERLIN MORGAN   WMA   Page 1   L
    1 May 1853   Parents: Elbert S. & Elizabeth McNew

McQUOWN, JOHN M   WMA   Page 4   F
    29 December 1853   Parents: Isaac A. & Nancy McQuown

McQUOWN, ROBT. F   WMA   Page 43   F
    13 October 1858   Parents: J.A. & N.K. McQuown

McQUOWN, WM. PARKER   WMA   Page 18   F
    12 March 1855   Parents: Isaac A. & Nancy McQuown

McREYNOLDS, C.M.   WFA   Page 37   F
    2 April 1857   Parents: Steven & Nancy McReynolds

McREYNOLDS, JAMES A   WMA   Page 47   F
    8 May 1859   Parents: Stephen P. & Nancy McReynolds

McTHENIA, LUCY A   WFA   Page 63   MC
    10 April 1892   Parents: C.W. & Nancy McThenia

McVEY, [n.n.]   WMA   Page 1   L
    October 1853   Parents: Anderson & Lydia McVey
    Reported by James K. Smyth

McVEY, MARY ANN   WFA   Page 3   F
    2 November 1853   Parents: Gideon & Ann McVey

McVEY, MARY C   WFA   Page 62   L
    28 September 1892   Parents: L.A. & Josephine McVey

McVEY, NANCY JANE   WFA   Page 17   F
    23 September 1855   Parents: Gideon & Jane McVey

McVEY, ROSE   WFA   Page 62   L
    14 May 1892   Parents: John & Julia McVey

McVEY, SERRA C   WFA   Page 47
    22 February 1859   Mother: Jane McVey

McVEY, WILLIAM   WMA   Page 5
    May 1853   Mother: Betsy McVey

MADISON, [n.n.]   CMA   Page 73   MC   Near Abingdon
    28 October 1892   Parents: D.P. & Minter Madison

MAHAFFEY, PAUL   WMA   Page 70   F   Abingdon Dist.
    June 1892   Parents: E.C. & Sarah MEHAFFEY

MAHALA   SFA   Page 43
    15 May 1858   Owner: W.W. Stickley

MAIDEN, ANN W   WFA   Page 47   F
    7 November 1859   Parents: John & Sharley Maiden

MAIDEN, ELIZABETH S   WFA   Page 43   F
    4 [April] 1858   Parents: Samuel & Nancy Maiden

MAIDEN, FRANCIS E   WMA   Page 37   F
    25 November 1857   Parents: Danl. W. & Rebecca E. Maiden

MAIDEN, FRANK   WMA   Page 55   C   Saltville Twp.
    10 October 1870   Parents: John C. & Bettie Maiden

MAIDEN, JAMES T   WMA   Page 47   F
    1 December 1859   Parents: Daniel W. & Elizabeth Maiden

MAIDEN, JOHN   WMA   Page 2   F
    21 January 1853   Parents: Henry A. & Elizabeth Maiden

MAIDEN, MARGARET R.S.   WFA   Page 54   F   Northfork Twp.
    10 April 1871   Parents: George H. & Elizabeth Maiden

MAIDEN, MARY ALICE   WFA   Page 3   F
    1 April 1853   Father: Samuel S. Maiden

MAIDEN, MARY B. (twin)   WFA   Page 47   F
    12 February 1859   Parents: Wm. S. & Rebecca Maiden

MAIDEN, MARY ELIZABETH
    10 November 1855
WFA   Page 17   F
Parents: Daniel W. & Rebecca Maiden

MAIDEN, MILTON W
    4 December 1854
WMA   Page 10   F
Parents: William S. & Rebecca Maiden

MAIDEN, ROBERT KING
    17 December 1855
WMA   Page 16   F
Parents: Sam'l L. & Nancy Maiden

MAIDEN, SARAH A. (twin)
    12 February 1859
WFA   Page 47   F
Parents: Wm. S. & Rebecca Maiden

MAIDEN, SUSAN JANE
    26 December 1853
WFA   Page 3   F
Parents: Daniel W. & Rebecca Maiden

MALICOTE, [n.n.]
    28 September 1853
WFA   Page 2   T
Parents: Augustine K. & Elizabeth Mal

MALLICOTE, [n.n.]
    March 1855
WFD   Page 17   T
Parents: Augustine R. & Elizabeth Mal

MALLICOTE, ELIZ. C
    27 June 1892
WFA   Page 63   F
Parents: A.R. & Amanda Mallicote

MALONE, HARIET J
    16 September 1857
WFA   Page 33   F
Parents: Dulany & E. Malone

MANN, JOSEPH H
    13 June 1854
WMA   Page 13   F   Poor Valley
Parents: Henry A. & Susan Mann

MANTZ, [n.n.]
    January 1853
WMD   Page 3   SH
Father: Geo. W. Mantz

MANTZ, SARAH VIRGINIA
    5 January 1855
WFA   Page 16   SH   Cedarville
Parents: Geo. W. & Mary S. Mantz

MARGARET
    16 April 1853
SFA   Page 2
Mother: Minerva
Master: Jno. N. Humes

MARGARET
    1 August 1853
SFA   Page 8
Owner: Jno. F. Preston

MARGARET
    7 March 1854
SFA   Page 12
Mother: Caty
Owner: David Rambo

MARGARET
    August 1854
SFA   Page 12
Mother: Mary
    Reported by Jas. W. Davis, [hirer]; Sam'l M. Snodgrass, owner

MARGARET P
    1 January 1858
SFA   Page 43
Owner: W. Clark

MARIA
    20 October 1857
SFA   Page 34
Owner: Gasper Fleenor

MARIAH
    5 October 1853
SFA   Page 3
Mother: Sarah
Owner: Philip Kesner

MARIAH
    18 May 1855

SFA   Page 16
Mother: Eve
Owner: Absalom Beatie

MARSH, ALICE A
    15 June 1857

WFA   Page 33   F
Parents: Warren C. & Mary Marsh

MARSH, JANE
    15 December 1855

WFA   Page 22   F
Parents: Warner C. & Dicey Marsh

MARSH, MARTHA A
    September 1853

WFA   Page 7   F
Father: Warren C. Marsh

MARSH, WASH. A
    28 November 1858

WMA   Page 40   F
Parents: W.C. & Dicy R. Marsh

MARSHAL, MIRTLE
    9 August 1892

WFA   Page 71   F   Goodson
Parents: John & Allie Marshal

MARTAIN, [n.n.]
    11 July 1859

CFA   Page 51   BA
Parents: Christ. & Mariah MARTIN

MARTHA
    15 June 1855

SFA   Page 23
Owner: Jno. S. Parrott

MARTHA
    4 July 1858

SFA   Page 43
Owner: John Byars

MARTHA
    1 October 1858

SFA   Page 41
Owner: Henry Roberts

MARTIN, J.T.
    20 September 1892

WMA   Page 67   F   Kinderhook
Parents: J.F. & Martha Martin

MARTIN, ROBT. MILTON
    23 May 1853

WMA   Page 23   ML
Father: Archibald Martin

MARY
    7 December 1853

SFA   Page 3
Mother: Martha
Owner: Thos. M. Preston

MARY
    28 December 1853

SFA   Page 8
Owner: Samuel W. Montgomery

MARY
    6 February 1854

SFA   Page 9
Mother: Mary
Owner: Robert Clark

MARY
    31 May 1854

SFA   Page 11
Mother: Mary
Owner: John Maiden

MARY
    15 November 1854
Ben. K. Buchanan, overseer; Wyndham Robertson, owner

SFA   Page 9
Mother: Evelina

MARY
    15 September 1855

SFA   Page 20
Mother: Mariah
Owner: Whitly Fullen

MARY
    25 October 1856

SFA   Page 27
Owner: John Preston

MARY
    22 February 1857

SFA   Page 37
Owner: David Clark

MARY
    20 May 1857

SFA   Page 36
Owner: Henry Mock

MARY
    12 December 1857

SFA   Page 37
Owner: A.R. Malicote

MARY
    20 May 1859

SFA   Page 47
Reported by Ann Campbell, 'witness'

MARY A
    26 December 1854

SFA   Page 13
Mother: Ann
Master: Martin Hagy

MARY E
    27 February 1855

SFA   Page 23
Owner: Mary Gray

MARY JANE
    3 February 1853

SFA   Page 8
Owner: Jno. H. Wallace

MASON, IRVING
    15 December 1892

WMA   Page 63   F
Parents: J.T. & Sarah Mason

MASON, JOSEPHINE
    25 December 1892

WFA   Page 62   M
Parents: Jas. P. & Anna B. Mason

MASSEY, HENRIETTA
    9 March 1853

WFA   Page 6   F
Parents: Wm. & Pauline Massey

MASSEY, WM. JAS
    28 August 1854

WMA   Page 14   F
Parents: Wm. & Pauline Massey

MASSIE, ALICE J
    15 September 1856

WFA   Page 24
Parents: Wm. & Paulina Massie

MASSIE, EDWIN C.F.
    7 July 1856

WMA   Page 24
Parents: Granville & Ann Massie

MASSY, [n.n.]
    4 January 1857

WFA   Page 33
Father: Geo. W. Massy
Mother: Mary C. MASSEY

MASSY, ALICE J
    30 October 1857
    Reported by Wm. MASSEY, father

WFA   Page 33
Parents: Wm. & Paulina Massy

MASSY, JNO. F
    27 June 1858

WMA   Page 40
Parents: W. & Paulina Massy

MATHEWS, [n.n.]
    24 February 1892

CMD   Page 63   L
Parents: Saml. & Rach. Mathews

MAXWELL, FRANK A
    7 November 1855

WMA   Page 20   PH
Parents: Alex'r C. & C.A. Maxwell

MAXWELL, JULIET E
    29 May 1858

WFA   Page 40   PH
Parents: A.C. & C.A. Maxwell

MAXWELL, LORENIA
    15 May 1871

WFA   Page 53   F   Abingdon Twp
Parents: Alex M. & Isabella Maxwell

MAXWELL, THOMAS
    16 September 1853

WMA   Page 6   PH
Parents: A.C. & C.A. Maxwell

MAYS, [n.n.]
    17 February 1859

WMA   Page 51   F
Parents: Flem. & Mary Mays

MAYS, JNO. B
    1 November 1853

WMA   Page 7   F
Father: Fleming Mays

MAZE, JOSEPHINE
    11 March 1892

WFA   Page 71   F   Goodson
Parents: T.J. & Elizabeth Maze

MEADE, IRENE
    28 February 1892

CFA   Page 63   L
Parents: Walter & Maria Meade

MEADLY, SUSAN A
    15 May 1857

WFA   Page 33   F
Father: Wm. H. MEADLEY
Mother: Emily MEDLEY

MEDLEY, ANN E
    15 October 1854

WFA   Page 14   F
Parents: Wm. H. & Emily Medley

MERCHANT, SARAH A
    3 October 1859

CFA   Page 51   MR
Parents: Samuel & Olivia Merchant

MESSERSMITH, JOHN M
    2 August 1871

WMA   Page 53   F   Abingdon Twp.
Parents: William & Ellen A. Messersmith

METCALF, GUY L
    5 July 1892

WMA   Page 71   MR   Goodson
Parents: C.E. & Nannie Metcalf

MIKEL, MAG. A
    9 March 1892

WFA   Page 63   F
Parents: C.M. & Lorena Mikel

MILES, JOHN
    8 August 1892

WMA   Page 67   F   Kinderhook
Parents: William & Alice Miles

MILES, SARAH J
    24 March 1858

WFA   Page 40   F
Parents: Wm. & Cath Miles

MILLARD, A.M.
    22 December 1858

WFA   Page 40   P
Parents: S.H. & M.M. Millard

MILLARD, HUGH D (twin)
    13 August 1856

WMA   Page 26   F
Parents: Alfred J. & Martha Millard

MILLARD, JOHN W
    2 June 1855

WMA   Page 22   F
Parents: Sam'l H. & Maria S. Millard

MILLARD, JONT. F (twin)
    13 August 1856

WMA   Page 26   F
Parents: Alfred J. & Martha Millard

MILLARD, SARAH A
    13 March 1857

WFA   Page 33   F
Parents: Saml. H. & Mariah Millard

MILLER, [n.n.]
    July 1856
    Reported by Jno. Miller, grandfather

WFD   Page 24   F
Parents: Henry & Susan Miller

MILLER, [n.n.]
    11 September 1856

WMD   Page 26   L
Parents: Wm. & R.L. Miller

MILLER, [n.n.]
    27 July 1892

WFA   Page 71   MC   Goodson
Parents: J.F. & Mary C. Miller

MILLER, E.F.
    4 August 1853
WMA   Page 8   W
Father: Wm. S. Miller

MILLER, EDNA W
    21 May 1892
CFA   Page 63   L
Parents: John & Eunice Miller

MILLER, ELIZABETH FRANCES
    9 August 1855
WFA   Page 17   F
Parents: Samuel A. & Elizabeth Mille

MILLER, G.E.
    28 January 1892
WMA   Page 67   F   Kinderhook
Parents: F.E. & R. Bell Miller

MILLER, GEORGE
    23 February 1856
WMA   Page 25   F
Parents: Jessee H. & E. Miller

MILLER, JNO. JAS. CAMPBELL
    22 July 1856
WMA   Page 25   F
Parents: John & Nancy Miller

MILLER, JOHN R
    29 November 1859
WMA   Page 47   F
Parents: James & Mary R. Miller

MILLER, JOHN WESLEY
    19 March 1853
WMA   Page 2   L
Father: Samuel Miller

MILLER, NANCY
    22 July 1858
WFA   Page 43   F
Parents: John & M.S. Miller

MILLER, SADIA
    25 April 1892
WFA   Page 73   MC   Near Abingdc
Parents: Emmet & Mary B. Miller

MILLER, UMBERSON
    13 March 1857
WMA   Page 37   F
Parents: Umberson & Catherine Mille

MILLER, WALTER W
    19 September 1858
WMA   Page 40   L
Parents: William & Rachel L. Miller

MILLER, WM. J
    6 June 1858
WMA   Page 43   F
Parents: Jas. A. & S.C. Miller

MILLER, WILLIAM W
    13 August 1854
WMA   Page 11   F
Parents: James & Mary R. Miller

MILLIANDER, FANNIE
    12 December 1871
WFA   Page 53   F   Abingdon Tw
Parents: James & Sallie Milliander

MILLINOR, HENRY
    10 May 1858
WMA   Page 43   F
Parents: W.P. & Laura Millinor

MILLY
    August 1855
SFA   Page 23
Owner: John Preston

MILNER, JOSEPHINE
    15 March 1855
WFA   Page 17   CL
Parents: Wm. P. & Laura Milner

MILTON
    12 April 1853
SMA   Page 1   Saltville
Mistress: Louisa P. King

MINERVA
    28 May 1855
SFA   Page 16
Mother: Mary
Owner: Amanda C. Hutton

MINK, AND. M.P.F.
    6 June 1856
WMA   Page 29   F
Parents: Wm. & Eliz'th Mink

MINK, ELLEN SOPHRONIA   WFA   Page 3   F
     13 November 1853   Parents: James & Elizabeth Mink

MINK, ROBT. B   WMA   Page 63   F
     22 August 1892   Parents: Jno. G. & Nancy E. Mink

MINK, SUSAN JANE   WFA   Page 4   F
     19 October 1853   Parents: Wm. & Elizabeth Mink

MINICK, ANN E   WFA   Page 33   F
     17 August 1857   Parents: Rica. & Nancy Minick

MINICK, MARTHA M   WFA   Page 33
     11 December 1857   Mother: E. Minick

MINICK, RACHEL A   WFA   Page 40   F
     16 September 1858   Parents: John W. & Sarah E. Minick

MINICK, SARAH J   WFA   Page 22   F
     10 November 1855   Parents: Richard & Nancy B. Minick

MINICK, SUSAN E   WFA   Page 33   F
     1 December 1857   Parents: L.J. & Jane Minick

MINNICK, [n.n.]   WFA   Page 51   F
     11 June 1859   Parents: Henry & Rosannah Minnick

MINNICK, [n.n.]   WMD   Page 63   F
     15 May 1892   Parents: W.F. & Susy Minnick

MINNICK, ANNIE W   WFA   Page 71   F   Goodson
     15 January 1892   Parents: Andrew & Eva Minnick

MINNICK, HARRIET E   WFA   Page 23   F
     20 July 1855   Parents: L.J. & Jane Minnick

MINNICK, J.F.   WMA   Page 7   F
     28 January 1853   Father: Richard Minnick

MINNICK, PETER   WMA   Page 6
     26 October 1853   Mother: Elizabeth Minnick

MINNICK, ROSANNA   WFA   Page 6
     1 January 1853   Mother: Susan Minnick

MINNICK, W.W.   WMA   Page 7   F
     29 August 1853   Parents: Benj'n & Jemima Minnick

MINNICK, WILLIAM   WMA   Page 22
     5 May 1855   Mother: Susan Minnick

MINNICK, WM. C   WMA   Page 7   F
     27 March 1853   Parents: Leander J. & Jane Minnick

MITCHEL, SUSAN   WFA   Page 69   F   North Fork Dist.
     18 March 1892   Parents: Wesley & Mary Mitchel

MITCHELL, [n.n.]   WMD   Page 22   F
     1 January 1855   Parents: John & E. Mitchell

MITCHELL, HARDY   WMA   Page 25   F
     1 December 1856   Father: Hiram Mitchell
                         Mother: Nancy MITCHEL

MITCHELL, JNO. A   WMA   Page 25   F
    1 May 1856   Father: James Mitchell
                                    Mother: M. MITCHEL

MITCHELL, ROBT. G   WMA   Page 63   F
    8 December 1892   Parents: P.H. & Susan C. Mitchell

MITCHELL, SUSAN   WFA   Page 44   F
    4 August 1858   Parents: Col. & Margaret Mitchell

MOCK, ELIZABETH   WFA   Page 71   F   Goodson
    20 July 1892   Parents: William & Mary Mock

MOCK, ELLEN   WFA   Page 25   F
    15 October 1856   Parents: Jno. W. & Mary J. Mock

MOCK, M.C.   WFA   Page 43   F
    20 September 1858   Parents: Peter B. & Lidda Mock

MOCK, MARY   WFA   Page 56   F
    24 March 1857   Parents: D. [J.] & M. Mock

MOCK, MILTON FLOYD   WMA   Page 63   F
    3 March 1855   Parents: Henry & Mary Mock

MOCK, NANCY   WFA   Page 12   F
    31 August 1854   Parents: John W. & Mary J. Mock

MOCK, ROBT.   WMA   Page 47   F
    12 July 1859   Parents: Henry & Mary Mock

MOCK, ROBT. J   WMA   Page 43   F
    12 July 1858   Parents: Henry & Mary Mock

MOCK, SUSANAH   WFA   Page 47   F
    12 July 1859   Parents: Daniel & Margaret Mock

MOCK, VIRGINIA FRANCES   WFA   Page 56   F   Glade Spring
    1870   Parents: Henry & Mary K. Mock

MOFIELD, [n.n.]   WFA   Page 47   F
    15 September 1859   Parents: Benjamin & Louisa Mofield

MOON, ALBERT G   WMA   Page 40   MR
    25 March 1858   Parents: R.L. & Mary E. Moon

MOON, MARY J   WFA   Page 23   F
    4 February 1857   Parents: Wm. F. & Mary E. Moon

MOON, WM. H   WMA   Page 44   F
    20 October 1859   Parents: R.H. & Martha Moon

MONGLE, JAS. L.A.   WMA   Page 41   F
    14 October 1858   Parents: Elijah & Sarah Mongle

MONGLE, MARY C   WFA   Page 23   F
    12 July 1857   Parents: James H. & S.I. Mongle

MONTGOMERY, ANN   WFA   Page 43   F
    1 June 1858   Parents: Hugh & O.V. Montgomery

MONTGOMERY, LILLIE   WFA   Page 59   North Fork D
    20 April 1892   Parents: Wm. & Jennie Montgomery

MONTGOMERY, OLIVER   WMA   Page 70   F   Abingdon Dist.
    September 1892   Parents: W.M. & Mattie Montgomery

MONTGOMERY, R.T.   WMA   Page 50   F
    16 October 1859   Parents: A.J. & M.J. Montgomery

MONTGOMERY, WM. TRA.   WMA   Page 56   F   Glade Spring Twp.
    1870   Parents: John H. & Sarah Montgomery

MOORE, [n.n.]   WMA   Page 70   F   Abingdon Dist.
    20 February 1892   Parents: Milton & Elizabeth Moore

MOORE, A.B.   WMA   Page 51   F
    14 May 1859   Parents: Isaac & S.J. Moore

MOORE, A.S.   WMA   Page 67   F   Kinderhook
    29 April 1892   Parents: J.B. & Amanda Moore

MOORE, ABRAM   WMA   Page 47   F
    20 May 1859   Parents: William & Sarah Moore

MOORE, AND. J   WMA   Page 37   F
    12 July 1857   Parents: Wm. & S.J. Moore

MOORE, BENJAMIN   WMA   Page 67   F   Kinderhook
    10 August 1892   Parents: Charles & Mary Moore

MOORE, CHARLES E   WMA   Page 47   F
    20 November 1859   Parents: Andrew F. & Martha Moore

MOORE, CLARENCE   WMA   Page 67   F   Kinderhook
    5 January 1892   Parents: S.L. & Jane Moore

MOORE, CORDELIA   WFA   Page 53   F   Abingdon Twp.
    6 June 1871   Parents: Joseph & Synthia Moore

MOORE, DAVID R   WMA   Page 62   F
    16 September 1892   Parents: John & Adeline Moore

MOORE, ELIZABETH   WFA   Page 33   F
    8 March 1857   Parents: Isaac & Sarah Moore

MOORE, [HARREY] G   WMA   Page 10   F
    16 March 1854   Parents: William S. & Susan Moore

MOORE, JACOB S   WMA   Page 62   L
    12 March 1892   Parents: Ed. C. & Agnes Moore

MOORE, JOHN   WMA   Page 25   F
    8 August 1856   Parents: Jos. & Ann Moore

MOORE, LUCY J   WFA   Page 67   F   Kinderhook
    28 April 1892   Parents: W.W. & Eugenia Moore

MOORE, MARGARET E   WFA   Page 21   F
    31 March 1855   Parents: Martin & Elizabeth Moore

MOORE, MARIAH E   WFA   Page 26   MC
    13 November 1856   Parents: Jno. E. & Margret L. Moore

MOORE, MARY E   WFA   Page 30   F
    25 or 28 March 1856   Parents: W.A. & Sarah I. Moore

MOORE, MARY JANE   WFA   Page 11   F
     20 July 1854   Parents: Allen & Mary Moore

MOORE, MARY JANE   WFA   Page 10   F
     17 Dec. 1854   Parents: Joseph & Martha J. Moore

MOORE, NANCY   WFA   Page 63   F
     15 June 1892   Parents: Eldridge & Eliz. Moore

MOORE, NANCY J   WFA   Page 6   F
     16 Sept. 1853   Parents: Isaac & Elizabeth Moore

MOORE, NANNIE   WFA   Page 67   F   Kinderhook
     10 July 1892   Parents: John & Lou Moore

MOORE, RICHARD   WMA   Page 21   F
     10 May 1855   Parents: Isaac & Sarah A. Moore

MOORE, ROBT. LEE   WMA   Page 62   F
     14 Aug. 1892   Parents: T.J. & Nannie Moore

MOORE, S.E.   WMA   Page 67   F   Kinderhook
     8 June 1892   Parents: James & Gill Moore

MOORE, SAMUEL   WMA   Page 30   F
     22 June 1857   Parents: Jno. B. & Sarah Moore

MOORE, SARAH ANN   WFA   Page 1   F
     16 May 1853   Father: Joseph Moore

MOORE, STUART V   WMA   Page 62   F
     10 Nov. 1892   Parents: Thomas & Ann Moore

MOORE, SUSAN   WFA   Page 70   F   Abingdon Dis
     22 June 1892   Parents: R.S. & Jennie Moore

MOORE, SUSAN JANE   WFA   Page 18   F
     31 July 1855   Parents: John E. & Marg't L. Moore

MOORE, WM. JAMES   WMA   Page 11   F
     18 June 1854   Parents: Andrew F. & Bethial Moore

MOORE, WILLIAM M   WMA   Page 47   F
     16 Dec. 1859   Parents: Allen & Mary Moore

MOOREFIELD, MARTHA E   WFA   Page 54   F   Northfork Tw
     13 May 1871   Parents: J.M. & Mary A. Moorefield

MOORFIELD, BENJAMIN   WMA   Page 30   F
     6 Dec. 1856   Parents: Jas. & Jane Moorfield

MORGAN, [n.n.]   WMA   Page 9   OV   Near Saltvil
     11 Aug. 1854   Parents: Henry L. & Louisa P. Morgar

MORGAN, [n.n.]   WMA   Page 16   Saltville
     21 Nov. 1855   Parents: Henry L. & Louisa Morgan

MORGAN, ANN R   WFA   Page 24   F
     28 March 1856   Parents: M.R. & Mary E. Morgan

MORGAN, CAROLINE A   WFA   Page 40   F
     24 March 1858   Parents: Alex & Adaline Morgan

MORGAN, DAVID
    5 October 1892
CMA   Page 73   L   Near Abingdon
Parents: Allen & Lucinda Morgan

MORGAN, ELIZA E
    28 November 1857
WFA   Page 33   F
Parents: W.F. & M.E. Morgan

MORGAN, JNO. H
    24 January 1857
WMA   Page 36   F
Parents: Verlin & Cath Morgan

MORGAN, MARY E
    6 September 1855
WFA   Page 16   L   Saltville
Parents: John & Ilsa Morgan

MORISON, [n.n.]
    24 October 1853
WFA   Page 4   L
Father: Jno. Morison

MORISON, MARGRET J
    18 May 1856
WFA   Page 29   F
Parents: Jas. & Sarah Morison

MORISON, MARY L
    December 1854
WFA   Page 9   CL
Parents: William M. & Jennett Morison

MORISON, SARAH JANE
    11 August 1853
WFA   Page 3   F
Father: James Morison

MORRIS, JOHN
    4 September 1858
WMA   Page 43   F
Parents: J. & Cath. Morris

MORRIS, NANNIE B
    1870
WFA   Page 56   F   Glade Spring Twp.
Parents: Marion M. & Elizabeth Morris

MORRIS, WM. P
    18 July 1892
    born in Lee Co., Va.
WMA   Page 62   F
Parents: Alex C. & S.E. Morris

MORRISON, EVA
    5 April 1892
WFA   Page 62   F
Parents: Geo. G. & Eliz. Morrison

MORRISON, LEWIS M
    22 February 1859
WMA   Page 47   F
Parents: John & Merienda Morrison

MORTON, EMMA A
    18 July 1892
WFA   Page 71   F   Goodson
Parents: Steven & Mary Morton

MOSER, JNO. W
    14 January 1856
WMA   Page 29   ML
Parents: Wm. & Dicy Moser

MOTERN, [n.n.]
    14 January 1858
WFA   Page 40   F
Parents: W. & E. Motern

MOTERN, E.C. TESTER
    14 March 1855
WMA   Page 20   F
Parents: Wm. C. & Elizabeth Motern

MOTTERN, J.H.
    7 September 1853
WMA   Page 6   F
Parents: Wm. C. & Betsy Mottern

MOTTERN, MARY E
    6 August 1856
WFA   Page 24   F
Parents: W. [A.] & Elizabeth Mottern

MOUNTAIN, WILLIAM
    12 August 1855
WMA   Page 19   B
Parents: Jesse & Lydia Mountain

MUMPOWER, LAURA J
    3 October 1892
WFA   Page 72   F   Goodson
Parents: Henry & Malisie Mumpower

MUMPOWER, REVANAH   WFA   Page 72   F   Goodson
 December 1892   Parents: W.H. & N.E. Mumpower

MUMPOWER, W.E.   WMA   Page 71   F   Goodson
 11 October 1892   Parents: J.W. & Nancy Mumpower

MUMPOWERS, [n.n.]   WFD   Page 40   F
 13 March 1858   Parents: A. & M. Mumpowers

MURRAY, REBECCA   WFA   Page 13   F
 8 May 1857   Parents: James & Rebecca Murray

MURRY, KATIE   WFA   Page 69   F   North Fork Dis
 18 March 1892   Parents: Aaron & Lulu Murry

MURRY, LUTHUR   WMA   Page 69   F   North Fork Dis
 28 September 1892   Parents: Belvin & Mollie Murry

MURRY, MARY   WFA   Page 14   F
 20 June 1854   Father: James Murry
         Mother: Rebecca MURRAY

MUSIC, ARTHUR C   WMA   Page 73   Near Abingdon
 16 August 1892   Mother: Polly MUSIC

MUSIC, HENRY L.W.   WMA   Page 69   F   North Fork Dis
 30 March 1892   Parents: A.G. & Sarah E. Music

MUSICK, GEORGE F. (twin) WMA   Page 22   F
 11 February 1855   Parents: Eleenor & Mary Musick

MUSICK, HENRY   WMA   Page 22   F
 18 October 1855   Parents: Isaac & Mary Musick

MUSICK, SUSAN (twin)   WFA   Page 22   F
 11 February 1855   Parents: Eleenor & Mary Musick

MUSSELWHITE, HARRIET   WFA   Page 55   B   Saltville Twp.
 25 August 1870   Parents: Morley & Sally Musselwhite

MUSSELWHITE, WM. HENRY   WMA   Page 1   B   Saltville
 25 May 1853   Parents: Morley & Sally Musselwhite

MUSSER, ELIZABETH   WFA   Page 13   B
 27 July 1854   Parents: Adam & Corinna Musser

MUSSER, L.A.   WFA   Page 13   B
 15 November 1856   Parents: Adam & Corinna Musser

MUSSER, SOPHIA   WFA   Page 73   MC   Abingdon
 8 April 1892   Parents: Wm. H. & E.M. Musser

MUSSER, WILLIAM E   WMA   Page 13   F
 5 October 1858   Parents: Adam & Lycena Musser

MYERS, ISABELLA   WFA   Page 14
 27 December 1854   Mother: Martha Myers
 Reported by Christo. Myers, grandfather

MYERS, JOHN   WMA   Page 67   F   Kinderhook
 February 1892   Parents: J.M. & Susan Myers

NAFF, ARTHUR R   WMA   Page 47   F
    20 December 1859   Parents: Jacob & Jane Naff

NAFF, MARGARET H   WFA   Page 15   LW
    22 March 1854   Parents: Geo. E. & M.C. Naff

NAFF, PETER F   WMA   Page 37   F
    5 October 1857   Parents: Jacob & Jane NEFF

NANCY   SFA   Page 6
    24 May 1853   Mother: Jane
    Owner: David Campbell; reported by Ann Campbell, 'wife of owner'

NANCY   SFA   Page 10
    6 June 1854   Parents: Edmund & Ann
                                         Owner: Jacob Morell

NATHAN   SMA   Page 41
    8 October 1858   Owner: John Preston

NEAL, JAS. A.F.   WMA   Page 27   F
    22 December 1856   Father: Jno. H.F. Neal
    Reported by Jno. H.F.   Mother: H E. NEEL
       NEEL, father

NEAL, JAMES G   WMA   Page 56   F   Glade Spring Twp.
    1870   Parents: William G. & Eliza Neal

NEAL, MARGARET E.H.   WFA   Page 18   F
    17 December 1855   Parents: John H.F. & Harriet Neal

NEAL, OLIVER VOSS   WFA   Page 18   F
    17 March 1855   Parents: Daniel & Fanny Neal

NEAL, SARAH ANN   WFA   Page 56   Glade Spring Twp.
    1870   Parents: Isaac B.D. & Liddia Neal

NEAL, SARAH MARGARET   WFA   Page 18   F
    22 April 1855   Parents: William & Levisa Neal

NECESSARY, [n.n.]   WF_   Page 58
    1 November 1870   Parents: Singleton & Sarah Necessary

NECESSARY, J.W.   WMA   Page 67   F   Kinderhook
    12 January 1892   Parents: Georg & Susan Necessary

NECESSARY, W.V.   WMA   Page 67   F   Kinderhook
    15 May 1892   Parents: J.W. & N.C. Necessary

NEEL, HETTY B.V.   WFA   Page 28   F
    28 July 1856   Parents: Wm. & Louisa E. Neel
    Reported by Cath Collings, grandmother

NEEL, ISAAC W   WMA   Page 43   F
    5 October 1859   Parents: Daniel & Ellen Neel

NEEL, JNO. J.D.   WMA   Page 37   F
    26 December 1857   Parents: Jno. L.F. & Harriett E. Neel

NEEL, JNO. R   WMA   Page 28   F
    2 September 1856   Parents: O. & Amanda Neel

NEEL, OBIDIAH   WMA   Page 11   SM
     8 May 1854   Parents: Obidiah & Amanda Neel

NEELEY, ELIZA J   WFA   Page 28   F
     25 April 1856   Parents: Isaac & Mary J. Neeley

NEELY, [n.n.]   WMA   Page 43   F
     24 October 1858   Parents: Isaac & Mary J. Neely

NEELY, W.H.   WMA   Page 24
     5 June 1856   Mother: Malinda Neely

NEFF, LAFAYETTE   WMA   Page 17   F
     4 August 1855   Parents: Jacob & Jennette Neff

NEFF, SUSANNAH R   WFA   Page 53   F   Abingdon Twp
     4 April 1871   Parents: Andrew M. & Sarah M. Neff

NEIL, AMANDA J   WFA   Page 12   F
     13 October 1854   Parents: John H.F. & Harriet Neil

NEIKIRK, RACHEL   WFA   Page 2   L
     29 March 1853   Parents: John H. & Frances Neikirk

NELSON, NANCY E   WFA   Page 30   F
     17 May 1856   Parents: Marshall & Eliz'th Nelson

NELSON, NEOMA J   WFA   Page 37   F
     5 or 11 April 1857   Parents: Andrew & Francis Nelson

NEWLAND, SARAH F   WFA   Page 29   F
     2 September 1856   Parents: Thos. D. & Nancy R. NOWLANI
     Reported by Thos. D. NOULAND, father

NEWMAN, FRANK H   WMA   Page 63   F
     19 August 1892   Parents: Asa B. & Millie Newman

NEWTON   SMA   Page 1   Saltville
     27 April 1853   Mistress: Louisa P. King

NICHOLAS, SARAH A   WFA   Page 37   F
     1 October 1857   Parents: Carter & Sarah W. Nicholas

NICHOLAS, VIRGINIA VICTORIA   WFA   Page 19   B
     9 December 1855   Parents: Edward & Justine Nicholas

NICHOLS, F.E.   WFA   Page 43   F
     15 August 1858   Parents: Ed. & J. Nichols

NICHOLS, MATILDA   WFA   Page 4   B
     19 December 1853   Father: Edmund Nichols

NIDERMAIER, [n.n.]   WFA   Page 73   MR   Abingdon
     15 November 1892   Parents: L.J. & L.R. Nidermaier

NOLAND, W. KING N   WMA   Page 44   F
     24 September 1858   Parents: Thos. & Mary Noland

NORRIS, [n.n.]   WMA   Page 1   CP   Near Saltv
     20 December 1853   Parents: Isaiah & Catherine Norris

NUCKELS, RICD. F   WMA   Page 33   F
     2 April 1857   Parents: Richd. & Mary A.F. Nuckel

NUCKLES, JOSEPH B   WMA   Page 21   F
  6 July 1855   Parents: Richard & M.A. Nuckles

NUCKOLS, EUGINE G   WMA   Page 51   F
  19 May 1859   Parents: Richard & Mary A.F. Nuckols

NUNLEY, [n.n.]   WMD   Page 48   F
  16 May 1859   Parents: Richard & Mary Nunley

NUNLEY, [n.n.]   WFA   Page 48   F
  20 December 1859   Parents: William & Nancy Nunley

NUNLEY, FRANCIS   WFA   Page 63   F
  7 August 1892   Parents: J.H. & Mary Nunley

NUNLEY, MILTON H   WMA   Page 33   F
  25 August 1857   Parents: Jas. M. & Virginia Nunley

NUNN, SARAH J.E.   WFA   Page 56   F   Glade Spring Twp.
  1870   Parents: John A. & Margaret Nunn

NUTTER, ONEY M   WFA   Page 63   F
  23 May 1892   Parents: W.J. & Fannie Nutter

NYE, LIZZIE K   WFA   Page 63   MR
  15 June 1892   Parents: W.B. & M.A. Nye

OADOM, NANCY E.S.   WFA   Page 44   F
  23 March 1858   Parents: Laten & Isabella ODEM
  Reported by L. OADEM, father

ODLE, FRANK W.R.   WMA   Page 51   F
  15 November 1859   Parents: Levi & Susan Odle

ODLE, MARTHA A   WFA   Page 72   F
  10 May 1892   Parents: Richard & Betsy Odle

ODUM, JNO. H. (twin)   WMA   Page 69   F   North Fork Dist.
  10 January 1892   Parents: James & Alice Odum

ODUM, MARGARET   WFA   Page 4   F
  3 December 1853   Father: Latin Odum

ODUM, MARY J. (twin)   WFA   Page 69   F   North Fork Dist.
  10 January 1892   Parents: James & Alice Odum

ODUM, MATILDA   WFA   Page 69   F   North Fork Dist
  2 April 1892   Parents: Lafayet & Nannie Odum

ODUM, SARAH   WFA   Page 31   F
  12 December 1856   Father: Latin Odum
                           Mother: Margret ODAM

OGLE, MARY E   WFA   Page 69   F   North Fork Dist.
  20 August 1892   Parents: F.M. & Martha Ogle

OGLETON, ROSELIE   CFA   Page 73   F   Near Abingdon
  13 October 1892   Parents: Chas. & Josie Ogleton

ONEY, BETTIE D   WFA   Page 44   F
  24 August 1858   Parents: Jas. W. & Laurey Oney

ORFIELD, SARAH J   WFA   Page 33   F
     15 December 1857   Parents: Isaac & Eliza Orfield

ORFIELD, WM. B   WMA   Page 51   F
     20 February 1859   Parents: Preston & E.L. Orfield

ORNDUFF, [n.n.]   WFA   Page 33   F
     18 May 1857   Parents: James & Barbary Ornduff

ORNDUFF, CHARLES A   WMA   Page 33   F
     18 October 1857   Parents: Thos. & Ann E. Ornduff

ORNDUFF, LARENIA A   WFA   Page 33   F
     31 December 1857   Parents: Joseph & Susan E. Ornduff

ORNDUFF, SARAH J   WFA   Page 51   F
     1 November 1859   Parents: Lewis & Elizabeth Ornduff

ORR, LORA   WFA   Page 44   F
     21 October 1858   Parents: Campbell E. & Mary Orr

ORR, MARTHA VIRGINIA   WFA   Page 3   MR   Cedarville
     24 May 1853   Parents: James & Eliza Orr

ORR, MARY   WFA   Page 48   F
     7 January 1859   Parents: James H. & Martha Orr

OVERBAY, MARTH. J.E.   WFA   Page 63   MC
     21 December 1892   Parents: H.G. & Susan R. Overbay

OVERLEY, NANCY JANE   WFA   Page 56   MC   Glade Spring
     1870   Parents: Howard & Nancy Overley

OWEN, [n.n.]   WFA   Page 51   F
     31 May 1859   Parents: Jas. G. & Caroline Owen

OWEN, JAS. BUCHANAN   WMA   Page 10   F
     29 August 1854   Parents: David C. & Sarah A. Owen

OWEN, MARIAH   WFA   Page 25   F
     22 March 1856   Parents: Thos. & Nancy Owen
     Reported by Jas. Crabtree, grandfather

OWEN, MARK   WMA   Page 19   L
     26 April 1855   Parents: Alex'r & Elizabeth OWENS

OWENS, [n.n.]   WMD   Page 37   F
     20 October 1857   Parents: Jas. & Sarah Owens

OWENS, ANDREW E   WMA   Page 48   F
     14 August 1859   Parents: David & Sarah Owens

OWENS, BATANA B   WFA   Page 4   F
     23 April 1853   Parents: Alexander & Betsey Owens

OWENS, GEORGE W   WMA   Page 51   F
     10 February 1859   Parents: Thomas & Nancy Owens

OWENS, JOHN   WMA   Page 67   F   Kinderhook
     15 April 1892   Parents: G.W. & Sally Owens

OWENS, MARY FRANCES   WFA   Page 19   F
     4 July 1855   Parents: James & Sarah Owens

PAINTER, [n.n.]   WMA   Page 44   F
    15 October 1858   Parents: William & Judith Painter

PAINTER, JAMES A   WMA   Page 15   F
    24 December 1854   Parents: John & Rachel Painter

PAINTER, THOS. JAMES   WMA   Page 27   B
    15 June 1856   Parents: Wm. & Judith Painter

PALMER, [n.n.]   WMA   Page 51   MR
    7 October 1859   Parents: J.B. & Sarah A. Palmer

PALMER, BENJ'N   WMA   Page 11   F
    20 February 1854   Parents: Jacob & Ellen Palmer

PALMER, EDMUND M   WMA   Page 3   F
    4 January 1853   Parents: Holbert & Mary J. Palmer

PARAGEN, MARGARET   WFA   Page 40   F
    2 April 1858   Parents: Alfred & Mary Paragen

PARAGEN, WM. T   WMA   Page 51   F
    1 December 1859   Parents: Alfred & Mary Paragen

PARAGIN, WALTER   WMA   Page 24   F
    12 August 1856   Parents: James & Cath. Paragin

PARIGEN, FRANK   WMA   Page 21
    10 May 1855   Mother: Ellen Parigen

PARIGEN, JAMES C   WMA   Page 21   F
    8 April 1855   Father: Joseph Parigen
                                   Mother: Amelia PARRIGEN

PARKS, JAS. BOWEN   WMA   Page 4   B
    4 February 1853   Parents: Granville C. & Nancy Parks

PARKS, LULA M   WFA   Page 70   MC   Abingdon Dist.
    27 July 1892   Parents: Jeff. & Nancy F. Parks
    'moved recently to Florida'

PARKS, MARY J   WFA   Page 48   F
    29 May 1859   Parents: Wm. L. & Sarah Parks

PARRIS, SARAH C   WFA   Page 40   F
    2 May 1858   Parents: Alex & S.E. Parris

PARTHEMY, MARGRET   WFA   Page 30   F
    24 January 1856   Parents: Wm. S. & Nancy Parthemy

PATISON, SUSAN   CFA   Page 73   L   Near Abingdon
    9 November 1892   Parents: Rufus & Susan Patison

PAYNE, CALLEY E   WFA   Page 72   F   Goodson
    23 August 1892   Parents: Enock & L.M. Payne

PEACO, MARY E   WFA   Page 63   F
    11 April 1892   Parents: James & Rhoda Peaco

PEARIGIN, EPHRAIM F   WMA   Page 33   F
    6 January 1857   Parents: John & L. PARAGIN

PEARIGIN, JOSEPH   WMA   Page 33   F
    1 April 1857   Parents: Jno. F. & Sarah PARAGIN

PEARIGIN, SYLVANUS   WMA   Page 33   F
    4 April 1857   Parents: Jos. & Ann A. PARAGIN

PEARSON, OLEY   WFA   Page 56   F   Glade Spring Twp
    1870   Parents: Rufus & Nancy Pearson

PENDLETON, CHAS. M   WMA   Page 69   F   North Fork Dist.
    10 November 1892   Parents: C.C. & Marg. Pendleton

PENDLETON, CLARA   WFA   Page 63   F
    10 September 1892   Parents: W.R. & Alice Pendleton

PENNICK, DOLPHIA   WMA   Page 58
    1870   Parents: Jno. W. & Susan Pennick

PENNINGTON, AMAN. L   WFA   Page 63   F
    27 October 1892   Parents: Walt & P.C. Pennington

PEPPER, JNO. W   WMA   Page 40   TN
    15 April 1858   Parents: J.E. & F.E. Pepper

PERDUE, JOHN R   WMA   Page 10   F   Northfork Twp.
    10 March 1871   Parents: Andrew G. & Julia A. Perdue

PERKINS, ROBT. H   WMA   Page 63   F
    5 December 1892   Parents: F.F. & Henrietta Perkins

PERRIGEN, DELANEY   WFA   Page 72   F   Goodson
    5 May 1892   Father: Saml. Perrigen
                                   Mother: Sally PERREGIN

PERRY, [n.n.]   CFA   Page 74   F   Goodson
    October 1892   Father: John Perry

PERRY, ERRISTUN R   CMA   Page 73   L   Near Abingdon
    27 September 1892   Parents: Wm. & Emma Perry

PETER   SMA   Page 27
    15 August 1856   Owner: Jno. Gibson

PETERMAN, P.P.   WFA   Page 51   F
    15 April 1859   Parents: Wm. B. & Angeline Peterman

PETTYJOHN, MARY C   WF_   Page 58
    2 April 1870   Parents: G.W. & Sarah Pettyjohn

PETTYJOHN, [REMO]   WFA   Page 67   F   Kinderhook
    9 December 1892   Parents: C.H. & Martha Pettyjohn

PHELPS, [n.n.]   WFA   Page 26   F
    14 July 1856   Parents: John & Patsy Phelps

PHELPS, JOHN   WMA   Page 54   F   North Fork Twp.
    29 November 1871   Parents: James & Nancy J. Phelps

PHELPS. LUCY A   WFA   Page 22   F
    5 December 1855   Parents: James & E.J. Phelps

PHELPS, MARTHA W   WFA   Page 41   F
    15 April 1858   Parents: Jno. & May Phelps

PHELPS, NEWTON   WMA   Page 33   F
    15 March 1857   Parents: Martin & Malinda Phelps

PHELPS, WM. L   WMA   Page 22   F
    7 April 1855   Parents: Martin & M. Phelps

PHELPS, WM. M   WMA   Page 25   F
    6 July 1856   Parents: Geo. & Mary Phelps

PHILIPS, ANN E   WFA   Page 41   F
    1 October 1858   Parents: M. & Nancy Phillips

PHILIPS, GARLAND   CMA   Page 73   L   Near Abingdon
    10 April 1892   Parents: Ben & Jane PHILIPPS

PHILIPS, ROBERT   CMA   Page 73   L   Near Abingdon
    10 August 1892   Father: Robert PHILIPS
                      Mother: Caroline PHILIPPS

PHILLIS   SMA   Page 27
    15 September 1856   Owner: S.W. Montgomery

PHIPPS, CYNTHIA   WFA   Page 3   F
    9 August 1853   Father: Elijah Phipps

PICKENS, RUBY S   WFA   Page 72   MC   Goodson
    10 April 1892   Parents: W.C. & Sally R. Pickens

PICKLE, [n.n.]   WFA   Page 73   EL   Abingdon
    8 December 1892   Parents: T.L. & Sally Pickle

[PIERCE], FRANCIS   WFA   Page 44
    30 August 1858   Mother: Rebecca BARLOW

PINKSTON, [n.n.]   WFA   Page 40   F
    9 February 1858   Parents: Jas. W. & Rachel Pinkston

PINKSTON, M.J.   WFA   Page 6   F
    11 March 1853   Father: Jas. Pinkston

PIPPIN, [n.n.]   WMD   Page 25   F
    28 November 1856   Parents: Rob't & Sarah Pippin

PIPPIN, [n.n. twin]   WFA   Page 26   F
    18 December 1856   Parents: Elisha & Nancy Pippin

PIPPIN, [n.n. twins]   WF_   Page 58
    16 November 1870   Parents: Jno. H. & Mattie Pippin

PIPPIN, CAMPBELL C   WMA   Page 33   F
    1 November 1857   Parents: Robt. S. & Sarah Pippin

PIPPIN, CHARLES CAMPBELL (twin)   WMA   Page 14   F
    2 April 1854   Parents: John H. & Mary Pippin

PIPPIN, CHARLES M   WM_   Page 58
    21 September 1870   Parents: Robert & Laura Pippin

PIPPIN, CRAIG   WMA   Page 25   F
    4 July 1856   Parents: Jno. H. & Mary Pippin
       Reported by Matt Talbert, grandfather

PIPPIN, ELIZABETH J   WF_   Page 58
    September 1870   Parents: Robert & Mary E. Pippin

PIPPIN, HENRY A   WMA   Page 22   F
    1 September 1855   Parents: Benj. E. & Susan Pippin

PIPPIN, J.G. (twin)   WMA   Page 6   F
    16 August 1853   Parents: Elisha & Nancy Pippin

PIPPIN, JNO. W   WMA   Page 22   F
    5 March 1855   Parents: Wm. P. & Catharine Pippin

PIPPIN, LAURIA A   WFA   Page 54   F   Northfork Twp.
    6 August 1871   Parents: Thomas & Mary Pippin

PIPPIN, MARGRET C (twin)   WFA   Page 26   F
    18 December 1856   Parents: Elisha & Nancy Pippin

PIPPIN, MARY J   WFA   Page 33   F
    15 June 1857   Parents: Jos. & E. Pippin

PIPPIN, MIRTLE   WFA   Page 67   F   Kinderhook
    4 March 1892   Parents: Patten & Mary Pippin

PIPPIN, R.C. (twin)   WMA   Page 6   F
    16 August 1853   Parents: Elisha & Nancy Pippin

PIPPIN, SADIE   WFA   Page 67   F   Kinderhook
    October 1892   Parents: W.M. & [Hannes] Pippin

PIPPIN, SARAH J   WFA   Page 33   F
    15 May 1857   Parents: Benj. E. & Susan Pippin

PIPPIN, WM.   WMA   Page 22   F
    15 May 1855   Parents: James & E. Pippin

PIPPIN, WM. M   WMA   Page 6   F
    1 December 1853   Parents: Robt. P. & Malinda Pippin

PIPPIN, WM. M. (twin)   WMA   Page 14   F
    2 April 1854   Parents: John H. & Mary Pippin

PITTS, EULA   WFA   Page 67   F   Kinderhook
    20 September 1892   Parents: Robert & Nannie Pitts

PITTS, VIRGINIA E   WFA   Page 51   F
    7 January 1859   Parents: Lewis & Louisa Pitts

POFF, CHARLES   WMA   Page 51   F
    4 September 1859   Parents: John & Sarah A. Poff

POLLY   SFA   Page 27
    15 July 1856   Owner: John Preston

POOL, ELIZA MARG'T   WFA   Page 4   L
    28 July 1853   Parents: Claiborne & Ann Pool

POOL, JOHN   WMA   Page 44   F
    16 March 1858   Parents: Claborn & Vina A. Pool

POOL, NANCY ANN   WFA   Page 20   F
    28 August 1855   Parents: Claiborne & Ann Pool

POOR, WILLIAM   WMA   Page 44   F
    30 July 1858   Parents: Jerry & Isabella Poor

POPE, EARL B   CMA   Page 73   L   Near Abingdon
    15 July 1892   Parents: James B. & Mary A. Pope

PORTER, DALE S   WMA   Page 73   MC   Abingdon
    2 October 1892   Parents: D.T. & Lula Porter

PORTERFIELD, THOS. M   WMA   Page 38   F
    30 April 1859   Parents: Jas. C. & Jane Porterfield

PORTERFIELD, WILSON GRAHAM   WMA   Page 16   F
    15 October 1855   Parents: Lilburn B. & Rachel C. Porterfield

POSTON, [n.n.]   WFA   Page 10   F
    23 October 1854   Parents: James & Eliza Poston

POSTON, [n.n.]   WFD   Page 37   F
    15 February 1857   Parents: Jos. & Sarah Poston

POSTON, [n.n.]   WMA   Page 2   L   North Fork
    April 1863   Parents: Joseph & Sally Poston

POSTON, GROVER C   WMA   Page 63   F
    14 November 1892   Father: K.H. Poston
                         Mother: Rebecca POSTEN

POSTON, JOHN   WMA   Page 30   F
    4 March 1856   Parents: Jos. & Sarah Poston

POTTER, REUBEN   WMA   Page 41   F
    14 May 1858   Parents: Jos. & Sarah E. Potter

POWERS, MARY   WFA   Page 14   F
    11 February 1854   Parents: Henry & Catharine Powers

POWERS, WILLIAM   WMA   Page 41   F
    1 September 1858   Parents: David & Susan Powers

PRATER, [n.n.]   WFA   Page 10   F
    June 1854   Parents: Carrington & Jane Prater

PRATER, FLORENCE   WFA   Page 30   F
    7 March 1856   Parents: Joseph & Martha Prater

PRATOR, [n.n.]   WFA   Page 1   F
    22 December 1853   Parents: Joseph & Jane Prator

PRESTON   SMA   Page 51
    11 October 1859   Owner: John H. Wallace

PRESTON, ELIZABETH M   WFA   Page 54   F   Northfork Twp.
    26 March 1871   Parents: Robert A. & Amelia C. Preston

PRESTON, FARNCIS   WMA   Page 6   F
    4 December 1853   Parents: Francis & Virginia Preston

PRESTON, M.E.   WFA   Page 40   F
    14 December 1858   Parents: W.S. & N.J. Preston

PRESTON, MARGARET B   WFA   Page 22   F
    9 September 1855   Parents: Henry & Ann C. Preston

PRESTON, ROBT. P   WMA   Page 33   F
    1 April 1857   Parents: James F. & Fannie Preston

PRESTON, WILLIAM   WMA   Page 56   F   Glade Spring Twp.
    1870   Parents: Samuel & Catharine Preston

PRESTON, WM. A   WMA   Page 23   F
    19 April 1855   Parents: Francis & Mary V. Preston

PRESTON, WM. K
    20 May 1859
WMA   Page 51   F
Parents: Wm. A. & Elizabeth Preston

PRICE, ANN
    10 June 1892
WFA   Page 67   F   Kinderhook
Parents: James & Alice Price

PRICE, ANNIE L
    20 December 1892
WFA   Page 63   F
Parents: Wm. & Alice Price

PRICE, C.R.
    20 December 1892
WMA   Page 67   F   Kinderhook
Parents: T.C. & Mollie Price

PRICE, ELIZABETH
    25 May 1853
WFA   Page 2   L
Father: John Price

PRICE, JNO. W
    13 July 1858
WMA   Page 41   F
Parents: R.P.A. & Sidney Price

PRICE, MARTHA J
    7 July 1853
WFA   Page 6   MR
Parents: Dan'l E. & Mary Price

PRICE, NOAH
    17 November 1892
WMA   Page 69   F   North Fork Dist.
Parents: Francis & Sarah Price

PRICE, RUFUS K
    5 April 1854
WMA   Page 14   MC
Parents: James T. & Maria Price

PRICE, SARAH E
    18 July 1856
    Reported by Nathan Price, grandfather
WFA   Page 25   F
Parents: Jas. F. & Mariah Price

PROTER, DORCAS A
    6 August 1859
WFA   Page 51   F
Parents: John & Elizabeth Proter

PUCKETT, [n.n.]
    September 1855
WMD   Page 20   F
Parents: Wm. S. & Elizabeth Puckett

QUESENBERRY, [n.n.]
    23 January 1853
WMA   Page 5   F
Parents: Wm. & Frances Jane Quesenberry

QUESENBERRY, IDA B
    20 August 1892
WFA   Page 72   F   Goodson
Parents: John & Mary Quesenberry

QUINSBURRY, [n.n.]
    19 March 1856
    Reported by Amos
        QUEISENBURY, father
W D   Page 29   F
Father: Amos Quinsburry
Mother: Mahalia QUISNBURY

RACHEL
    2 May 1856
SFA   Page 29
Owner: Jno. Byars

RACHEL, MARTHA S
    18 January 1858
WFA   Page 41   F
Parents: Jas. J. & Isabella Rachel

RACHEL, SARAH E
    28 December 1856
WFA   Page 26   F
Parents: Jas. J. & Isabella Rachel

RACHEL, WILLIAM [G]
    5 March 1870
WM_   Page 58
Parents: Nathan J. & Sarah Rachel

RACHELS, N.W.
    10 September 1892
WMA   Page 67   F   Kinderhook
Parents: H.A. & S.E. Rachels

RAE, [n.n.]
    17 December 1855
WFA   Page 18   B
Parents: Arthur S. & Hannah Rae

118

RAE, MARY JANE   WFA   Page 5   B
     22 December 1853   Parents: Arthur & Nancy Rae

RAMBO, JOHN   WMA   Page 56   F   Glade Spring Twp.
     1870   Parents: Wm. D. & Mary A. Rambo

RAMBO, NANCY MATILDA   WFA   Page 56   Glade Spring Twp.
     1870   Parents: James K. & Virginia E. Rambo

RAMBO, WM. E   WMA   Page 27   F
     20 May 1856   Parents: David & Matilda Rambo

RAMBO, WM. JAMES   WMA   Page 5   F
     20 November 1853   Parents: John L. & Eliza Rambo

RAMSEY, HIRAM F   WMA   Page 5   F
     21 October 1853   Parents: John & Nancy Ramsey

RAMSEY, IRBY L   WMA   Page 63   F
     15 March 1892   Parents: M.B. & Mat. E. Ramsey

RAMSEY, JACOB A   WMA   Page 28   F
     24 April 1856   Parents: John & Cath Ramsey

RAMSEY, JNO. F   WMA   Page 7   F
     23 June 1853   Parents: James & Marg't E. Ramsey

RAMSEY, LAFAYETTE   WMA   Page 44   F
     19 October 1858   Parents: John & Catherine Ramsey

RAMSEY, THOMAS J   WMA   Page 23   F
     18 September 1855   Parents: James & R. Ramsey

RANDOLPH, RUFUS   CMA   Page 73   MC   Near Abingdon
     14 September 1892   Parents: Chas. & Mary Randolph

RASNICK, LULA   WFA   Page 72   F   Goodson
     20 December 1892   Parents: Wm. E. & Emily Rasnick

RATLIFF, HUBBARD   WMA   Page 63   F
     6 June 1892   Parents: G.R. & F.M. Ratliff

RATLIFF, E.E.N.   WFA   Page 51   F
     2 April 1859   Parents: James & Mary Ratliff

RAY, AMERICA F   WFA   Page 27   F
     7 September 1856   Parents: Jno. W. & Susan C. Ray

RECTOR, THOS. B   WMA   Page 37   F
     23 December 1857   Parents: Henry & L. Rector

REED, E.J.   WFA   Page 44   F
     4 April 1858   Parents: David B. & Margaret Reed

REED, JOHN J   WMA   Page 56   F   Glade Spring Twp.
     1870   Parents: Benjamin & Mary E. Reed

REED, LUCRETIA   WFA   Page 3   F
     27 May 1853   Parents: David B. & Margaret Reed

REEDY, RACHEL   WFA   Page 48   F
     5 May 1859   Parents: Elijah & Catharine Reedy

REID
8 March 1854
SMA   Page 12
Mother: Nancy
Owner: Margaret Hawthorne

REMINE, CATHARINE
13 September 1859
WFA   Page 48   F
Parents: Harry B. & Margaret Remine

REMINE, JAS. H.B.
8 November 1853
WMA   Page 3   F
Parents: William & Mary Remine

REMINES, MARY L
15 September 1857
WFA   Page 37   F
Parents: Harry B. & Margret Remines

REYNOLDS, MAGGIE
30 May 1892
WFA   Page 69   F   North Fork Dist
Parents: R.C. & Mollie Reynolds

REYNOLDS, W.H.
15 July 1892
WMA   Page 69   F   North Fork Dist
Parents: John C. & Kate Reynolds

RHEA, ELIZABETH M
14 February 1858
WFA   Page 44   F
Parents: Jacob & H.E. Rhea

RHEA, FRANCIS J
1 May 1856
WFA   Page 27   F
Parents: Jos. W. & E.C.P. Rhea

RHEA, HETTY
26 December 1853
WFA   Page 4   F
Father: Jacob H. Rhea

RHEA, ISAAC E
6 April 1854
WMA   Page 14   F
Parents: Wm. R. & Louisa Rhea

RHEA, JOSEPH
1870
WMA   Page 56   F   Glade Spring T
Parents: James & Ruth Ann Rhea

RHEA, MARY EMELINE
1 October 1853
WFA   Page 3   MW
Parents: Robt. H. & Fanny Rhea

RHEA, NANCY M.P.
15 November 1853
WFA   Page 6   F
Parents: Joseph W. & Eliz. C. Rhea

RHEA, ROBT. H
30 March 1858
WMA   Page 44   F
Parents: John W. & Susanah Rhea

RHEA, SARAH MARGARET
1870
WFA   Page 56   F   Glade Spring T
Parents: John W. & Susan Rhea

RHEA, W.F.
20 April 1858
WMA   Page 41   F
Parents: Jos. W. & E.P.C. Rhea

RHEA, W.J.
6 January 1856
WMA   Page 28   F
Parents: Jacob H. & Hariet E. Rhea

RHODA
17 October 1853
SFA   Page 9
Owner: John Preston

RICHARDS, ELIZA
20 February 1855
WFA   Page 21   F
Parents: Amos & Elizabeth Richards

RICHARDS, JNO. WESLEY
31 September 1855
WMA   Page 18   F
Parents: Wm. T. & Malinda Richards

RICHARDS, M.R.E.
10 November 1858
WFA   Page 41   F
Parents: Wm. & Ruth Richards

RICHARDS, MARY E   WFA   Page 24   F
    1 November 1856   Parents: Amos & Elizabeth Richards

RICHARDS, WM. C   WMA   Page 28   F
    28 March 1853   Parents: Amos & Elizabeth Richards

RICHARDSON, S.E.   WFA   Page 63   F
    22 October 1892   Parents: Rufus E. & M.J. Richardson

RICHARDSON, WM. JOSIAH   WMA   Page 56   F
    1870   Parents: Charles N. & Catharine Richardson
    Born in Smyth Co., Va.,; residence in Glade Spring Twp.

RICHMOND   SMA   Page 23
    4 November 1855   Owner: Wm. R. Rhea

RICHMAN, SARAH   WFA   Page 55   F   Saltville Twp.
    1 October 1870   Parents: George & Emily Rickman

RIDDLE, MARY B   WFA   Page 63   F
    17 July 1892   Parents: Wm. S. & Evaline Riddle

RILEY, SUSAN   WF_   Page 53   F   Abingdon Twp.
    31 August 1871   Parents: Charles & Susan Riley

RINGLEY, [n.n.]   SMA   Page 33   F
    30 September 1857   Parents: J.D. & Mary Ringley

RINGLEY, BARBARA   WFA   Page 14   F
    12 March 1854   Parents: [Jessie] D. & Mary Ringley

RINGLEY, DAVID   WMA   Page 22   F
    10 September 1855   Parents: John M. & Sarah Ringley
    Reported by E. Ringley, grandfather

RITCHIE, [n.n.]   WMD   Page 63   CL
    15 November 1892   Parents: T.F. & Laura L. Ritchie

RITCHIE, MARTHA J.F.   WFA   Page 53   F   Abingdon Twp.
    19 April 1871   Parents: James L. & Rosannah M. Ritchie

ROBERTS, ALFRED B   WMA   Page 63   F
    24 June 1892   Parents: Thos. M. & Lelia Roberts

ROBERTS, AMANDA   WFA   Page 54   F   Northfork Twp.
    11 January 1871   Parents: Wm. W. & Juila A. Roberts

ROBERTS, CHARLES C   WMA   Page 24   F
    10 February 1856   Parents: Charles & Jane Roberts

ROBERTS, EMELINE   WFA   Page 48   F
    15 May 1859   Parents: Charles & Lincy Roberts

ROBERTS, EZEKIEL   WMA   Page 37   F
    1 February 1857   Father: Wm. Roberts

ROBERTS, JNO. L.B.   WMA   Page 8   F
    16 March 1853   Father: Charles Roberts

ROBERTS, JULIA C   WFA   Page 33   F
    1 August 1857   Parents: Geo. & Martha Roberts

ROBERTS, KELLEY   WMA   Page 63   F
    24 June 1892   Parents: W.B. & Mary J. Roberts

ROBERTS, MARGRET A
    20 October 1857
WFA   Page 33   F
Parents: Charles & Jane Roberts

ROBERTS, MARTHA D
    18 March 1871
WFA   Page 54   F   Northfork Twp.
Parents: John W. & Levina Roberts

ROBERTS, MARY (twin)
    September 1853
WFA   Page 2   F   Near Saltville
Parents: William & Rosanna Roberts

ROBERTS, MARY
    28 February 1857
WFA   Page 33   F
Parents: Saml. & S.J. Roberts

ROBERTS, MARTHA
    1 November 1855
WFA   Page 16   F   Near Saltville
Parents: William & Susannah Roberts

ROBERTS, PRESTON
    31 August 1892
CMA   Page 63   F
Parents: Andrew & Fran. Roberts

ROBERTS, SARAH (twin)
    September 1853
WFA   Page 2   F   Near Saltville
Parents: William & Rosanna Roberts

ROBERTS, SARAH E
    15 August 1859
WFA   Page 48   F
Parents: George & Martha Roberts

ROBERTS, SUSANNAH
    June 1855
WFA   Page 16   F   Near Saltville
Parents: Chapman & Mary Roberts

ROBERTSON, [n.n.]
    10 November 1892
    Also noted as 'stillborn.'
WMA   Page 69   F
Parents: W.F. & Alice C. Robertson

ROBERTSON, VIRGINIA
    16 July 1859
WFA   Page 48   C
Parents: Samuel & Elizabeth Robertson

ROBERTSON, WM. W
    16 May 1859
WMA   Page 48   F
Parents: David E. & Temperance Robertso

ROBINSON, JAS. A
    28 October 1858
WMA   Page 44   F
Parents: Jas. & L.J. Robinson

ROBINSON, JAS. E.A.
    5 April 1854
WMA   Page 12   W
Parents: David E. & Temperance Robinson

ROBINSON, JAS. E.T.
    23 December 1856
WMA   Page 28   F
Parents: Jno. C. & Mary C. Robinson

ROBINSON, JNO. W.P.
    1 October 1855
WMA   Page 18   F
Parents: Jas. L. & Sarah M. Robinson

ROBINSON, JNO. WESLEY C.
    9 January 1853
WMA   Page 4   F
Father: David E. Robinson

ROBINSON, M.C.A.
    7 July 1858
WFA   Page 44   F
Parents: Samuel & Mahela Robinson

ROBINSON, MATILDA J
    6 May 1858
WFA   Page 44   F
Parents: James L. & S.M. Robinson

ROBINSON, MISSOURI ANN
    24 June 1853
WFA   Page 4   WE
Parents: James & Hannah Robinson

ROBINSON, NANCY ANN
    10 November 1853
WFA   Page 5   F
Parents: Jas. L. & Sarah M. Robinson

ROBINSON, PETER CLARK   WMA   Page 9   C
    March 1854   Parents: Samuel W. & Elizabeth Robinson

ROBINSON, RACHEL H.V.   WFA   Page 29   F
    16 March 1856   Parents: David E. & Temperance Robinson

ROBINSON, ROB'T A   WMA   Page 29   F
    17 Oct. 1856   Parents: Saml. W. & Eliza. Robinson

ROBINSON, SAMPSON H   WMA   Page 19   F
    14 July 1855   Parents: Sam'l & Mahala Robinson

ROBINSON, WILLIAM THOS. J.   WMA   Page 12   F
    4 Dec. 1854   Parents: James & Mary Ann Robinson

ROCK, [METTIE]   WFA   Page 67   F   Kinderhook
    10 Jan. 1892   Parents: Sam & Nannie Rock

ROCK, SAMUEL J   WM_   Page 58   MC
    1870   Parents: Boston G. & Rachel J. Rock

RODAFER, JAS. D.   WFA   Page 8   C
    15 June 1853   Parents: Emmanuel & Frances Rodafer

ROE, DELANIA   WMA   Page 56   F   Glade Spring Twp.
    1870   Parents: John E. & Susan E. Roe

ROE, FRANCIS ANN   WFA   Page 56   Glade Spring Twp.
    1870   Parents: Edmond F. & Mary C. Roe

ROE, HENRY C   WMA   Page 63   F
    16 Dec. 1892   Parents: Robt. L. & Eliza M. Roe

ROE, JACKSON   WMA   Page 44   F
    19 April 1858   Parents: Robert S. & Sarah E. Roe

ROE, JAMES   WMA   Page 48   F
    2 July 1859   Parents: Arthur S. & Hannah Roe

ROE, LEANDER   WMA   Page 28   ML
    15 Ap 1 1856   Parents: Jno., Jr., & Susanah Roe

ROE, MARTHA I   WFA   Page 37   F
    2 Nov. 1857   Parents: Thos. J. & Emaline Roe

ROE, SARAH M.J.   WFA   Page 63   F
    11 June 1892   Parents: John & Eunice J.V. Roe

ROE, WASHINGTON E   WMA   Page 58   F
    15 Feb. 1859   Parents: Thomas & Emeline Roe

ROE, WILLIAM C   WM_   Page 58
    8 Dec. 1870   Parents: Elisha & Margaret Roe

ROMINE, MARY A   WFA   Page 63   F
    30 April 1892   Parents: A.J. & Elvira Romine

ROSANAH   WFA   Page 16
    14 Feb. 1855   Owner: James A. Bailey

ROSANAH   SFA   Page 44
    15 Oct. 1858   Owner: Job Clark

ROSANNA
2 March 1853

SFA   Page 8
Owner: Jno. Fleenor

ROSANNAH
10 Aug. 1859

SFA   Page 51
Owner: Russell B. Rogers

ROSE
June 1855

WFA   Page 20
Mother: Rachel
Owner: Geo. V. Litchfield

ROSE, ELEANOR SARAH FIELDS
17 Jan. 1854

WFA   Page 13   CM   Near Abingdon
Parents: John D. & Julia Elma Rose

ROSE, JANE
12 May 1857

WFA   Page 34   CM
Parents: J.M. & E.W. Rose

ROSE, LEWIS W
12 July 1856

WMA   Page 26   CM
Parents: Jackson M. & Ellen W. Rose

ROSE, RUSSELL C
20 Jan. 1854

WMA   Page 15   MC
Parents: J.M. & Ellen W. Rose

ROSENBALM, [n.n.]
31 Oct. 1858

WFD   Page 44   F
Parents: J.H. & S. Rosenbalm

ROSENBALM, AARON
24 Dec. 1857

WMA   Page 37   F
Parents: Joel & Nancy Rosenbalm

ROSENBALM, ADELLA
9 Sept. 1871

WFA   Page 53   F   Abingdon Twp.
Parents: James A. & Susannah Rosenbalm

ROSENBALM, CHARLES
1870

WMA   Page 56   F   Glade Spring Tw
Parents: Aaron & Margaret E. Rosenbalm

ROSENBALM, CYNTHIA ANN
25 July 1853

WFA   Page 3
Mother: Sarah Rosenbalm

ROSENBALM, DUDLEY F
1870

WMA   Page 56   F   Glade Spring Tw
Parents: Joel F. & Mary Rosenbalm

ROSENBALM, E.W.F.
14 May 1857

WMA   Page 37   F
Parents: James & O.K. Rosenbalm

ROSENBALM, F.C.
31 Sept. 1858

WFA   Page 44   F
Parents: James & N. Rosenbalm

ROSENBALM, GEORGE
29 April 1859

WMA   Page 48   F
Parents: Isaac & Catharine Rosenbalm

ROSENBALM, HENRY C
7 April 1857

WFA   Page 37
Mother: Sarah Rosenbalm

ROSENBALM, HUMBERSON
2 March 1859

WMA   Page 48   F
Parents: Daniel & Mary Rosenbalm

ROSENBALM, JACOB E
10 May 1854

WMA   Page 12   F
Parents: David & Jenny Ann Rosenbalm

ROSENBALM, JAMES
11 April 1853

WMA   Page 5   F
Parents: Jack & Nancy Rosenbalm

ROSENBALM, JNO.
23 April 1856

WMA   Page 29   F
Parents: Jno. W. & Dorcus Rosenbalm

ROSENBALM, JNO. W   WMA   Page 28   F
    17 March 1856   Parents: John & Mary Rosenbalm

ROSENBALM, MARGARET   WFA   Page 5   F
    12 August 1853   Parents: Jno. W. & Dorcas Rosenbalm

ROSENBALM, MARY F.V.   WFA   Page 48   F
    25 February 1859   Parents: Adam & Hetty Rosenbalm

ROSENBALM, MATTHEW   WMA   Page 48   F
    16 July 1859   Parents: Matthew & Elizabeth Rosenbalm

ROSENBALM, NANCY J   WFA   Page 28   F
    18 January 1856   Parents: Jas. & Mary A. Rosenbalm

ROSENBALM, RACHEL   WFA   Page 18   F
    5 July 1855   Parents: Isaac & Cath. Rosenbalm

ROSENBALM, SARAH V   WFA   Page 44
    25 May 1858   Mother: Priscilla Rosenbalm

ROSENBALM, THOS. JEFFERSON   WMA   Page 3   F
    17 October 1853   Parents: Jno. & Louisa Rosenbalm

ROSENBALM, VIRGINIA CAROLINE   WFA   Page 18   F
    31 August 1855   Parents: Joel & Nancy Rosenbalm

ROSENBALM, VIR. E   WFA   Page 63   F
    17 August 1892   Parents: Fayett & Alice Rosenbalm

ROSENBALM, WALTER F   WMA   Page 48   F
    23 July 1859   Parents: Aaron & Margaret Rosenbalm

ROSENBALM, WM.   WMA   Page 18   L
    December 1855   Parents: And'w & Sally Rosenbalm

ROSS, [n.n.]   WMD   Page 14   F
    23 July 1854   Parents: Andrew & Sena Ross

ROSS, CAMPBELL S   WMA   Page 21   F
    10 October 1855   Parents: Andrew & S.L. Ross

ROSS, FRANCIS C   WMA   Page 63   U
    1 August 1892   Parents: D.G. & Nancy M. Ross

ROSS, JOHN   WMA   Page 56   F   Glade Spring Twp.
    1870   Parents: Alexander & Susan Ross

ROSS, SARAH L   WFA   Page 51   F
    12 December 1859   Parents: Andrew & S.L. Ross

ROUS, [n.n.]   WFD   Page 37   F
    29 October 1857   Parents: Isaac D. & Margret Rous

ROUSE, BENJ. P   WMA   Page 63   F
    10 September 1892   Parents: J.H. & Dora A. Rouse

ROUSE, C.C.   WMA   Page 67   F   Kinderhook
    5 March 1892   Parents: James & Mary Rouse

ROUSE, NICKERSON SNEAD   WMA   Page 13   F   Rush Creek
    5 August 1854   Parents: Isaac & Margaret Rouse

ROUTH, NEWELL   WMA   Page 63   F
    16 October 1892   Parents: W.N. & Mollie Routh

RUDY, SARAH C — WFA Page 12 F
11 January 1854 — Parents: Samuel & Patsey Rudy

RUDY, WILEY — WMA Page 48 F
9 May 1859 — Parents: Samuel & Martha Rudy

RUMBLEY, MARG. — WFA Page 63 F
20 March 1892 — Parents: J.C. & Alice Rumbley

RUMBLY, JAMES — WMA Page 53 F Abingdon Twp.
14 August 1871 — Father: Henry RUMBLEY
Mother: Catharine Rumbly

RUSH, ARTHUR V — WMA Page 69 F North Fork Dist
14 October 1892 — Parents: J.J. & Mary E. Rush

RUSH, EMMET — WMA Page 25 F
9 July 1856 — Father: David Rush
Mother: Elizabeth RUST

Reported by DAVID RUST, father

RUSH, F.C. — WFA Page 6 B
20 September 1853 — Parents: Jno. C. & Catharine Rush

RUSH, J.V. — WMA Page 6 F
12 July 1853 — Parents: Jas. & Amanda Rush

RUSH, JOHN C — WMA Page 21 F
12 January 1855 — Parents: James & A.E. Rush

RUSH, MARY — WFA Page 67 F Kinderhook
April 1892 — Parents: J.W. & Margaret Rush

RUSH, SARAH C — WFA Page 41 B
31 January 1858 — Parents: Jno. C. & R.R. Rush

RUSH, SUSAN J — WFA Page 21 B
7 November 1855 — Parents: John C. & R.P. Rush

RUST, [n.n.] — WMD Page 24 L
20 September 1856 — Parents: David & McCagy Rust

RUST, [n.n.] — WMA Page 41 F
1 May 1858 — Parents: Dan. & E. Rust

RUST, DANIEL C — WMA Page 14 F
17 June 1854 — Parents: Daniel & Elizabeth Rust

RUST, SUSANNA — WFA Page 14 F
30 June 1854 — Parents: Jeremiah & Ann Rust

RUTHERFORD, BERTY G — WFA Page 72 F Goodson
May 1892 — Parents: James & C.L. Rutherford

RUTHERFORD, FRANCIS — WMA Page 51 F
5 December 1859 — Parents: Wm. R. & A.J. Rutherford

RUTHERFORD, MARTHA V — WFA Page 72 F Goodson
11 July 1892 — Parents: George & Mag. Rutherford

RUTLEDGE, ALEXANDER — WMA Page 27 F
26 October 1856 — Parents: Anthony & Cath. Rutledge

RUTLEDGE, HETTY — WFA Page 5 F
29 November 1854 — Parents: Matthias & Catharine Rutledg

RUTLEDGE, JOSEPH   WMA   Page 18   F
    23 June 1855   Parents: Anthony & Catharine Rutledge

RUTLEDGE, MARY   WFA   Page 44   F
    20 January 1858   Parents: Mathias & Rachel Rutledge

RUTLEDGE, TIMOTHY   WMA   Page 28   F
    29 January 1856   Parents: Matthias & Rachel Rutledge

RUTLEDGE, WILLIAM   WMA   Page 18   F
    April 1855   Parents: Robert & Jane Rutledge

RUTLEDGE, CHRISTLEY   WMA   Page 5
    11 March 1853   Mother: Elizabeth Rutledge

RUTLEDGE, LUCINDA   WFA   Page 3   F
    16 May 1853   Parents: Antony & [Sarah] Rutledge

RUTTER, MARY O   WFA   Page 72   F   Goodson
    11 June 1892   Parents: Steven & Nancy Rutter

RUTTER, SARAH L   WFA   Page 24   L
    12 November 1856   Parents: Jno. A. & R.J. Rutter

RYAN, ADAM HICKMAN   WMA   Page 17   T
    December 1855   Parents: James & Barbara Ryan

RYAN, DAVID H   WMA   Page 11   C
    20 July 1854   Parents: James & Barbary H. Ryan

RYAN, FRANK B   WMA   Page 63   F
    31 October 1892   Parents: D.C. & Susan Ryan

RYAN, NANCY M   WFA   Page 28   MC
    26 November 1856   Parents: James & Martha Ryan

RYAN, STELLA   WFA   Page 63   F
    15 June 1892   Parents: J.A.P. & Susan M. Ryan

RYAN, W.F.   WMA   Page 31   F
    5 April 1856   Parents: Dan'l C. & Sarah W. Ryan

RYBURN, DAVID KING   WMA   Page 15   F
    2 March 1854   Parents: John & Jane Ryburn

RYBURN, E.J.   WFA   Page 44   F
    20 July 1858   Parents: W.S. & Rebecca J. Ryburn

RYBURN, ISABELLA J   WFA   Page 48   F
    10 December 1859   Parents: James O. & Margaret Ryburn

RYBURN, JOHN D.G.   WMA   Page 11   F
    5 March 1854   Parents: William S. & Rebecca Ryburn

RYBURN, MARY E.C.   WFA   Page 26   F
    18 March 1856   Parents: Jno. & Jane Ryburn

RYBURN, MARY M   WFA   Page 28   F
    9 June 1856   Parents: Wm. & Rebecca J. Ryburn

RYBURN, MATTHEW   WMA   Page 9   F
    21 March 1854   Parents: James O. & Margaret Ryburn

SADDLER, JAS. E.
    10 April 1857
    Born in North Carolina

WMA   Page 34   F
Father: Henry SADLER
Mother: J. Saddler

SAILER, JAMES
    14 February 1858

WMA   Page 41   SH
Parents: L.W. & Adaline Sailor

ST. JOHN, ELIZA M
    2 February 1892

WFA   Page 64   F
Parents: A.D. & Julia St. John

ST. JOHN, ELIZABETH
    17 March 1855

WFA   Page 17   F
Parents: Campbell B. & Martha St. John

ST. JOHN, JOHN B
    6 March 1859

WMA   Page 48   F
Parents: William & Rachel St. John

ST. JOHN, WM. B
    4 June 1854

WMA   Page 11   F
Parents: Wm. C. & Rachel St. John

SALLY
    17 November 1853

SFA   Page 9
Owner: John Preston

SALTS, VIOLA
    17 June 1871

WFA   Page 53   B   Abingdon Twp.
Parents: William & Nancy Salts

SAM
    13 January 1855

SMA   Page 23
Owner: M.H. Buchanan

SAM
    20 September 1857

SMA   Page 34
Owner: Jas. M. Jones

SAMUEL
    15 July 1858

SMA   Page 44
Owner: B. Talbert

SAMUEL
    27 June 1853

SMA   Page 8
Owner: Rob't F. Preston

SAMUEL
    8 March 1855

SMA   Page 18
Mother: Nancy
Owner: Jacob Clark

SANDERS, AMANDA VIRGINIA
    26 June 1855

WFA   Page 17   F
Parents: Henry & Mary Sanders

SANDERS, HUGH GRIM
    1870

WMA   Page 56   F   Glade Spring T
Parents: H.W. & Hettie F. Sanders

SANDIFER, [n.n.]
    13 May 1853

WMA   Page 2   F
Father: William Sandifer

SANDOE, J.G. KREGER
    24 Apirl 1858

WMA   Page 41   T
Parents: W.M.G. & Margaret Sandoe

SANDOE, JAS. L.D.
    24 April 1856

WMA   Page 26   T
Parents: Wm. M.G. & M.A. Sandoe

SANDOE, THOMAS P.H.
    1 July 1871

WMA   Page 53   MR   Abingdon Twp.
Parents: Wm. M.G. & Margaret Sandoe

SANDS, ALEY
    15 April 1857

WFA   Page 37   F
Parents: Jno. M. & Sarah Sands

SANDS, JOSEPH
    19 July 1855

WMA   Page 20   F
Parents: John M. & Sarah Sands

SANDS, MARY
    18 January 1853
WFA   Page 2   L   Poor Valley
Parents: John M. & Sally Sands

SARAH
    15 September 1853
SFA   Page 8
Owner: Jas. Fields

SARAH
    3 August 1854
SFA   Page 15
Master: Edward E. Lathim

SARAH
    2 January 1855
SFA   Page 17
Mother: Octavia
Owner: Jas. S. Buchanan

SARAH
    31 September 1858
SFA   Page 38
Owner: Alfred Carmack

SARAH
    12 October 1858
SFA   Page 44
Master: J.H. Smyth

SARAH
    15 October 1858
SFA   Page 44
Owner: David Rambo

SARAH
    10 January 1859
SFA   Page 48
Master: Jacob Morell

SARAH
    1 September 1859
SFA   Page 48
Master: Joseph Keller

SARAH
    3 November 1853
SFA   Page 2
Mother: Clara
Owner: Whitley Fullen

SARAH A
    1 June 1856
SMA   Page 34
Owner: Jno. H. Clark

SARAH EMALINE
    20 December 1856
SFA   Page 28
Mother: Ann
Owner: John Roe, Sr.

SAUL, SUSAN
    26 March 1859
WFA   Page 51   F
Parents: Stephen & Nancy Saul

SAULLS, LAURA
    30 December 1892
WFA   Page 70   F   Abingdon Dist.
Parents: A.J. & L.E. SALLS

SAULS, MARGARET
    28 March 1871
WFA   Page 53   F   Abingdon Twp.
Parents: Thomas & Lucinda Sauls

SAWYERS, BENJ. M
    10 April 1892
WMA   Page 64   MC
Parents: Baxter & Mol. R. Sawyers

SCOTT
    12 February 1856
SMA   Page 27
Owner: Jno. Gray

SCOTT, CLAUDE S.W.
    22 November 1892
WMA   Page 64   F
Parents: J.F. & Mary Scott

SCOTT, GEO.
    29 April 1859
WMA   Page 51   F
Parents: Andrew & Sarah Scott

SCOTT, GEO. W
    15 December 1857
    Reported by J. Scott, uncle
WMA   Page 34   F
Parents: Solomin & Eliza Scott

SCOTT, HARRIET   WFA   Page 1   F
    23 July 1853   Parents: Grandison & Elizabeth Scott

SCOTT, JAMES   WMA   Page 16   F
    25 March 1855   Parents: Grandison & Elizabeth Scott

SCOTT, JAS. F.H.   WMA   Page 37   F
    5 March 1857   Parents: And. J. & Nancy S. Scott

SCOTT, JAMES W   WMA   Page 53   F   Abingdon Twp.
    17 July 1871   Parents: William & Margaret Scott

SCOTT, JESSEE S   WMA   Page 51   F
    6 May 1859   Parents: Solamon & Elizabeth Scott

SCOTT, LYDIA B   WFA   Page 69   F   North Fork Dist
    2 April 1892   Parents: J.F.I.C. & Martha Scott

SCOTT, MARTIN C   WMA   Page 7   F
    13 September 1853   Father: John J. Scott

SCOTT, MARY A   WFA   Page 30   F
    27 October 1856   Parents: Josiah & Nancy Scott

SCOTT, MARY E   WFA   Page 48   F
    3 December 1859   Parents: Samuel & Margaret Scott

SCOTT, RMILDA   WFA   Page 48   F
    2 December 1859   Parents: Joseph & Sarah Scott

SCOTT, SOLOMON C   WMA   Page 22   F
    24 December 1855   Parents: John J. & Martha Scott

SCOTT, SUSAN   WFA   Page 10   F
    17 July 1854   Father: Robert H. Scott

SCOTT, VERLIN   WMA   Page 37   F
    21 March 1857   Parents: Saml. P. & Margret Scott

SCYPHERS, OSCAR D   WMA   Page 64   F
    3 September 1892   Parents: W.J. & Alice Scyphers

SEALS, CHARLES B   CMA   Page 56   F   Glade Spring T
    1870   Parents: Philip & Saphronia Seals

SEARS, [n.n.]   WFD   Page 6   F
    August 1853   Father: Wm. T. Sears

SEARS, ANN M.P.   WFA   Page 9   TN   Near Saltville
    30 January 1854   Parents: David N. & Mary Sears

SELESTIAL   SFA   Page 27
    15 April 1856   Owner: Jos. W. Rhea

SELF, J.S.   WMA   Page 67   F   Kinderhook
    21 June 1892   Parents: W.T. & Martha Self

SENNIKER, JOSEPH   WMA   Page 34   F
    6 September 1857   Father: Wm. B. Senniker
    Reported by Wm. B.   Mother: Margret SENEKER
        SENAKER, father

SENTRE, MARY V   WFA   Page 29   F
    31 July 1856   Parents: Wm. T. & Sarah B. Sentre

SETSER, JOHN HENRY   WMA   Page 20   F
    22 July 1855   Parents: Abner & Sarah Setser

SHAFFER, EDWARD W   WMA   Page 14   F
    15 May 1854   Parents: Jackson & Elizabeth Shaffer

SHAFFER, ELIZABETH   WFA   Page 25   F
    7 July 1856   Parents: Geo. & Polly Shaffer

SHAFFER, SARAH R   WFA   Page 41   F
    20 January 1858   Parents: Geo. H. & Polly A. Shaffer

SHAFFER, ZACHARIAH   WMA   Page 67   F   Kinderhook
    5 December 1892   Parents: D. & Eliza Shaffer

SHANKLE, [n.n.]   WFA   Page 22   F
    25 December 1855   Parents: Jno. M. & Mary Shankle

SHANKLE, CATHERINE   WFA   Page 72   B
    24 April 1856   Parents: Granville & Sarah A. Shankle

SHANKLE, CLAY R   WMA   Page 72   F   Goodson
    6 August 1892   Parents: W.K. & A.J. Shankle

SHANKLE, D.C.   WMA   Page 34   F
    10 December 1857   Parents: A.L. & Ann Shankle

SHANKLE, JEREMIAH L   WMA   Page 14   F
    22 March 1854   Parents: A.L. & Ann Shankle

SHANKLE, SARAH J   WFA   Page 24   B
    12 March 1856   Parents: A.L. & Ann M. Shankle
    Reported by A.L. SHANKEL, father

SHANNON, ANDREW   WMA   Page 19   S
    21 February 1855   Parents: James D. & Marg't Shannon

SHARER, MARY I   WFA   Page 24   L
    8 April 1856   Parents: Martin & Eliza Sharer

SHARP, JOSEPH R   WMA   Page 44   F
    3 February 1858   Parents: Benj. B. & Margaret E. Sharp

SHARP, MARGARET A   WFA   Page 12   F
    10 August 1854   Parents: William C. & Nancy Sharp

SHARP, MARY MARTHA M   WFA   Page 18   F
    26 December 1855   Parents: William C. & Nancy R. Sharp

SHARP, RICHARDS W   WMA   Page 44   F
    14 October 1858   Parents: W.C. & Nancy R. Sharp

SHARRETT, A.C.   WFA   Page 6   F
    7 May 1853   Parents: Daniel & Eliz. Sharrett

SHARRETT, ANN E   WFA   Page 41   F
    24 January 1858   Parents: Danl. & Margaret Sharrett

SHARRETT, ARTHUR D   WMA   Page 24   F
    20 January 1856   Parents: Daniel & Margret Sharrett
    Reported by Daniel SHARRET, father

SHARRETT, BENJ.   WMA   Page 72   F   Goodson
         4 May 1892   Parents: Robt. W. & Mary E. Sharrett

SHARRETT, JACOB   WMA   Page 24   F
         5 March 1856   Parents: James & Susan Sharrett

SHARRETT, JAS. E   WMA   Page 34   F
         15 March 1857   Parents: Benj. & Rachel Sharrett

SHARRETT, THOS.   WMA   Page 41   F
         19 January 1858   Parents: Jas. & Susan Sharrett

SHEETS, [n.n.]   WMA   Page 73   F   Abingdon
         23 December 1892   Mother: Mary Sheets

SHEETS, WILLIE JOSEPHINE   WFA   Page 57   F   Glade Spring Tw
         1870   Parents: David & Mary J. Sheets

SHEFFEY, CLARENCE   WMA   Page 72   F   Goodson
         10 July 1892   Parents: Charles & C.H. Sheffey

SHEFFIELD, GORD. C   WMA   Page 64   F
         8 July 1892   Parents: T.P. & Rhoda Sheffield

SHELBY, WILLIAM   WMA   Page 67   F   Kinderhook
         5 December 1892   Parents: J.S. & Nancy Shelby

SHELLEY, CLAUD M   WMA   Page 64
         24 April 1892   Parents: D.A. & Sarah J. Shelley

SHELTON, SAMUEL L   WMA   Page 72   F   Goodson
         23 December 1892   Parents: Ed. & Mag. Shelton

SHEPHARD, C.B.   WMA   Page 21   F
         12 December 1855   Parents: S.F. & Frances Shephard

SHERMAN, SAMUEL F   WM_   Page 58
         April 1870   Parents: Leroy S. & Sarah Sherman

SHERWOOD, FRANCIS M   WMA   Page 44   F
         15 November 1858   Parents: Caleb & Susan Sherwood

SHERWOOD, JAMES M   WMA   Page 48   F
         15 January 1859   Parents: Caleb & Susanah Sherwood
         Reported by CLABURN Sherwood, father

SHERWOOD, NANCY MARGARET RUTH PRISCILLA ANN   WFA   Page 19
         20 November 1855   Parents: Levi & Rebecca Sherwood

SHERWOOD, SARAH N   WFA   Page 53   F   Abingdon Twp.
         18 November 1871   Parents: Noah St. John & Martha Sherwo

SHERWOOD, WM. CAMPBELL   WMA   Page 4   F
         22 September 1853   Parents: Levi & Rebecca Sherwood

SHOEMAKER, NAOMI L   WFA   Page 6   F
         5 April 1853   Parents: Jacob & Malinda Shoemaker

SHORES, SARAH K   WFA   Page 72   F   Goodson
         27 June 1892   Parents: James & Mary V. Shores

SHORT, NANNIE E   WFA   Page 70   F   North Fork Dis
         24 July 1892   Parents: Floyd & Susan Short

SHOUSE, RENA MARY   WFA   Page 68   MC   Kinderhook
    10 July 1892   Parents: J.L. & Ida Shouse

SHOUSE, SALLY   WFA   Page 68   MC   Kinderhook Dist.
    2 September 1892   Parents: F.L. & Manerva Shouse

SHUFF, DAVID J   WMA   Page 64   F
    28 March 1892   Parents: D.E. & Barbara Shuff

SHUFFIELD, [n.n.]   WMD   Page 37   MR
    12 March 1857   Parents: Benj. R. & Margret Shuffield

SHUFFIELD, BEATIE JOSIE   WFA   Page 56   MC   Glade Spring Twp.
    1870   Parents: Benjamin & Mary SHEFFIELD

SHUFFIELD, BENJ'N   WMA   Page 18   F
    3 January 1855   Parents: John & Caroline Shuffield

SHUFFIELD, FRANCIS W   WMA   Page 44   F
    4 July 1858   Parents: Benj. & Mary Shuffield

SHUFFIELD, SARAH V   WFA   Page 29   F
    1 October 1856   Parents: John & Caroline Shuffield
    Reported by J.A. [McQuouan], neighbor

SHUFFIELD, THOS. W   WMA   Page 44   F
    6 August 1858   Parents: John & Caroline Shuffield

SHUGART, MARY C   WFA   Page 48   F
    6 June 1859   Parents: Claburn L. & Mary Shugart

SHUGART, MINERVA ELIZABETH   WFA   Page 10   F
    16 February 1854   Parents: Claiborn L. & Mary C. Shugart

SHULTZ, EDWARD A   WMA   Page 48   F
    22 November 1859   Parents: Adam & Eliza Schultz

SHUPE, BESSIE (twin)   WFA   Page 72   F   Goodson
    22 December 1892   Parents: Andrew & Mary Shupe

SHUPE, MAGGIE (twin)   WFA   Page 72   F   Goodson
    22 December 1892   Parents: Andrew & Mary Shupe

SHUPE, WILLIAM   WMA   Page 72   F   Goodson
    8 February 1892   Parents: Andrew & Mary Shupe

SHUTTER, [n.n.]   WFA   Page 72   F   Goodson
    October 1892   Parents: Jacob & Amanda Shutter

SHUTTERS, MALINDA   WFA   Page 21   F
    15 April 1855   Parents: John & Malinda Shutters

SHUTTERS, MARGRET E   WFA   Page 34   F
    29 August 1857   Parents: Jno. & Malinda Shutters

SHUTTLE, FRANK   WMA   Page 72   F   Goodson
    15 November 1892   Parents: Isaac & Cath. Shuttle

SIFERS, JNO. R   WMA   Page 41   F
    21 May 1858   Parents: William & Susan E. Sifers

SIFERS, MARTHA E   WFA   Page 34   F
    29 October 1857   Parents: Harry G. & L.A. Sifers

SIMMONS, MAUD A   WFA   Page 69   F   North Fork Dist.
     5 March 1892   Parents: John & Sally Simmons

SIMMS, DAN'L   SMA   Page 4
     1 January 1853   Owner: Jas. E. Hayter

SIMPSON, JNO. K   WMA   Page 64   L
     15 November 1892   Parents: W.A. & An. B. Simpson

SINGLETON, [n.n.]   WMA   Page 69   MC   North Fork Dist.
     17 June 1892   Parents: W.G. & Eliz. Singleton

SINGLETON, [n.n.]   WFA   Page 60   MC   North Fork Dist.
     16 November 1892   Parents: Thos. C. & S.C. Singleton

SINGLETON, JAMES B   WMA   Page 69   MC   North Fork Dist.
     12 March 1892   Parents: Thos. C. & S.C. Singleton

SIRA, JOHN F   WMA   Page 48   F
     1 August 1859   Parents: Thomas & Elizabeth Sira

SIRIAH - see THOMAS

SISK, FRS. E   WMA   Page 31   F
     22 December 1856   Parents: Timothy & Francis Sisk

SISK, LULA MAY   WFA   Page 64   MR
     15 December 1892   Parents: N.B. & Sarah A. Sisk

SISK, NUTON   WMA   Page 44   F
     12 November 1858   Parents: Timothy & Frances Sisk

SLAGLE, [n.n.]   WFA   Page 21   F
     6 March 1855   Parents: George & Mary Slagle
     Reported by A.C. Maxwell, physician

SLAUGHTER, ALFRED S   WM_   Page 58   MC
     December 1870   Parents: Jno. J. & Aline B. Slaughter

SLAUGHTER, JAMES   WMA   Page 24   F
     16 January 1856   Parents: John & Alice Slaughter

SMELTSON, LEE   WMA   Page 72   F   Goodson
     1 September 1892   Father: Semore SMELTSER
                         Mother: Cal. SMELTZER

SMILEY, [n.n.]   WMD   Page 13   F   North Fork
     August 1854   Parents: James & Sally Smiley

SMILEY, MARY   WFA   Page 20   F
     14 July 1855   Parents: James & Sally Smiley

SMITH, [n.n.]   WFA   Page 5   F
     14 October 1853   Father: Peter S. Smith

SMITH, [n.n.]   WMD   Page 34
     20 October 1857   Mother: E. Smith
     Reported by Jas. Smith, grandfather

SMITH, ALEX P   CMA   Page 74   F   Goodson
     16 December 1892   Parents: Aron & Caroline Smith

SMITH, ANDREW M   WMA   Page 9   F
     12 September 1854   Parents: David D. & Rachel Smith

SMITH, CHS. M
    13 August 1856
WMA   Page 30   F
Parents: Jas. O. & Mary B. Smith

SMITH, ELIZA A
    22 February 1858
WFA   Page 41   F
Parents: Eml. & E.A. Smith

SMITH, ELIZABETH
    30 March 1854
WFA   Page 10   F
Father: Robert Smith
Mother: Sarah HENDERSON

SMITH, H.D.
    10 June 1892
WFA   Page 67   F   Kinderhook
Parents: L.H. & Rebecca Smith

SMITH, HUGH
    17 November 1870
WMA   Page 55   PH   Saltville Twp.
Parents: William & Elizabeth Smith

SMITH, JAMES R
    1 February 1855
WMA   Page 21
Mother: Louisianna Smith

SMITH, JOHN T
    18 May 1871
CMA   Page 53   F   Abingdon Twp.
Parents: James & Hellen Smith

SMITH, JOHN W
    30 August 1858
WMA   Page 41   F
Parents: Jno. & Elizabeth Smith

SMITH, JULIA
    23 January 1892
CFA   Page 73   L   Near Abingdon
Parents: Crocket & Mary Smith

SMITH, LOUISA
    18 September 1871
WFA   Page 53   F   Abingdon Twp.
Parents: Moses B. & Elizabeth Smith

SMITH, MAMIE A
    25 June 1892
WFA   Page 64   F
Parents: W.F. & Mary Smith

SMITH, MARTHA
    2 October 1856
WFA   Page 25   F
Parents: Isaac T. & Martha Smith

SMITH, MARTHA
    2 October 1856
WFA   Page 25   L
Parents: J.T. & Tiny Smith

SMITH, MARTHA W
    20 December 1854
WFA   Page 15   C
Parents: Frans. & Eliza Smith

SMITH, MILTON Y.H.
    23 April 1857
WMA   Page 34   C
Parents: Frs. & Eliza Smith

SMITH, MINNIE
    27 December 1892
WFA   Page 68   F   Kinderhook Dist.
Parents: Robert & Betty Smith

SMITH, NANCY C
    30 December 1858
WFA   Page 41   F
Parents: Henry & Nancy Smith

SMITH, PALLIE
    1 October 1892
WFA   Page 64   F
Parents: Saml. & Alice Smith

SMITH, REBECCA S
    December 1870
WF_   Page 58
Parents: Jno. C. & Elvira Smith

SMITH, THOS. L
    21 September 1856
WMA   Page 30   F
Parents: Jno. H. & Eliz'th Smith

SMITH, W.S.
    5 September 1892
WMA   Page 67   F   Kinderhook
Parents: John & Margret Smith

SMITH, WM. M   WMA   Page 72   F   Goodson
    July 1892   Parents: Wm. M. & Anna Smith

SMITH, ZILLS V   WMA   Page 41   F
    30 December 1858   Parents: E.S. & Eliza Smith

SMYTH, ALICE MARIA   WFA   Page 1   F
    10 July 1853   Parents: James K. & Jane B. Smyth

SMYTH, ELIZA   WFA   Page 37   F
    24 May 1857   Father: John Smyth

SMYTH, GEORGE W.H.   WMA   Page 10   F
    18 June 1854   Parents: John S. & Elizabeth Smyth

SMYTH, ISABELLA FRANCES   WFA   Page 16   F
    10 October 1855   Parents: James K. & Jane B. Smyth

SMYTH, JAMES   WMA   Page 1   L
    27 August 1853   Father: John DOUGHERTY

SMYTH, JAMES WALLACE   WMA   Page 16   F
    10 April 1855   Parents: William & Eliza Smyth
    Father's residence in Tennessee

SMYTH, JOHN   W/C MA Page 48   F
    30 March 1859   Mother: Ann Smyth
    Reported by Ann Smyth, 'free negro'

SMYTH, MARY ELIZABETH   WFA   Page 1   F   Near E&H Colleg
    16 October 1853   Parents: John H. & Elizabeth Smyth

SMYTH, WILLIAM F   WMA   Page 10   F
    1 June 1854   Parents: James O. & Mary B. Smyth

SMYTH, WILLIAM L   WMA   Page 48   F
    11 November 1859   Parents: Ballard P. & Mary SMITH

SNAPP, CHARLES O   WMA   Page 9   MR
    25 June 1854   Parents: Philip B. & Mary D. Snapp

SNAPP, L. Mc.   WMA   Page 63   F
    24 October 1892   Parents: C.O. & L.K. Snapp

SNEAD, MALINDA   WFA   Page 64   F
    29 December 1892   Parents: D.C. & Mary Snead

SNEAD, STELLA E   WFA   Page 64   F
    22 June 1892   Parents: O.N. & Mary A. Snead

SNIDER, MARGRET A   WFA () Page 31   F
    12 August 1856   Parents: Abram & Eliz'th LINDER

SNODGRASS, [n.n.]   WMA   Page 2   F
    13 April 1853   Parents: James M. & Ann Snodgrass

SNODGRASS, BETTIE P   WFA   Page 56   F   Glade Spring T
    1870   Parents: Wm. & Mary Snodgrass

SNODGRASS, ELIZA M   WFA   Page 44   F
    20 November 1858   Parents: Joseph & Nancy Snodgrass

SNODGRASS, HENRY F .   WMA   Page 48   F
    15 December 1859   Parents: James & Amelia Snodgrass

136

SNODGRASS, [IONA]   WFA   Page 44   F
        15 November 1858   Parents: J.M. & F. Snodgrass

SNODGRASS, JAS. C   WFA   Page 64   MR
        10 April 1892   Parents: Wm. J. & S.T. Snodgrass

SNODGRASS, JOHN   WMA   Page 41   F
        31 July 1858   Parents: W. & Cath Snodgrass

SNODGRASS, JOSEPH   WMA   Page 5   F
        8 July 1853   Parents: James & Catharine Snodgrass
        Reported by Jas. Snodgrass, grandfather

SNODGRASS, JULINA O   WFA   Page 20   F
        16 February 1855   Parents: Jas. M. & Ann Snodgrass

SNODGRASS, MAHALA   WFA   Page 55   F   Saltville Twp.
        17 August 1870   Parents: C.C. & Amanda Snodgrass

SNODGRASS, MARGARET ANN   WFA   Page 20   F
        November 1855   Parents: Joseph R. & Taymer Snodgrass

SNODGRASS, MARY A   WFA   Page 29   F
        27 April 1856   Parents: Jas. & Cath Snodgrass

SNODGRASS, REBECCA C   WFA   Page 25   F
        8 September 1856   Parents: Wm. & Cath Snodgrass

SOPHIA   SFA   Page 6
        November 1853   Owner: Jas. W. Sheffey

SORAH, J.C.   WMA   Page 68   F   Kinderhook Dist.
        13 July 1892   Parents: J.F. & Nancy Sorah

SORAH, JOHN   WMA   Page 68   F   Kinderhook Dist.
        5 April 1892   Parents: J.H. & Mary Sorah

SORAH, SARAH A   WF_   Page 58
        13 July 1870   Parents: Francis C.M. & Lucy Sorah

SOUBER, [n.n.]   WFA   Page 72   F
        25 July 1892   Parents: A.J. & Susan B. Souber

SOUTH, JOHN   WMA   Page 70   F   North Fork Dist.
        15 July 1892   Parents: W.F. & Elizabeth South

SOUTH, JUDA E   WFA   Page 44   F
        10 May 1858   Parents: A.C. & P.A. South

SOUTH, LACY   WMA   Page 64   F
        22 July 1892   Parents: Chas. E. & Caroline South

SOUTH, MATTHEW C   WMA   Page 27   SH
        22 November 1856   Parents: Sam'l D. & Charlotte South

SOUTH, SARAH M   WFA   Page 11   L
        11 December 1854   Parents: Samuel & Elizabeth South

SPAHR, D.B.   WMA   Page 41   F
        16 June 1858   Parents: Geo. W. & Mary A. Spahr

SPARKS, [n.n.]   WMA   Page 16   CP
        9 September 1855   Parents: Jacob & Minerva Sparks

SPARKS, MARGARET L
    2 February 1853
                   WFA   Page 9   CO
                   Parents: James & Julia Sparks

SPEAR, [n.n.]
    30 May 1858
                   WMD   Page 44   F
                   Parents: W.T. & Margaret Spear

SPEAR, MARTHA O
    5 April 1892
                   WFA   Page 70   TC   Abingdon Dist.
                   Parents: N.V. & Nannie V. Spear

SPEER, ANDREW
    24 March 1858
                   WMA   Page 44   F
                   Parents: Alfred & Ann SPEAR

SPEER, NANCY M
    2 March 1856
                   WFA   Page 27   B
                   Father: A.W. Speer
                   Mother: Ann SPEAR

SPENCE, MARY ELIZABETH
    13 May 1853
                   WFA   Page 2   F
                   Parents: George & Mary A. Spence

SPHAR, MILLARD FILLMORE
    6 May 1856
                   WMA   Page 24   F
                   Parents: Geo. W. & Mary A. Sphar
    Reported by Geo. W. SPAHR, father

SPRIGGS, [n.n.]
    1870
                   WMA   Page 56   F   Glade Spring Twp
                   Parents: A.J. & Mary Spriggs

SPRIGGS, MAR. W
    2 February 1892
                   WMA   Page 63   J
                   Parents: A.J. & Amer. Spriggs

SPRIGGS, PRISSA E
    10 November 1856
                   WFA   Page 29   F
                   Parents: Andrew & Eliz'th SPRIGS

SPRIGS, NOAH C. BALDWIN
    5 May 1855
                   WFA   Page 16
                   Parents: Cary & Mary SPRIGGS

SPRINKLE, MAURICE E
    10 April 1892
                   WMA   Page 64   F
                   Parents: G.W. & M.A. Sprinkle

SPROLES, ALBERT
    February 1870
                   WM_   Page 58
                   Parents: Moses & Serilda Sproles

SPROLES, ALVIN
    1870
                   WM_   Page 58   F
                   Parents: Joseph & Susan Sproles

SPROLES, CHARLES B
    10 December 1855
                   WMA   Page 22   F
                   Parents: Jno. & Elizabeth Sproles

SPROLES, E.L.
    8 July 1892
                   WMA   Page 68   F   Kinderhook Dist
                   Parents: W.J. & Martha Sproles

SPROLES, ELISHA
    10 November 1859
                   WMA   Page 51   F
                   Parents: Thomas & Elizabeth Sproles

SPROLES, JOS. R
    7 February 1857
                   WMA   Page 34   F
                   Parents: Thos. & E. Sproles

SPROLES, MARY L
    7 February 1855
                   WMFA   Page 22   F
                   Parents: Thos. & E. Sproles

SPROLES, WM. W
    8 January 1853
                   WMA   Page 6   F
                   Father: Thos. Sproles

SPROULE, [n.n.]
    20 August 1856
                   WMA   Page 25
                   Father: Noah Sproule
                   Mother: Mary SPROLES

SPURGEON, JOSEPH WMA Page 26 F
 19 November 1856 Parents: [Wm.] & Mary Spurgeon
 Reported by Jno. Gobble, neighbor

SPURRIER, NANCY ELIZABETH WFA Page 20 F
 16 September 1855 Parents: John & Sally Spurrier

[SPURYER], RACHEL WFA Page 48 F
 3 July 1859 Parents: John B. & Sarah [Spuryer]

STAMPER, JOSIE WFA Page 72 TC Goodson
 30 April 1892 Parents: Harvey & Nannie Stamper

STAPLETON, E.C. WMA Page 67 F Kinderhook
 10 January 1892 Parents: H.T. & Martha Stapleton

STARKS, EVELINE WFA Page 7 F
 2 January 1853 Parents: Wm. & Barbara Starks

STARKS, WM. D WMA Page 34 F
 15 December 1857 Parents: Wm. & Barbary STARK

STARNES, HELEN VIRGINIA WFA Page 9 F
 22 December 1854 Parents: William H. & Rebecca Starnes

STATA, [n.n.] WMA Page 69 F North Fork Dist.
 16 November 1892 Parents: A.B. & Sarah Stata

STATZER, CALEDONIA WFA Page 14
 11 March 1854 Mother: Catharine Statzer

STATZER, EDWIN C WMA Page 41 F
 23 October 1858 Parents: Martin & E.A. Statzer

STATZER, MARGRET V WFA Page 24
 3 April 1856 Mother: Eliz'th Statzer

STATZER, NANCY J WFA Page 41
 10 May 1858 Mother: Alcy H. Statzer

STEEL, LILLY MAY WFA Page 72 F Goodson
 20 April 1892 Parents: F.J. & Eliz. Steel

STEVENS, [n.n.] WMA Page 15 F
 1 August 1854 Parents: D.C. & Sarah A. Stevens

STEVENS, L.C. WMA Page 7 F
 8 April 1853 Parents: Thos. & Susan Stevens

STEVENS, M.E. (twin) WFA Page 51 F
 10 February 1859 Parents: William C. & Margaret Stevens

STEVENS, MARY E.C. (twin) WFA Page 51 F
 10 February 1859 Parents: William C. & Margaret Stevens

STEVENS, ONEY G WFA Page 64 F
 16 September 1892 Parents: Jas. M. & Alice Stevens

STEVENS, SALLY J WFA Page 72 F Goodson
 28 October 1892 Parents: William & Marg. Stevens

STEVENS, SARA A WFA Page 34 F
 25 November 1857 Parents: D.C. & L. Stevens

STEVENS, WM. H
27 January 1859
WMA   Page 51   F
Parents: D.C. & Lucretia Stevens

STEVENS, WM. P
21 August 1854
WMA   Page 15   F
Parents: Nathan'l & Dorotha Stevens

STEWART, ARTHUR WM
15 February 1854
WMA   Page 14   F
Parents: Wm. C. & Sarah Stewart

STEWART, CAL (twin)
15 March 1892
CFA   Page 64   BN
Parents: James & Caro. Stewart

STEWART, LOU (twin)
15 March 1892
CFA   Page 64   BN
Parents: James & Caro. Stewart

STICKLEY, ROSA D
21 February 1858
WMA   Page 44   MN
Parents: W.W. & M.J. Stickley

STOFFEL, ISAAC
6 September 1857
WMA   Page 34   F
Parents: E.C. & E.J. STOFFLE

STOFFEL, NANCY B
8 January 1859
WFA   Page 51   F
Parents: E.C. & E.J. Stoffel

STOFFLE, JAS. B
15 June 1855
WMA   Page 22   F
Parents: Edw'd C. & E.J. Stoffle

STONE, CLAUD H
10 February 1892
WMA   Page 72   F   Goodson
Parents: James M. & S.C. Stone

STOUT, ALICE
31 December 1892
WFA   Page 70   F   North Fork Dist
Parents: A.J. & Eliza Stout

STOUT, CAMNA
5 June 1892
WMA   Page 69   F   North Fork Dist
Parents: J.W. & Alcey Stout

STOUT, EDW. CAMPBELL
5 October 1853
WMA   Page 5   F
Parents: Geo. W. & Julia Ann Stout

STOUT, JOHN R
14 November 1858
WMA   Page 44   F
Father: G.W. Stout
Mother: J. Ann STOUGHT

STOUT, RUTHA A
15 September 1857
Reported by A. Gobble, neighbor
WFA   Page 34   F
Parents: Saml. & Hannah Stout

STOUT, SARAH JANE
23 January 1855
WFA   Page 18   F
Parents: Geo. W. & Julia Ann Stout

STRATTON, DORA
10 July 1892
WFA   Page 67   F   Kinderhook
Parents: Moses & Harriet Stratton

STRATTON, F.S.
10 February 1892
WMA   Page 68   F   Kinderhook Dis
Parents: A.D. & Martha Stratton

STRINGER, MARGARET ANN
19 October 1854
WFA   Page 12   L
Parents: Winsten & Elizabeth Stringer

STROUP, ELECTA MAY
15 September 1892
WFA   Page 70   F   Abingdon Dist
Parents: James & Jemima Stroup

STUART, [n.n.]
10 April 1855
WFA   Page 16   F   Cedarville
Parents: David M. & Ellen Stuart

STUART, HESTER   WFA   Page 68   F   Kinderhook Dist.
    24 December 1892   Parents: Andrew & Jane Stuart

STUART, MARGARET   WFA   Page 44   F
    25 October 1858   Parents: D.M. & Ellen A. Stuart

STUART, WILLIAM J   WM_   Page 58
    1870   Parents: Thomas & Sarah M. Stuart

STURGEON, [n.n.]   WMA   Page 30   F
    27 October 1856   Parents: Saml. & Margret Sturgeon

STURGEON, JOEL   WMA   Page 16   F
    11 August 1855   Parents: Harvey & Mary Sturgeon

STURGEON, MARY C   WFA   Page 30   F
    11 September 1856   Parents: Harry & Mary Sturgeon

STURGEON, [TIVES]   WMA   Page 10   F
    17 August 1854   Parents: Harvey & Mary Sturgeon

STURGILL, ONAN B   WMA   Page 64   F
    26 April 1892   Parents: Melvill & Celia Sturgill

SUIT, BERTY   WFA   Page 68   F   Kinderhook Dist.
    27 December 1892   Parents: John D. & Betty Suit

SULIVAN, MARY EMELINE   WFA   Page 18   F
    14 December 1855   Parents: Wiley & Sarah Sulivan

SULIVAN, SOPHRONIA E   WFA   Page 12   L
    27 February 1854   Parents: Wiley & Sarah Sulivan

SULLENS, MARGARET   WFA   Page 3   L
    26 June 1853   Father: Joab Sullens

SULLINS, MARTHA ANN   WFA   Page 19   F
    3 February 1855   Parents: Wm. P. & Catharine Sullins

SULLIVAN, MARY E   WFA   Page 28   F
    16 November 1856   Parents: Wiley & Sarah C. Sullivan

SUMMERFIELD, JULIUS   WMA   Page 73   F   Abingdon
    5 May 1892   Parents: C. & M.L. Summerfield

SUSAN   SFA   Page 20
    14 July 1855   Mother: Cynthia
                                 Owner: John W. Price

SUSAN   SFA   Page 44
    15 October 1858   Master: David Stuart

SUSONG, AMANDA A   WFA   Page 14   F
    7 July 1854   Parents: Mahlen & Mary E. Susong

SUSONG, W.J.   WFA   Page 34   F
    20 January 1857   Parents: Walon & Mary E. Susong

SUTHERLAND, A.E.H.   WFA   Page 44   F
    20 August 1858   Parents: Jas. K. & Catherine Sutherland

SUTHERLAND, MARTHA A   WFA   Page 19   F
    30 March 1855   Parents: Jas. K. & Cath. C. Sutherland
    Reported by Martha Horne, grandmother

SUTHERLAND, SARAH E WFA Page 12 F
 31 Jan. 1854 Parents: James K. & Catharine C. Suther

SUTTON, JOHN WMA Page 51 F
 22 Nov. 1859 Parents: John F. & Mary E. Sutton

SUTTON, NANCY A WFA Page 31 F
 12 March 1856 Parents: John & Nancy Sutton

SWATTS, JANE WFA Page 67 F Kinderhook
 20 Jan. 1892 Parents: W.T. & Martha Swatts

SWEAT, WILLIAM K WMA Page 44 F
 5 April 1858 Father: T.P. Sweat
 Reported by F.P. SWEET, father Mother: Charity A. SWEET

SWEENY, CHARLES WMA Page 72 F Goodson
 1 Jan. 1892 Parents: Thos. & Jane SWEENEY

SWEET, MARY M.C. WFA Page 53 F Abingdon Twp.
 7 March 1871 Parents: Henry S. & Elizabeth Sweet

SWEET, THOS. E.A. WMA Page 23 F
 5 Oct. 1855 Parents: F.P. & C.A. Sweet

SWINK, ARCHA. B. WMA Page 72 F
 24 July 1892 Parents: Peter & Eliza Swink

SYKES, LUCY WFA Page 69 F North Fork Dist
 17 July 1892 Parents: Noah & Jane Sykes

SYPES, [n.n.] WMA Page 70 F Abingdon Dist.
 June 1892 Parents: David & Emeline Sypes

SYPHERS, [n.n.] WFA Page 54 F Northfork Twp.
 2 April 1871 Parents: John T. & Maty E. Syphers

SYRIA, MARY E WFA Page 29 F
 17 Oct. 1856 Parents: Thos. & Eliz'th Syria

TADLOCK, DAISY WFA Page 64 F
 9 May 1892 Parents: W.A. & Sarah Tadlock

TALLY, [n.n.] WFD Page 2 L
 7 Nov. 1853 Father: Evan Tally

TALLY, [n.n.] WMA Page 10 L
 Nov. 1854 Parents: Evan & Delila Tally
 Reported by And'w D. Grubb, neighbor

TALLY, [n.n.] WFD Page 34 PA
 23 Oct. 1857 Parents: C. & Nancy Tally
 Reported by Nancy TALLEY, mother

TALBERT, [n.n.] WFA Page 20 F
 13 May 1855 Parents: Thomas & Mariah Talbert

TALBERT, A.W. WFA Page 41 F
 18 Oct. 1858 Parents: T.J. & H.J. Talbert

TALBERT, AMANDA V WMA Page 68 F Kinderhook Dis
 6 Dec. 1892 Parents: Trigg & Amanda Talbert

TALBERT, CLARA
    5 July 1892

WFA   Page 64   F
Parents: David & Mary A. Talbert

TALBERT, JAMES
    5 July 1892

WMA   Page 68   F
Parents: John & Nancy Talbert

TALBERT, JAMES GRANDISON
    8 October 1853

WMA   Page 2   W   North Fork
Parents: David M. & Mahala Talbert

TALBERT, SAML
    9 April 1857

WMA   Page 37   F
Parents: B.S. & Mary Talbert

TALBERT, SARAH ANN
    13 April 1853

WFA   Page 2   L
Parents: Thomas & Maria Talbert

[TARY], JOHN
    29 December 1853

WMA   Page 3   B
Parents: Wm. S. & Sarah A. [TARY]

TATE, [n.n.]
    15 March 1855

WFA   Page 22   F
Parents: D.L. & Mariah Tate

TATE, A.G.
    14 May 1892

WMA   Page 70   F   North Fork Dist.
Parents: B.F. & Susan F. Tate

TATE, AMANDA E
    27 December 1892

WFA   Page 70   F   North Fork Dist.
Parents: A.W. & Nannie Tate

TATE, C.A.
    28 April 1892

WMA   Page 70   F   North Fork Dist.
Parents: John & Julia Tate

TATE, HUMPHREY
    25 July 1856
    Reported by Canada Tate, grandfather

WMA   Page 25   L
Parents: D.L. & Mariah Tate

TATE, JOS.
    5 June 1892

WMA   Page 68   F
Parents: Sam'l & Sally Tate

TATE, JULIA A
    12 Nov. or Dec. 1856
    Reported by Canada Tate, grandfather

WFA   Page 25   L
Parents: Drury & Ellen Tate

TATE, NANCY
    9 July 1855

WFA   Page 21   F
Parents: John C. & Nancy Tate

TATE, NEWTON T
    25 November 1859

WMA   Page 51   F
Parents: Drury & Ellen Tate

TATE, SARAH E
    1 December 1853

WFA   Page 7   F
Parents: Jas. & Patsy Tate

TAYLOR, [n.n.]
    11 November 1858

WFD   Page 45   F
Parents: Jonathan & Margaret Taylor

TAYLOR, BERTHA V
    6 August 1892

WFA   Page 64   F
Parents: Chas. A. & Ellen Taylor

TAYLOR, FRANCIS
    15 December 1859

WMA   Page 48   F
Parents: Andrew J. & Nancy Taylor

TAYLOR, JONATHAN
    15 July 1854

WMA   Page 13   F   North Fork
Parents: Andrew & Nancy Taylor

TAYLOR, LAVINIA
    29 August 1854

SFA   Page 15
Mistress: S.H. Teeter

TAYLOR, LEVI   WMA   Page 48   F
    10 November 1859   Parents: Henry & Mary Taylor

TAYLOR, MARGARET   WFA   Page 11   F
    3 April 1854   Parents: [Levi] & Amanda J. Taylor

TAYLOR, MARY   WFA   Page 2   L   North Fork
    27 August 1853   Parents: Jonathan & Mary Taylor

TAYLOR, THOMAS A   WM_   Page 58
    3 July 1870   Parents: Lafayette & Susannah Taylor

TEETER, SOPHIA A   WFA   Page 34   PH
    15 November 1857   Parents: E.C. & Frs. J. Teeter

TERRY, ANN M   WFA   Page 29   B
    10 August 1856   Parents: Wm. & Sarah A. Terry

TERRY, GEORGE A   WMA   Page 45   B
    20 December 1858   Parents: William & Sarah A. Terry

THARE, CATH H   WFA   Page 37   F
    13 February 1857   Parents: James & May Thare
    Reported by James THAYER, father

THAYER, ANDREW JACKSON (twin)   WMA   Page 17   F
    5 July 1855   Parents: James & Mary Ann Thayer

THAYER, LEONARD   WMA   Page 64   F
    19 February 1892   Parents: A.J. & Nannie Thayer

THAYER, THOMPSON McCONNELL (twin)   WMA   Page 17   F
    5 July 1855   Parents: James & Mary Ann Thayer

THAYER, VIRGIE L   WFA   Page 64   F
    17 March 1892   Parents: J.G. & Annie Thayer

THOMAS, [n.n.]   WMA   Page 13   F
    26 February 1854   Parents: Andrew J. & Charlotte Thomas

THOMAS, [n.n.]   WFAD   Page 19   F
    20 June 1855   Parents: Andrew & Mary Ann Thomas

THOMAS, [n.n.]   WMD   Page 34
    15 January 1857   Mother: Sarah Elizabeth Thomas
    Reported by Thos. SIRIAH, father

THOMAS   SMA   Page 34
    16 August 1857   Owner: Wm. B. Campbell

THOMAS   S_A   Page 37
    1 November 1857   Owner: A.R. Malicote

THOMAS, [n.n.]   WFA   Page 45   B
    4 June 1858   Parents: S.B. & M.J. Thomas

THOMAS, [n.n.]   WMA   Page 44   F
    10 December 1858   Parents: Isaac & [Tena] Thomas

THOMAS, AMANDA K   WFA   Page 10   B
    21 February 1854   Parents: Sam'l & Matilda Thomas

THOMAS, AMERICA FRELOVE   WFA   Page 16   L
    25 February 1855   Parents: James V. & Rachel Thomas

THOMAS, BENJ. P   WMA   Page 64   F
    29 May 1892   Parents: J.D. & Mary J. Thomas

THOMAS, CATHERINE   WFA   Page 26   MR
    20 April 1856   Parents: D.G. & S.J. Thomas

THOMAS, CATHERINE SOPHRONIA   WFA   Page 1   CP
    18 February 1853   Father: John Thomas

THOMAS, CLIFFORD   WMA   Page 64   F
    24 April 1892   Parents: J.W. & Rachel Thomas

THOMAS, DAVIS JESSE   WMA   Page 4
    9 October 1853   Mother: Nancy Thomas
    Reported by Henry Doss, 'said to be the father'

THOMAS, GEORGE   WMA   Page 64   F
    10 May 1892   Parents: R.E. & Mary Thomas

THOMAS, GEO. V   WMA   Page 64   F
    17 November 1892   Parents: J.M. & Amanda Thomas

THOMAS, GEO. W   WMA   Page 28   F
    29 June 1856   Parents: And. E. & Mary A. Thomas

THOMAS H   SMA   Page 23
    20 April 1855   Owner: Susannah Baker

THOMAS, H.B.   WMA   Page 68   F   Kinderhook Dist.
    5 August 1892   Parents: J.W. & Amanda Thomas

THOMAS, IRA   WMA   Page 9   F
    August 1854   Parents: Presley & Patsey Thomas

THOMAS, JAMES   WMA   Page 12   SH
    29 September 1854   Parents: Isaac & Catharine Thomas

THOMAS, JAMES B   WMA   Page 48   F
    13 June 1859   Parents: James & Sarah Thomas

THOMAS, JEMIMA   WFA   Page 37   F
    25 March 1857   Parents: Lewis & Nancy Thomas

THOMAS, JESSIE   CFA   Page 64   F
    20 December 1892   Parents: Geo. & Nancy Thomas

THOMAS, JOHN S   WMA   Page 54   F   Northfork Twp.
    28 February 1871   Parents: C.A. & Charlotte A. Thomas

THOMAS, JOHN S   WMA   Page 72   F   Goodson
    10 November 1892   Parents: Lewis J. & Jennie Thomas

THOMAS, JNO. W   WMA   Page 64   F
    6 April 1892   Parents: Jas. H. & Lav. Thomas

THOMAS, JOSEPH   WMA   Page 44   F
    27 October 1858   Parents: John & M.J. Thomas

THOMAS, LEVIA CAROLINE   WMA   Page 19   F
    24 May 1855   Parents: Stephen & Elizabeth Thomas

THOMAS, LEWIS (twin)   WMA   Page 64   F
    14 February 1892   Parents: J.W. & Minerva E. Thomas

THOMAS, LEWIS J   WMA   Page 5   F
    23 March 1853   Parents: Andw. & Mary Thomas

THOMAS, LILBURN P   WMA   Page 16   L
    10 May 1855   Parents: David & Mary Thomas

THOMAS, LUCY   WFA   Page 44   F
    14 February 1858   Parents: A.J. & Charlotte Thomas

THOMAS, MARGARET   WFA   Page 3   F
    April 1853   Father: Isaac Thomas

THOMAS, MARY (twin)   WFA   Page 64   F
    14 February 1892   Parents: J.W. & Minerva E. Thomas

THOMAS, MARY C   WFA   Page 17   L
    13 December 1855   Parents: David & Malinda Thomas

THOMAS, PAUL E   WMA   Page 64
    8 April 1892   Mother: Jane Thomas

THOMAS, RACHEL   WFA   Page 53   F   Abingdon Twp.
    14 April 1871   Parents: Mathew B. & Catharine Thomas

THOMAS, RACHEL M   WFA   Page 64   F
    1 March 1892   Parents: J.B. & Nancy E. Thomas

THOMAS, RO. C   WMA   Page 37   F
    8 July 1857   Parents: David & Mary A. Thomas

THOMAS, ROBERT   WMA   Page 10   F
    13 January 1854   Parents: David J. & Melinda Thomas

THOMAS, RODA VIRGINIA   WFA   Page 57   F   Glade Spring Tv
    1870   Parents: Henry & Emaline Thomas

THOMAS, S.V.C.   WMA   Page 45   F
    17 July 1858   Parents: Stephen & Elizabeth Thomas

THOMAS, SARAH C   WFA   Page 48   F
    15 May 1859   Parents: Presley & Martha Thomas

THOMAS, SARAH E   WFA   Page 37   F
    7 June 1857   Parents: David T. & Melinda Thomas

THOMAS, SARAH F   WFA   Page 44   F
    21 November 1858   Parents: William & Ann E. Thomas

THOMAS, SUSAN   WFA   Page 30
    15 February 1856   Mother: Sarah Thomas
    Reported by W.J. Bishop, neighbor

THOMAS, WM. J   WMA   Page 34   F
    10 December 1857   Parents: J.W. & R.A. Thomas

THOMAS, WM. JAMES   WMA   Page 18   F
    5 May 1855   Parents: Andrew J. & Catharine E. Thon

THOMBLESON, UNAS CAHARINE   WFA   Page 57   F   Glade Spring T
    1870   Parents: Wm. & Ann Thombleson

THOMELSON, WM. E   WMA   Page 37   F
    22 January 1857   Parents: Wm. & Ann TOMELSON

THOMPSON, [n.n.]   WFA   Page 1   F
    1 April 1853   Parents: James & Susan Thompson

THOMPSON, ADA L   WFA   Page 64   F
    11 May 1892   Parents: J.H. & Eva Thompson

THOMPSON, BEN   WMA   Page 70   North Fork Dist.
    18 January 1892   Parents: W.C. & Florence Thompson

THOMPSON, CHARLES   WMA   Page 48   F
    4 October 1859   Parents: James A. & Martha Thompson

THOMPSON, JOHN T   WMA   Page 49   F
    20 March 1859   Parents: James H. & Susanah Thompson

THOMPSON, MARY   WFA   Page 31   F
    1 December 1856   Parents: Frs. & Sarah J. Thompson

THOMPSON, MARY E   WFA   Page 48   F
    10 June 1859   Parents: William & Mary A. Thompson

THOMPSON, SARA C   WFA   Page 31   F
    24 or 28 October 1856   Parents: Jas. H. & Susan E. Thompson

THOMPSON, SARAH   WFA   Page 48   F
    15 October 1859   Parents: A.G. & Sarah Thompson

THOMPSON, WM. C   WMA   Page 54   F   Northfork Twp.
    27 October 1871   Parents: James H. & Susan E. Thompson

THORNTON (twin of Collin)   SMA   Page 15
    15 August 1854   Master: John Preston

THORNTON, SINAH   CFA   Page 73   L   Near Abingdon
    21 June 1892   Parents: Charles & Victoria Thornton

TILLSON, RICHARD   WMA   Page 34
    16 March 1857   Mother: Sarah Tillson

TILSON, ABBY   WFA   Page 48   F
    7 January 1859   Parents: Stephen J. & Elizabeth Tilson

TILSON, MARY E   WFA   Page 29   F
    5 December 1856   Parents: Stephen & Eliz'th Tilson

TILSON, MARY E   WFA   Page 64   F
    13 February 1892   Parents: Wm. T. & Mary F. Tilson

TILSON, NANCY CATHARINE   WFA   Page 5   F
    2 January 1853   Parents: David & Lucretia Tilson

TILSON, SUSAN   WFA   Page 19   F
    8 October 1855   Parents: David & Lucretia Tilson

TIPTON, A.D.   WMA   Page 6   F
    16 August 1853   Parents: Wm. R. & B. Tipton

TIPTON, DAVID   WMA   Page 26   F
    15 December 1856   Parents: Isaac & Lucinda Tipton

TIPTON, ISAAC H   WMA   Page 41   F
    9 December 1858   Parents: Isaac & Lucinda Tipton

TODD, AMANDA F   WFA   Page 51   F
    14 November 1859   Parents: Wm. & A.J. Todd

TODD, MARY J
    23 November 1855

WFA   Page 22   F
Parents: Wm. & Jane Todd

TODD, WM. J
    24 September 1853

WMA   Page 7   F
Parents: Wm. & Jane Todd

TOLAR, NEWTON
    8 March 1892

CMA   Page 73   Near Abingdon
Mother: Amelia Tolar

TOLBERT, ANN E
    15 September 1859

WFA   Page 48   F
Parents: David & Mehala Tolbert

TOLBERT, THOMAS T
    27 August 1859

WMA   Page 48   F
Parents: Russell S. & Mary Tolbert

TOM
    May 1853

SMA   Page 3
Owner: Mary Edmondson

TOM
    1 March 1855

SMA   Page 23
Owner: Wm. Fields

TOMLINSON, HATTIE
    12 September 1892

WFA   Page 64   MC
Parents: J.M. & Caro. Tomlinson

TOMLINSON, JAMES C
    21 March 1855

WMA   Page 19   F
Parents: Wm. & Ann Eliza Tomlinson

TOMLINSON, LEONIDAS LOVE
    7 October 1853

WMA   Page 4   F
Parents: Wm. & Sarah A. Tomlinson

TOMLINSON, SOPHIA
    15 March 1892

WFA   Page 64   MC
Parents: L.L. & Sarah F. Tomlinson

TOWNSEN, NANCY E
    14 January 1859

WFA   Page 51   F
Parents: Geo. T. & M.A. Townsen

TOWNSEND, JOHN R.M.
    8 May 1871

WMA   Page 54   F   Northfork Twp.
Parents: George F. & Mary Townsend

TOWNSEND, MAGGIE
    5 May 1892

WFA   Page 68   F
Parents: G.W. & Mary L. Townsend

TRAMELL, JNO. B
    12 June 1856
    Reported by Wm. TRAMEL,
      father

WMA   Page 24   L
Father: Wm. Tramell
Mother: Lucy W. TRAMEL

TRAMMELL, [n.n.]
    20 December 1858

WFA   Page 41   F
Parents: W.H. & Lucy Trammell

TRENT, D.H.
    24 August 1858

WMA   Page 44   F
Parents: Lewis & Isabella Trent

TRENT, GROVER C
    29 December 1892

WMA   Page 64   MC
Parents: Jas. J. & Callie Trent

TRENT, JAMES J
    15 September 1859

WMA   Page 48   F
Parents: Lewis & Isabella Trent

TRENT, NANCY JANE
    15 August 1855

WFA   Page 19   L
Parents: Kindrick & Sally Trent

TRENT, NOAH C.J.
    29 November 1856

WMA   Page 28   F
Parents: Lewis & Isabella J. Trent

TRIGG, ELIZA MITCHELL
    13 February 1853
WFA   Page 2   F
Parents: Jas. E.C. & Rachel Trigg

TRIGG, JOSEPHINE C
    27 April 1854
WFA   Page 15   LW
Parents: Connally F. & Mary C. Trigg

TRIGG, MARY
    8 November 1892
CFA   Page 64   L
Parents: Floyd & Sallie Trigg

TRIGG, PETER BRANCH
    11 July 1855
WMA   Page 17   F
Parents: Joseph E.C. & Rachel Trigg

TRIVITT, JOHN F
    4 June 1855
WMA   Page 20   BR
Parents: Thompson & Mary Trivitt

TROXIL, ELIZA A
    3 October 1856
WFA   Page 29   F
Father: Geo. W. Troxil
Mother: Eliz'th TROXILL

TROXWELL, MARTHA V.O.
    27 March 1859
WFA   Page 48   F
Parents: George W. & Isabella Troxwell

TUCKER, MARY
    18 October 1871
WFA   Page 53   F   Abingdon Twp.
Parents: John L. & Martha Tucker

TUCKER, RAY (twin)
    20 December 1892
WMA   Page 68   F   Kinderhook Dist.
Parents: Thomas & Amanda Tucker

TUCKER, ROBERT (twin)
    20 December 1892
WMA   Page 68   F   Kinderhook Dist.
Parents: Thomas & Amanda Tucker

TUCKER, WORTH
    1870
WMA   Page 57   F
Parents: Moses & Mary J. Tucker
    Born in Ash Co., N.C.; father's residence in Glade Spring Twp.

TURLEY, EMORY G
    22 August 1892
WMA   Page 64   F
Parents: R.T. & Mary Turley

TURNER, ELIZA
    November 1854
SFA   Page 13   Brook Hall
Mother: Delsey Turner
Master: Col. Wm. Byars

TURNER, JOSEPH T
    2 September 1870
WM_   Page 58   F
Parents: Joseph & Eliza J. Turner

TURNER, MARY A
    30 June 1892
WFA   Page 64   F
Parents: G.A. & Mis. C. Turner

TURNER, MINNIE
    28 June 1892
CFA   Page 64   F
Parents: Shep & Emme Turner

TUSLER, JAMES A
    10 May 1892
WFA   Page 70   F   Abingdon
Parents: Thomas & Eva Tusler

VAIL, SUSAN
    31 May 1892
WFA   Page 64   MC
Parents: J.H. & M.M. Vail

VANCE, DECK
    10 June 1892
WMA   Page 68   F
Parents: P.F. & Martha Vance

VANCE, HARRIET
    20 August 1853
WFA   Page 1   F
Parents: John A. & Angeline Vance

VANCE, JAMES A   WMA   Page 34   F
    3 January 1857   Parents: Jno. A. & E. Vance

VANCE, JOHN M   WMA   Page 51   F
    15 January 1859   Parents: James & Mary Vance

VANCE, MARY L   WFA   Page 20   F
    2 February 1855   Parents: John A. & Emeline E. Vance

VANCE, NANCY (twin)   WFA   Page 27   F
    13 January 1856   Parents: Patten & Cath Vance

VANCE, NANCY D   WFA   Page 31   F
    23 October 1856   Parents: James & Mary D. Vance

VANCE, PETER (twin)   WMA   Page 27   F
    13 January 1856   Parents: Patten & Cath Vance

VANCE, VIRGINIA   WFA   Page 37   F
    1 June 1857   Parents: James A. & Mary Vance

VANHOOK, W.C.   WMA   Page 68   F
    5 November 1892   Parents: H.J. & Sarah Vanhook

VANHOSS, DANL. H   WMA   Page 45   F
    18 May 1858   Parents: Valentine & Julia A. Vanhoss

VANHOSS, MARY   WFA   Page 45   F
    24 July 1858   Parents: Anthony & Dorcas Vanhoss

VANHUSS, BENJAMIN   WMA   Page 49   F
    23 October 1859   Parents: Valentine & Julia Vanhuss

VANHUSS, CATHARINE ANN   WFA   Page 19   F
    7 November 1855   Parents: Anthony & Dorcas Vanhuss

VANHUSS, JACOB   WMA   Page 5   F
    23 April 1853   Father: Anthony Vanhuss

VANHUSS, MARY   WFA   Page 57   F   Glade Spring Tw
    1870   Parents: John M. & Sallie Vanhuss

VANNOY, FRANK   CMA   Page 65
    11 November 1892   Mother: Hannah Vannoy

VAUGHAN, ELLEN   WFA   Page 64   BO
    8 December 1892   Father: Chas. C. Vaughan
                                  Mother: Lorena VAUGHN

VAWTER, CLAY V   WMA   Page 57   PF   Glade Spring Tw
    1870   Parents: Charles E. & Virginia L. Vawte

VENABLE, JOSEPH.   WFA   Page 64   F
    12 March 1892   Parents: Geo. W. & Kate Venable

VENABLE, MARY E.L.   WFA   Page 30   F
    15 September 1856   Parents: Thos. & Jane Venable

VESS, ISAAC   WMA   Page 51   F
    15 June 1859   Parents: Jacob & Mary R. Vess

VEST, JOHN   WMA   Page 68   F
    10 June 1892   Parents: B.W. & Delia Vest

VESTAL, [n.n.]   WMA   Page 12   PR
      18 September 1854   Parents: Jesse & Elizabeth J. Vestal

VESTAL, [n.n.]   WMA   Page 53   F   Abingdon Twp.
      1 December 1871   Parents: Jessee & Elizabeth Vestal

VESTAL, ADEN   WMA   Page 53   F   Abingdon Twp.
      15 May 1871   Parents: Bartholomew & Nancy Vestal

VESTAL, GEO. B   WMA   Page 37   F
      8 June 1857   Parents: Jessee & E.J. Vestal

VESTAL, HENRY B   WMA   Page 64   F
      28 October 1892   Parents: Alex & Callie Vestal

VESTAL, JAS F   WMA   Page 28   F
      7 July 1856   Parents: Jessee & Eliz. J. Vestal

VESTAL, JOHN M   WMA   Page 18   F
      17 December 1855   Parents: Simon S. & Rebecca Vestal

VESTAL, MARY A.N.   WFA   Page 28   F
      2 June 1856   Parents: Bartholamew & Nancy Vestal

VESTAL, SAMUEL L   WMA   Page 45   F
      6 August 1858   Parents: Simon S. & Rebecca Vestal

VESTILL, [n.n.]   WMD   Page 3   PR
      September 1853   Parents: Thos. & Grace Vestill

VESTILL, CATHERINE   WFA   Page 3   PR
      27 December 1853   Father: Simon S. Vestill

VINCENT, MARY   WFA   Page 64   F
      13 October 1892   Parents: James & Sarah Vincent

VINEY   SFA   Page 4
      1 November 1853   Mother: Letha
      Reported by Martha Beatie, wife of owner

VIRGINIA   SFA   Page 20
      July 1855   Mother: Hannah
                                   Owner: Ellen White

WALDEN, MARY   WFA   Page 65   F
      18 January 1892   Parents: L.J. & Marg. Walden

WALKER, HENRY see EDMONDSON, HENRY WALKER

WARD, JAMES N   WMA   Page 49   F
      11 March 1859   Parents: Ota. H., Jr., & Sarah Ward

WARD, JOSEPH F   WFA   Page 54   F   Northfork Twp.
      1 December 1871   Parents: Ota H. & Martha L. Ward

WARD, WM. R.M.   WMA   Page 31   F
      28 December 1856   Parents: Ota H. & Sarah E. Ward

WARDEN, THEODOSIA   WFA   Page 3   B
      13 June 1853   Parents: John J. & Martha Warden

WARREN, BESS M   WFA   Page 65   F
      7 July 1892   Parents: J.H. & Martha Warren

WARREN, EWEL
21 April 1892
WMA Page 70 F North Fork Dist.
Parents: W.H. & Mary Warren

WARREN, MARTHA
15 September 1859
WFA Page 52 F
Parents: William & Taressa Warren

WARREN, MARY J
16 April 1892
WFA Page 70 F
Parents: J.D. & Melvina Warren

WARRICK
1 June 1858
SMA Page 40
Owner: L.C. Newland

WARSHAM, ALAMAN C
17 December 1853
WFA Page 1 F
Parents: William & Rebecca Warsham

WARSHAM, JOHN R.W.
27 April 1855
WMA Page 20 F
Parents: Wm. F. & Rebecca Warsham

WARSHAM, JONAS M
26 August 1854
WMA Page 10 F
Parents: Robert & Elizabeth Warsham

WASHAM, L.D.
24 March 1857
WMA Page 38 F
Parents: Wm. F. & Rebecca Washam

WASHAM, MARY S.L.E.
6 May 1857
WFA Page 38 F
Parents: Robt. R. & E. Washam

WASHINGTON
1 September 1856
SMA Page 30
Owner: Wm. Byars

WATERMAN, DAVID W.C.
26 January 1855
WMA Page 21 F
Parents: Wm. W. & M.F. Waterman

WATSON, [n.n.]
11 January 1855
WMFA Page 20 F
Parents: Robert & Jane Watson

WATSON, [n.n.]
15 December 1858
WMA Page 41 F
Parents: Henry & Jane Watson

WATSON, DAVID
10 May 1857
WMA Page 34 F
Parents: Robt. & Jane Watson

WATSON, DAVID C
14 December 1892
WMA Page 72 F Goodson
Parents: James & Mattie Watson

WATSON, JAS.
15 January 1853
WMA Page 7 F
Parents: Rob't & Jane Watson

WATSON, JAS. A.B.
11 September 1856
WMA Page 31 F
Parents: Henry & Mary J. Watson

WATSON, MARGARET ELIZ.
6 May 1853
WFA Page 3 F
Parents: Henry & Eliza Watson

WATSON, MARTIN
15 October 1892
WMA Page 68 F
Parents: Wm. & Harriet Watson

WATSON, MEREDITH
11 June 1892
WMA Page 73 EN Abingdon
Parents: J.C. & Maud Watson

WATSON, NANCY
6 May 1854
WFA Page 10 F
Parents: Henry & Mary Jane Watson

WATSON, REBECCA
13 January 1855
WFA Page 23 F
Parents: Rob't & Jane Watson

WATSON, ROB'T C
    5 October 1853
    WMA   Page 7   F
    Parents: Jubal & Rebecca Watson

WEATHERLEY, JOHN A
    September 1854
    WMA   Page 12   L
    Parents: Hosea M. & Ann WEATHERLY

WEATHERLEY, MARTHA A
    20 September 1853
    WFA   Page 14   F
    Parents: Preston & Martha Weatherley

WEATHERLY, ISAAC L
    5 October 1856
    WMA   Page 25   F
    Parents: Preston & Ann Weatherly

WEATHERLY, JULIA A.R.
    15 April 1857
    WFA   Page 37   F
    Parents: H.M. & Ann Weatherly

WEATHERLY, NANCY C
    23 December 1858
    WFA   Page 41   F
    Parents: Press. & Ann Weatherly

WEATHERS, E.C.T.
    March 1854
    WMA   Page 14   F
    Parents: M.W. & Mary A. Weathers

WEATHERS, M.A.E.
    19 April 1859
    WFA   Page 52   F
    Parents: M.W. & Mary A. Weathers

WEATHERS, SAML. P
    23 September 1856
    WMA   Page 25   F
    Parents: M.W. & Mary A. Weathers

WEBB, [n.n.]
    10 January 1870
    WMA   Page 55   F   Saltville Twp.
    Parents: William & Priscilla Webb

WEBB, BERTHA
    16 September 1892
    WFA   Page 65   F
    Parents: F.N. & Susan Webb

WEBB, C.E.
    30 October 1892
    WMA   Page 70   F   North Fork Dist.
    Parents: C.G. & Laura Webb

WEBB, MILTON K
    30 April 1855
    WMA   Page 20   SE
    Parents: Chas. W. & Louisa Webb

WEBB, NANCY
    17 June 1870
    WFA   Page 55   F   Saltville Twp.
    Parents: John A. & Mary Webb

WEBB, SARAH
    13 December 1870
    WFA   Page 55   F   Saltville Twp.
    Parents: Newton & Julina Webb

WEBSTER, MARY C
    25 March 1892
    CFA   Page 65   F
    Parents: Thomas & Nancy Webster

WEEKS, JOHN
    5 May 1854
    SMA   Page 15
    Master: A.F. Bradley

WEEKS, MARY E
    25 February 1856
    WFA   Page 26   F
    Parents: Jno. & Sarah J. Weeks

WEEKS, SARAH J
    1 August 1859
    WFA   Page 52   F
    Parents: John & Sarah J. Weeks

WELLS, SAVANNAH
    1 August 1892
    Born in Johnson City, Tn.
    WFA   Page 65   F
    Parents: Jno. W. & Jelia Wells

WEST, DAIRY
    8 August 1892
    Reported by E.W. West
    WFA   Page 68
    Mother: Nancy West

WEST, VIRGINIA   WF_   Page 58
    21 December 1870   Parents: Jno. & Sarah West

WETHERLY, NEWMAN   WMA   Page 68   F
    10 April 1892   Parents: John & Sarah Wetherly

WETZELL, BENJ. F   WMA   Page 24   L
    12 September 1856   Father: Jefferson Wetzell
                                        Mother: Cath WETZEL

WETZELL, DAVID L.C.   WMA   Page 14   F
    21 June 1854   Parents: Jefferson & Catharine Wetzell

WETZELL, GEO. W   WMA   Page 34   F
    9 October 1857   Parents: Jeff & Cath Wetzell

WHEATLEY, JOHN   WMA   Page 34   F
    14 September 1857   Parents: Wm. & L. Wheatley

WHEATLY, M.J. (twin)   WMFA   Page 41   F
    12 October 1858   Parents: W. & Lou Wheatly

WHEATLY, W.J. (twin)   WMFA   Page 41   F
    12 October 1858   Parents: W. & Lou Wheatly

WHEELER, ALPHONSO   WMA   Page 65   F
    8 August 1892   Parents: Ward & Eliz. Wheeler

WHEELER, HARRIET A   WFA   Page 15   L
    1 February 1854   Parents: B.F. & Susannah Wheeler

WHICKER, EDWIN C   WMA   Page 24   F
    20 February 1856   Parents: Sam'l & Mary Whicker
    Reported by Sam'l WHISKER, father

WHICKER, EMMA V   WFA   Page 72   F   Goodson
    25 August 1892   Parents: Josiah & Marg. L. Whicker

WHICKER, MALVINA A   WF_   Page 58
    7 May 1870   Parents: Benj. & Martha Whicker

WHICKER, MARY I   WF_   Page 58
    November 1870   Parents: George & Lucy Whicker

WHICKER, SAML.   WMA   Page 42   F
    4 October 1858   Parents: Saml. & Elizabeth Whicker

WHICKER, SARAH A   WFA   Page 54   F   North Fork Twp
    19 April 1871   Parents: Thomas P. & Mary Whicker

WHICKER, W.E.   WMA   Page 24   F
    1 December 1856   Parents: Neuell & Malinda Whicker

WHITAKER, ABEL W   WMA   Page 25   F
    20 April 1856   Parents: Calvin & Phebe Whitaker

WHITAKER, CAROLINE V   WFA   Page 20   F
    2 October 1855   Parents: Rufus & Elizabeth Whitaker
    Reported by Moses Whitaker, grandfather

WHITAKER, LOUISA   WFA   Page 34   F
    16 September 1857   Parents: D.A. & Caroline Whitaker
    Reported by M. Davidson, grandfather

WHITAKER, S.E.   WFA   Page 6   F
    16 September 1853   Parents: Calvin & Phebe Whitaker

WHITE, [n.n.]   WM_   Page 58
    12 September 1870   Parents: R.H. & Elizabeth White

WHITE, A.B.   WMA   Page 7   F
    17 May 1853   Parents: Jno. M. & Hannah White

WHITE, ALSEY   WFA   Page 45   F
    17 October 1858   Parents: Joseph & Sarah J. White

WHITE, DAVID M   WMA   Page 26   F
    14 March 1856   Parents: Jno. M. & Hannah White

WHITE, FRANK C   WMA   Page 25   L
    8 April 1856   Parents: Spencer & E.J. White

WHITE, FREEMAN   WMA   Page 52   F
    3 April 1859   Parents: John & Eliza A. White

WHITE, J.N.   WMA   Page 68   F
    6 April 1892   Parents: Fred & Mary White

WHITE, JNO. N   WMA   Page 65   F
    6 March 1892   Parents: W.D. & Mag. A. White

WHITE, JOS. F   WMA   Page 34   F
    24 November 1857   Parents: Henry C. & Mary White

WHITE, JULIA A   WFA   Page 51   F
    8 September 1859   Parents: Spencer & Elizabeth White

WHITE, JULIA F   WFA   Page 70   F   North Fork Dist.
    15 February 1892   Parents: R.E. & Mary White

WHITE, LEANDER J   WMA   Page 41   F
    11 December 1858   Parents: Geo. W. & J.A.C. White

WHITE, MARVEL   WMA   Page 23   F
    2 April 1855   Parents: P.H. & M. White

WHITE, MARY   WFA   Page 70   F   North Fork Dist.
    22 October 1892   Parents: Robert & Mary White

WHITE, MARY C   WFA   Page 38   F
    11 May 1857   Parents: Patrick & E. White

WHITE, NATHANIEL   WMA   Page 68   F
    9 August 1892   Parents: N.P.H. & Delia White

WHITE, NEWTON   WMA   Page 21   F
    6 November 1855   Parents: Joseph & Mary E. White

WHITE, NEWTON   WMA   Page 54   F   Northfork Twp.
    1 April 1871   Parents: Washington & Sarah A. White

WHITE, PAULINIA   WFA   Page 54   PH   Abingdon Twp.
    23 September 1871   Parents: William & Elizabeth White

WHITE, RYBURN   WMA   Page 1   L
    18 October 1853   Father: James White

WHITE, THOMAS   WMA   Page 45   F
    17 May 1858   Parents: Patrick & Isabella White

WHITE, THURSY
    29 November 1857
WFA   Page 34   F
Parents: Spencer & E.J. White

WHITEAKER, JAS. M
    17 October 1859
WMA   Page 49   F
Parents: Rufus & Elizabeth Whiteaker

WHITT, CALONIA
    14 February 1870
WFA   Page 55   F   Saltville Twp.
Parents: Full. & Sintha Whitt

WIDENER, [n.n.]
    July 1854
    Reported by Henry Mock, neighbor
WFD   Page 12   L
Parents: James & Martha Widener

WIDENER, [n.n.]
    August 1854
WMD   Page 12   F
Parents: Sam'l B. & M. Widener

WIDENER, [n.n.]
    14 October 1892
WFD   Page 65   F
Parents: Jas. J.A. & Maggie Widener

WIDENER, AMANDA
    21 April 1854
WFA   Page 13   F   Widener Valley
Parents: Elias & Mary Widener

WIDENER, AND. B
    17 May 1857
WMA   Page 38   F
Parents: Lilburn & Mary Widener

WIDENER, AND. BUCHANAN
    25 May 1853
WMA   Page 5   F
Parents: Philip & Winny Widener

WIDENER, AND. W
    20 July 1857
WMA   Page 38   F
Parents: J.R. & Ann Widener

WIDENER, ANDREW
    4 November 1853
WMA   Page 5   F
Parents: Jacob & Wato. Widener

WIDENER, ANDW.
    15 December 1853
WMA   Page 5   F
Parents: Jacob & Ann Widener

WIDENER, BERTHA C
    20 September 1892
WFA   Page 65   F
Parents: Jas. P. & Martha Widener

WIDENER, BESS H
    8 March 1892
WFA   Page 65   F
Parents: Michael & Sallie Widener

WIDENER, BESS J
    30 November 1892
WFA   Page 65   F
Parents: Emanuel & Martha Widener

WIDENER, BETTIE CORDELIA
    1870
WFA   Page 57   F   Glade Spring T
Parents: William & Ellen Widener

WIDENER, CHARLES P
    1870
WMA   Page 57   MC   Glade Spring T
Parents: James J. & Rachel Widener

WIDENER, CORDELIA
    20 May 1892
WFA   Page 65   F
Parents: John & Missouri Widener

WIDENER, DAVID C
    4 March 1855
WMA   Page 17   F
Parents: Nelson & Rachel Widener

WIDENER, ELIZA
    25 November 1855
WFA   Page 19   F
Parents: Joel & Catharine Widener

WIDENER, ELIZA
    30 December 1892
WFA   Page 65   F
Parents: Fayett & Ann Widener

WIDENER, EMALINE
 4 November 1857
WFA Page 37 F
Parents: Nelson & Rachel Widener

WIDENER, EMANUEL
 30 March 1856
WMA Page 28 F
Parents: Elias & Mary Widener

WIDENER, EMANUEL W
 15 October 1856
WMA Page 28 F
Parents: F.H. & Eliza A. Widener

WIDENER, EMELINE
 31 September 1855
WFA Page 19 F
Parents: Philip & Winney Widener

WIDENER, FREELOVE
 1 March 1856
WFA Page 28 F
Parents: Elijah & Mary A. Widener

WIDENER, GROVER C
 18 January 1892
WMA Page 65 MC
Parents: Wm. D. & Eliz. J.S. Widener

WIDENER, GUY
 3 March 1892
WMA Page 65 F
Parents: J.A. & Fannie Widener

WIDENER, ISAAC A
 20 December 1892
WMA Page 65 F
Parents: Elijah & Minerva Widener

WIDENER, JAMES
 4 April 1859
WMA Page 49 F
Parents: John & Margaret Widener

WIDENER, JAMES A
 March 1854
WMA Page 12 F
Parents: [Fairman] & Eliza Widener

WIDENER, JAS. C
 22 January 1857
WMA Page 37 F
Parents: Calvin & Rebecca Widener

WIDENER, JAS. S
 15 November 1856
WMA Page 28 F
Parents: Danl. & Nancy Widener

WIDENER, JOHN
 15 June 1859
WMA Page 49 F
Parents: Elias & Mary Widener

WIDENER, JOHN FRANKLIN
 26 July 1853
WMA Page 5 F
Parents: Elijah & Mary Widener

WIDENER, JOSEPH
 20 December 1857
WMA Page 37 F
Parents: Jacob & Susan Widener

WIDENER, JOSIAH FRANKLIN
 January 1855
WMA Page 19 B
Parents: Elijah & Elizabeth Widener

WIDENER, LACY P
 14 November 1892
WMA Page 65 F
Parents: Joel & Marg. Widener

WIDENER, LUCY
 17 October 1853
WFA Page 3 F
Parents: John J. & Frances Widener

WIDENER, MARTHA I.B.E.
 11 January 1859
WFA Page 49 F
Parents: John & Nancy Widener

WIDENER, MARY
 16 January 1853
WFA Page 5 F
Parents: Jock & Catharine Widener

WIDENER, MARY J
 11 March 1858
WFA Page 45 F
Parents: W.S. & E.A. Widener

WIDENER, MENEROY
 9 May 1859
WFA Page 49 F
Parents: Philip & Winney Widener

WIDENER, NEWTON FITZHUGH 1870	WMA Page 57 MC Glade Spring Tw Parents: Wm. M. & Mary V.C. Widener
WIDENER, ORA MAY 18 June 1892	WFA Page 65 F Parents: J. & Nancy M. Widener
WIDENER, OSCAR 10 June 1892	WMA Page 65 F Parents: D.C. & Rachel Widener
WIDENER, PELEG J 30 July 1856	WMA Page 29 F Parents: Jno. A. & Nancy I. Widener
WIDENER, PRUDY 10 November 1858	WFA Page 45 Parents: Daniel & Nancy Widener
WIDENER, RACHEL 26 February 1859	WFA Page 49 Mother: Martha Widener
WIDENER, RACHEL E 18 April 1859	WFA Page 49 F Parents: Elijah & Elizabeth Widener
WIDENER, SARAH June 1854	WFA Page 11 F Parents: Palser & Catharine Widener
WIDENER, SARAH 14 September 1855	WFA Page 19 F Parents: Sam'l B. & Unice Widener
WIDENER, SARAH C 22 May 1856	WFA Page 28 F Parents: Elijah & Eliza. Widener
WIDENER, [SILLER] 1 May 1858	WFA Page 45 F Parents: Elijah & Mary A. Widener
WIDENER, SUSAN 25 April 1856	WFA Page 28 F Parents: Jas. & Eliza Widener
WIDENER, WALT J 20 July 1892	WMA Page 65 F Parents: J.W. & Nancy C. Widener
WIDENER, WILLIAM 8 December 1859	WMA Page 49 F Parents: William & Eliza Ann Widener
WIDENER, WILLIAM LANE 17 March 1854	WMA Page 13 F Widener Valley Parents: Jonas & Elizabeth Widener
WIDNER, ANDREW 1870	WMA Page 57 F Glade Spring T Parents: Felix & Mary WIDENER
WIDNER, ELBERT 1870	WMA Page 57 Glade Spring T Mother: Elizabeth Widner
WIDSON 20 March 1857	SMA Page 34 Owner: F.P. Clapp
WILDS, MARY D 14 March 1855	WFA Page 21 MR Parents: Henry A. & Jane G. Wilds
WILDS, SARAH D 4 March 1857	WFA Page 34 F Parents: Henry A. & Jane G. Wilds
WILEY 20 December 1857	SMA Page 38 Owner: Arthur Orr
WILEY, [n.n.] 31 October 1854	WMA Page 10 PF E&H College Parents: Ephraim & Elizabeth Wiley

WILEY, MARY E   WFA   Page 38   F
16 May 1857   Parents: Wm. E. & Mary F. Wiley

WILLIAM   SMA   Page 4
August 1853   Owner: Geo. V. Litchfield

WILLIAM   SMA   Page 23
24 September 1855   Owner: Rachel Fickle

WM.   SMA   Page 27
15 December 1856   Owner: Henry Preston

WILLIAM   SMA   Page 38
5 May 1857   Owner: A.R. Malicote

WILLIAM   SMA   Page 38
4 January 1858   Owner: Mary Bondurant

WILLIAM   SMA   Page 50
12 February 1859   Owner: R.J. Legard

WILLIAM   SMA   Page 51
15 August 1859   Owner: Wm. A. Preston

WM. C   SMA   Page 8
6 December 1853   Owner: Alex'r Susong

WM. F   SMA   Page 15
6 November 1854   Master: Wm. B. Campbell

WILLIAMS, LOUISA   WFA   Page 22   F
23 February 1855   Parents: And'w & Martha Williams

WILLIAMS, NANCY M   WFA   Page 17   F
14 March 1854   Parents: Amos & Rhoda Williams

WILLIAMS, ROBT. H   WMA   Page 65   F
3 December 1892   Parents: R.E. & Mary Williams

WILLIAMS, SARAH A   WFA   Page 52   F
3 April 1859   Parents: C.G. & Elizabeth Williams

WILLIS, B.H.   WMA   Page 41   F
20 November 1858   Parents: H.D. & Elizabeth Willis

WILLOUGHBY, [n.n.]   WMA   Page 21   F
30 March 1855   Parents: And. J. & Matilda C. Willoughby
Reported by A.C. Maxwell, physician

WILLOUGHBY, CAROLINE   WFA   Page 41   F
15 October 1858   Parents: W. & Mary Willoughby

WILLOUGHBY, MARY R   WFA   Page 41   F
20 July 1858   Parents: A.J. & M.C. Willoughby

WILSON, [n.n.]   WFA   Page 23   F
15 May 1855   Parents: Nat & Elizabeth Wilson

WILSON, [n.n.]   WFA   Page 45   F
12 January 1858   Parents: John M. & Mary Wilson

WILSON, AMELIA C   WFA   Page 42   F
27 February 1858   Parents: Abel & Lucinda Wilson

WILSON, ANDREW
    25 May 1854
WMA   Page 9   SH
Parents: John B. & Mary Wilson

WILSON, CARIE
    1 March 1892
WFA   Page 72   F   Goodson
Parents: Wm. & Florrence Wilson

WILSON, DAVID
    1 April 1853
WMA   Page 5   F
Parents: John M. & Mary Wilson

WILSON, DAVID JEFFERSON
    1870
WMA   Page 57   F   Glade Spring
Parents: David R. & Nancy Wilson

WILSON, ELLEN D
    29 September 1856
WFA   Page 24   MR
Parents: A.T. & Mary Wilson

WILSON, GEORGE
    31 October 1858
WMA   Page 41   F
Parents: Jas. P. & Nancy Wilson

WILSON, ISAAC F
    24 May 1856
WMA   Page 26   F
Parents: N.D. & Eliz. Wilson

WILSON, ISAAC L
    2 July 1854
WMA   Page 12   F
Parents: John M. & Mary E. Wilson

WILSON, JOHN
    October 1853
    Reported by Jacob Widener
WMA   Page 6
Mother: Mary Wilson

WILSON, JNO. F
    17 March 1858
WMA   Page 42   F
Parents: A.H. & Lucinda Wilson

WILSON, KITTIE B
    10 October 1892
CFA   Page 74   F   Goodson
Parents: Jim & Rose Wilson

WILSON, MARGRET J
    15 October 1856
WFA   Page 28   F
Parents: Jno. M. & Mary E. Wilson

WILSON, MARY J
    1 February 1857
WFA   Page 37   F
Parents: Jno. M. & Mary E. Wilson

WILSON, MARY V
    10 October 1858
WFA   Page 41   F
Parents: N.D. & Eliza Wilson

WILSON, NANCY
    6 October 1892
WFA   Page 68   F
Parents: C.A.L. & Abbey Wilson

WILSON, NANCY J
    29 March 1859
WFA   Page 49   F
Parents: Hesikiah & Jane Wilson

WILSON, RICE A
    17 February 1892
WMA   Page 65   F
Parents: C.C. & N.J. Wilson

WILSON, WILLIAM A
    1 September 1854
WMA   Page 12   F
Parents: James & Nancy Wilson

WINTON
    14 July 1856
SMA   Page 27
Owner: Susan Baker

WISE, AMANDA
    27 January 1892
WFA   Page 65   F
Parents: Isaac & Macedonia Wise

WISE, ALEX.
    15 March 1892
WMA   Page 65   F
Parents: J.W. & Eliza J. Wise

WISE, GEO. C
    9 July 1892
WMA   Page 65   F
Parents: Chas. C. & Mary J. Wise

WISE, MARY I.S.
    10 November 1856
WFA   Page 30   F
Parents: William & Susan Wise

WISELY, EMILY M
    27 February 1855
WFA   Page 17   F
Parents: William S. & Nancy Wisely

WITHERSPOON, [n.n.]
    21 February 1892
WMA   Page 70   F   North Fork Dist.
Parents: S.J. & Laura Witherspoon

WIZE, MAZELLA
    9 February 1892
WFA   Page 65   F
Parents: G.W. & M.E. Wise

WOHLFORD, HARRIET S
    4 April 1854
WFA   Page 15   S
Parents: George & Jane Wolhford

WOLF, JOSEPH T
    7 December 1859
WMA   Page 49   F
Parents: Peter & Mary Wolf

WOLFE, EZRA
    10 May 1892
WMA   Page 65   F
Parents: Wm. F. & Jennie Wolfe

WOLFE, LEE
    8 August 1892
WMA   Page 65   F
Parents: S.L. & Ellen W. Wolfe

WOOD, DORA LEE
    April 1870
WF_   Page 58
Parents: Dempsey & Margaret Wood

WOOD, JAMES J
    2 December 1856
WFA   Page 25   F
Parents: Dempsey & Margret Wood

WOOD, MARY J
    11 September 1854
WFA   Page 14   F
Parents: Dempsey & Margaret Wood

WOODS, [n.n.]
    1853
W_D   Page 7   F
Father: Demssey Woods

WOODS, CHARLES
    10 January 1892
WMA   Page 68   F
Parents: Craig & A.G. Woods

WOODS, S.M.
    5 April 1858
WMA   Page 41   F
Parents: J.M. & Mary A. Woods

WOODS, W.A.
    11 October 1892
WMA   Page 68   F
Parents: W.B. & Nannie Woods

WOODSON, POLINIA
    1 May 1871
CFA   Page 53   F   Abingdon Twp.
Parents: James & Mary Woodson

WOODWARD, IRBY
    7 June 1892
WMA   Page 65   F
Parents: J.W. & Mol. J. Woodward

WOODWARD, JAMES MONROE
    9 October 1853
WMA   Page 2   L
Parents: Jacob & Rachel Woodward

WOODWARD, NANCY
    21 June 1855
WFA   Page 20   L
Parents: Jacob & Lavinia Woodward

WOODWARD, RACHEL B
    10 May 1858
WFA   Page 45   F
Parents: Bartholomew & Isabella Woodward

WOODWARD, SALLIE
    20 December 1892
WFA   Page 65   F
Parents: Jno. H. & Sallie Woodward

WOOLF, MARGRET E
    1 January 1857
    WFA   Page 38   F
    Parents: Peter & Rachel WOOLFE

WOOTEN, EM
    21 April 1859
    WFA   Page 49   F
    Parents: James T. & Charity Wooten

WOOTEN, FRANCES CATHARINE
    21 March 1855
    WFA   Page 18   PR
    Parents: James J. & Charity Wooten

WOOTEN, H.M.
    5 January 1892
    WMA   Page 68   MC
    Parents: J.T. & Hettie Wooten

WOOTON, MARY R
    22 December 1871
    WFA   Page 53   F   Abingdon Twp.
    Parents: John W. & Ellen Wooton

WORLEY, BERTHA
    5 December 1892
    WFA   Page 68   F
    Parents: William & Martha Worley

WORLEY, CHARLES
    27 February 1858
    WFA   Page 42   F
    Parents: G.L. & Amanda Worley

WORLEY, GEO.
    24 February 1892
    WMA   Page 73   KL   Abingdon
    Parents: Wm. & Marg. Worley

WORLEY, ISAAC ROB'T
    27 November 1854
    WMA   Page 13   F   North Fork
    Parents: David & Elizabeth C. Worley

WORLEY, JAMES
    10 January 1892
    WMA   Page 68   F
    Parents: Wm. & Mary Worley

WORLEY, JOHN
    10 February 1892
    WMA   Page 68   F
    Parents: Charles & Eliza Worley

WORLEY, MAHALA E
    27 August 1858
    WFA   Page 45   F
    Parents: David & Elizabeth Worley

WORLEY, MARTHA W
    20 April 1855
    WFA   Page 22   F
    Parents: Jno. W. & Elizabeth Worley

WORLEY, MARY V
    14 November 1856
    WFA   Page 30   F
    Parents: David & Eliz'th C. Worley

WORLEY, NANCY B
    27 January 1855
    WFA   Page 22   F
    Parents: Geo. L. & Amanda Worley

WORLEY, NAT R
    9 April 1858
    WMA   Page 41   F
    Parents: J.W. & E.D. Worley

WORLEY, PETER EARL
    11 March 1853
    WMA   Page 2   L   North Fork
    Parents: David & Elizabeth Worley

WORLEY, SARAH E
    20 September 1858
    WFA   Page 41   F
    Parents: Leander & Mima Worley

WORLEY, WM
    20 October 1858
    WMA   Page 41   F
    Parents: Francis & Alcy Worley

WORLEY, WILLIAM
    5 February 1892
    WMA   Page 68   F
    Parents: Nathan & Martha L. Worley

WORLEY, WILLIAM L
    10 June 1859
    WMA   Page 49   F
    Parents: A.G. & Elizabeth Worley

WORSHAM, FLORENA C
    21 December 1858
    WFA   Page 45   F
    Parents: Alfred & Nancy Worsham

WORSHAM, JOSEPH
    25 March 1870
WMA   Page 55   F   Saltville Twp.
Parents: Alfred & Nancy Worsham

WRIGHT, [n.n.]
    10 November 1855
WMA   Page 18   F
Parents: Andrew & Dorcas Wright

WRIGHT, [n.n.]
    24 October 1857
W_D   Page 37   F
Parents: James H. & Francis P. Wright

WRIGHT, ANDREW E
    21 December 1853
WMA   Page 5   F
Parents: Wm. S. & Eveline Wright

WRIGHT, CHARLES
    8 September 1892
WMA   Page 70   F   Abingdon Dist.
Parents: Andrew & Louvenia Wright

WRIGHT, DAVID
    17 October 1859
WMA   Page 49   F
Parents: Thomas & Sarah Wright

WRIGHT, DAVID W
    3 April 1858
WMA   Page 45   F
Parents: William & Emeline Wright

WRIGHT, ELLIOTT R
    8 June 1892
WMA   Page 65   MC
Parents: P.W. & A.J.M. Wright

WRIGHT, FERDENAND
    1870
WMA   Page 57   MR   Glade Spring Twp.
Parents: Robert & Sally Wright

WRIGHT, JESSEE H.C.
    13 September 1856
WMA   Page 28   F
Parents: Andrew & Dorcas R. Wright

WRIGHT, JOHN C
    18 November 1854
WMA   Page 13   F
Parents: Sam'l H. & Ann Wright

WRIGHT, JOHN C
    4 November 1858
WMA   Page 45   F
Parents: Andrew K. & Margaret A. Wright

WRIGHT, JOHN J
    6 April 1854
WMA   Page 12   F
Parents: Robert & Dicey Wright

WRIGHT, MARGARET R.E.
    19 August 1855
WFA   Page 18   F
Parents: James H. & Frances Wright

WRIGHT, MARY E
    5 December 1871
WFA   Page 53   F   Abingdon Twp.
Parents: John W. & Margaret Wright

WRIGHT, MARY J
    30 April 1857
WFA   Page 37   F
Parents: Saml. & Ann Wright

WRIGHT, PETER WALTER
    28 March 1855
WMA   Page 18   PH
Parents: And'w K. & Marg't Ann Wright

WRIGHT, REBECCA
    15 December 1870
WF_   Page 58
Parents: Richard A. & Rebecca Wright

WRIGHT, ROB'T H
    7 September 1853
WMA   Page 5   F
Parents: Jno. & Mahala Wright
    Reported by Polly Carr, 'sister to father'

WRIGHT, SARAH B
    22 April 1854
WFA   Page 12
Mother: Polly Wright

WRIGHT, SUSANAH J
    6 December 1856
WFA   Page 28   PH
Parents: And. K. & Margret A. Wright

WRIGHT, THOS. EVAN   WMA   Page 5   PH
     14 November 1853   Parents: Andw. K. & Sally Wright

WYATT, [n.n.]   WMA   Page 10   L
     December 1854   Parents: [Adrich] & Lucinda Wyatt

WYATT, JNO. W   WMA   Page 38   F
     19 October   Parents: P.W. & Margret Wyatt
     Reported by [Pinkey] WIATT, father

WYETT, [n.n.]   SFD   Page 13   Brook Hall
     November 1854   Mother: Mariah Wyett
                        Master: Col. Wm. Byars

WYETT, MARTHA J   WFA   Page 16   L
     7 December 1855   Parents: Pinkney W. & Margaret Wyett

WYNDHAM   SMA   Page 5
     6 August 1853   Mother: Julia
                        Owner: Capt. Wm. Duff

YANCY, ALICE JULIA   WFA   Page 11   F
     10 or 15 April 1854   Parents: Stephen L. & Catharine Yancy

YANCY, MILTON   WFA   Page 45   F
     8 January 1858   Parents: Stephen & Mary Yancy

YARBER, JOHN M   WMA   Page 70   F   North Fork Dist.
     31 December 1892   Parents: W.A. & Ellen Yarber

YEATES, GEORGE B   WMA   Page 57   MC   Glade Spring Twp.
     1870   Father: J.D. Yeates
     Reported by J.D. YATES,   Mother: Shelly YATES
        father

YEATTS, PRESTON L   WMA   Page 65   F
     9 December 1892   Parents: W.A.J. & Bessie Yeatts

YODER, BESSIE   WFA   Page 55   MW   Saltville Twp.
     30 August 1870   Parents: J.S. & Sallie Yoder

ZIMERMAN, BENJ'N F   WMA   Page 22   F
     29 May 1855   Parents: Benj. F. & Martha Zimerman

ABLE, LEANDER (27y)   WM   Page 28   North Fork
    25 Dec. 1892 - Hemorhage   Parents: Valentine & Lucy Able
    Born in Johnson Co., Tn.

ADAM (47y)   SM   Page 17
    24 Feb. 1858 - Flux   Owner: S.W. Montgomery

ADKINS, LYDIA (2y)   WF   Page 3
    1 Oct. 1854 - Dysentery   Parents: Jno. & Nancy Adkins

AGNES (65y)   SF   Page 4
    Aug. 1854 - Old age   Master: John Morell

ALDERSON, GEORGE C. (2y)   WM   Page 19
    10 Apr. 1859 - Scarlet Fev.   Parents: Geo. & Lydia Alderson

ALEXANDER (4y)   CM   Page 12
    1 Dec. 1856 - Fever

ALEXANDER (30y)   SM   Page 2
    15 Sept. 1853 - Typhoid Fev. Owner: Jacob Morell

ALEXANDER, ELIZABETH (34y)   WF   Page 18
    25 Oct. 1858 - Typhoid Fev.   Spouse: Geo. Alexander
    Reported by John Smith, brother

ALFRED, SARAH I. (6y)   WF   Page 11
    11 Sept. 1856 - Dysentery   Parents: Isaac & M.J. Alfred

ALICE (9m)   SF   Page 21
    9 Feb. 1859 - Fever   Owner: Humberson Miller

ALLEN, ELIZ. JANE (28y)   WF   Page 3
    5 Oct. 1854 - Dysentery   Parents: Jno. & Mary Allen
    Reported by Parker Hall   Spouse: Moses Allen

ALLEN, JAMES (80y)   WM   Page 8   F
    15 Dec. 1855 - Dropsey   Parents: Daugherty & Rebecca Allen
    Born in Orange Co., N.C.   Spouse: Mariah Allen

ALLEN, JOHN (66y)   WM   Page 12   F
    10 June 1856 - Infla'on Brain Father: Geo. Allen
    Reported by Dan'l Smith, friend

ALLEN, SARAH E. (42y)   WF   Page 28   Kinderhook
    6 Jan. 1892 - Hart disease   Reported by M.J. Kennedy, neighbor

ALLEN, SUSANNAH (22y)   WF   Page 1
    15 June 1853   Parents: Parker & Ruth Hall
                                  Spouse: Moses Allen

AMANDA (4y)   SF   Page 4
    30 Nov. 1854 - Dysentery   Owner: Capt. Wm. Duff

ANDERSON, EASTER (34y)   CF   Page 30   Town of Abingdc
    12 April 1892 - Consumption   Reported by Henry Anderson

ANDERSON, GEO. (52y)   CM   Page 30   L
    8 May 1892 - Parelsis   Reported by Martha Cotten, daughter

ANDERSON, JNO. C. (56y 4m)   WM   Page 10   F
    27 May 1856 - Consumption   Parents: Jas. & R. Anderson
                                  Spouse: Jane C. Anderson

ANDERSON, LUCY (10y) CF Page 30 Town of Abingdon
 1 Nov. 1892 - Bronchitis Parents: Henry & Easter Anderson

ANDERSON, TOM (54y) CM Page 30 Town of Abingdon
 20 April 1892 - Kidney dis. Father: William Anderson

ANDY (38y) SM Page 1 Saltville
 Nov. 1853 - Fever Owner: James C. Hayter

ANETTE (2y) SF Page 7
 Sept. 1855 - Dysentery Owner: Henry L. Morgan
 Born in Saltville, Va.

ASTRAP, JESSEE (5y) WM Page 19
 9 Dec. 1859 - Croup Parents: Andrew J. & Mary T. Astrap

ASTROP, OLIVER (1y) WM Page 13
 23 June 1856 - Croup

AUTHENWREATH, MARY (6d) WF Page 25
 5 June 1892 - Not known Parents: Frank & Mary Authenwreath

AYRES, MARY F. (18y) WF Page 2
 4 June 1853 - Consumption Father: Isaac Ayres

BAKER, EMMA I. (1y 2m) WF Page 14
 17 Feb. 1857 - Unknown Parents: Henry Wm. & N.S.F. Baker

BAKER, EMMA J. (1y 3m) WF Page 16
 17 Feb. 1858 - Fitts Parents: Henry W. & L.F. Baker

BAKER, JOHN (59y 1m 21d) WM Page 2 F
 19 Feb. 1853 - Fever Parents: Isaac & Elizabeth Baker
  Spouse: Susannah Baker

BALDWIN, NANCY (32y 4m) WF Page 6
 26 Oct. 1854 - Fever Parents: Jno. & Narcissa M. Miller
  Spouse: N.C. Baldwin

BALL, ALTA (28y 7m) WF Page 25
 5 June 1892 - Consumption Reported by O.B. Kindrick, brother
 Born in Russell Co., Va.

BARBARY, REBECCA (36y) WF Page 8
 1 April 1855 - Consumption Parents: Jno. & Sally Robinson
 Born in Smyth Co., Va. Spouse: Smittack Barbary

BARKER, BEBECCA (6y 7m) WF Page 9
 2 June 1855 - Flux Parents: Geo. & M. Barker

BARKER, ELIZABETH WF Page 23 Kinderhook Twp.
 13 April 1871 - Unknown

BARKER, IRA (9y 5m 13d) WM Page 11
 4 April 1856 - 'Killed' Parents: Edmund & Sarah Barker

BARKER, J.S. (5y) WM Page 28
 8 Feb. 1892 - Flux Parents: S.L. Barker

BARKER, JOEL (75y) WM Page 14
 29 May 1857 - White swelling Parents: Thos. & Rebecca Barker
 Reported by Joel Barker, son Spouse: Ellen Barker

BARKER, L.V. (7y) WF Page 6
    29 Sept. 1854 - Flux Parents: Jno. & Susan Barker

BARKER, MEZORAH WF Page 23 Kinderhook Twp.
    7 March 1871 - Unknown Spouse: Joseph Barker

BARKER, NANCY (1d) WF Page 11
    14 Feb. 1856 - Unknown Parents: Edmund & Sarah Barker

BARKER, SHERWOOD (55y) WM Page 6
    24 May 1854 - Fever Parents: Thos. & Rebecca Barker
    Spouse: Rachel Barker

BARLO, MEMBER (35y) WF Page 13
    22 March 1857 - Consumption Father: Micheal Widener
    Reported by Rebecca Barlo, daughter Spouse: Jno. Barlo

BARLOW, [n.n.] (14d) W_ Page 12
    April 1856 - Unknown Parents: Jacob Barlow & wife

BARLOW, [n.n.] WF Page 19
    30 Dec. 1858 Mother: Rebecca Barlow

BARLOW, BENJ'N (5y 11m) WM Page 5 Widener Valley
    15 Aug. 1854 - Dysentery Parents: Jno. & Remember Barlow

BARLOW, FAIRMAN (1y 8m) WM Page 3
    13 Aug. 1854 - Dysentery Parents: Jacob & Sally Barlow

BARLOW, MARANDA J. (5y) WF Page 12
    15 Feb. 1856 - Unknown Parents: Jacob & Sarah Barlow

BARLOW, MARSEM A. (1y 8m) WF Page 8
    3 Jan. 1855 - Inflammation of brain Parents: Joseph & Sarah Barl[

BARLOW, WILLIAM C. (17m) WM Page 19
    28 Nov. 1859 - Scarlet Fev. Father: James Barlow
    Reported by JOSEPH Barlow, father

BARR, FRANKLIN (2y) WM Page 12
    20 Dec. 1856 - Unknown

BARR, GEO. R. (82y) WM Page 29 MN Town of Abingdo[
    27 Aug. 1892 - Blood poisonong Parents: Wm. & Reb. Barr
    Reported by son

BARR, REBECCA (72y) WF Page 14 F
    18 June 1857 - Old age Parents: Geo. R. & Mary Rhea
    Reported by Geo. R. Barr, son Spouse: Wm. Barr

BARRETT, JULIA (16y) WF Page 25
    31 May 1892 - Typhoid fev. Father: W.G. BARNETT

BAYS, MARY (38y 8m) WF Page 25
    6 March 1892 - Consumption Spouse: J.H. Bays

BEATIE, AVERY (17y) CF Page 4
    28 Aug. 1854 - Scrofula Parents: Ab & Celia BEATY

BEATIE, SAMUEL (15y) CM Page 4
    25 Nov. 1854 - Scrofula Parents: Ab & Celia BEATY

BEATIE, WINSTON (2m)   CM   Page 4
    Sept. 1854   Parents: Avery BEATY
    Reported by Celia BEATY, grandmother

BEATTIE, AMANDA J. (16y 8m 17d)   WF   Page 19
    1 Dec. 1859 - Typhoid fev.   Father: Absalom Beattie

BEATY, [n.n.] (6m)   WF   Page 4
    1 Dec. 1854   Parents: Nelson J.M. & Eliz. Beaty

BENJAMIN (40y)   SM   Page 1
    Oct. 1853 - Typhoid Fev.   Owner: Andrew Patterson

BERDINE, E.C. (11y)   CF   Page 28
    10 Feb. 1892 - Burned   Father: Robert BURDINE

BERRY, ELLEN (6y)   WF   Page 3
    6 Sept. 1854 - Dysentery   Parents: John & Sarah Berry

BERRY, NAT. (42y)   WM   Page 10   F
    25 Aug. 1856 - Brain fev.   Parents: Wm. & Jane Berry
    Reported by Hugh Berry, brother

BERRY, NATH'L M. (2y 2m)   WM   Page 6
    14 Oct. 1854 - Hooping cough   Parents: Nath'l & Isabella Berry

BERRY, SARAH (73y)   WF   Page 8
    21 April 1855 - Old age   Spouse: David Berry
    Reported by Alexr. R. Berry, grandson

BISHOP, JOHN (4m)   WM   Page 5   Near Mill Creek
    5 Sept. 1854 - Dysentery   Parents: Madison & Eunice Bishop

BISHOP, LEVI C. (22y 1m 21d)   WM   Page 18   F
    22 May 1858 - Dropsy   Father: Samuel D. Bishop

BISHOP, MARGARET ANN (23y)   WF   Page 23   Glade Spring
    April 1871 - Fever   Parents: John & Mary Hawthorn

BISHOP, MARY E. (3y 5m)   WF   Page 5   Near Mill Creek
    11 Oct. 1854 - Dysentery   Parents: Madison & Eunice Bishop

BISHOP, RACHEL (2y)   WF   Page 13
    24 Oct. 1857 - Disentary   Father: Madison Bishop

BITTIE (56y)   SF   Page 11
    9 Jan. 1856 - Palpt. heart   Owner: David Baltzell

BITTLE, MARY M. (23y 5m)   WF   Page 16
    24 Aug. 1858 - Scrofula   Parents: D.G. & E. Bittle

BLACK, CHERRY (57y)   WF   Page 18
    11 May 1858 - Appoplexy   Father: John Cash
                                   Spouse: Jas. C. Black

BLACK, DAVID (21y)   CM   Page 30   L   Town of Abingdon
    18 Dec. 1892 - Consumption   Parents: David & Cora Black

BLACK, ELIZABETH (18y)   WF   Page 18
    15 Dec. 1858 - Typhoid fev.   Mother: Mary Black

BLACK, JAS. (21y)   WM   Page 11   F
    15 Oct. 1856 - Fever   Parents: Jno. & Susan Black

BLACK, JOHN H. (4m)   WM   Page 9
    3 Sept. 1855   Parents: Wm. H. & E.C. Black

BLACK, OVEL (80y)   CM   Page 30   L   Town of Abingdo
    1 Dec. 1892 - Rheumatism   Reported by Angeline Black, daughter

BLACKWELL, MILLY (17y)   WF   Page 24   Saltville
    1871   Parents: Wm. & Jane Blackwell

BLACKWELL, VICTORIA (3m 4d) WF   Page 25
    15 Feb. 1892 - Croup   Parents: J.A. & Mag. Blackwell

BLACKWELL, WILLIAM (56y)   WM   Page 4
    12 May 1854 - Consumption Parents: Wm. & Mary Blackwell
    Reported by wife

BLAIR, JAMES (2y 1d)   WM   Page 9
    2 March 1855 - Flux   Parents: Jas. & M. Blair

BLAND, ANNIE L. (9m)   WF   Page 29   Goodson Dist.
    7 May 1892 - Not known   Parents: Howard & M. Bland

BOGLE, DERRY (75y)   CF   Page 30   F   Town of Abingdo
    16 Dec. 1892 - Old age   Reported by Bob Stewart, son in law

BONDURANT, MARY G. (58y 1m 8d) WF   Page 21
    12 March 1859 - Pneumonia Parents: Jno. & Cisley Ayce
    Born in Buckingham, Va.   Spouse: Jos. Bondurant
    Reported by Mary A. Nuckols, daughter

BOOHER, [n.n.]   WF   Page 6
    4 July 1854 - Stillborn   Parents: Fred D. & Ann Booher

BOOHER, ANN (35y)   WF   Page 6
    4 July 1854 - Fever   Parents: Jacob & Polly Mumpower
                         Spouse - F.D. Booher

BOOHER, ANN E. (1y 7d)   WF   Page 6
    29 Oct. 1854 - Flux   Mother: Jane Booher

BOOHER, C. (24d)   WM   Page 21
    8 Aug. 1859 - Unknown   Parents: Jno. S. & Mary Booher

BOOHER, CLARACH (24d)   WF   Page 21
    8 Aug. 1859 - Unknown   Parents: Jno. S. & Mary Booher

BOOHER, JAMES (6m)   SM   Page 14
    15 Feb. 1857 - Croup   Owner: Isaac Booher

BOOHER, JAS. H. (5m 5d)   WM   Page 10
    22 March 1856 - Fever   Parents: L.A. & Sarah Booher

BOOHER, MARY (60y)   WF   Page 6
    Aug. 1854 - Fever   Reported by F.D. Booher, son

BOTT, JAS. A. (1y 10m)   WM   Page 9
    15 Sept. 1855 - Fever   Parents: Wm. & N. Bott

BOUSER, EMANUEL (48y 4m 16d) WM   Page 8   F
    10 May 1855 - Consumption

BOWERS, CATHARINE (20y)   WF   Page 23   HK
    8 May 1871 - Unknown   Father: Laton Odum
    Born in Northfork Twp.   Spouse: Edmomd Bowers
    Reported by Martha Bowers, mother in law

BOWERS, JOHN (1d)   WM   Page 25
    25 June 1892 - Not known   Parents: Henry & Martha Bowers

BOWERS, ROBT. (1d)   WM   Page 25
    25 June 1892 - Not known   Parents: Henry & Martha Bowers

BOWERS, SUSAN T. (20y)   WF   Page 21
    27 June 1859 - Consumption   Parents: William & Temperance Bowers

BOWERS, TEMPERANCE (56y)   WF   Page 21
    27 Sept. 1859 - Consumption   Parents: John & Dorcas Brewer
                                     Spouse: William Bowers

BOWLING, [n.n.] (1d)   WM   Page 29
    8 June 1892 - Not known   Parents: And. & Sallie Bowling

BOWLS, JOHN PELL (8m 26d)   WM   Page 23
    26 Dec. 1857 - Enlargement of throat   Parents: George W. & Martha Bowls
    Born in Abingdon Twp.

BOWMAN, BENJ. (84y)   WM   Page 16   F
    18 July 1858 - Flux   Parents: Isiah & Ann Bowman
                                     Spouse: Mary A. Bowman

BOWMAN, CATHARINE A. (2y 6m)   WF   Page 8
    15 Aug. 1855 - Dysentery   Parents: Alexr. & Lucinda Bowman

BOWMAN, ELIZABETH (63y)   WF   Page 23   HK
    20 Sept. 1871 - Dropsy   Spouse: Samuel Bowman
    Born in Northfork Twp.   Reported by Elijah Bowman, son

BOWMAN, JAMES W. (2y)   WM   Page 21
    26 June 1859 - Flux   Parents: Harrison & E. Bowman

BOWMAN, ROBERT (1y 6m)   WM   Page 8
    22 Jan. 1855 - Not known   Parents: Matthias & Susan Bowman
    Reported by MATTHAS Bowman, father

BOYD, CHAS. (27y)   CM   Page 30   L   Town of Abingdon
    10 May 1892 - Not known   Parents: Points Boyd

BOYD, HATTIE (3y)   CF   Page 30   Town of Abingdon
    29 Sept. 1892 - Hooping cough   Father: Charles Boyd

BRADLEY, [n.n.]   WF   Page 16
    27 Dec. 1858 - Dead born   Parents: Jas. H. & S.J. Bradley
    Reported by Jas. L. Bradley, grandfather

BRADLEY, C.S. BEKEN (1y 2m)   WM   Page 16
    22 Sept. 1858 - Flux   Parents: A.F. & Mary E. Bradley

BRADLEY, JAS. L. (59y)   WM   Page 21
    16 Oct. 1859 - Hung himself   Parents: Reuben & Elizabeth Bradley
    Reported by James H. Bradley, son   Spouse: Mary C. Bradley

BRADLEY, JAS. W.W. (8y 6m)   WM   Page 16
    28 June 1858 - Flux   Parents: A.F. & Mary E. Bradley

BRADLEY, POLLY (77y)   WF   Page 16
    15 Sept. 1858   Parents: Jas. & Mary Fulkerson
    Reported by A.F. Bradley, son   Spouse: Abram Bradley

BRADLEY, SARAH V. (22y)   WF   Page 21
    15 Jan. 1859 - Consumption   Parents: Jas. L. & M.C. Bradley
    Reported by James H. Bradley, brother

BRADLEY, W.P. (4y 7m)   WM   Page 16
    12 July 1858 - Flux   Parents: A.F. & Mary E. Bradley

BRAGGS, [n.n.] (4d)   WF   Page 4
    14 Oct. 1854   Parents: Wm. & Nancy Braggs
    Reported by Andw. D. Grubb, neighbor

BRANSON, ABSALOM (75y)   WM   Page 30   Goodson Dist.
    7 May 1892 - Heart disease Spouse: Sarah Branson

BRANSON, JONATHAN (49y)   WM   Page 21
    16 April 1859 - Fever   Father: Henry Branson
                                Spouse: Mary Branson

BREWER, SUSAN (60y)   WF   Page 28   Kinderhook
    8 Feb. 1892 - Flux   Reported by husband

BREWER, WM. A. (9y)   WM   Page 13
    15 July 1856 - Typhoid fev. Father: Jesse G. Brewer

BRICE, ROBT. M. (32y)   WM   Page 30   Town of Abingdon
    8 Aug. 1892 - Tumer of brain   Reported by wife

BRIGGS, FRED (60y 6m)   WM   Page 14   F
    18 Oct. 1857 - Fever   Reported by Martin Phelps, neighbor

BRIGGS, VIRGINIA (1m)   WF   Page 11
    11 Dec. 1856 - Unknown   Parents: Fred & Mary Briggs

BRIM, JOSEPH P. (5y)   WM   Page 3
    15 Sept. 1854 - Dysentery   Parents: James & Martha Brim

BROOKS, LOUCINDA (65y)   WF   Page 29   Goodson Dist.
    10 Aug. 1892 - Fever   Parents: Henry & Sally Moore
    Reported by Jno. Brooks

BROOKS, MARY (7y)   WF   Page 13
    8 Oct. 1857 - Flux   Father: Moses Brooks

BROWN, ETHEL (1y)   CF   Page 30   Town of Abingdon
    12 Jan. 1892 - Not known   Parents: Steven & Susan Brown

BROWN, JANE (72y)   WF   Page 18
    15 Feb. 1858 - Old age   Father: Moses McSpaddin
    Reported by John Brown, son   Spouse: Mather Brown

BROWN, JOHN (5m 99d)   CM   Page 23
    16 May 1871 - Not ascertained   Parents: Mark & Hettie Brown
    Born in Abingdon Twp.

BROWN, MARIAH (50y)   CF   Page 30   L   Town of Abingdon
    July 1892 - Cold   Reported by Sarah Robinson

BROWN, POLLY A. (6y 2m)   WF   Page 6
    27 Nov. 1854 - Flux   Parents: Andw. & Mahaley Brown

BROWN, REBECCA A. (3y)   WF   Page 6
    Nov. 1854 - Flux   Parents: Andw. & Mahaley Brown

BUCHANAN, [n.n.]   WF   Page 16
      17 Oct. 1858 - Consumption   Parents: Jno. P. & Elizabeth Buchanan

BUCHANAN, ANDW. E.F. (8y 7d)   WM   Page 8
      5 June 1855 - Scarlet fev.   Parents: Russell M. & Rosanna Buchanan
      Reported by And. Edmundson, uncle

BUCHANAN, L.J. (24y)   WF   Page 16
      17 Oct. 1858 - Consumption   Parents: Jno. P. & Elizabeth Buchanan

BUCHANAN, LAVINIA C. (37y 3m)   WF   Page 25
      12 May 1892 - Consumption   Spouse: M.S. Buchanan

BUCHANAN, MARGARET (74y)   WF   Page 8
      25 March 1855 - Unknown   Parents: Jno. & Ann Buchanan
      Reported by Andw. Edmundson, son in law   Spouse: Wm. Buchanan

BUCHANAN, MARY Y. (66y 2m)   WF   Page 25
      22 Sept. 1892 - Paralysis   Spouse: Jas. A. Buchanan

BUCHANAN, MINERVA (35y 10m)   WF   Page 10
      27 July 1856 - Dropsy   Parents: Jas. & Nancy Buchanan

BUCHANAN, MYRTHA A. (2y)   WF   Page 6
      9 Oct. 1854 - Flux   Parents: Jno. & Elizabeth Buchanan

BUCHANAN, NANCY (65y)   WF   Page 18
      30 June 1858 - Dropsy   Father: Arthur Joseph
      Reported by A. Buchanan, son   Spouse: Isaac Buchanan

BUCHANAN, RUSSELL M. (43y 2m 10d) WM   Page 8   F
      12 April 1855 - Inflammation of brain   Parents: Wm. & Sarah Buchanan
      Reported by And. Edmundson, brother in law   Spouse: Rosanna Buchanan

BUCHANAN, TOBY (1y 10m 7d)   WM   Page 1   Saltville
      21 Sept. 1853 - Fever   Parents: Benj. K. & Rachel Buchanan

BULLEN, SARAH (64y)   _F   Page 4
      11 Dec. 1854   Reported by Wilcher Bullen, son
      Born in Stokes Co., N.C.

BUMBGARDNER, [n.n.]   WM   Page 23   Abingdon Twp.
      5 April 1871 - Still born   Parents: Franklin & Emeline Bumbgardner

BURCH, LEVI (78y)   WM   Page 3   F
      20 April 1854 - Old age   Reported by John Burch, son
      Born in Craven Co., N.C.

BURK, MARTHA (23y)   WF   Page 5
      March 1854   Parents: Martin & Nancy Hagy
                                   Spouse: Thos. M. Burk

BUTT, SARAH H. (51y 6m)   WF   Page 14   F
      29 Dec. 1857 - Consumption   Parents: Jacob & Jane Bondurant
                                   Spouse: Rignal Butt

BUTT, THOMAS (30y 2m 15d)   WM   Page 2
      25 July 1853 - Fever   Parents: Regnal & Sarah Butt
                                   Spouse: Mary Butt

BYARS, SARAH A.A. (9y)   WF   Page 12
      31 Dec. 1856 - Infla'n lungs Parents: Jno. & Jane Byars

CALDWELL, ANDREW (7y)   WM   Page 3
        12 Aug. 1854 - Dysentery   Parents: Jno. S. & Margt. Caldwell

CALDWELL, DAVID (9y)   WM   Page 3
        7 Aug. 1854 - Dysentery   Parents: Jno. S. & Margt. Caldwell

CALDWELL, FELIX (7y)   WM   Page 5   South Fork
        12 Sept. 1854 - Dysentery   Parents: Jesse H. & Mary Caldwell

CALDWELL, FRANCES ISABELLA (3y)   WF   Page 5   South Fork
        11 Sept. 1854 - Dysentery   Parents: Jesse H. & Mary Caldwell

CALDWELL, ROBT. (79y)   WM   Page 12
        5 Oct. 1856 - Plurasy   Parents: James Caldwell & wife
        Reported by Dorcas Foster, daughter   Spouse: Jane Caldwell

CALDWELL, SATINA (16y 9m)   WF   Page 13
        5 Nov. 1857 - Infla. brain   Parents: Jno. & Margaret Caldwell

CALLIHAN, JAS. (4y)   WM   Page 12
        7 April 1856 - Unknown   Father: Wm. Callihan

CAMPBELL, DANIEL T. (23y)   WM   Page 9
        1 Oct. 1855 - Fever   Parents: E. & R. Campbell
        Reported by E.M. Campbell, brother

CAMPBELL, DAVID (60y 1m 3d)   WM   Page 1   F
        13 Sept. 1853   Parents: James & Ann Campbell
                                         Spouse: Ann Campbell

CAMPBELL, ELIZA N. (1y 6m)   WF   Page 14
        1 Dec. 1857 - Disentary   Parents: Jno. C. & N.J. Campbell
        Reported by Jno. E. Campbell, father

CAMPBELL, FANNIE (3m)   CF   Page 30   L   Town of Abingdo
        10 March 1892 - Not known   Parents: David & Martha Campbell

CAMPBELL, FRANCES J. (4y 4d)   WF   Page 9
        1 Aug. 1855 - Flux   Parents: Jno. C. & M. Campbell

CAMPBELL, HANNAH (41y)   CF   Page 23
        23 June 1871 - Cancer in throat   Born in Abingdon Twp.

CAMPBELL, JACK (68y)   CM   Page 25   F
        28 Aug. 1892 - Heart disease   Spouse: East. Campbell

CAMPBELL, JANE E. (3y)   WF   Page 3
        13 Sept. 1854 - Dysentery   Parents: Jas. L. & Eliza Campbell

CAMPBELL, JEFFERSON   WM   Page 25   F
        4 Nov. 1892   Spouse: Rebec. Campbell

CAMPBELL, R.E. (31y 3m 9d)   WF   Page 21
        25 Feb. 1859 - Fever   Parents: Abram & S.B. McConnell
                                         Spouse: Jas. L.F. Campbell

CAMPBELL, RHODA ANN (1y 6m 21d)   WF   Page 10
        15 March 1856 - Unknown   Parents: J.L.F. & R.E. Campbell

CAMPBELL, ROSA (5y)   CF   Page 30   Town of Abingd
        5 Jan. 1892 - Disease of bowels   Reported by Wm. Campbell

CANTER, ALFRED (1m)   WM   Page 9
        31 Aug. 1855 - Inflamation   Parents: Wm. & Elizabeth Canter

CAROLINE (6y 3m 10d)   SF   Page 8
        2 June 1855 - Scarlet fev.   Mother: Malinda
        Reported by And. Edmundson   Owner: Rosanna Buchanan

CARRELL, W.O. (51y)   WM   Page 11   PA
        13 Sept. 1856 - Shot himself   Reported by Mary Low, friend

CARSON (1y)   SM   Page 12
        1 Sept. 1856   Owner: Jno. Byars

CARSON, SAML. H. (2y 4m)   WM   Page 8
        26 Oct. 1855 - Scarlet fev.   Parents: Wm. & Margaret Carson
        Born in Ash Co., N.C.

CARTER (17y)   SM   Page 19
        25 Dec. 1859 - Inflamation   Master: William Clark

CARTER, DILCEY (26y)   CF   Page 25
        3 Sept. 1892 - Consumption   Spouse: Abram Carter

CARTER, LEWIS (29y 10m)   CM   Page 25
        18 April 1892 - Blood poison   Parents: Jerry & Maria Carter

CARTER, LINCOLN (9m 4d)   CM   Page 25
        4 Aug. 1892 - Bronchitis   Parents: Abram & Dilcey Carter

CASEY, MARGARET JANE (1y 7m)   WF   Page 5
        9 Sept. 1854 - Dysentery   Parents: Wm. & Marg't Casey

CASSELL, CATHARINE (54y)   WF   Page 5   Cedarville
        24 July 1854   Parents: Jno. & Cath Repass
        Born in Wythe Co., Va.   Spouse: Adam Cassell

CATO, ANDREW   CM   Page 9   W
        25 April 1853 - Fever   Spouse: Susan Cato
        Reported by Joseph Crabtree

CATRON, CHRISTOPHER (68y)   WM   Page 3   F
        8 Sept. 1854 - Dysentery   Parents: Philip & Elizabeth Catron

CATRON, DAVID (6y)   WM   Page 3
        1 Oct. 1854 - Dysentery   Parents: Philip W. & Delila Catron

CATRON, DAVID G. (30y)   WM   Page 20   F
        11 May 1859 - Consumption   Father: Christian Catron

CATRON, NANCY R. (63y)   WF   Page 1
        20 April 1853   Parents: Francis & Ann Kincannon
        Reported by Francis K. Catron, son   Spouse: Francis Catron

CATRON, PHILIP W. (38y)   WM   Page 19   F
        30 March 1859 - Thrown from horse   Father: Christian Catron
                                      Spouse: Delila Catron

CATRON, WALTER J. (3y 6m)   WM   Page 13
        16 Feb. 1857 - Drowned   Father: Philip W. Catron

CAYWOOD, MOSES (74y)   WM   Page 12   F
        3 July 1856 - Old age   Reported by Berry Caywood, son

CHANDLER, BLANCH (6y)   WF   Page 29   Goodson Dist.
        16 Nov. 1892 - Croup   Parents: L.S. & A.J. Chandler

CHAPMAN, JAMES (6m 16d) WM Page 2
    17 July 1853 Father: Joseph Chapman

CHAPMAN, NANCY L. (1y 16d) WF Page 28 Kinderhook
    20 Nov. 1892 - Flux Parents: C.C. & Nancy Chapman

CHARLES (24y) SM Page 18 F
    15 Sept. 1858 - Typhoid fev. Owner: Parker Smythe

CHARLEY (2m 6d) SM Page 7 Cedarville
    6 April 1855 - Croup Parents: Sidney & Ann
    Born in Cedarville Arthur D. Hutton, owner & physician

CHILDERS, JULIA ANN (18y) WF Page 2
    5 June 1853 - Thrown from horse Reported by Robert Clark

CHURCH, WILLIAM M. (2m 1d) WM Page 1
    18 Jan. 1853 Father: Sampson Church

CLAPP, CAROLINE (13y 6m) SF Page 14 F
    15 June 1857 - Consumption Father: Jno.
      Owner: Theophilis D. Clapp

CLAPP, E.B. (81y) WM Page 6 DO
    11 Sept. 1854 - Fever Reported by T.P. Clapp, son

CLAPP, ELIZA (35y) (S)F Page 14 F
    15 May 1857 - Consumption Owner: Theophilis D. Clapp

CLARK (15y 6m) SF Page 11
    11 Nov. 1856 - Disentary Owner: Robt. R. Preston

CLARK, [n.n.] WF Page 16
    15 Sept. 1858 - Dead born Parents: Wm. & C. Clark

CLARK, CHESTER L. (6y 3m) WMF Page 25
    2 Nov. 1892 - Croup Parents: Jas. H. & S.A. Clark

CLARK, EMILY (18y) WF Page 23 Glade Spring
    1871 - Fever Parents: John & Isabella Clark

CLARK, HARRIS L.F. (1y 10m) WM Page 6
    4 Aug. 1854 - Flux Mother: Margaret Clark

CLARK, JACOB J. (38y) WM Page 18 F
    28 June 1858 - Consumption Father: John B. Clark
      Spouse: Martha Clark

CLARK, JAMES K. (19y 6m 15d) WM Page 8
    7 Aug. 1855 - Dysentery Parents: Peter H. & Mary Clark
    Born in Green Co., Illinois

CLARK, JOB (76y 1d) WM Page 25 F
    19 May 1892 - Bronchitis Spouse: Amanda Clark

CLARK, JOHN S. (46y) WM Page 4
    10 Oct. 1854 - Dysentery Parents: Rob't & Martha Clark
    Born in Scotland Spouse: Isabella Clark

CLARK, MARGARET (1y 8m) WF Page 16
    20 June 1858 - Flux Parents: Jas. & Elizabeth Clark

CLARK, MARTHA (2d) WF Page 25
    25 Feb. 1892 - Not known Parents: Jno. H. & Miriam Clark

CLARK, MARTHA A. (70y)   WF   Page 29   Abingdon Dist.
    2 April 1892 - Fever   Reported by Nick Speer

CLARK, MARY (64y)   WF   Page 18
    20 June 1858 - Typhoid fev.   Father: David Beattie
                                  Spouse: John Clark

CLARK, MARY (1m 10d)   WF   Page 25
    3 April 1892 - Not known   Parents: Jno. H. & Miriam Clark

CLARK, MILLY C.   WF   Page 8
    June 1855 - Consumption   Parents: Jacob & Elizabeth Clark

CLARK, MIRIAM (41y 22d)   WF   Page 25
    18 April 1892 - Consumption   Spouse: Jno. H. Clark

CLARK, P.S. (39y)   WF   Page 29   Abingdon Dist.
    3 Sept. 1892 - Consumption   Parents: W.B. & Martha Clark
    Reported by Nick Speer

CLARK, PLEASANT (3y)   WM   Page 18
    18 Nov. 1858 - Typhoid fev.   Father: Francis Clark

CLARK, ROBERT [41y]   CM   Page 30   L   Town of Abingdon
    12 Oct. 1892 - Consumption   Father: Robert Clark
                                  Spouse: Alcy Clark

CLARK, ROBT. W. [4 or 11y]   WM   Page 13
    8 April 1857 - Inflamation   Parents: Jas. A. & Mary Clark

CLARK, SAML. (26y)   WM   Page 25   F
    5 May 1892 - Pneumonia Fever   Reported by Ryburn Clark, brother

CLARK, WILLIAM (87y)   WM   Page 39
    1 July 1853 - Old Age   Reported by John J. Clark, son
    Born in North Carolina

CLARK, WILLIAM (5y)   WM   Page 16
    3 June 1858 - Flux   Parents: Jas. & Elizabeth Clark

CLARK, WILLIAM (55y)   WM   Page 19
    15 Sept. 1859 - Consumption   Spouse: Delila Clark

CLAYMAN, JACOB (78y 8m)   WM   Page 10   F
    10 Oct. 1856 - Disentary   Parents: Jno. & Catherine Clayman
                                  Spouse: Mary Clayman

CLOUD, LENA (11y)   CF   Page 30   L   Town of Abingdon
    5 Dec. 1892 - Hooping cough   Parents: Henry & Martha Cotten

COCHRAN, C.C. (4y 4d)   WM   Page 9
    19 June 1855 - Cough   Parents: R.B. & Mary Cochran

COCHRAN, MARTHA (2y)   WF   Page 9
    27 March 1855 - Cough   Parents: R.B. & Mary Cochran

COLE, ANDREW C. (41y)   WM   Page 18   F
    28 Feb. 1858   Father: James Cole
                                  Spouse: Eliza Cole

COLE, CALDWELL (1y 5m)   CM   Page 25
    28 Sept. 1892 - Phtisic   Parents: Eli & Julia Cole

COLE, JEMIMAH (35y)   WF   Page 23   Glade Spring
   1871 - Inflamation   Parents: David & Martha Rambo

COLE, JOHN (24y 3m)   WM   Page 3
   1 Dec. 1854   Parents: Peleg & Polly Cole

COLE, JOHN (34y)   WM   Page 23   Glade Spring
   1871 - Consumption   Parents: Nathaniel & Jane Cole
   Born in Smyth Co., Va.

COLE, PELEG (65y)   WM   Page 19   F
   15 Aug. 1859 - Dropsey   Father: John Cole
                                   Spouse: Martha Cole

COLE, SAMUEL G. (3y 1m)   WM   Page 1
   15 Feb. 1853 - Inflamation of lungs   Parents: Andw. & Eliza Cole

COLEMAN, JAS. (5y)   WM   Page 11
   13 Aug. 1856 - Disentary   Parents: Frank & Millie Coleman

COLEMAN, JOSEPH   CM   Page 30   L   Town of Abingdc
   23 Feb. 1892 - Gun shot   Spouse: Ann Coleman

COLEMAN, ROBT. A. (2y)   WM   Page 11
   15 March 1856 - Disentary   Parents: Frank & Millie Coleman

COLLEY, CHAS. (25y 7m)   WM   Page 25   F
   5 Aug. 1892 - Pneumonia   Parents: W.E. & Martha Colley

COLLEY, SHADRICH (69y)   WM   Page 18   F
   1 Oct. 1858 - Mortification of leg   Spouse: Mary Colley

COLLINGS, SARAH M. (13y)   WF   Page 11
   22 June 1856 - Unknown   Parents: Jno. D. & N. Collings

COLLINS (8m)   SM   Page 10
   Aug. 1855 - Flux   Owner: John Preston

COLLINS, [n.n.] (1d)   WM   Page 14
   4 June 1857 - Disentary   Parents: Henry & Margret Collins

COLLINS, JOHN H. (5m)   WM   Page 14
   12 Nov. 1857 - Disentary   Parents: Jno. D. & Nancy Collins

COLLINS, MARTHA (65y)   WF   Page 10
   2 Aug. 1856 - Dropsy   Reported by Isaac Lewis, son in law

COLLY, THOMAS (85y 5m)   WM   Page 8   BP
   14 Feb. 1855 - Palsey   Parents: Thos. & Rhoda COLLEY
   Born in Albemarle Co., Va.   Reported by Margret COLLEY, daughter

CONANALY, JOHN (17y)   WM   Page 10   F
   27 Aug. 1856 - Killed by horse Parents: Steven & R. CONALY

COOK, ALEXR. B. (17y)   WM   Page 8
   19 Sept. 1855 - Congestive chills   Parents: Wm. & Ann Cook
   Born in Bottetourt Co., Va.   Reported by Alexr. J. Findlay,
                                        brother in law

COOK, OLLY (14y)   WF   Page 29   Goodson Dist.
   15 May 1892 - Consumption   Parents: J.W. & Eliz. Cook

CORNELIUS, GEO. W. (1m)   WM   Page 30   Town of Abingdc
   27 July 1892 - Information brain Parents: G.P. & M.R. Cornelius

CORRY, JOHN (82y)   WM   Page 9
     20 April 1855 - Cold   Reported by Wallace Maxwell, son in law

COTTEN, CATHARINE (5m)   CF   Page 30   Town of Abingdon
     4 April 1892 - Hooping cough   Parents: Jas. & Adaline Walace

COTTEN, KATY (5m)   CF   Page 30   Town of Abingdon
     10 May 1892 - Fever   Father: Henry Cotten

COUNTS, [n.n.] (24d)   WF   Page 25
     9 Nov. 1892 - Not known   Parents: W.E. & M.E. Counts

COWAN, [n.n.]   W_   Page 13
     27 June 1856 - Unknown   Father: Andrew J. Cowan

COXBY, JANE E. (42y 7m 5d)   WF   Page 1
     13 June 1853   Parents: Wm. & Jane Bekem
     Born in Nashville, Tn.   Spouse: Lewis F. Coxby

CRABTREE, [n.n.]   WM   Page 16
     15 March 1858 - Dead born   Parents: Z. & Caroline Crabtree

CRABTREE, JAS. S. (60y)   WM   Page 23   F   Kinderhook Twp.
     24 July 1871 - Unknown   Reported by Zackariah Crabtree, son

CRABTREE, MARIA (17y)   WF   Page 9
     19 Nov. 1855 - Fever   Parents: Jas. S. & E. Crabtree

CRABTREE, REBECCA (16y)   WF   Page 16
     15 June 1858 - Flux   Parents: J.S. & O. Crabtree

CRAFT, EMMA V. (1y)   WF   Page 23   Kinderhook Twp.
     7 March 1871 - Unknown   Parents: Daniel H. & Eliza Craft

CRAFT, JAMES P. (25y 7m)   WM   Page 23   Kinderhook Twp.
     20 Nov. 1871 - Bleeding at the nose   Parents: Daniel H. & Eliza Craft
     Born in Bedford Co., Va.

CRAIG, JAMES (5y)   WM   Page 16
     22 Oct. 1858 - Flux   Parents: R.C. & M.J. Craig

CRAIG, VIRGINIA K.H. (7y 5m)   WF   Page 16
     8 July 1858 - Flux   Parents: R.C. & M.J. Craig

CRAWFORD, ARTHUR O. (37y)   WM   Page 2
     24 June 1853 - Pateecha   Parents: Benjn. & Mary Crawford
     Reported by Levi Oak, father in law   Spouse: Mary Crawford

CROSS, [n.n.] (1m 10d)   WM   Page 29   Goodson Twp.
     31 March 1892 - Not known   Parents: Cinklain & Alice Cross

CROW, JAMES (31y)   SM   Page 6
     21 Sept. 1854 - Consumption   Master: Jacob Lynch

CROW, MARY E. (4y 10m)   WF   Page 8
     12 Aug. 1855 - Fever   Parents: Wm. & Eliza M. Crow

CUNNINGHAM, ABRAM (10m)   WM   Page 11
     16 Feb. 1856 - Unknown   Parents: Thos. B. & Martha Cunningham

CUNNINGHAM, BIRD (25y)   WM   Page 28   F   Kinderhook
     27 Dec. 1892 - Stabed   Reported by wife

CUNNINGHAM, JOSEPH (2d)   WM Page 9
  19 Feb. 1855   Parents: Robt. & M. Cunningham

CUNNINGHAM, M.A. (2y 7m) WF Page 16
  20 June 1858 - Flux   Parents: G.F. & M.D. Cunningham

CUNNINGHAM, [MARY] J. (6m) WMF Page 9
  20 Sept. 1855 - Flux Parents: Thos. & M.A. Cunningham

CUDDY, WM. A. (1y 6m)   WM Page 14
  20 Sept. 1857 - Disentary Parents: Jno. & Judith Cuddy

DADMEY, ELLEN (40y)   CF Page 23
  2 April 1871 - Consumption Born in Abingdon Twp.

DADMEY, HENRY (42y)   CM Page 23
  20 Aug. 1871 - Consumption Born in Abingdon Twp.

DANIEL (40y)   SM Page 17
  30 Sept. 1858 - Fever Owner: Jno. M. Ropp

DAVENPORT, [n.n.]   WM Page 19
  10 April 1859 - Dead born Father: James Davenport

DAVENPORT, FRANKLIN P. (2y 2m) WM Page 8
  13 June 1855 - Pneumonia Parents: Jas. N. & Lydia Davenport

DAVID (1y)   SM Page 10
  Aug. 1855   Owner: Jno. F. Preston

DAVIS, [n.n.] (1d)   WF Page 28   North Fork
  26 Jan. 1892 - Not known Mother: Alice Davis

DAVIS, G. (2y 1m)   WM Page 9
  1 Aug. 1855 - Flux   Parents: A. & M.V. Davis

DAVIS, JAS. C. (34y)   WM Page 25 F
  4 Aug. 1892 - Typhoid fev. Spouse: Lucinda Davis

DAVIS, JOHN (79y)   WM Page 16
  23 July 1858 - Flux   Parents: Jno. & Isabella Davis
  Reported by D.O. Bradley, son in law Spouse: Catherine Davis

DAVIS, JOSEPH (30y)   WM Page 28   North Fork
  4 Nov. 1892 - Typhoid fev. Reported by wife

DAVIS, M.J. (53y)   WF Page 28   North Fork
  19 Jan. 1892 - Dropsy Reported by husband

DAVIS, MARY A. (77y 6m) WF Page 25
  6 Dec. 1892 - General debility Reported by Eli Davis, son

DAVIS, WILLIAM (70y)   WM Page 13 F
  26 March 1856 - Old age Spouse: Mary A. Davis

DEBOSE, FLORA (36y)   CF Page 30 L Town of Abingc
  10 Aug. 1892 - Consumption Parents: Jack & Mary Dixon

DEBUSK, DORCAS ALMEDA (15y) WF Page 24   Glade Spring
  1871 - Sudden death Parents: Isaac E. & Martha J. Debusk

DEBUSK, EASTER (25y)   WF Page 19
  15 May 1859 - Consumption Father: Andrew Debusk

DEBUSK, JANATTE A. (4m)   WF   Page 12
    20 June 1856 - Affection brest   Father: Sam'l Debusk

DEBUSK, MARY E. (8y 8m 28d)   WF   Page 8
    7 July 1855 - Scarlet fev.   Parents: James & Jane Debusk

DECK, GEO. (88y 11m 22d)   WM   Page 14   F
    2 Feb. 1857 - Old age   Parents: Abram & Susan Deck
    Reported by Jos. Deck, nephew

DECK, MICHEAL (76y)   WM   Page 17   F
    21 Nov. 1857 - Dropsy   Parents: Abram & Susan Deck
    Reported by Joseph Deck, son   Spouse: Barbary Deck

DECK, SARAH C. (4y 8m)   WF   Page 16   F
    22 Oct. 1858 - Fever   Parents: Jos. & Susan Deck

DELAP, ROSIE (31y)   CF   Page 30   Town of Abingdon
    1 Dec. 1892 - Consumpation   Father: Madison Delap
    Reported by Chas. Delap

[DENISON], JAMES (70y)   WM   Page 5   Near Saltville
    1854   Spouse: Deby Denison
    Reported by W. Braddy, sister

[DENTON], [n.n.]   WF   Page 16
    29 April 1858 - Dead born   Parents: Danl. & M.A. Denton

DENTON, ALEXANDER (9y)   WM   Page 3
    29 Sept. 1854 - Dysentery   Parents: Wm. & Eliza Denton
    Reported by Jno. Denton, uncle

DENTON, DAVID (70y)   WM   Page 12   F
    23 Dec. 1856 - Consumption   Father: Jas. Denton
    Reported by David Denton, son

DENTON, E.B. (3y 5m)   WM   Page 14
    19 May 1857 - Fever   Parents: Robt. & S. Denton

DENTON, ELIZABETH (7y)   WF   Page 3
    13 Oct. 1854 - Dysentery   Parents: Wm. & Eliza Denton
    Reported by Jno. Denton, uncle

DENTON, JAS. F. (15y 9m)   WM   Page 21
    21 Nov. 1859 - Fever   Parents: Daniel & M.A. Denton

DENTON, M.W.P. (6y 5m)   WF   Page 14
    24 May 1857 - Fever   Parents: Robt. & S. Denton

DENTON, MARY C. (11y)   WF   Page 3
    27 Oct. 1854 - Dysentery   Parents: Wm. & Eliza Denton
    Reported by Jno. Denton, uncle

DENTON, SARAH (1y)   WF   Page 19
    4 May 1859 - <u>Phthisich</u>   Father: David Denton

DINKINS, HENDERSON (22y)   WM   Page 29   Abingdon Dist.
    4 July 1892 - Killed by Berg Shortt   Father: King Y. Dinkins
    Reported by brother

DINKINS, HUGH (14y)   WM   Page 3
    4 Oct. 1854 - Dysentery   Parents: [Welcom] & Betsey Dinkins

DINSMORE, [n.n.]   WM   Page 21
    24 May 1859   Parents: G.L. & S.C. Dinsmore

DINSMORE, LILBURN (7m)   WM   Page 4
    8 Dec. 1854   Parents: Jas. & Nancy Dinsmore

DINSMORE, WM. J. (7m 21d)   WM   Page 2
    26 June 1853 - Diarrhoea   Father: James Dinsmore

DISHNER, JNO. (80y)   WM   Page 29   Goodson Dist.
    2 Dec. 1892 - Old age   Father: John Dishner
    Reported by E.P. Dishner

DIXON, [n.n.]   WF   Page 21
    6 Nov. 1859 - Dead born   Parents: Isaac W. & Rachel Dixon

DIXON, FRANK (58y)   CM   Page 30   L   Town of Abingdc
    March 1892 - Pneumonia   Reported by Edna Dixon

DIXON, LOUCINDA (45y)   WF   Page 28   North Fork
    28 Feb. 1892 - Child birth   Parents: Levy & Mary Fleenor
    Reported by husband

DIXON, LUCY (30y)   CF   Page 30   L   Town of Abingdc
    Feb. 1892 - La gripp   Parents: Jack & Marg. Dixon

DIXON, MARTHA E. (2y 2m)   WF   Page 16
    16 April 1858 - Flux   Parents: Ed & Margaret Dixon

DIXON, WILLIAM (21y)   CM   Page 34   Goodson Dist.
    17 May 1892 - Dropsy   Parents: Robt. & Marg. Dixon

DOLAN, THOMAS (60Y)   WM   Page 5   North Fork
    2 Nov. 1854 - Supposed apoplexy   Parents: Jas. & Sarah Dolan
    Reported by Isiah Posten, friend

DOLINGER, [n.n.]   WM   Page 18
    17 Aug. 1858 - Born dead   Father: Wm. Dolinger

DOOLEY, SARAH (19y 11m)   WF   Page 14
    16 Oct. 1857 - Tetanus   Parents: H.S. & Sarah Dooley

DORCAS (16y)   SF   Page 11
    30 Oct. 1856 - Disentary   Owner: C.J. Cummings

DUFF, [n.n.] (7m)   WF   Page 8
    Dec. 1855 - Croup   Mother: Rebecca Duff
    Reported by Jno. N. Duff, grandfather

DUFF, MARY H. (3y 4m)   WF   Page 13
    9 May 1857 - S. fever   Father: Wm. K. Duff

DUFF, THOS. J. (83y 4m)   WM   Page 25   F
    22 Aug. 1892 - Flux   Reported by F.C. Duff, son

DUFF, WILLIAM (90y)   WM   Page 13   F
    8 Jan. 1857 - Gravel   Father: Saml. Duff
    Reported by Thos. J. Duff, son   Spouse: [Eloner] Duff

DUNCAN, ELIZA JANE (7y 9m)   WF   Page 7
    24 Sept. 1855 - Dysentery   Parents: John & Susan Duncan

DUNCAN, GABRIEL (65y)   WM   Page 7
    18 Oct. 1844 - Dysentery   Father: Jacob Duncan
    Born in Buckingham Co.

DUNCAN, JNO. HENRY (10m)   WM   Page 7
    25 Sept. 1855 - Dysentery Parents: John & Susan Duncan

DUNCAN, SENA (71y)   WF   Page 2
    7 Oct. 1853 - Old age   Spouse: Gabriel Duncan

DUNGAN, ANN (17y)   WF   Page 13
    30 May 1857 - S. fever   Mother: Mary J. Dungan

DUNN, JNO. D. (10y)   WM   Page 11
    29 Aug. 1856 - Disentary Parents: J.B. & Mary H. Dunn

DUNN, [SIZEE] (28y)   (S)F   Page 14
    20 Sept. 1857 - Fever   Owner: D.C. Dunn

DUTTON, MARY E. (29y)   WF   Page 18
    2 Nov. 1858 - Typhoid fev. Father: John Miller
                            Spouse: Peter Dutton

EAKIN, ALEX'R. (23y)   WM   Page 1
    23 April 1853 - Consumption Father: James Eakin
    Reported by James Grant

EAKIN, ELLEN (58y)   WF   Page 3
    29 Oct. 1854 - Dysentery Parents: Samuel & Sarah Eakin

EAKIN, SARAH (3y)   WF   Page 19
    3 Sept. 1859 - Scarlet fev. Father: John Eakin

EARLS, CATHARINE (20y)   WF   Page 24   Saltville
    1871 - Dropsy   Parents: J.L. & Ann EARLES

EDMONDSON, MARGARET (74y 2m 15d) WF   Page 1
    19 Feb. 1853   Parents: Robt. & Jane Buchanan
    Reported by Robt. B. Edmondson, son   Spouse: Thos. Edmondson, dec'd

EDMONDSON, MARY (86y)   WF   Page 19
    20 April 1859   Father: James Glenn
    Reported by J.L.G. Edmondson, son   Spouse: Robt. Edmondson

EDMONDSON, WM. M. (9m)   WM   Page 24   Glade Spring
    1871 - Croup   Parents: Saml. P. & Catharine Edmondson

EDMUNDSON, [n.n.] (1d)   WF   Page 8
    16 July 1855   Parents: Wm. & Elizabeth Edmundson

EDMUNDSON, ANDREW (2y)   WM   Page 13
    2 Sept. 1857 - Inflamation Father: Jas. Edmundson

EDMUNDSON, JAMES B. (4y)   WM   Page 5
    22 Sept. 1854 - Dysentery Parents: Jno. D. & Marg't Edmundson

EDUARD (3y 3m)   SM   Page 18
    2 Feb. 1858   Owner: B.P. Smith

EDWARDS, ANN (90y)   WF   Page 5   Abingdon
    1854   Spouse: Capt. Edwards
    Born in Massachusetts   Reported by Chas. G. Fitzgerald, friend

EDWARDS, RACHEL (18y)   SF   Page 15
    20 Nov. 1857 - Fever   Owner: Arthur Edwards

ELIZA (5y)   SF   Page 4
    1854 - Dysentery or flux   Parents: Lewis & Viney
                                      Owner: Gardner Grant

ELIZA (32y)   SF   Page 19
    1 Jan. 1859 - Consumption   Reported by Martha Horn, 'witness'

ELIZABETH (2y 1d)   SF   Page 10
    4 June 1855 - Fever   Owner: Alexr. Susong

ELLA (7m)   SF   Page 21
    7 March 1859 - Fever   Owner: Mary G. Bondurant
    Reported by Mary A. Nuckols, daughter of owner

ELLEN (30y)   CF   Page 1   Poor house
    June 1853   Reported by John L. Caldwell,
                                          Steward - poor house

ELLEN (6y)   SF   Page 4
    1854 - Pneumonia   Mother: Asaline
    Reported by Harriet Bailey, mistress   Owner: Jas. A. Bailey

ELLEN (5y)   WF   Page 4
    June 1854 - Scrofula   Master: Jacob Morell

ELLEN (3y)   S_   Page 7
    15 Sept. 1854 - Flux   Owner: Jnot. T. Hanby

ELLEN (3m)   SF   Page 17
    11 March 1858 - Flux   Owner: Isaac Fleenor

ELLINGTON, JOHN C. (14y)   WM   Page 14
    28 Aug. 1854 - Flux   Parents: Frans. & Rebecca Ellington

ELLINGTON, MATTHEW (24y)   WM   Page 6
    24 Aug. 1854 - Flux   Parents: Frans. & Rebecca Ellington

ELMORE, HUGH A. (10y)   WM   Page 12
    3 May 1856 - Fever

EMELINE (35y)   SF   Page 2   CO
    26 March 1853 - Fever   Owner: Jacob Lynch

EMELINE (30y)   SF   Page 5   South Fork
    15 Sept. 1854 - Consumption   Owner: Andw. C. Cole

ESTRIGE, MARTHA (4m)   WF   Page 28   North Fork
    26 Jan. 1892 - Hives   Parents: David & Loucinda ESTRIDGE

EVANS, WM. S. (1y)   WM   Page 3
    24 Dec. 1854 - Unknown   Parents: Jno. & Margaret Evans

EWING, JAMES (47y)   WM   Page 16
    24 Aug. 1858 - Flux   Parents: S. & Patsey Ewing
                                      Spouse: Patsey Ewing

FANNY (65y)   SF   Page 20
    15 Sept. 1859 - Hemorrhage   Master: John Clark

FARIS, BETTIE J. (21y 3m)   WF   Page 25
    12 Feb. 1892 - Consumption   Spouse: S.W.R. Faris

FARIS, ETHEL V. (9m)   WF   Page 25
    13 Feb. 1892 - La grippe   Parents: S.W.R. & Bet. J. Faris

FARIS, THOS. (80y)   WM   Page 12   F
    20 Dec. 1856 - Fever

FARRAS, NANCY (80y)   WF   Page 24   Saltville
    1871

FARRIS, ELIZ'TH (71y)   WF   Page 12
    15 June 1856 - Consumption   Spouse: Jas. Farris

FARRIS, JANE (79y)   WF   Page 19
    5 Oct. 1859   Spouse: Sam'l Farris

FARRIS, JOHN (2y)   WM   Page 21   F
    25 Dec. 1859 - Scarlet fev. Father: David Farris

FARRIS, WM. (17y)   WM   Page 13   F
    4 Feb. 1857 - Typhoid fev.   Father: Thos. Farris
    Reported by Thos. FARIS, father

FELTY, ELIZABETH (32y 1m)   WF   Page 9
    15 Aug. 1855 - Flux   Parents: George & Sarah Houser
                      Spouse: Wm. Felty

FELTY, LUCINDA J. (9y 2m)   WF   Page 15
    27 Aug. 1857 - Fever   Parents: Malon & D. Felty
    Reported by B.F. Felty, uncle

FICKLE, ISAAC (3y)   WM   Page 10
    30 Aug. 1854 - Disentary   Parents: Reuben & Eliza Fickle

FIELDS, MARY (7y)   WF   Page 2
    4 Jan. 1853 - Fever   Father: Wm. B. Fields

FIELDS, SARAH (13y)   WF   Page 2
    9 Dec. 1853 - Fever   Father: Wm. B. Fields

FLANIGAN, JOHN (8y)   WM   Page 19
    27 Sept. 1859   Mother: Elizabeth Flanigan

FLEENOR, [n.n.] (1d)   WF   Page 15
    25 Nov. 1857 - Fever   Parents: Isaac & W.J. Fleenor

FLEENOR, [n.n.]   M   Page 17
    6 July 1858 - Dead born   Parents: Gasper & M. Fleenor

FLEENOR, [n.n.]   WF   Page 21
    27 March 1859 - Dead born   Parents: Jasper & M. Fleenor

FLEENOR, ADELINE (34y 10m 19d)   WF   Page 2
    6 Oct. 1853 - Unknown   Parents: Adam & Sarah Fleenor

FLEENOR, AMANDA C. (4y)   WF   Page 21
    27 Oct. 1859 - Fever   Parents: Jno. Q. & Julia A. Fleenor

FLEENOR, BENJ. (13y 4m 2d)   WM   Page 15
    15 Oct. 1857 - Flux   Parents: Allen & Sarah Fleenor

FLEENOR, CAMPBELL J. (11y 8m)   WM   Page 17
    26 June 1858 - Flux   Parents: Gasper & M. Fleenor

FLEENOR, CATHERINE (48y 6m)   WF   Page 15
    25 July 1857 - Fever   Parents: Daniel & E. Kaylor
                                       Spouse: Peter Fleenor

FLEENOR, ELLEN (4y)   SF   Page 15
    21 March 1857   Owner: Isaac Fleenor

FLEENOR, GILBERT B. (6y 3m)   WM   Page 17
    8 July 1858 - Flux   Parents: Joel & M.A. Fleenor

FLEENOR, H.C. (23y 6m 15d)   WM   Page 15
    22 Jan. 1857 - Flux   Parents: Thos. W. & Deida Fleenor

FLEENOR, HENRY (79y 9m 9d)   WM   Page 17
    5 July 1858 - Flux   Parents: N. & Mary Fleenor
                                       Spouse: Letta Fleenor

FLEENOR, JAS. B. (1y 5m)   WM   Page 17
    8 Aug. 1858 - Flux   Parents: Joel & M.A. Fleenor

FLEENOR, JOHN (1y 11m)   WM   Page 15
    7 May 1857 - Flux   Parents: David & M. Fleenor

FLEENOR, JULIA A. (33y 3m)   WF   Page 18
    12 Oct. 1858 - Fever   Parents: M. & E. Talbert
                                       Spouse: J.Q. Fleenor

FLEENOR, LEVI C. (2y)   WM   Page 17
    28 June 1858 - Flux   Parents: Gasper & M. Fleenor

FLEENOR, LIDDIA A. (3y)   WF   Page 17
    28 June 1858 - Flux   Parents: Gasper & M. Fleenor

FLEENOR, MARTHA L. (6m)   WF   Page 28   Kinderhook
    1 May 1892 - Croup   Parent: J.R. Fleenor

FLEENOR, MARY (33y)   SF   Page 15
    4 Feb. 1857 - Fever   Owner: Isaac Fleenor

FLEENOR, MARY (87y)   WF   Page 17
    19 June 1858 - Flux   Parents: A. & Elizabeth Hudson
    Reported by Nancy Fleenor, daughter

FLEENOR, MARY A. (4y 3m)   WF   Page 15
    15 Sept. 1857 - Flux   Parents: Allen & Sarah Fleenor

FLEENOR, MATILDA (6y)   WF   Page 9
    8 Aug. 1855 - Flux   Parents: David & M. Fleenor

FLEENOR, NANCY C. (9y 6m)   WF   Page 17
    6 July 1858 - Flux   Parents: Gasper & M. Fleenor

FLEENOR, NANNIE (2y)   WF   Page 28   Kinderhook
    Oct. 1892 - Croup   Father: Milton Fleenor

FLEENOR, PETER H. (56y)   WM   Page 21
    24 April 1859 - Dropsey   Parents: Christhy & Mary Fleenor
                                       Spouse: Elizabeth Fleenor

FLEENOR, SARAH (83y 1d)   WF   Page 2
    9 July 1853 - Fever   Reported by John Fleenor, son

FLEENOR, SOLOMON (74y 5m)   WM   Page 16
    15 June 1858 - Flux   Parents: G. & M. Fleenor
                       Spouse: Susan Fleenor

FLEENOR, SUSAN E. (7y 10m)   WF   Page 17
    19 June 1858 - Flux   Parents: Gasper & M. Fleenor

FLEENOR, W.J.L. (3y 2m)   WM   Page 17
    3 July 1858 - Flux   Parents: Joel & M.A. Fleenor

FLEENOR, W.M. (1m)   WM   Page 28   Kinderhook
    1 Nov. 1892 - Flux   Parents: Robert & Sallie Fleenor

FLORANCE (7y)   SF   Page 19
    30 April 1859 - Scarlet fev. Master: Claburn L. Shugart

FORESTER, WILLIAM (1y)   WM   Page 5   South Fork
    8 Sept. 1854 - Dysentery   Parents: Joseph & Dorcas Fleenor

FOSTER, [n.n.] (21d)   WM   Page 25
    13 July 1892 - Not known   Parents: R.C. & S.M. Foster

FOSTER, MARTHA I. (1y)   WF   Page 12
    17 June 1856 - Inflamation lungs   Parents: Joseph T. & Dorcas Foster

FOSTER, SARAH M. (37y)   WF   Page 25
    22 Aug. 1892 - Dropsy   Spouse: R.C. Foster

FOUST, JOHN (6m)   SM   Page 15
    20 Nov. 1857 - Fever   Owner: Henry Foust

FRANKLIN, WILLIAM D. (21y)   WM   Page 18
    15 Feb. 1858 - Consumption   Father: Elisha Franklin

FRACTION, WILLIE B. (14y)   CM   Page 23
    16 June 1871 - Consumption   Parents: John & Hannah Fraction
    Born in Abingdon Twp.

FRY, RACHEL L. (1y 3m 10d)   WF   Page 7   Saltville
    6 Oct. 1855 - Dysentery   Geo. N. & Sarah A. Fry
    Born in Saltville

FULLEN, JOHNSON (49y)   WM   Page 16
    24 June 1858 - Flux   Parents: F. & Jane Fullen

FULLER, DICIE (20y)   WF   Page 28   Kinderhook
    10 July 1892 - Consumption

FURGUSON, WILLIAM (90y)   WM   Page 18
    30 Dec. 1858 - Old Age   Father: Joel Furguson
    Born in Virginia   Spouse: Mary Furguson

GALLIHER, ANN E. (6y)   WF   Page 20
    16 Sept. 1859 - Scarlet fev. Father: William Galliher

GALLIHER, JANE (43y)   WF   Page 7
    25 Jan. 1855 - Consumption   Parents: Wm. & Nancy Galliher
                       Spouse: Joel ADAMS

GALLIHER, WM. J. (73y)   WM   Page 25   F
    22 Aug. 1892 - Liver disease Spouse: Nan. M. Galliher

GARDNER, THOMAS H.   WM   Page 5   ST   E&H College
    Oct. 1854   Father: Wm. C. Gardner
    Born in Pulaski Co., Va.   Reported by E.E. Wiley, president

GARNER, JOHN M. (13y 7m)   WM   Page 2
    2 Sept. 1853 - Drowned   Parents: Saml. & Jane Garner

GARNES, ELIZABETH (64y)   WF   Page 8
    11 Sept. 1855 - Consumption   Parent: Cane
    Born in Bottetourt Co., Va.   Spouse: Benjn. T. Garnes

GARRETT, CAMPBELL (7m)   WM   Page 4
    26 Aug. 1854 - Dysentery   Parents: Henry C. & Nancy J. Garrett
    Reported by Henry C. Garrett, Arthur D. Hutton, physician

GARRETT, CHARLES R. (3y 2m)   WM   Page 21
    18 Nov. 1859 - Fits   Parents: Thos. & Nancy J. Garrett

GARRETT, ELIZABETH (71y)   WF   Page 21
    15 Oct. 1859 - Old age   Parents: Saml. & Mary A. Bond
    Reported by Henry S. Garrett, son   Spouse: Geo. Garrett

GARRETT, FRANCES (3y)   WM   Page 4
    26 Aug. 1854 - Dysentery   Parents: Henry C. & Nancy J. Garrett
    Reported by Henry C. Garrett, Arthur D. Hutton, physician

GARRETT, HENRY C. (4y)   WM   Page 6
    6 Dec. 1854 - Flux   Parents: Wm. & Asa GRANT

GARRETT, HENRY L. (39y)   WM   Page 20
    13 Jan. 1859 - Consumption   Father: Henry Garrett
                                    Spouse: Nancy Garrett

GARRETT, LEGRAND (7y 4m)   WM   Page 4
    15 Sept. 1854 - Dysentery   Parents: Henry C. & Nancy J. Garrett
    Reported by Henry C. Garrett, Arthur D. Hutton, physician

GEORGE   SM   Page 2
    Feb. 1853 - Inflamation of lungs   Owner: James A. Bailey

GIBSON, MARY (50y)   CF   Page 23
    20 May 1871 - Dropsy   Born in Abingdon Twp.

GILBERT (45y)   SM   Page 20   F
    15 Feb. 1859 - Disease of heart   Master: Ballard P. Smith

GILES, FRANK L. (2y 6m)   WM   Page 25
    22 Nov. 1892 - Burned   Parents: G.W. & S.C. Giles

GILL, ANN E. (11m)   WF   Page 13
    30 Aug. 1857 - S. fever   Father: Wm. W. HILL

GILL, THOS. C. (1y 1m)   WM   Page 13
    15 Aug. 1857 - Cholera morbus   Father: Thos. GILL

GILLENWATER, WM. A. (1y 3m)   WM   Page 15
    19 Oct. 1857 - Fever   Parents: Geo. L. & Sarah Gillenwater

GILLENWATERS, JOHN L. (59y)   WM   Page 23   F
    15 Nov. 1871 - Liver   Parents: Joel & Lucy Gillenwaters
                                    Spouse: Louisa Gillenwaters

GILLENWATERS, M.E. (1y 1m)   WF   Page 21
   17 Aug. 1859 - Fever   Parents: Geo. L. & Sarah Gillenwaters

GILLEY, PHEBY (50y)   WF   Page 12
   15 May 1856 - Inflamation lungs   Spouse: Peter Gilley
   Reported by daughter   Born in North Carolina

GILLILAND, JOHN K. (56y 8m)   WM   Page 15
   26 June 1857 - Consumption   Parents: Jas. & M. Gilliland
   Reported by David Gilliland, son   Spouse: Martha Gilliland

GLENN, BENJAMIN (68y)   WM   Page 1
   5 Dec. 1853 - Erysipelas

GLOVER, JNO. F. (5y)   WM   Page 30   Town of Abingdon
   9 July 1892 - Pneumonia   Parents: C.W. & L.E. Glover

GOBBLE, ABRAM (79y 5m 6d)   WM   Page 6   F
   16 June 1854 - Cancer   Parents: Fred. & E. Gobble
   Reported by Wm. M. Gobble, son

GOBBLE, JESSEE (1y 4m)   WM   Page 15
   17 Oct. 1857 - Fever   Parents: Henry & M. Gobble
   Reported by Jont. Gobble, uncle

GOBBLE, LOUISA F. (2m)   WF   Page 15
   22 Dec. 1857 - Fever   Parents: Abram & Cath Gobble

GOBBLE, MARY E. (12y)   WF   Page 17
   17 Sept. 1858 - Flux   Parents: Abram & C. Gobble

GOBBLE, SAMUEL (79y)   WM   Page 28   North Fork
   Oct. 1892 - Palsey   Reported by son

GOBBLE, WM. (1y 4m)   WM   Page 15
   17 Oct. 1857 - Fever   Parents: Henry & M. Gobble
   Reported by Jont. Gobble, uncle

GOFF, ELIJAH (2y 7m)   WM   Page 11
   13 June 1856 - Cramp   Parents: Jacob & E. Goff

GOFF, JAS. K.P. (12y)   WM   Page 17
   17 July 1858 - Shot himself   Parents: Wilson F. & M.A. Goff

GOFF, L.M. (59y)   WM   Page 25   F
   25 Sept. 1892 - Cramp colic   Reported by F.G. Goff, son

GOFF, WILSON H. (9y 17d)   WM   Page 11
   2 Aug. 1856 - Flux   Parents: Jacob & E. Goff

GOODMAN, [n.n.]   WF   Page 15
   1 Sept. 1857 - Still born   Parents: J.S. & E. Goodman

GOODMAN, [n.n.]   WF   Page 17
   11 April 1858 - Dead born   Parents: Jas. B. & J. Goodman

GOODMAN, SUSAN (70y)   WF   Page 2
   7 July 1853 - Fever   Reported by Isaac Goodman, son

GRACE, DORCAS (2y)   WF   Page 12
   24 Oct. 1856 - S. fever   Parents: Wm. & Mary Grace

GRACE, WILLIAM (42y)   WM   Page 12
   28 Apr. 1856 - Pneumonia   Spouse: Mary Grace

GRAHAM, ELIZABETH (58y 8m 19d)   WF   Page 23
    31 Nov. 1871   Parents: James & Jane Graham
    Born in North Fork Twp.   Reported by Martha Graham, sister

GRANT, ELIZABETH (49y)   WF   Page 1
    26 July 1853   Parents: Robert & Mary Edmondson
    Spouse: James Grant

GRANT, ELIZABETH (87y)   WF   Page 3
    26 May 1854 - Old age   Parents: Isaac & Mary Grant
    Born in Lenoir Co., N.C.   Reported by Charlotte Miller, daughter

GRANT, ELIZABETH H. (1y 21d)   WF   Page 3
    28 Aug. 1854   Parents: Jno. C. & Theodocia Grant
    Reported by Gardner Grant, grandfather of dec'd

GRANT, ISAAC A. (73y 9m)   WM   Page 25   PH
    1 Feb. 1892 - Cramp colic   Spouse: Nancy Grant

GRANT, LUCINDA J. (14y)   WF   Page 18
    13 May 1858 - Typhoid fever   Father: Gardner Grant

GRANVILLE (2y 3m)   SM   Page 1
    20 Feb. 1853   Parents: Samuel & Harriet
    Owner: Robt. B. Edmondson

GRAVES, GEO. (3m)   CM   Page 30   Town of Abingd
    1 June 1892 - Yellow jaundice   Parents: W.P. & Cor. Graves

GRAY, FRANCES J. (18y 6m)   WF   Page 6
    17 Oct. 1854 - Flux   Parents: Frans. W. & Jane Irby

GRAY, JOHN (84y)   WM   Page 9   F
    16 Aug. 1855 - Old age   Parents: Jno. & Margaret Gray
    Reported by John Gray, son

GRAY, MARGRET E. (27y 4m)   WF   Page 15
    23 Nov. 1857 - Fever   Parents: Jas. & Jane Lowry
    Spouse: F.T. Gray

GRAY, NANCY I. (21y)   WF   Page 11
    29 May 1856 - Shot herself   Parents: Jas. L. & E.J. Davis
    Spouse: Wm. M. Gray

GRAY, WILLIAM (1y 11m)   WM   Page 2
    20 July 1853   Father: John Gray

GRAY, WILLIAM (2y 11m)   WM   Page 15
    12 Dec. 1857 - Fever   Parents: F.T. & M.E. Gray

GREENWAY, JOHN H. (26y)   WM   Page 9
    24 June 1855 - Consumption   Parents: Jno. C. & M.C. Greenway

GREER, BETSEY (30y)   CF   Page 30   Town of Abingc
    1 Oct. 1892 - Dropsy   Reported by John Greer

GREER, NANCY (39y)   WF   Page 20
    19 Feb. 1859 - Consumption   Father: James Speer
    Born in Tennessee   Spouse: Elijah Greer

GRINSTEAD, WILLIAM (3y)   WM   Page 13
     9 April 1857 - Typhoid fev. Father: Benj. F. Grinstead

GRUBB, ANDREW D. (60y)   WM   Page 18   F
     14 Oct. 1858 - Fall from a tree   Father: Nicholas Grubb
     Reported by W.H. Grubb, son Spouse: Elizabeth Grubb

GRUBB, JOSEPH (5y)   WM   Page 20
     19 Aug. 1859 - Cholera morbus   Father: Martain H. Grubb

GRUBB, LILLIAN R. (3y 6m)   WF   Page 25
     3 Dec. 1892 - Tonsilitis   Parents: W.P. & H.N. Grubb

HAGY, [n.n.] (1d)   WM   Page 30   Town of Abingdon
     19 Dec. 1892 - Not known   Parents: J.L.P. & Roxy Hagy

HAGY, ADORA (7m)   WF   Page 24   Glade Spring
     1871 - Inflamation   Parents: Jas. & Mary A. Hagy

HAGY, DELILAH (29y)   WMF   Page 13   F
     18 April 1857 - Typhoid fev.   Father: Joseph Hagy

HALL, DANIEL J. (16y)   WM   Page 3
     19 Oct. 1854 - Dysentery   Parents: Parker & Ruth Hall

HAM, EMANUEL (18y)   WM   Page 25
     26 July 1892 - Typhoid fev. Parents: Ezekiel & Marth. Ham

HAMILTON, ABRAM (1y 7m 6d)   WM   Page 6
     27 Nov. 1854 - Flux   Parents: Robt. B. & M.M. Hamilton

HAMILTON, ADAM F. (32y)   WM   Page 4
     16 June 1854 - Bleeding at lungs   Reported by John Minnick

HAMILTON, NANCY E. (19y)   WF   Page 4
     1 Sept. 1854 - Dysentery   Parents: Jno. C. & Sarah Hamilton

HAMILTON, SARAH (4y)   WF   Page 17
     18 June 1858 - Flux   Parents: J.M. & S. Hamilton

HAMMONS, ALFRED (5y)   WM   Page 12
     1 June 1856 - Fever

HAMMONS, JNO. (5y)   WM   Page 12
     1 June 1856 - Fever

HAMMONS, LORETTA (2y)   WF   Page 12
     2 June 1856 - Fever

HAMMONS, MARY (45y)   WF   Page 12
     9 June 1856 - Fever

HANBY, JONATHAN T. (1y 10m)   WM   Page 6
     29 Aug. 1854 - Flux   Parents: Peter S. & C.N. Hanby

HANBY, JULIA (80y)   WF   Page 29   Goodson Dist.
     20 April 1892 - Old age   Reported by son

HANBY, PETER S. (52y)   WM   Page 11   F
     22 Jan. 1856 - Consumption   Parents: Geo. & Cath Hanby
                                  Spouse: Cath. H. Hanby

HANBY, VIRGINIA (6y 8m)   WF   Page 6
     1 Sept. 1854 - Flux   Parents: Peter S. & C.N. Hanby

HAND, HOPE W. (3m 16d)   CM Page 25
  9 July 1892 - Not known Parents: W.T.S. & M.E. Hand

HAND, JOHN (7y)   WM Page 5
  5 Oct. 1854 - Dysentery Mother: Mary Hand

HAND, MARG. E. (33y)   CF Page 25
  10 May 1892 - Heart disease Spouse: W.T.S. Hand

HANFORD, SAML. W. (32y)   WM Page 10 CL
  28 Dec. 1856 - Fever   Reported by Geo. C. Langhorn, friend

HANKLEY, MARY ANN (26y 8m) WF Page 7
  19 March 1855 - Fever Parents: Geo. & Mary Burkhart
  Born in Smyth Co., Va. Spouse: Jas. H. Hankley

HANNAH   SF Page 1
  Sept. 1853 - Burnt   Owner: Thomas Wilkerson

HARKINS, MARY (15d)   WF Page 17
  24 Dec. 1858 - Flux   Parents: Peter & S. Harkins

HARLOW, JAMES (13y)   WM Page 6
  22 Nov. 1854 - Flux   Parents: Thos. & Jane Harlow

HARRIET (36y)   SF Page 7 CO
  April 1855   Parents: Peter & Rose
  Owner: Robt. B. Edmundson Spouse: Sam

HARRIS, ARCEY (22y)   WF Page 8
  4 Oct. 1855 - Consumption Parents: Jas. & Sarah Harris
  Reported by John Miller, neighbor

HARRIS, REBECCA (74y)   WF Page 3
  13 May 1854 - Hemorrhage - lungs Parents: John & Ruth Evans
  Reported by John Wright, son in law

HARRISON, WM. (18m)   WM Page 9
  24 Aug. 1855 - Flux   Reported by Frans. Smith, friend

HARTSOCK, CHARLES (74y)   WM Page 15 F
  17 April 1857 - Consumption Parents: Saml. & Eliza Hartsock
  Reported by E.L. Booher, son in law

HARTSOCK, SARAH (7y)   WF Page 6
  28 July 1854 - Flux   Parents: Isaac & N. Hartsock

HAWKINS, NANCY (38y)   WF Page 18
  15 Dec. 1858 - Flux   Reported by Reuben Thomas, neighbor
  Born in North Carolina

HAWTHORN, LYDIA (43y 6m 7d) WF Page 7
  31 Aug. 1855 - Dysentery Mother: Martha Cole
  Born in Smyth Co., Va. Spouse: David S. Hawthorn

HAWTHORNE, MARTH. J. (28y) WF Page 12
  17 May 1856 - Unknown Parents: Jas. & Ann Hawthorne

HAYTER, TABITHA (72y)   WF Page 1   Russell Co.
  4 June 1853 - Typhoid Fev. Father: James Fullen
            Spouse: James C. Hayter

HAYTON, MARY (52y)   WF   Page 25
    1 Sept. 1892 - Flux   Spouse: Thos. Hayton

HEATH, ABRAM (10y 6m)   WM   Page 5
    <u>31</u> Sept. 1854 - Dysentery Parents: Jno. & Alcey Heath

HEATH, ELIZABETH (4y)   WF   Page 20
    15 March 1859 - Scarlet fev. Father: John Heath

HEATH, JOHN (12y 3m)   WM   Page 5
    2 Oct. 1854 - Dysentery   Parents: Jno. & Alcey Heath

HEATH, JOHN (2y)   WM   Page 20
    12 March 1859 - Scarlet fev. Father: John Heath

HELTON, CAROLINE M. (2d)   WF   Page 8
    5 June 1855   Parents: Saml. & Caroline Helton

HELYARD, C.W. (19y)   WM   Page 30   Town of Abingdon
    1 Jan. 1892 - Consumption Parents: S.L. & Sarah Helyard

HELYARD, J.W. (17y)   WM   Page 30   Town of Abingdon
    4 Feb. 1892 - Fever   Parents: S.L. & Sarah Helyard

HENDERSON, NANCY (3y)   WF   Page 13
    6 May 1857 - Typhoid fev. Father: Robt. Henderson

HENDERSON, ROBERT H. (37y) WM   Page 18   F
    16 Aug. 1858 - Typhoid fev. Father: Thomas Henderson
    Born in Va.   Spouse: Mary Henderson

HENRIETTA (2y 7m)   SF   Page 11
    7 Nov. 1856 - Poisoned   Owner: Jacob Lynch

HENRITZE, CYNTHIA (25y 1m 4d) WF   Page 2
    27 Aug. 1853 - Fever   Parents: Samuel & Jane Keller
                    Spouse: P.E.B.C. Henritze

HENRY (53y)   SM   Page 2   F
    20 March 1853 - Fever   Owner: Margaret R. White

HENRY (6d)   SM   Page 10
    Aug. 1855 - Cough   Owner: John F. Preston

HERNDON, EDWD. (62y)   WM   Page 25   F
    5 Feb. 1892 - Consumption Spouse: M.H. Herndon

HERNDON, WALTER (1y)   WM   Page 28   North Fork
    29 Dec. 1892 - Not known Parents: J.N. & Florence Herndon

HERRON, NANCY M. (12y)   WF   Page 1   Poor House
    8 April 1853   Mother: Elizabeth Herron
    Reported by John L. Caldwell, steward, Poor House

HILLIARD, ANN (57y)   WF   Page 13   F
    5 May 1857 - Consumption Father: Jas. Anderson
                    Spouse: Saml. Hilliard

HILLIARD, ROSANNAH (15y)   WF   Page 23   F
    7 July 1871 - Not ascertained Father: Joel Hilliard
    Born in Abingdon Twp.

HIRAM (9y)   SM   Page 18
    30 Aug. 1858 - Inflamation   Owner: Louisa Kelly
    Born in Va.

HISKELL, [n.n.] (1d)   SM
    15 March 1857 - Killed   Owner: Wm. King Heskell
    Reported by Geo. C. Langhorne, neighbor

HITE, THOMAS J. (1y)   WM   Page 21
    22 Aug. 1859 - Killed   Parents: Nicholas & M.L. Hite

HOBBS, A.E. (10y)   WM   Page 28   Kinderhook
    4 Oct. 1892 - Fever   Father: Harvey Hobbs

HOBBS, JAS. K.P. (10y 9m)   WM   Page 11
    30 Oct. 1856 - Disentary   Parents: Harrison & Maria Hobbs

HOBBS, MARY A.C. (3m 20d)   WF   Page 23   Kinderhook Twp
    3 Aug. 1871 - Croup   Parents: Jefferson H. & M.J. Hobbs

HOBBS, RHODA G. (2y 7m)   WF   Page 6
    24 Nov. 1854 - Flux   Parents: Henry B. & M.A. Hobbs

HOBBS, SALLIE (65y)   WF   Page 28   Kinderhook
    Jan. 1892 - Heart disease   Reported by R.M. Hensley

HOBBS, THOMAS P. (13y)   WM   Page 28   Kinderhook
    5 March 1892 - Killed by a log   Father: Thomas Hobbs

HOCKETT, WILLIAM (31y 15m)   WM   Page 1   F
    2 Oct. 1853   Parents: Jno. & Catherine Hockett
                                    Spouse: Eleanor Hockett

HOGSTON, CORA B. (7y)   WF   Page 25
    14 Sept. 1892 - Croup   Parents: Jno. & N.J. Hogston

HOLAWAY, SERENA (15d)   WF   Page 20
    29 Dec. 1859   Father: Wells Holaway
    Reported by WILLS Holaway, father

HOLLEY, ELLEN (16y)   WF   Page 7
    Dec. 1855 - Consumption   Parents: Madison & Elizabeth Holley

HOLLY, MADISON Y. (6y)   WM   Page 4
    15 Jan. 1854   Parents: Madison Y. & Eliz. Holly
    Reported by Madison Y. HOLLEY, father

HOLMES, JAS. (45y)   WM   Page 25   F
    17 July 1892 - Scroffula   Reported by Jas. M. Lee, friend

HOLT, [n.n.]   WM   Page 10
    23 Sept. 1856 - Still born   Parents: Wm. & Mary A. Holt

HORNE, MARY JANE (3y 19d)   WF   Page 5   Middle Fork
    19 Aug. 1854 - Dysentery   Parents: Jno. E. & Mary Horne

HORTENSTINE, MARGRET (54y 3m)   WF   Page 15   F
    19 March 1857 - Fever   Parents: Jas. & Phoebe Wilson
                                    Spouse: Jno. Hortenstine

HOUSTON, MATTHEW P. (6y)   WM   Page 5   Mill Creek
    23 Jan. 1854 - Consumption   Parents: James & May Houston

HOUSTON, WM. (66y)   WM   Page 12   F
        13 Sept. 1856 - Accidental injury   Parent: M.V. Houston
        Reported by Jas. Buchanan, son in law

HOWELL, W.T. (4m)   WM   Page 13
        26 Feb. 1856 - Unknown   Father: Wm. Howell

HUDSON, CAROLINE (15y)   WF   Page 4
        22 May 1854 - Inflammation of lungs   Parents: Wm. & Rachel Hudson

HUMPHREY, REUBEN (59y)   WM   Page 14   F
        4 May 1857 - Consumption   Spouse: Rizziah Humphrey

HUMPHREYS, MARY C. (1y 6m)   WF   Page 15
        6 Sept. 1857 - Flux   Parents: A.H. & N.A. Humphreys

HURLEY, ABNER (1y 3m)   WM   Page 25
        18 Sept. 1892 - Diarhoea   Parents: W.H. & Eliz. Hurley

HURT, JAMES (9y 6m)   WM   Page 17
        10 April 1858 - Croup   Parents: J.D. & Ann E. Hurt

HURT, MARY (6y)   WF   Page 15
        15 Sept. 1857 - Flux   Parents: Geo. W. & R. Hurt

HURT, SARAH E. (4y)   WF   Page 15
        15 Sept. 1857 - Flux   Parents: Geo. W. & R. Hurt

HUTTON, MARY REBECCA (4y 11m 19d)   WF   Page 8
        10 Aug. 1855 - Dysentery   Parents: Jno. & Jane Hutton

HUTTON, R.S.C. (61y)   WM   Page 25   F
        26 Nov. 1892 - Rheumatism   Reported by Wm. E. Hutton, son

INMAN, SALLY (20y)   WF   Page 8
        15 Nov. 1855 - Consumption   Parents: Edmond & Sally Inman
        Born in Surry Co., N.C.

IRESON, GEO. A. (1y)   WM   Page 17
        14 Sept. 1858 - Flux   Parents: Wm. & L. Ireson

IRESON, JAMES D. (8y 2m)   WM   Page 8
        Aug. 1855 - Dysentery   Parents: James C. & Ellen Ireson

ISAAC (5y 6m)   SM   Page 7
        29 Aug. 1854 - Flux   Owner: Peter S. Hanby

ISAAC (73y)   SM   Page 7
        28 Oct. 1854 - Rupture   Master: Jas. C. Campbell

ISAAC (1y 6m)   WM   Page 18
        29 March 1858   Owner: John Byars

ISAAC (5m)   SM   Page 18
        15 Dec. 1858 - Burned to death   Owner: Jas. C. Hayter

ISABELLA (28y)   SF   Page 18
        17 Oct. 1858 - Inflamation of brain   Owner: B.P. Smith

JACKSON, DORCAS (3y 9m)   WF   Page 4
        7 July 1854 - Dysentery   Parents: John R. & Mary Jackson

JACKSON, EPHARIN (80y)   WM   Page 22
        17 July 1859 - Fever   Reported by Wm. Massy, son-in-law

JACKSON, EPHARIN (16y)   WM   Page 22
    15 Oct. 1859 - Fever   Parents: John & Matilda Jackson

JACKSON, FLORENCE (3y)   WF   Page 12
    30 Aug. 1856 - Dysentary   Father: Jno. J. Jackson

JACKSON, JULIA (1m 15d)   WF   Page 25
    30 July 1892 - Not known   Parents: F.M & S.E. Jackson
    Born in Smyth Co., Va.

JAMES, [n.n.] (1d)   WM   Page 29   Goodson Dist.
    17 June 1892 - Not known   Parents: Sidney & Lucy James

JAMES, ELIZ. V. (10m)   WF   Page 13
    19 Oct. 1857 - Typhoid fev.   Father: James James

JAMES, JONATHAN (20y)   WM   Page 10
    19 Nov. 1856 - Fever   Parents: Jno. & Nancy James

JAMISON, C.D. (47y 9m 13d)   WM   Page 25
    28 March 1892 - Consumption   Spouse: 'Mrs. Jamison'
    Born in Smyth Co., Va.

JANE (15y)   SF   Page 1
    1 Oct. 1853   Parents: Sonny & Melly
                           Mistress: Jane Porterfield

JAQUES, MARY (72y)   WF   Page 7
    14 March 1855 - Inflammation in lungs
    Born in Westmoreland Co., Eng.   Parents: Wm. & Margaret Hudson
    Reported by Wm. Hudson, brother   Spouse: Wm. Jaques

JENNINGS, RACHEL   WF   Page 5   Near Cedarville
    1854 - Consumption   Reported by Arthur D. Hutton, physician

JESSEE (22y 10m)   SM   Page 21
    17 Dec. 1859 - Killed   Owner: Edward E. Lathan

JOHN (2y 1m)   SM   Page 11
    22 Feb. 1856 - Fever   Owner: Joseph W. Rhea

JOHN (2y 6m)   SM   Page 11
    1 April 1856 - Fever   Owner: Jno. Worley

JOHN (4y)   SM   Page 18
    7 Dec. 1858 - Inflamation of bowels   Owner: Louisa Kelly

JOHN (2y)   SM   Page 20
    3 June 1859 - Croup   Master: James Hathorn

JOHNSON, [n.n.]   WF   Page 17
    14 Aug. 1858 - Dead born   Parents: W.J. & Susan Johnson

JOHNSON, ARAMINTA E.O. (11y)   WF   Page 13
    12 Aug. 1856 - Inflamation brain   Father: Robt. Johnson

JOHNSON, BENJN.   SM   Page 1   F
    19 March 1853 - Fever   Spouse: Mary Johnson
    Reported by Samuel Dunn, physician

JOHNSON, DORCAS (20y)   WF   Page 4
    May 1854 - Consumption   Parents: John & Eliz'th Johnson

JOHNSON, EGBERT (53y)   WM   Page 8
     May 1855 - Dispepsia   Mother: Elizabeth Johnson
     Reported by Saml. Moore, neighbor

JOHNSON, ISAAC (8y)   WM   Page 5
     April 1854 - Consumption   Parents: Jesse. & Eleanor Johnson
     Reported by W. Johnson, wife of Jno. C. Johnson

JOHNSON, JNO. W. (14y)   CM   Page 30   Town of Abingdon
     2 Aug. 1892 - Not given   Father: Flem. Johnson

JOHNSON, MARY (11y 9m)   WF   Page 13
     19 Sept. 1857 - Typhoid fev.   Father: Jno. Johnson

JOHNSON, MARY J. (34y)   CF   Page 30   Town of Abingdon
     21 Jan. 1892 - Not given   Father: Wesley Cotten
     Reported by Fleur Johnson

JOHNSON, THOMAS (4y)   WM   Page 12
     3 Sept. 1856 - S. fever   Father: Wm. Johnson

JOHNSON, THOS. C. (75y)   WM   Page 30   Town of Abingdon
     5 March 1892 - Pneumonia   Father: Hugh Johnson
     Reported by sister

JOHNSTON, THOMAS (4m or 4y)   CM   Page 23
     6 July 1871 - Infermation of stomach   Born in Abingdon Twp.

JONES, [n.n.] (13d)   WF   Page 4
     20 July 1854   Parents: Furney & Rebecca Jones

JONES, ISAAC (3y 10m)   WM   Page 5   Rush Creek
     22 Sept. 1854 - Dysentery   Parents: Wm. B. & Cath Jones

JONES, ISAAC (95y)   SM   Page 15   F
     15 Aug. 1857 - Unknown   Owner: James M. Jones

JONES, SARAH (6y 3m)   SF   Page 15
     15 July 1857 - Unknown   Owner: James M. Jones

JONES, SARAH (12y)   CF   Page 23
     12 June 1871 - Billious fever   Born in Abingdon Twp.

JOSEPH (1y)   SM   Page 7
     15 Aug. 1854 - Flux   Owner: John H. Wallace

JULIA (3y)   SF   Page 7
     1 July 1855 - Scrofula   Mother: Caroline
     Born in Saltville, Va.   Owner: Henry L. Morgan

KASTNER, MARGARET (5y)   WF   Page 20
     15 Jan. 1859 - Croup   Father: Jacob KESTNER

KATRON, MARGARET (63y)   WF   Page 20
     15 Jan. 1859 - Disease liver   Father: David Gileland
                                   Spouse: Christian CATRON

KATRON, MARGARET A. (63y 6m)   WF   Page 18
     26 Jan. 1858 - Liver complaint   Father: David Gilliland
                                   Spouse: C. Katron

KAYLOR, MARIAH J. (12y 4m)   WF   Page 17
     4 July 1858 - Flux   Parents: Danl. & H. Kaylor

KAYLOR, ELIZABETH (3m)   WF   Page 15
    15 Sept. 1857 - Fever   Parents: Daniel & Hulda Kaylor

KAYLOR, ELIZABETH (96y)   WF   Page 21
    15 Oct. 1859 - Old age   Parents: John & Elizabeth Weeks
    Reported by A.B. Kaylor, son   Spouse: Daniel Kaylor

KELLER, DANIEL W. (3y 2m 26d)   WM   Page 7
    Dec. 1855 - Croup   Parents: Geo. & Nancy Keller

KELLER, EVA J. (41y 4m)   WF   Page 26
    28 Oct. 1892 - Consumption   Spouse: W.H.H. Keller

KELLER, JOHN C. (1y 6m)   WM   Page 15
    18 Oct. 1857 - Fits   Parents: Wm. N. & Ann R. Keller
    Reported by Jno. C. Campbell, grandfather

KELLEY, ELIZTH. F. (2y 3m 10d)   WF   Page 10
    18 Sept. 1856 - Fever   Parents: H.R. & A. FELTY

KELLEY, MARG. (79y)   WF   Page 26
    4 Nov. 1892 - Gen. debility   Reported by Andrew Kelley, son

KENEDY, J.E. (21y)   WM   Page 28   F   North Fork
    7 Jan. 1892 - Killed by gun shot   Parents: M.J. & Eliz. Kenedy

KENT, EUGENE (2m 22d)   WM   Page 25
    1 Sept. 1892 - Not known   Parents: J.C. & Fannie Kent

KESNER, E.B. (21y)   WM   Page 21
    16 July 1859 - Fever   Parents: David & Catharine Kesner

KESNER, JOHN B. (7m)   WM   Page 18
    24 Jan. 1858 - Cramp   Father: John Kesner
    Born in Va.

KESNER, LEVINIA (88y)   WF   Page 7
    12 March 1855 - Old age   Parents: Wentle & Dolly Wolf
    Born in Hagerstown, Penn.   Spouse: Henry CASNER

KESNER, SARAH A. (27y 3m)   WF   Page 17
    8 Sept. 1858 - Flux   Parents: H. & Catherine Forrest
    Reported by Catherine FOREST, mother   Spouse: John Kesner

KEYS, GEORGE B. (40y)   WM   Page 2   F
    28 July 1853 - Fever   Spouse: Sarah B. Keys

KEYS, GEO. H. (1m)   WM   Page 29   Goodson Dist.
    10 March 1892 - Not known   Parents: T.G. & Susan R. Keys

KEYS, ISABELLA (32y)   WF   Page 20
    23 Jan. 1859 - Inflamation brain   Father: James Lowrey
                                     Spouse: Robt. Keys, Jr.

KEYS, JAMES C. (24y)   WM   Page 23   F
    13 Sept. 1871 - Consumption   Father: Robert Keys
    Born in Abingdon Twp.

KEYS, JULIA C. (11y)   WF   Page 11
    25 Aug. 1856 - Disentary   Parents: Geo. B. & Sarah Keys

KEYS, MARTHA (74y)   WF   Page 23
    20 May 1871 - Infermation of bowels   Born in Abingdon Twp.

KEYS, SUSAN E. (13y)   WF   Page 11
    7 Aug. 1856 - Disentary   Parents: Geo. B. & Sarah Keys

KING, DINAH (110y)   CF   Page 23
    14 June 1871 - Old age   Born in Abingdon Twp.

KING, JAS. A.D. (8y 6m 7d)   WM   Page 11
    25 Oct. 1856 - Disentary   Parents: Jas. A. & E.M. King

KING, JNO. R. (5y)   WM   Page 11
    13 Nov. 1856 - Disentary   Parents: Jas. A. & E.M. King

KING, SARAH M. (7y 1m)   WF   Page 11
    10 Nov. 1856 - Disentary   Parents: Jas. A. & E.M. King

KNOTT, PETER (24y)   WM   Page 23   C   Kinderhook
    4 June 1871   Parents: James & Susan Sproles
    Reported by Mrs. Henritze, sister

KYLE, MILLY (112y)   CF   Page 30   L   Town of Abingdon
    25 Jan. 1892 - Old age   Reported by Angeline Black, her granddaughter

LANGLEY, ELI S. (18d)   WM   Page 8
    10 Feb. 1855 - Palsey   Parents: Jas. O. & Margaret Langley

LARGE, [n.n.]   WF   Page 15
    27 Dec. 1857 - Still born   Parents: James & Eady Large

LARIMER, ANDW. W. (2y)   WM   Page 8
    22 Sept. 1855 - Not known   Parents: Robt. & Rachel Larimer

LARIMER, HETTY K. (6y)   WF   Page 4
    6 Aug. 1854 - Dysentery   Parents: John & Sarah Larimer

LARIMER, MARIAH L. (1y 4m)   WF   Page 3
    Sept. 1854 - Dysentery   Parents: Robert E. & Mary Larimer

LARIMER, MARY (56y)   WF   Page 8   F
    17 Dec. 1855 - Consumption   Parents: Andw. & Elizabeth McKee
                                        Spouse: John Larimer

LARIMER, SARAH E. (3y)   WF   Page 4
    12 Aug. 1854 - Dysentery   Parents: Jno. & Sarah Larimer

LARIMORE, ANN (68y)   WF   Page 20   F
    8 May 1859 - Dysentery   Father: John Larimore
    Reported by Robert Larimore, brother

LARIMORE, DAVID (7y)   WM   Page 19
    9 Jan. 1858 - Scarlet fev.   Father: Robert LARIMER

LARIMORE, FEBY (14y)   WF   Page 20
    15 June 1859   Father: Andrew Larimore
    Reported by Robert Larimore, grandfather

LARIMORE, JOHN (44y)   WM   Page 20   F
    9 June 1859 - Consumption   Father: Robt. Larimore
                                        Spouse: Salley Larimore

LARIMORE, MARGARET (7y)   WF   Page 20
    15 May 1859 - Scarlet fev.   Father: William Larimore

LARIMORE, MATHEW M. (3y)   WM   Page 19
    15 Dec. 1858 - Scarlet fev.   Father: Robert LARIMER

LATHAN, DANIEL H. 92y 6m)   WM   Page 21
    15 Sept. 1859 - Fever   Parents: J.H. & Sarah M. LATHIN

LATHIM, DANIEL C. (2m)   WM   Page 6
    23 Nov. 1854 - Croup   Parents: M.H. & Ellen Lathim

LATHIM, F.M. (3y 6m)   WF   Page 17
    8 April 1858 - Fever   Parents: J.H. & S.M. Lathim

LAWSON, [n.n.] (2d)   W_   Page 23   North Fork Twp.
    11 Apr. 1871 - Infancy   Parents: Wm. B. & Sarah Lawson

LEAH (33y)   SF   Page 7
    17 Sept. 1855 - Scrofula   Mother: Peggy
                                   Owner: Madison Beatie

LEANARD, BENJ. F. (6m)   WM   Page 10
    10 Aug. 1856 - Disentary   Parents: Geo. & Martha Leanard
    Reported by Henry Shaffer, friend

LEE, CALDONIA (11m)   WF   Page 20
    13 July 1859   Father: James Lee

LEGARD, ELIZA (21d)   SF   Page 15
    11 Oct. 1857 - Fever   Owner: R.T. Legard

LENTICUM, JAMES (19y)   WM   Page 4
    March 1854 - Paralasis   Reported by Abram Smith, step-father

LEONARD, [n.n.] (1d)   WF   Page 29   Goodson
    6 March 1892 - Not known   Parents: Jack & Mary Leonard

LEONARD, ELIZABETH (1y 2m)   WF   Page 21
    5 July 1859 - Fever   Parents: Wm. & Sarah Leonard

LEONARD, JOS. (25y)   WF   Page 29   Goodson Dist.
    8 Sept. 1892 - Fever   Parents: Jas. & Lucinda Brooks
    Reported by husband

LEONARD, NANCY (28y)   WF   Page 17
    4 Dec. 1858 - Fever   Parents: Wm. & Sarah Blair
    Reported by Mima Leonard, MOTHER   Spouse: Geo. Leonard

LEONARD, NEWELL (1y 5m 6d)   WM   Page 9
    8 Aug. 1855 - Whooping cough   Parents: Jno. & M. Leonard

LEONARD, SARAH (40y)   WF   Page 9
    6 June 1855 - Flux   Parents: A. & C. Grubb
                                   Spouse: Wm. Leonard

LESTER, ANDW. D. (7y 6m)   WM   Page 5   Glade Spring
    Sept. 1854 - Dysentery   Parents: David & Eliz'th Lester
    Born in Smyth Co., Va.

LESTER, ANDREW J. (2y)   WM   Page 20
    20 July 1859 - Scarlet fev.   Father: Levi Lester

LESTER, JOHN M. (9y 8m 8d)   WM   Page 5   Glade Spring
    Oct. 1854 - Dysentery   Parents: David & Eliz'th Lester
    Born in Smyth Co., Va.

LESTER, LUCY (1y 7d)   WF   Page 26
    17 Sept. 1892 - Whooping co.   Parents: Z.T. & Eliz. Lester

LESTER, NANCY J. (56y 3m)   WF   Page 26
    26 Oct. 1892 - Consumption   Reported by Ryburn Lester, son

LESTER, ROBT. (1y)   WM   Page 20
    20 July 1857 - Scarlet fev. Father: Levi Lester

LEWIS, [n.n.]   WF   Page 15
    15 March 1857 - Still born Parents: Isaac & Frns. Lewis

LIGGIN, JOHN (3y)   CM   Page 30   Town of Abingdon
    1 Nov. 1892 - From a burn Parents: Robt. & Lucinda Liggin

LILLY, DAVID (82y)   WM   Page 23   F
    9 Jan. 1871 - Paralysis   Reported by David Lilly, son
    Born in North Fork Twp.

LILLY, RACHEL (2y)   WF   Page 12
    27 Dec. 1856 - Fever

LINDER, J.B. (74y)   WM   Page 28   Kinderhook
    11 July 1892 - Old age

LINDER, MARY V. (3y 1m 15d)   WF   Page 9
    27 March 1855 - Fever   Parents: J.D. & Isabella Linder

LINDER, REBECCA E. (11y 7m 12d) WF   Page 1
    16 Aug. 1853   Father: Abram Linder

LITCHFIELD, E.P. (49y)   WF   Page 30   Town of Abingdon
    14 Oct. 1892 - Information liver Parents: Jas. N. & Ann D. Pierce
    Reported by husband

LITTLE, JAMES (20y 1m)   WM   Page 1   L
    18 March 1853 - Fall of tree Father: William Little

LITTON, JAS. HARREY (10y)   WM   Page 7
    July 1855 - Dysentery   Parents: Harvey & Emily Litton

LITZ, WILLIAM (50y 5d)   WM   Page 5   Near Glade Spring
    7 Dec. 1854 - Consumption Parents: Wm. & Catharine Litz
    Born in Wythe Co., Va.   Reported by wife

LIVINGSTON, NATHAN L. (27y)   WM   Page 2   T
    13 July 1853 - Hemorrhage of lungs
    Reported by Hugh Johnston, father in law

LIVINGSTON, NATHAN L. (12d)   WM   Page 2
    16 July 1853 - Unknown   Parents: Nathan L. & Sarah C. Livingston
    Reported by Hugh Johnston, grandfather

LOCK, MARY A. (5y 11d)   WF   Page 6
    15 Dec. 1854 - Pneumonia Parents: Wm. J. & Caroline Lock
    Reported by Abram F. Bradley, neighbor

LOCKHART, FAN. A. (2m 1d)   CF   Page 26
    25 Aug. 1892 - Not known Parents: Walt. & E. Lockhart

LOCKHART, WM. (1y 2m)   CM   Page 26
    20 July 1892 - Not known Parents: Thos. & Mag. Lockhart

LOGAN, JOHN S. (33y)   WM   Page 1   F
    4 Nov. 1853 - Consumption Parents: Jno. G. & Elizabeth Logan
    Reported by Alfred B. Logan, brother   Spouse: Elizabeth Logan

LOGAN, MARY A. (17y)   WF   Page 20   F
        4 Aug. 1859 - Flux   Father: Joseph Logan

LOGAN, RHODA N. (7m 18d)   WF   Page 1
        4 March 1853 - Hives   Father: Alfred B. Logan

LOVE, A.K. (63y)   WM   Page 26
        27 Oct. 1892 - Typhoid fev.   Reported by Jas. R. Love, son

LOVE, LAURA G. (23y 4m)   WF   Page 26
        30 Aug. 1892 - Typhoid fev.   Spouse: Jas. R. Love

LOVE, MARTHA (3y)   WF   Page 20
        3 July 1859 - Scarlet fev.   Father: Andrew Love

LOVE, SUSAN N.M. (25y)   WF   Page 2
        24 Oct. 1853 - Consumption   Parents: John J. & Sarah Love
        Reported by Sarah Love, sister

LOVEM, BELLE (1y 5m)   WF   Page 26
        5 May 1892 - Flux   Parents: J.J. & T.P. Lovem

LOWERY, JNO. M. (76y 6m)   WM   Page 26
        14 Jan. 1892 - Blood poison   Reported by Jno. G. LOWREY, son

LOWREY, [n.n.] (1d)   WF   Page 9
        30 March 1855   Parents: Jas. K. & E. Lowrey

LOWREY, JANE (49y)   WF   Page 1
        20 Dec. 1853 - Consumption   Parents: Thos. & Elizabeth McSpadden
        Reported by Eliza Lowrey   Spouse: James Lowrey

LOWREY, ROSANNA (40y)   WF   Page 9
        20 Feb. 1855 - Pneumonia   Parents: Wm. & E. McConnell
                                        Spouse: John Lowrey

LOWRY, JAS. M. (6y)   WM   Page 11
        11 Sept. 1856 - Flux   Parents: Jno. M. & E. Lowry

LOWRY, MARTH. L. (17y)   WF   Page 13   F
        6 May 1857 - Consumption   Father: James Lowry

LOYD, SALLY (17d)   WF   Page 24   Glade Spring
        1871 - Inflamation   Parents: Saml. N. & Martha J. Loyd

LUCY (1m 11d)   SF   Page 2
        20 March 1853   Owner: Jacob Tool

LUCY (72y 6m 5d)   SF   Page 7   CO
        20 July 1855 - Dropsey   Parents: Geo. & Phoebe
                                        Owner: Jno. R. Nye

LUTZ, MARG. (91y)   WF   Page 26
        9 Aug. 1892 - La grippe   Reported by D. Dolinger, friend
        Born in Wythe, Va.

LYNCH, ELIZTH. (13y)   WF   Page 11
        11 June 1856 - Disentary   Parents: Danl. & S. Lynch
        Reported by Daniel G. Thomas, friend

LYTZ, JOHN WESLEY   SM   Page 23
        28 Aug. 1871 - Phneumonia   Parents: W.B. & E. Lytz
        Born in North Fork Twp.

MACKELRAS, META (8y)   WF   Page 20
    11 Feb. 1892 - Burned   Parents: H. & S. Mackelras

MAIDEN, JOHN (5m)   WM   Page 2
    25 Jan. 1853   Parents: Henry A. & Jane Maiden

MALLICOATE, [n.n.)   WF   Page 2
    5 Oct. 1853   Parents: Augustin R. & Eliz. MALLICOTE

MANTZ, SARAH VIRGINIA (9m)   WF   Page 7
    20 Sept. 1855 - Unknown   Parents: Geo. W. & Mary S. Mantz
    Born in Cedarville, Va.

MARGARET (30y 2m)   S_   Page 7
    20 Dec. 1854 - Fever   Owner: John Preston

MARIAH (27y)   SF   Page 19
    16 Oct. 1858 - Inflamation of brain   Owner: Louisa Kelly

MARK (23y)   SM   Page 13   F
    22 April 1857 - Consumption   Master: Jno. S. Caldwell

MARSHAL, THOS. (16y)   WM   Page 29   Goodson Dist.
    27 Dec. 1892 - Fever   Parents: Jno. & Allie MOORE

MARTHA (32y)   SF   Page 12   CO
    30 March 1856 - Unknown   Owner: Jno. Byars

MARY (31y)   SF   Page 2   CO
    Feb. 1853 - Consumption   Owner: Thos. W. Warren

MARY (21y)   SF   Page 2   CO
    20 July 1853 - Fever   Owner: Rebecca Sandoe

MARY (19y)   SF   Page 6
    Oct. 1854 - Flux   Master: Mosby Davison

MARY (20y)   SF   Page 10
    Sept. 1855 - Flux   Owner: Saml. W. Montgomery

MARY (1y)   SF   Page 11
    20 Dec. 1856 - Cough   Owner: S.W. Montgomery

MARY (33y 3m)   SF   Page 17
    4 Feb. 1858 - Flux   Owner: Isaac Fleenor

MARY (22y)   SF   Page 16
    15 July 1858 - Flux   Owner: Isaac Booker

MARY (33y)   SF   Page 20   F
    15 May 1859 - Rheumatism   Master: James Hawthorn

MARY (55y)   SF   Page 20   F
    4 July 1859 - Scrofula   Master: Jas. Porterfield

MARY LIZ (20y)   SF   Page 2
    26 June 1853 - Typhoid fev.   Owner: Jacob Morell

MASSY, [n.n.]   WM   Page 22
    24 Dec. 1859 - Dead born   Parents: Geo. W. & Mary Massy

MATILDA (14y)   SF   Page 3
    18 Oct. 1854 - Dysentery   Master: Andw. K. Love

MAYS, [n.n.]   WM   Page 21
    17 Feb. 1859 - Dead born   Parents: Fleming & Mary Mays

MAYS, MARY (30y)   WF   Page 21.
    7 March 1859 - Scrofula   Parents: Henry & Lucy Wilson
                                    Spouse: Fleming Mays

McCALL, JANE (36y 5m)   WF   Page 8
    .5 June 1855 - Dysentery   Parents: Robt. & Sally Larimer
                                    Spouse: James McCall

McCALL, NANCY (74y)   WF   Page 1
    31 March 1853   Spouse: Thos. McCall, dec'd
    Born in Pennsylvania   Reported by James McCall

McCALL, ROBT. D. (18y)   WM   Page 26   F
    16 Nov. 1892 - Typhoid fev.   Parents: M.H. & M.A. McCall

McCANN, [n.n.]   W_   Page 12
    28 Sept. 1856   Parents: James & Lydia McCann

McCHESNEY, SARAH (96y)   WF   Page 6
    9 Dec. 1854 - Palsey   Parents: Hugh & Ann McChesney
    Reported by Julia Hanby, daughter

McCLELLEN, H.P.T. (2y)   WM   Page 29   Goodson Dist.
    2 Aug. 1892 - Flux   Parents: R.H. & H.C. McClellen

McCLELLEN, JNO. E.   WM   Page 29   Goodson Dist.
    25 Sept. 1892 - Flux   Parents: R.H. & H.C. McClellen

McCLOUD, [n.n.] (3y)   WF   Page 14
    7 June 1857 - Consumption   Father: John McCloud

McCLOUD, CALEDONIA (15y)   WF   Page 13
    7 June 1857 - Consumption   Father: John MOORE
    Reported by B.K. Buchanan, neighbor   (note: reported as unmarri

McCLOUD, D.O. (4y)   WM   Page 21
    8 Aug. 1859 - Fever   Parents: James & Elizabeth McCloud

McCLOUD, HANNAH (47y)   WF   Page 4
    13 Jan. 1854 - Consumption   Parents: Cyrinius & Agnes Johnson
                                    Spouse: Andw. McCloud

McCLOUD, JNO. L. (42y 3m)   WM   Page 26   F
    8 April 1892 - Consumption   Reported by D.A. McCloud, brother

McCLURE, [APPIAH] (50y)   WF   Page 4
    30 Oct. 1854 - By eating arsnick   Parents: Sam'l & Jemima Kelly
                                    Spouse: Nathaniel McClure

McCOLLUM, MARY V. (13y)   W_   Page 30   Town of Abing
    10 Nov. 1892 - Fits   Reported by Jno. McClellen

McCONKEY, JANE (81y)   WF   Page 6
    8 March 1854 - Palsey   Parents: John & E. Sharp
    Reported by Jane Ryburn, daughter

McCONNELL, [n.n.]   WM   Page 11
    28 Sept. 1856 - Still born   Parents: Thos. G. & Rachel E. McConne

McCONNELL, ABRAM (65y 3m)   WM   Page 22
    26 March 1859 - Fever   Parents: A. & Rosannah McConnell
                                    Spouse: Susan B. McConnell

McCONNELL, ELIZABETH (56y 1m 5d)   WF   Page 9
    1 April 1855 - Paralysis of brain   Parents: Andw. & Jennette Willoughby
                                    Spouse: Thos. McConnell

McCONNELL, S.J.R. (4y 10d)   WF   Page 21
    9 July 1859 - Fever   Parents: Abram A. & Mary A. McConnell

McCORMACK, JAS. E. (9y)   WM   Page 13
    20 May 1857 - Fever   Father: Wm. McCormack

McCORMACK, M.L. (3y 2m)   WF   Page 26   Grayson Co., Va.
    12 Sept. 1892 - Dyptheria   Parents: C.C. & B. McCormack

McCORMACK, MICAJAH (70y)   WM   Page 5
    July 1854 - Dropsey   Reported by John W. Price, friend
    Born in Bedford Co., Va.

McCORMICK, NANCY V. (1y)   WF   Page 12
    13 Oct. 1856 - Fever   Father: Micajah McCormick

McCRACKEN, [n.n.] (1d)   W_   Page 23   North Fork Twp.
    March 1871 - Infancy   Mother: Mary McCracken

McCRACKEN, AILSEY (75y)   WF   Page 19
    30 Dec. 1858 - Consumption   Father: Latin Odum
    Reported by Madison McCracken, son   Spouse: John McCracken

McCRACKEN, CATHARINE (5y)   WF   Page 13
    20 Aug. 1857 - Dropsy   Father: Wm. McCracken

McCRACKEN, HUGH (50y)   WM   Page 8   L
    12 Jan. 1855 - Dysentery   Parents: Hugh & Mary McCracken
    Reported by James Lowrey, neighbor

McCREADY, ELIZ. (75y 1m)   WF   Page 26
    27 Feb. 1892 - Consumption   Reported by Mary J. Walden, daughter

McCREADY, SCOTT (42y)   WM   Page 26   F
    10 June 1892 - Fever   Spouse: Eliza McCready

McCROSKEY, REBECCA (66y)   WF   Page 21
    31 Oct. 1859 - Consumption   Parents: Allen & Bersheba Aven
    Reported by Timothy Aven, son-in-law   Spouse: Jas. McCroskey

McCROSKY, M.A.C. (8y)   WF   Page 17
    24 July 1858 - Flux   Parents: Jno. B. & M. McCrosky

McCULLOCK, SARAH (80y)   WF   Page 5   North Fork
    28 Dec. 1854 - Old age   Reported by Mary Dunn, daughter

McDANIEL, [n.n.] (1d)   WM   Page 9
    2 May 1855 - Stillborn   Parents: Jos. & S.J. McDaniel
    Reported by A.C. Maxwell, physician

McDANIEL, ELIZABETH (65y)   WF   Page 17
    20 Oct. 1858 - Unknown   Parents: Jno. & Rachel Gentle
                                    Spouse: Wm. McDaniel

McKEE, JAMES (65y)   WM   Page 8
    18 July 1855 - Consumption   Parents: And. & Elizabeth McKee
                                    Spouse: Sarah McKee

McNEW, CATE (21y)   WF   Page 24   Saltville
   1871   Parents: Elisha & Dorca McNew

McNEW, CATHARINE (40y)   WF   Page 4
   15 Aug. 1854 - Dysentery   Parents: Amos & Abigail Sutton
                                    Spouse: George McNew

McNEW, CATHARINE (47y)   WF   Page 7
   1855 - Dysentery   Parents: Wm. & Rebecca Ivett
   Reported by Jonathan McNew, Jr., son   Spouse: Jonathan McNew

McNEW, ELISHA (66y)   WM   Page 4
   26 Aug. 1854 - Dyspepsia   Parents: Elisha & Cath. McNew
   Reported by Elisha McNew, son & executor   Spouse: Jane McNew

McNEW, GEO. (26y)   WM   Page 4
   1 Aug. 1854 - Dysentery   Parents: Elisha & Jane McNew
   Reported by Elisha McNew, brother

McNEW, JANE (65y)   WF   Page 4
   15 Aug. 1854 - Dysentery   Parents: Amos & Abigail Sutton
   Reported by Elisha McNew, son & executor   Spouse: Elisha McNew

McNEW, MARTHA (43y)   WF   Page 20   F
   15 Oct. 1859   Spouse: John B. McNew

McNEW, SARAH (57y)   WF   Page 20   F
   15 May 1859 - Rheumatism   Spouse: James McNew

McNEW, THOMAS (62y)   WM   Page 12   F
   23 May 1856 - Inflamation brain

McQUOWN, JOHN (8m)   WM   Page 4
   11 Sept. 1854 - Dysentery   Parents: Isaac A. & Nancy McQuown

McQUOWN, MARGARET (81y)   WF   Page 3
   8 May 1854 - Old age   Parents: Nath'l & Myrd Dryden
   Reported by Isaac McQuown, son   Spouse: Isaac McQuown

[McTEER], ROBERT W. (5y)   WM   Page 4
   6 Sept. 1854   Parents: John M. & Eliza [McTeer]

McVEY, GIDEON (25y)   WM   Page 8   F
   19 Aug. 1855 - Dispepsia   Parents: Jno. & Polly McVey
                                    Spouse: Jane McVey

McVEY, MARY JANE (2y)   WF   Page 8
   8 May 1855   Parents: Anderson & Jane McVey

MEAD, JOHN (40y)   WM   Page 28   Kinderhook
   12 June 1892 - Flux

MEEK, JOHN W. (23y)   WM   Page 8   CM
   May 1855 - Consumption   Parents: Charles & Sarah Meek

MEEK, MARY E. (12y 1m)   WF   Page 13
   15 March 1857 - S. fever   Father: Charles Meek

MEEK, SALLY (30y)   WF   Page 24   Glade Spring
   1871 - Consumption   Parents: Chas. & Sally Meek

MEEK, VIRG. I. (8y 4m)   WF   Page 13
   8 March 1857 - Scarlet fever   Father: Charles Meek

MELINDA (23y)   SF   Page 1
    Feb. 1853   Owner: John W. Price

MILES, MARY I. (20y 6m)   WF   Page 13
    22 Sept. 1857 - Fever   Parents: Jno. & M. Miles

MILLARD, V.M. (4y)   WF   Page 29   Goodson Dist.
    28 Oct. 1892 - Bronchitis   Parents: D.B. Millard

MILLER, [n.n.]   WF   Page 11
    2 Sept. 1856 - Still born   Parents: William & R.L. Miller

MILLER, ALONZA A. (2y 16d)   WM   Page 19
    24 Sept. 1858 - Inflamation of brain   Father: James Miller

MILLER, AMANDA (23y)   WF   Page 20
    13 July 1859 - Consumption   Father: Isaac Miller
    Reported by Isaac MISER, brother

MILLER, CHAS. B. (8y)   WM   Page 3
    23 Oct. 1854 - Dysentery   Parents: Jno. L. & Charlotte Miller

MILLER, HUGH (76y)   WM   Page 2
    3 June 1853 - Gravel   Father: Hugh Miller
    Reported by John Miller, brother

MILLER, MARY J. (6y 6m)   WF   Page 17
    1 Aug. 1858 - Flux   Mother: Eliza Miller

MILLER, MELVINA (73y)   WF   Page 19
    28 Dec. 1858 - Consumption   Father: Stephen Graham
    Reported by Jas. A. Miller, son   Spouse: Sam'l L. Miller

MILLER, NORA L. (4m)   WF   Page 26
    21 Nov. 1892 - Whooping co.   Parents: S.P. & Jane Miller

MILLER, WILLIE M. (6m 10d)   WM   Page 26
    27 Sept. 1892 - Whooping co.   Parents: M.W. & Sarah Miller

MINICK, WM. C. (4y 9m)   WM   Page 15
    15 Oct. 1857 - Fever   Parents: L.J. & Jane Minick

MINK, THOS. (6y)   WM   Page 13
    30 May 1857 - Scrofula   Father: William Mink

MINNICK, [n.n.]   WF   Page 21
    11 June 1859 - Dead born   Parents: Henry & R. Minnick

MINNICK, BARBARY (9y)   WF   Page 4
    27 Dec. 1854 - Consumption   Parents: John & Eve Minnick

MINNICK, FANNIE J. (21y)   WF   Page 29   Goodson Dist.
    22 Sept. 1892 - Consumption   Parents: P.W. & Martha Minnick

MINNICK, JNO. W. (9m)   WM   Page 26
    29 July 1892 - Chol. infan.   Parents: J.P. & A. Minnick

MINNICK, L.P. (25y)   WF   Page 28   Kinderhook
    28 Nov. 1892 - Consumption   Reported by J.W. Morrison

MINNICK, M.E. (38y)   WF   Page 28   F
    23 Feb. 1892 - Consumption   Father: Elijah Phipps
    Reported by husband

MINNICK, PETER (88y 9m)   WM   Page 21
    9 July 1859 - Old age   Reported by Benjamin Minnick, son

MINOR, RICHARD (21y)   CM   Page 30   Town of Abing(
    23 April 1892 - La grippe   Parents: W.V. & L. Minor

MITCHEL, OSKER (75y)   CM   Page 30   Town of Abing(
    Sept. 1892 - Perelsis   Reported by Delpha Mitchel

MITCHELL, [n.n.]   WF   Page 9
    1 Jan. 1855 - Stillborn   Parents: Jno. & E. Mitchell

MOCK, MARY (34y)   WF   Page 12
    10 April 1856 - Infla. of bowels   Parents: Frs. & Mary Catron
                            Spouse: Henry Mock

MONTGOMERY, CATHARINE (3y)   WF   Page 9
    30 June 1855 - Cough   Parents: Jno. & S. Montgomery
    Reported by A.C. Maxwell, physician

MONTGOMERY, ELIZABETH (40y)   WF   Page 8
    15 Jan. 1855 - Consumption   Parents: Moses & Joannah Buchanan
                            Spouse: Richd. Montgomery

MONTGOMERY, ELIZTH. (38y)   WF   Page 11
    15 June 1856 - Consumption   Parents: Moses & Joanah Buchanan
                            Spouse: Richard Montgomery

MONTGOMERY, M.S. (22y)   WF   Page 17
    24 July 1858 - Flux   Parents: Wm. P. & Elizabeth Montgomer;

MONTGOMERY, [VERLIN] (1y 2m)   WM   Page 13
    14 May 1857 - S. Fever   Father: James Montgomery

MOON, WM. (69y 7m)   WM   Page 26   F
    19 Sept. 1892 - Cancer   Spouse: M.E. MOORE

MOORE, ACY (24y)   WM   Page 29   Goodson Dist.
    Sept. 1892 - Fever   Father: John Moore

MOORE, AMANDA (28y)   WF   Page 28   Kinderhook
    21 May 1892 - Heart disease

MOORE, BETHIAL (29y)   WF   Page 4
    18 June 1854   Parents: Wm. & Jane Buchanan
                            Spouse: And. F. Moore

MOORE, BETTIE (26y)   WF   Page 28   Kinderhook
    1 May 1892 - Consumption   Father: Samuel Moore
    Reported by J.B. Moore

MOORE, FRNS. (8y 9m)   WM   Page 15
    15 Sept. 1857 - Fever   Parents: Jno. & Cath Moore

MOORE, GEO. W. (75y)   WM   Page 26   F
    4 July 1892 - Consumption   Spouse: Sarah Moore
    Born in Henry Co., Va.

MOORE, MARGARET ANN (34y)   WF   Page 3
    7 Sept. 1854 - Dysentery   Parents: Wm. & Isabella Graham
                            Spouse: Jno. B. Moore

208

MOORE, SAMUEL (71y)　　　　　　　WM　　Page 1
　　5 Nov. 1853 - Bronchitis　　　Parents:　Wm. & Elizabeth Moore
　　　　　　　　　　　　　　　　　　Spouse:　Ann Moore

MOORE, SAML. (66y)　　　　　　　WM　　Page 13　　F
　　16 Nov. 1857 - Consumption　Father:　John Moore
　　Reported by Margret Greer, daughter

MOOREFIELD, JOHN (1y 4m)　　　　WM　　Page 7
　　15 April or Aug. 1855 - Whooping cough　　Parents:　James & Jane Moorefield
　　Born in Johnson Co., Tn.

MORGAN, LUCINDA (32y)　　　　　　CF　　Page 30　　　　　Town of Abingdon
　　2 Dec. 1892 - Child birth　　Parents:　Alex & Sarah Carter
　　　　　　　　　　　　　　　　　　Spouse:　Allen Morgan

MORGAN, WM. (30y)　　　　　　　　WM　　Page 26　　　　　Pulaski, Va.
　　18 Jan. 1892 - La grippe　　Parents:　J.H. & E. Morgan

MORISON, JOHN D. (19y)　　　　　WM　　Page 5　　ST　　Emory & Henry College
　　Sept. 1854 - Dysentery　　　Father:　John W.S. Morison
　　Reported by E.E. Wiley, Pres. of College　　Born in Lee Co., Va.

MORTON, EMMA (2d)　　　　　　　　WF　　Page 29　　　　　Goodson Dist.
　　21 July 1892 - Unknown　　　Parents:　Steve & M. Morton

MOTERN, [n.n.] (15d)　　　　　　WF　　Page 17
　　28 Jan. 1858 - Unknown　　　Parents:　Wm. C. & E. Motern

MOTERN, E.C.T. (4m)　　　　　　　WM　　Page 9
　　31 July 1855 - Inflamation　Parents:　Wm. C. & E.J. Motern

MOUNTAIN, JESS C. (73y 1m)　　　WM　　Page 26　　F
　　18 July 1892 - Bronchitis　Reported by D.P. Mountain, son

MULLIN, J. ELLEN (10y 1m)　　　WF　　Page 26
　　4 July 1892 - Spasms　　　　Parents:　J.S. & Ellen Mullin

MUMPOWERS, [n.n.]　　　　　　　　WF　　Page 17
　　11 March 1858 - Dead born　Parents:　A. & M. Mumpowers

MUNROE, MARY (50y)　　　　　　　　CF　　Page 30　　　　　Goodson Dist.
　　Sept. 1892 - Not known　　　Father:　Edward Ashley
　　　　　　　　　　　　　　　　　　Spouse:　Robt. Munroe

MURRY, JAMES M. (3y)　　　　　　WM　　Page 6
　　29 April 1854 - Flux　　　　Parents:　James & Ru. Murry

NAFF, MARGARET H. (7m)　　　　　WF　　Page 6
　　18 Nov. 1854 - Inflammation　Parents:　Geo. E. & Margt. E. Naff

NANCY (37y)　　　　　　　　　　　　SF　　Page 22
　　22 Feb. 1859 - Fever　　　　Owner:　Jerry Rush

NATHAN (16y)　　　　　　　　　　　WM　　Page 7
　　20 Nov. 1854 - Fever　　　　Owner:　Frans. Preston

NECESSARY, ELIZA V.　　　　　　　WF　　Page 23　　　　　Kinderhook Twp.
　　3 Aug. 1871　　　　　　　　　　Parents:　Wm. A. & Nancy Necessary

NEEL, JNO. L.F. (21y 1m)　　　　WM　　Page 14
　　5 Oct. 1857 - Consumption　Father:　Bartholomew Neel
　　　　　　　　　　　　　　　　　　Spouse:　Emily Neel

NEELEY, MARY (67y)   WF   Page 20
    30 April 1859   Father: Patrick Bollins
    Reported by John Neeley, son   Spouse: Hugh C. Neeley

NEWLAND, ELIZA (40y)   WF   Page 17
    1 Oct. 1858 - Consumption   Parents: S. & R. Hawthorn
                                   Spouse: L.C. Newland

NEWMAN, NANCY A. (65y)   WF   Page 29   Goodson Dist.
    15 Feb. 1892 - Pneumonia   Parents: Wm. Jen. Grubb
    Reported by husband

NORRIS, [n.n.] (1y)   WM   Page 2
    22 Dec. 1853   Father: Isaiah Norris

NORRIS, GEO. W. (3m)   WM   Page 12
    30 Dec. 1856 - Croup

NUNLEY, [n.n.]   WM   Page 20
    16 May 1859   Father: Richard Nunley

NUNLEY, [n.n.]   WF   Page 20
    30 Dec. 1859 - Born dead   Father: William Nunley

NUNLEY, MARTHA A. (16y)   WF   Page 20
    22 April 1859 - Flux   Father: John Nunley

NUNLEY, WILLIAM (3y)   WM   Page 20
    20 April 1859 - Flux   Father: John Nunley

NYE, JASPER K. (2y 2m)   WM   Page 26
    24 Dec. 1892 - Croup   Parents: W.R. & M.A. Nye

ODAM, SUSANNAH (5y)   WF   Page 20
    5 June 1859 - Flux   Father: Laton Odam

ODEM, LYCINEUS (2y)   WM   Page 1
    15 March 1853   Father: Laton Odem

ODUM, MARGARET (43y)   WF   Page 13   F
    27 Dec. 1856 - Unknown   Spouse: Latin Odum

ODUM, SUSAN (5y)   WF   Page 19
    15 July 1858 - Flux   Father: Laton Odum

OREAR, SALLY (9d)   WF   Page 24   Glade Spring
    1871 - Inflamation   Parents: Jno. C. & Martha Orear

ORFIELD, JAMES (6y)   WM   Page 17
    20 Feb. 1858 - Croup   Father: Isaac M. Orfield

ORFIELD, JAS. (8y)   WM   Page 22
    28 Feb. 1859 - Fever   Parents: Isaac & Mary Orfield
    Reported by JAMES Orfield, father

ORR, JANE (46y 1m 11d)   WF   Page 1
    9 April 1853 - Pneumonia   Parents: James & Margaret Hope
                                   Spouse: Arthur Orr

ORR, MARY C. (32y 8d)   WF   Page 5
    14 April 1854 - Consumption   Parents: Archd. & Polly Orr

ORR, POLLY M. (51y)   WF   Page 5
    27 Oct. 1854 - Consumption   Parents: Jas. & Mary Hope
                           Spouse: Archd. Orr

OWEN, JNO. (5y)   WM   Page 17
    15 June 1858 - Flux   Parents: Thos. & Nancy Owen

PAFFORD, MAUD L. (17y)   WF   Page 26
    8 Aug. 1892 - Consumption   Reported by Andrew Kelley, uncle

PAGE, ROBERT P.   WM   Page 1   Poor House
    Jan. 1853 - Inflamation of bowels
    Reported by Jno. L. Caldwell, Steward of Poor House

PALMER, [n.n.]   WM   Page 22
    15 Sept. 1859 - Dead born   Parents: J.B. & Sarah A. Palmer

PARIS, JAS. J. (19y 8m)   WM   Page 26   F
    10 July 1892 - Cholera mor. Parents: A.G. & C.M. Paris

PARKS, DAVID (74y)   WM   Page 9
    25 May 1855 - Consumption   Parents: Jas. & R. Parks
    Reported by David Parks, son

PARRIGEN, ELIZABETH (24y)   WF   Page 2
    15 Apirl 1853 - Fever   Spouse: John Parrigen

PARROTT, [ELCANA] D. (12y) WM   Page 11
    17 June 1856 - Fever   Parents: Wm. & Mary Parrott
    Reported by R.M. Parrott, uncle

PARROTT, MARGARET (69y)   WF   Page 6
    6 March 1854 - Consumption Parents: Jas. & Margt. Pipes
    Reported by R.M. Parrott, son

PATERSON, JAS. R. (14y)   CM   Page 30   Town of Abingdon
    28 May 1892 - Heart disease Parents: R. & S. PATESON

PATSEY (70y)   SF   Page 7
    4 May 1854 - Dropsey   Owner: Nancy Davis

PATSEY (50y)   SF   Page 7   CO
    23 March 1855 - Dysentery   Owner: Arthur D. Hutton, physician

PATTERSON, JNO. (2y)   WM   Page 24   Glade Spring
    1871 - Inflamation   Parents: S.E. & Elizabeth Paterson

PEMBERTON, JOHN K. (4y 11d) WM   Page 9
    15 May 1855 - Flux   Parents: B.F. & E. Pemberton

PERIGEN, ALFORD (67y)   WM   Page 29   Goodson Dist.
    Dec. 1892 - Cancer   Father: Wm. Perigen
    Reported by Powers Dickenson

PETERMAN, CROCKET (3y)   WM   Page 10
    6 Nov. 1856 - Fever   Parents: Wm. B. & A. Peterman

PETERMAN, M.V. (6y)   WF   Page 10
    2 Nov. 1856 - Fever   Parents: Wm. B. & A. Peterman

PETERMAN, MARY E. (8y)   WF   Page 10
    12 Nov. 1856 - Fever   Parents: Wm. B. & A. Peterman

PHELPS, [n.n.] (1d)
    14 July 1856 - Unknown
WF   Page 11
Parents: Jno. & Patsy Phelps

PHILPS, MALINDA (8y 6m)
    15 Sept. 1859 - Fever
WF   Page 22
Parents: Martin & M. Philps

PHOEBE (75y)
    1 Aug. 1854 - Dropsey
S_   Page 7
Owner: R.E. Cummings

PICKLE, DANIEL (47y)
    23 Sept. 1892 - Accident
WM   Page 26   F
Reported by D.W. Lethco, nephew

PIPPIN, [n.n.]
    28 Nov. 1856 - Stillborn
WM   Page 10
Parents: Robt. & Sarah Pippin

PIPPIN, C.R. (24y 8m)
    29 May 1859 - Fever
WM   Page 22
Parents: Robt. & Delila Pippin

PIPPIN, CALVIN (7m)
    1 June 1858 - Flux
WM   Page 17
Parents: W.P. & Cath. Pippin

PIPPIN, CHRISTOPHER F. (8y)
    2 July 1858 - Flux
WM   Page 17
Parents: E. & Nancy Pippin

PIPPIN, MELINDA (36y)
    9 Dec. 1853 - Fever
WF   Page 2
Spouse: Robt. P. Pippin

PIPPIN, SHANON (4y)
    1 Feb. 1859 - Fever
WM   Page 22
Parents: Zack & Nancy Pippin

PITTS, VIRGINIA E. (7m)
    14 July 1859 - Fits
WF   Page 22
Parents: Lewis & Louisa Pitts

POLLY (2y)
    7 June 1859 - Inflamation
SF   Page 22
Owner: A.T.F. Hanby

POOL, NANCY (70y)
    9 Jan. 1859 - Consumption
WF   Page 20   F
Reported by Isaac Orr, son-in-law

POOLE, ALICE (16y 4m)
    15 Feb. 1892 - Consumption
WF   Page 26
Parents: Simeon & M. Poole

POSTON, FANNIE (27y 6m)
    18 Oct. 1892 - Consumption
WF   Page 26
Reported by Dr. A. Hicks, brother in la

POWERS, JOHN H. (23y 11m)
    22 Sept. 1854 - Dysentery
    Born in Stokes Co., N.C.
WM   Page 5   Widener Valley
Parents: Jas. & Elizabeth Powers

PRATER, MARY (4y)
    27 June 1854
WF   Page 4
Parents: Joseph W. & Patsey Prater

PRESTON, ANN LOUISA (3y 5m)
    13 Sept. 1854 - Dysentery
WF   Page 3
Parents: Thos. M. & Evalina Preston

PRESTON, FRANCIS (70y)
    2 Jan. 1892 - Not given
WM   Page 29   Goodson Dist.
Reported by Daniel Haiden

PRESTON, JAS. (8y 2m)
    15 Oct. 1857 - Fever
SM   Page 15
Owner: John Preston

PRESTON, JOHN (76y)
    7 Oct. 1853
WM   Page 2   F
Reported by Samuel Preston, brother

PRESTON, JNO. (19d)   WM   Page 24   Glade Spring
    1871 - Inflamation   Parents: Rufus & Isabella Preston

PRESTON, LIZZIE (28y 1m 2d)   SF   Page 15   F
    20 Sept. 1857 - Fever   Owner: Robt. R. Preston

PRESTON, MARTHA (33y)   WF   Page 22
    23 July 1859 - Dispepsia   Parents: Robt. & Ellen Moffett
    Born in Loudon, Va.   Spouse: Frank Preston

PRESTON, REBECCA (62y 5m)   WF   Page 17
    11 June 1858 - Cancer   Parents: W. & C. Snodgrass
    Reported by A.J. Legard, daughter   Spouse: Saml. Preston

PRESTON, ROSE (80y)   SF   Page 15   F
    25 Feb. 1857 - Fever   Owner: Rebecca Preston

PRESTON, SAMUEL (81y 6m 2d)   WM   Page 15
    17 Feb. 1857 - Fever   Parents: Thos. & Nancy Preston
                                    Spouse: Rebecca Preston

PRESTON, SARAH ANN (6y 5m)   WF   Page 3
    21 Aug. 1854 - Dysentery   Parents: Thos. M. & Evalina Preston

PRESTON, THOS. M. (18y 8m 18d)   WM   Page 15   F
    6 Feb. 1857 - Consumption   Parehts: Saml. A. & N.A. Preston

PRESTON, WM. A. (4m)   WM   Page 9
    1 Aug. 1855 - Fever   Parents: Frans. & M.V. Preston

PRICE, ADALINE (72y)   WF   Page 26
    16 Jan. 1892 - Cancer   Spouse: E.F. Price

PRICE, ADELINE (70y)   WF   Page 28   Kinderhook
    1 April 1892 - Flux   Reported by husband

PRICE, ELISHA (56y)   WM   Page 11   F
    15 March 1856 - Consumption   Parents: Danl. & Juda Price
    Reported by Danl. E. Price, son

PRICE, ELIZABETH (38y)   WF   Page 28   F   North Fork
    11 Sept. 1892 - Consumption   Reported by husband

PRICE, GREEN (17y)   WM   Page 26
    17 March 1892 - Spinal affect.   Parents: M.A. & D. Price
    Reported by W.A. Price, father

PRIVETT, LETTIE E. (25y 2m)   WF   Page 26
    20 Oct. 1892 - Consumption   Reported by Mrs. Null, mother

QUEEN (36y)   SF   Page 10
    Sept. 1855   Owner: Saml. W. Montgomery

QUESENBERRY, [n.n.] (1d)   W   Page 12
    20 Dec. 1856 - Unknown   Parents: Amos & Mahale Quesenberry

RACHEL (64y)   SF   Page 1
    25 Aug. 1853 - Dropsy   Owner: Andrew Patterson

RACHEL, MARGARET (56y 24d)   WF   Page 17
    21 Jan. 1858 - Flux   Parents: H. & D. Vaughan
    Reported by Jas. J. Rachel, son   Spouse: Jas. V. Rachel

RACHEL, SARAH E. (2y 25d)   WF   Page 17
     24 Jan. 1858 - Flux   Parents: Jas. J. & Isabella RICHARDS
     Reported by Jas. J. RACHEL, father

RAMSEY, CATHARINE (34y)   WF   Page 8
     1855 - Pneumonia   Parents: Lewis & Jamima Thomas
                                  Spouse: Jesse Ramsey

RAMSEY, CATHARINE (65y)   WF   Page 7
     10 June 1855 - From a fall   Parents: Robt. & Mary Ramsey
     Reported by Mrs. Harris, daughter

RAMSEY, JACOB A. (3y)   WM   Page 20
     17 Dec. 1859 - Scarlet fev. Father: John Ramsey

RAMSEY, JAS. B. (8y 5m)   WM   Page 20
     1 Dec. 1859 - Scarlet fev.   Father: John Ramsey

RANSOM, ANN (45y)   WF   Page 14   F
     1 June 1857 - Consumption   Father: George Campbell
                                  Spouse: Nelson Ransom

RASNICK, JINNIE F. (1y)   WF   Page 29   Goodson Dist.
     28 Dec. 1892 - Not known   Parents: E. & C. Rasnick

REID, NANCY (54y)   WF   Page 3
     31 Aug. 1854 - Dysentery   Parents: Benj. & Elizabeth Keys
                                  Spouse: Hugh Reid

REMINE, JAMES O. (3y)   WM   Page 13
     13 Oct. 1856 - Unknown   Father: William Remine

REMINE, WILLIAM (64y)   WM   Page 23   F
     19 July 1871 - Billious colic   Born in Abingdon Twp.

RENSHAW, FEBY (76y)   WF   Page 20   F
     16 May 1859 - Disease of heart   Spouse: Joseph Renshaw
     Reported by Wm. Buchanan, son-in-law

REPASS, DANIEL (1y)   WM   Page 2
     1 Dec. 1853   Father: William A. Repass

REUBEN (82y 5m)   SM   Page 10
     Aug. 1855 - Old age   Owner: John Preston

RHEA, JOSEPH (75y 8m)   WM   Page 15
     3 Oct. 1857 - Fever   Father: Jos. Rhea
     Reported by Wm. R. Rhea, nephew

RHEA, NANCY M.P. (3y)   WF   Page 11
     1 Sept. 1856 - Fever   Parents: Jos. W. & E.C.P. Rhea

RHEA, ROBT. H. (55y)   WM   Page 8   Will wright
     7 July 1855 - Dropsey   Parents: Joseph & Margaret Rhea

RICHARD, A.J. (23y)   WM   Page 22
     24 April 1859 - Consumption Spouse: Ann RICHARDS

RICHARD, JOS. (1y 6m)   WM   Page 22
     15 Aug. 1859 - Consumption   Parents: A.J. & Ann RICHARDS

RICHARDS, ELIZA (6m)   WF   Page 9
     29 Nov. 1855 - Cough   Parents: A. & E. Richards

RICHARDS, JOHN (60y)   WM   Page 23   F
     June 1871 - Paralysis   Parents: Mathew & Susan Richards
     Born in North Fork Twp.   Spouse: Ann Richards
     Reported by James Rush, nephew

RICHARDS, MARY (7y)   WF   Page 15
     2 Sept. 1857 - Flux   Parents: And. & Alice Richards

RICHARDS, MARY E. (1y 10m)   WF   Page 17
     11 Sept. 1858 - Flux   Parents: Amos & E. Richards
     Reported by John W. Minick, uncle

RICHARDS, SALLY (65y)   WF   Page 30   Town of Abingdon
     4 March 1892 - Dropsy   Parents: Alf. & Rachel Richards
     Reported by Wm. Richards

RICHARDS, WM. (1y 11m)   WM   Page 9
     14 March 1855 - Cough   Parents: A. & E. Richards

RICHARDSON, LAURA (36y)   CF   Page 30   Town of Abingdon
     25 July 1892 - Pneumonia   Spouse: J.C. Richardson

RICHARDSON, WILLIE (4y)   CM   Page 30   Town of Abingdon
     24 Dec. 1892 - Pneumonia   Parents: J.C. & L. Richardson

RINGLEY, BARSHA (4y 5m 5d)   WF   Page 15
     4 Oct. 1857 - Flux   Parents: J.D. & Mary Ringley

RINGLEY, JAMES D. (10y)   WM   Page 9
     27 Sept. 1855 - Fever   Parents: E. & S. Ringley

RITCHIE, LAURA L. (24y 3m)   WF   Page 26
     1 Dec. 1892 - Puerpeal fever   Spouse: T.F. Ritchie

ROBT. (22y)   SM   Page 14   F
     20 July 1857 - Consumption   Owner: Jno. S. Caldwell

ROBERT (79y)   SM   Page 20   F
     12 June 1859 - Consumption   Master: Ballard P. Smith

ROBERSON, JANE (18m)   WF   Page 20
     12 March 1859 - Scarlet fev. Father: James ROBERTSON

ROBERTS, [n.n.]   WF   Page 15
     1 Aug. 1857 - Still born   Parents: Geo. & Martha Roberts

ROBERTS, F.E. (24y)   WM   Page 28   Kinderhook
     8 Aug. 1892 - Flux   Reported by A.J. Richards

ROBERTS, JOANNA (27y)   WF   Page 28   Kinderhook
     June 1892 - La gripp   Reported by S.W. Roberts

ROBERTS, MARY JANE (1y 10m 5d)   WF   Page 7
     12 Aug. 1855 - Dysentery   Parents: Wm. & Susannah Roberts

ROBERTS, NEWTON A. (2y)   WM   Page 10
     20 Aug. 1856 - Disentary   Parents: Chs. & Jane Roberts

ROBERTSON, ISABELLA (4y)   WF   Page 20
     15 March 1859 - Scarlet fev. Father: James Robertson

ROBINSON, [n.n.]   WM   Page 14
     30 Oct. 1857 - Consumption   Father: David E. Robinson

ROBINSON, CHARITY (4y 2m)   WF   Page 14
    20 May 1857 - S. fever   Father: James A. Robinson

ROBINSON, JAMES (62y)   WM   Page 14   F
    18 Nov. 1857 - Consumption   Spouse: Mary Robinson

ROBINSON, JAS. E.C.W. (4y)   WM   Page 14
    4 Jan. 1857 - S. fever   Father: David E. Robinson

ROBINSON, JNO. W.C. (6y 6m)   WM   Page 14
    28 May 1857 - S. fever   Father: David E. Robinson

ROBINSON, MOSES C. (61y)   WM   Page 14   F
    3 Aug. 1857 - Consumption   Reported by Mary Robinson

ROBINSON, RACHEL H. (2y)   WF   Page 14
    13 Jan. 1857 - S. fever   Father: David E. Robinson

RODEFER, JACOB (69y)   WM   Page 30   Town of Abingdor
    6 April 1892 - Kidney disease   Parents: Saml. & Mary Rodefer
    Reported by sister

ROE, NANCY (72y 13d)   WF   Page 1
    18 Nov. 1853   Parents: Peter & Ann Hypock
    Born in Craven Co., N.C.   Spouse: John Roe

ROPP, JOHN P. (20y 11m 6d)   WM   Page 15   F
    1 July 1857 - Fever   Parents: John M. & [Thersy] Ropp

ROSANNAH (52y)   CF   Page 4
    13 May 1854 - Consumption   Reported by Milly Walden

ROSE, FRAN. C. (1d)   WM   Page 26
    2 Aug. 1892 - Not known   Parents: D.G. & N.M. Rose

ROSE, JACK M. (9m)   WM   Page 26
    5 Feb. 1892 - Pneumonia   Parents: D.G. & Nan. M. Rose

ROSE, NANCY M. (37y)   WF   Page 26
    5 Aug. 1892 - Heart disease   Spouse: D.G. Rose

ROSENBALM, [n.n.]   WF   Page 19
    30 Oct. 1858   Father: J.H. Rosenbalm

ROSENBALM, ALEX'R (12y)   WM   Page 5   South Fork
    18 Aug. 1854 - Dysentery   Parents: David & Cath Rosenbalm

ROSENBALM, E.M.F. (18m)   WM   Page 19
    26 Aug. 1858 - Liver complaint   Father: J.H. Rosenbalm

ROSENBALM, JAMES (1y 8m)   WM   Page 3
    10 Oct. 1854 - Dysentery   Parents: Joel & Nancy Rosenbalm

ROSENBALM, [JEREMIAH] (21y)   WM   Page 5   South Fork
    13 Aug. 1854 - Dysentery   Parents: David & Cath Rosenbalm

ROSENBALM, JOPPA (17y)   WF   Page 5   South Fork
    17 Aug. 1854 - Dysentery   Parents: David & Cath Rosenbalm

ROSENBALM, M.A. (5m 4d)   WF   Page 19
    21 Feb. 1858 - Inflamation of B.   Father: Adam Rosenbalm

ROSENBALM, M.E. (1y)   WF   Page 26
    4 June 1892 - Brain dis.   Parents: Alf. & M. Rosenbalm

ROSENBALM, MARGARET (8y 2m)   WF   Page 4
    21 Sept. 1854 - Dysentery   Parents: Isaac & Cath Rosenbalm

ROSENBALM, REBECCA (19y)   WF   Page 5   South Fork
    18 Aug. 1854 - Dysentery   Parents: David & Cath Rosenbalm

ROUS, ELIZA (21y)   WF   Page 20   F
    12 Aug. 1859 - Billious fev. Father: William Moser
                                     Spouse: Philip Rous

RULEY, LILBURN (17y)   WM   Page 2
    10 March 1853 - Fever   Parents: Wm. N. & Eliza Ruley

RUMBLEY, DORCAS (77y 20d)   WF   Page 26
    29 Oct. 1892 - Paralysis   Spouse: Nath. Rumbley

RUSH, DABORA (56y)   WF   Page 22
    27 Jan. 1859 - Pneumonia   Parents: Geo. & Polly Brooks
                                     Spouse: Jerry Rush

RUSH, ISAAC V. (2y)   WM   Page 9
    31 July 1855 - Flux   Parents: Jas. & A.E. Rush

RUSH, MARY E. (5y 6m)   WF   Page 15
    31 Aug. 1857 - Fever   Parents: Jno. C. & Rachel Rush

RUST, [n.n.]   WF   Page 17
    30 Jan. 1858 - Born dead   Parents: Daniel & E. Rust

RUST, DAVID (1y 6m)   WM   Page 22
    24 Nov. 1859 - Fits   Parents: V.C. & Elizabeth Rust

RUST, ISAAC (5y 1m 2d)   WM   Page 6
    5 Aug. 1854 - Flux   Parents: Jeremiah & Ann Rust

RUTHERFORD, M.I.B. (23y 4m)   WF   Page 15   F
    23 Jan. 1857 - Fever   Parents: Arthur & Mary B. Stewart

RUTHERFORD, M.V. (18d)   WF   Page 29   Goodson Dist.
    24 July 1892 - Meningitis   Parents: Geo. & M. Rutherford

RUTLEDGE, BENJN. (2y)   WM   Page 2
    24 Dec. 1853 - Spinal affection   Father: Anthony Rutledge

RYAN, DAVID (5m)   WM   Page 4
    17 Nov. 1854 - Croup   Parents: James & Barbara Ryan

RYBURN, DAVID K. (2y 9m)   WM   Page 11
    29 Nov. 1856 - Fever   Parents: Jno. & Jane Ryburn

RYBURN, MARY (53y 2m)   WF   Page 26
    8 Feb. 1892 - La grippe   Spouse: W.S. Ryburn

RYBURN, MATTHEW (1y 1m 12d)   WM   Page 7
    2 May 1855 - Whooping cough   Parents: Jas. O. & Margaret Ryburn

RYBURN, SUSIE R. (1y 1m)   WF   Page 26
    19 March 1892 - Spasms   Parents: M.A. & M.A. Ryburn
    Reported by W.A. Ryburn, father

RYBURN, WILLIAM M. (3y 14d)   WM   Page 3
    9 Sept. 1854 - Dysentery   Parents: Wm. S. & Rebecca Ryburn

SAMUEL (20y)   SM   Page 2   F
    20 March 1853 - Consumption   Owner: Margaret R. White

SAML. (10y 5m)   SM   Page 11
    15 Aug. 1856 - Disentary   Owner: Abram McConnell

SAMUEL (70y)   SM   Page 19
    15 Sept. 1858 - Apoplectic fitt   Owner: W.G. Clark

SANDERS, AMANDA B. (1y)   WF   Page 12
    6 Sept. 1856 - Fever   Father: Wm. Sanders
    Reported by Wm. SAUNDERS, father

SANDERS, JAMES (13y)   WM   Page 6
    July 1854 - Lock jaw   Parents: Edwin & C. Sanders
    Reported by Francis Smith, uncle

SANDERS, MARGARET (1y)   WF   Page 1
    April 1853   Parents: Henry & Mary Sanders

SARAH (14y)   SF   Page 1
    17 June 1853 - Consumption   Master: Micajah McCormack

SARAH (4y)   SF   Page 17
    19 June 1858 - Flux   Owner: Gasper Fleenor

SARAH (35y)   SF   Page 20   F
    24 Feb. 1859 - Consumption   Master: Philip Anderson

SARAH (5y)   SF   Page 19
    10 May 1859 - Scarlet fev.   Master: Claburn L. Shugart

SCOTT, [n.n.]   WM   Page 17
    1 Dec. 1858 - Unknown   Parents: J.J. & Patsy Scott

SCOTT, ALEXANDER (25y)   WM   Page 19   F
    17 Dec. 1858 - Fever   Father: Alexander Scott
                                   Spouse: Elizabeth Scott

SCOTT, MARTHA (37y)   WF   Page 1
    4 June 1853 - Pneumonia   Parents: Obadiah & Jane Scott
                                   Spouse: Robert Scott

SCOTT, SAMUEL (26y 4m 24d)   WM   Page 1   F
    9 Oct. 1853   Reported by Wm. Scott

SCOTT, SARAH (80y)   WF   Page 27
    15 [March] 189] - La grippe   Reported by S.J. Henderson, daughter

SCOTT, WILLIAM (65y)   WM   Page 7   F
    28 Feb. 1855 - Consumption   Parents: Joseph & Mary Scott

SHAFFER, MARY (30y 15d)   WF   Page 9
    1 Sept. 1855 - Flux   Parents: E. & Sarah Pitts
                                   Spouse: Joel Shaffer

SHANKLE, LAFAYETTE M. (6y 10m)   WM   Page 18
    14 June 1858 - Flux   Parents: J.M. & M.A. Shankle

SHANKLE, LOW E.   WF   Page 23   Kinderhook
    3 Aug. 1871   Parents: George & Rebecca Shankle

SHARP, [n.n.] (15d)   WF   Page 20
    15 July 1859   Father: James Sharp

SHARP, EMMET B. (5y 5d)   WM   Page 3
    25 Sept. 1854 - Dysentery   Parents: Wm. C. & Nancy Sharp

SHARP, JAS. L. (71y)   WM   Page 26
    7 April 1892 - Paralysis   Reported by J.F. Jones, son in law

SHARP, MARGARET D. (17y)   WF   Page 8
    18 June 1855 - Consumption Parents: Benjn. & Mart. M. Sharp
    Reported by Wm. E. Sharp, brother

SHARP, MARGARET M. (56y)   WF   Page 8
    21 June 1855 - Consumption Parents: Robt. & Polly Edmundson
    Reported by Wm. E. Sharp, son   Spouse: Benjn. Sharp

SHARP, RICHARD E. (25y)   WM   Page 12   F
    24 Jan. 1856 - Consumption Parents: Richard E. & M. Sharp

SHARP, ROBT. E. (21y)   WM   Page 11   F
    19 Feb. 1856 - Consumption Parents: Benj. & Margret M. Sharp
    Reported by Wm. A. Sharp, brother

SHARRET, C.P. (70y)   WF   Page 28   Kinderhook
    31 Aug. 1892 - Old age   Reported by Y.W. South

SHARRETT, ELIZABETH (67y 8m) WF   Page 9
    14 Feb. 1855 - Rheumatism Parents: J. & C. Bealor
    Reported by Jacob Sharrett, son

SHARRITT, BETSY (45y 6m)   WF   Page 16   F
    9 Oct. 1857 - Dropsy   Parents: Abram & Cath Grubb
                       Spouse: Jacob SHARRETT

SHARRITT, ISAAC (34y)   WM   Page 16
    1 Nov. 1857 - Fever   Parents: Jno. & Eliz'th SHARRETT
    Reported by Benj. SHARRETT, brother

SHERWOOD, THOS. J. (5m 17d) WM   Page 19
    22 June 1858 - Liver complaint Father: Caleb Sherwood

SHUFFIELD, [n.n.]   WF   Page 14
    1 May 1857 - Still born   Father: Benjamine Shuffield

SHUPE, MARY (45y)   WF   Page 29   Goodson Dist.
    28 March 1892 - Consumption Mother: Malinda Breedlove
    Reported by husband

SHUPE, WILLIAM (1m 22d)   WM   Page 29   Goodson Dist.
    30 March 1892 - Fever   Parents: And. & M. Shupe

SHUPE, WM. F. (34y)   WM   Page 23   F
    26 Dec. 1871 - Assasenated Born in Abingdon Twp.; married

SIMMONS, LEANDER (25y)   WM   Page 29   Abingdon Dist.
    4 July 1892 - Killed by Berg Shortt   Father: William Simmons

SINGLETON, [n.n.] (16d)   WM   Page 28   North Fork
    1 July 1892 - Not known   Parents: W.G. & Eliz. Singleton

SINGLETON, [n.n.] (1d)   WF   Page 28   North Fork
    16 Nov. 1892 - Not known Parents: Thos. C. & S.C. Singleton

SINGLETON, RHODA (49y)   CF   Page 30   Town of Abingdon
    25 Aug. 1892 - Not known Parents: Peter & Eliz. Singleton
    Reported by Aron Longley

SINGLETON, S.C. (25y)   WF   Page 28   North Fork
    20 Nov. 1892 - Fever   Reported by husband
    Born in Dickenson Co., Va.

SISK, MARY (46y)   WF   Page 20   F
    26 June 1859 - Consumption   Spouse: John Sisk
    Reported by Timothy Sisk, son

SMITH, [n.n.] (1m)   WF   Page 1
    Oct. 1853   Father: Peter S. Smith

SMITH, [n.n.]   WF   Page 16
    20 Oct. 1857 - Still born   Mother: Elizabeth Smith

SMITH, ELIZTH. (30y 4m)   WF   Page 14   F
    24 May 1857 - Dropsy   Reported by Wm. Spears, son

SMITH, ELIZ. (81y)   WF   Page 26
    3 March 1892 - Gen. debility   Reported by A.M. Maxwell, nephew

SMITH, EPHRAIM F. (6y 6m)   WM   Page 11
    15 Nov. 1856 - Flux   Parents: Henry & Nancy Smith

SMITH, JAMES C.   WM   Page 2
    20 Oct. 1853 - Fever   Parents: Jas. K. & Isabella SMYTH
    Reported by Arthur D. Hutton, physician

SMITH, LOUISA (25d)   WF   Page 23
    13 Oct. 1871 - Enlargement of throat
    Born in Abingdon Twp.   Parents: Moses B. & Elizabeth Smith

SMITH, RUTH D. (6m)   CF   Page 27
    7 July 1892 - Not known   Parents: Saml. & Emma Smith

SMITH, SAMUEL (35y)   WM   Page 22
    4 April 1859 - Flux   Parents: Jas. & Martha Smith

SMITH, SARAH (99y)   WF   Page 17
    July 1858 - Flux   Parents: F. & S. Smith
    Reported by Susan Black, SON

SMITH, SUSAN (50y)   WF   Page 23   Kinderhook
    4 Nov. 1871   Parents: Daniel & Kate Smith
                                     Spouse: John Smith

SMYTH, ELIZ. F. (72y 2m)   WF   Page 26
    23 Jan. 1892 - Pneumonia   Reported by Jas. K. Smyth, brother

SNODGRASS, [n.n.] (1m)   WM   Page 2
    14 April 1853   Father: James M. Snodgrass

SNODGRASS, BENJAMIN (76y)   WM   Page 14   F
    22 Jan. 1857 - Diareah   Father: David Snodgrass
                                     Spouse: Elizth. Snodgrass

SNODGRASS, JAS. A. (11m)   WM   Page 10
    Oct. 1856 - Fever   Parents: Wm. & Cath Snodgrass

SNIDER, [JNS.] F. (21y)   WM   Page 24   F   Glade Spring
    1871 - Neuralgia   Parents: W.M. & America Snider
    Born in Smyth Co., Va.

220

SNODGRASS, RACHEL (44y 3m 27d)   WF   Page 19
    3 Nov. 1858 - Consumption   Father: Alexander Robertson
                                        Spouse: William Snodgrass

SNODGRASS, REBECCA C. (3y)   WF   Page 10
    8 Sept. 1856 - Fever   Parents: Wm. & Cath. Snodgrass

SNOW, ROBERT (4m)   WM   Page 28   Kinderhook
    5 June 1892 - Flux   Parent: M.C. Snow

SOURBEER, [n.n.] (1d)   WF   Page 29   Goodson Dist.
    26 July 1892 - Not known   Parents: A.J. & S.B. Sourbeer

SOURBEER, SUSAN B. (33y)   WF   Page 29   Goodson Dist.
    29 July 1892 - Disease of lungs   Parents: J.B. & Sally Wagner
    Reported by husband

SPAHR, HENRY (63y 7m)   WM   Page 9
    11 Aub. 1855 - Flux   Parents: H. & N. Spahr
    Reported by T.J. Spahr, son

SPEAR, ARTHUR (66y)   WM   Page 8
    24 Feb. 1855 - Dropsey   Parents: James & Jane SPEER
    Reported by Uns. Rae, sister

SPEAR, LUCY (18m)   WF   Page 28   Kinderhook
    10 April 1892 - Flux   Parent: T.H. Spear

SPEAR, MARY E. (20y)   WF   Page 4
    7 Oct. 1854 - Dysentery   Parents: Wm. & Milly Spear

SPEAR, WM. JAMES (16y 20d)   WM   Page 1
    28 May 1853 - Consumption   Parents: Wm. & Milley Spear

SPEARS, [n.n.]   WM   Page 19
    30 May 1858   Parent: W.T. Spears

SPEARS, NANCY (87y)   WF   Page 14   F
    24 May 1857 - Typhoid fev.   Reported by Wm. Spears, son

SPRIGGS, NOAH C. BALDWIN (1m 10d)   WM   Page 8
    25 June 1855 - Not known   Parents: Carey & Mary Spriggs
    Reported by CARY Spriggs, father

SPROLES, JANE (54y)   WF   Page 23   Kinderhook
    15 Sept. 1871 - Cancer   Spouse: Dempsey Sproles

SPROLES, JOHN C. (22y)   WM   Page 6   F
    5 Nov. 1854 - Flux   Parents: Jonathan & Nancy Sproles
    Reported by Abram F. Bradley, neighbor

SPROLES, RACHEL (63y 1m)   WF   Page 22
    8 Feb. 1859 - Rheumatism   Parents: Thos. & Rebecca Barker
                                        Spouse: James Sproles

SPROLES, SAMUEL (30y 4m)   WM   Page 22
    4 Aub. 1859 - Flux   Parents: Isaac & Susan Sproles

SPURGEON, ALLEN (3y 1d)   WM   Page 9
    11 Jan. 1855 - Flux   Parents: Wm. & Mary Spurgeon

SPURRIER, SALLIE (5y)   SF   Page 16
    20 Nov. 1857 - Fever   Owner: William Spurrier

STANFIELD, JAMES (19y)   WM   Page 28   F   North Fork D
    10 April 1892 - Fever   Parents: Jas. & Car. Stanfield

STARKS, D[?] (6y 4m)   WM   Page 16
    20 Sept. 1857 - Fever   Parents: Wm. & Barb Starks

STARKS, PARLINA (4y)   WF   Page 16
    20 Sept. 1857 - Fever   Parents: Wm. & Barb. Starks

STATA, [n.n.] (1d)   WM   Page 28   North Fork
    11 Nov. 1892 - Not known   Parents: Ap. & Sarah Stata

STATZER, JACOB (7y)   WM   Page 6
    1 Sept. 1854 - Flux   Parents: Jacob & Polly Statzer

STEVENS, CUMMINGS (35y)   WM   Page 29   Abingdon Dis
    June 1892 - Killed by lightning   Parents: Thos. & Susan Stevens
    Reported by brother

STEVENS, FRANS. C. (4y 4d)   WM   Page 6
    Sept. 1854 - Flux   Parents: Russell & Mary Stevens

STEVENS, TELITHA C. (18y 2m)   WF   Page 6
    10 Sept. 1854 - Flux   Parents: David & Rebecca Stevens

STEVENS, WM. C. (2y)   WM   Page 6
    Sept. 1854 - Flux   Parents: Russell & Mary Stevens

STEWART, ARTHUR (55y 11m)   WM   Page 10   F
    5 Sept. 1856 - Consumption   Parents: Wm. & Mary Stewart
                                   Spouse: Mary B. Stewart

STEWART, ROBT. R. (11y 5m)   WM   Page 16
    9 Jan. 1857 - Fever   Parents: Arthur & Mary B. Stewart

STEWART, SARAH (45y 1m)   WF   Page 22
    24 July 1859 - Flux   Parents: Wm. & Sarah Buchanan
                                   Spouse: James Stewart

STEWART, WM. B. (22y 4m)   WM   Page 22
    24 June 1859 - Flux   Parents: Arthur & Mary B. Stewart

STOUT, JAMES D. (11m)   WM   Page 1
    20 Nov. 1853   Parents: George W. & Julia Ann Stout

STUART, [n.n.] (4m 3d)   WF   Page 7   Near Cedarvi
    1855 - Dysentery   Parents: David & Ellen Stuart

STUART, D.M. (71y)   WM   Page 26   F
    1 Aug. 1892 - Paralysis   Reported by Geo. Stuart, son

STURGEON, LETITIA (65y)   WF   Page 1
    24 June 1853   Reported by Harvey Sturgeon

STURGEON, PETER (1y)   WM   Page 12
    7 Oct. 1856 - Fever   Parents: Harry & May Sturgeon

SULLIVAN, SOPHRONIA (6m 29d)   WF   Page 3
    25 Sept. 1854 - Dysentery   Parents: Wiley & Sarah SULIVAN

SUSONG, MARGARET B. (7y)   WF   Page 2
    9 Dec. 1843   Parents: Mahlon S. & E. Susong

SUTTON, MARGARET (62y)   WF   Page 6
    28 Sept. 1854 - Consumption Parents: Alex & Mary E. Eakin
                              Spouse: John Sutton

SWEENY, WM.   WM   Page 23
    11 June 1871 - Abscess on back   Parents: Thomas & Jane Sweeney
    Born in North Fork Twp.

SWEET, [n.n.] (3y)   W_   Page 10
    10 April 1856 - Cramp   Parents: F.P. & Charity Sweet

SWEET, R.M. (1y 7m)   WF   Page 26
    23 Aug. 1892 - Flux   Parents: W.L. & S. Sweet

SYKES, MARTHA E. (2y)   WF   Page 28   North Fork
    15 July 1892 - Not known Parents: Noah & Jane Sykes

SYPHER, ROBERT (8y)   WM   Page 29   Abingdon Dist.
    10 Nov. 1892 - Typhoid fev. Parents: David & E. SYPHIS

SYPHERS, [n.n.] (1d)   W_   Page 23
    7 June 1871 - Infancy   Parents: J.T. & M.E. Syphers

TALBERT, NANCY (65y)   WF   Page 5   Near Saltville
    24 June 1854   Parents: Thos. & Agatha Talbert
    Reported by Basil Talbert, brother

TALBERT, WILLIAM (1y)   WM   Page 12
    26 April 1856 - S. fever   Father: Basil Talbert

TALLEY, [n.n.]   WF   Page 16
    23 Oct. 1857 - Still born Parents: Cranford & Nancy Talley

TALLY, [n.n.] (14d)   WM   Page 4
    Nov. 1854   Parents: Iven & Delila Tally
    Reported by Andw. D. Grubb, neighbor

TARLTON (5m)   SM   Page 10
    Aug. 1855 - Flux   Owner: John Preston

TATE, [n.n.] (15d)   WM   Page 9
    30 March 1855   Parents: David & M. Tate

TATE, JULIA ANN (2y)   WF   Page 18
    14 July 1856 - Flux   Parents: Drury & Ellen Tate

TATE, SARAH E. (4y 6m)   WF   Page 18
    6 Sept. 1858 - Fever   Parents: Jas. & Martha Tate

TERRY, JOSEPH (6m)   WM   Page 27
    22 March 1892 - Pneumonia Parents: J.B. & Sarah Terry

TERRY, MARY E. (12y 7m) WF   Page 19
    8 Oct. 1858 - Neuralgia   Father: William Terry

THOMAS, [n.n.]   WM   Page 19
    10 Dec. 1858 - Born dead Father: Isaac Thomas

THOMAS, BARBARA (75y) WF   Page 5   Allisons Gap
    1854 - Old age   Father: Wm. Jennings
    Reported by Andw. Thomas, son   Spouse: John Thomas

THOMAS, DAVID (62y)   WM   Page 3   F
        25 Oct. 1854 - Dysentery   Parents: Jno. & Betsey Thomas
        Born in Smyth Co., Va.   Spouse: Lucy Thomas

THOMAS, DAVID J. (10m)   WM   Page 5   Widener Valle
        23 July 1854 - Dysentery   Mother: Nancy Thomas

THOMAS, DELILA JANE (4y 3m 13d)   WF   Page 7
        21 Feb. 1855 - Inflammation in brain
                                    Parents: Saml. & Matilda Thomas

THOMAS, FRANK (34y)   CM   Page 30   Goodson Dist.
        28 Dec. 1892 - Not known   Parents: Wm. & Sally Thomas
        Reported by Richard Brown, friend

THOMAS, JENIN. (11y)   WF   Page 27
        14 Aug. 1892 - Flux   Parents: Jas. & Ann Thomas
        Reported by F.C. Duff, friend

THOMAS, JOSEPH (3d)   WM   Page 20
        10 March 1859 - Scarlet fev. Father: Joseph Thomas

THOMAS, LOUISA (3y 2m)   WF   Page 19
        27 July 1858 - Diarrhea   Father: Stephen Thomas

THOMAS, SARAH F. (3d)   WF   Page 20
        28 Jan. 1859 - Scarlet fev. Father: William Thomas

THOMPSON, ADA L. (4m 13d)   WF   Page 27
        24 Sept. 1892 - Croup   Parents: J.H. & E.N. Thompson

THOMPSON, MARGARET E. (1y 5m)   WF   Page 5   Rich Valley
        Nov. 1854 - Dysentery   Parents: Jas. H. & Susan Thompson

TILLSON, [n.n.] (1m)   WF   Page 24   Glade Spring
        1871   Parents: A. & E. Tillson

TILLSON, DAVID (69y)   WM   Page 24   F   Glade Spring
        1871 - Pneumonia   Parents: Thos. & Unice Tillson
        Born in Smyth Co., Va.

TILLSON, SAMPSON (24y)   WM   Page 24   TC   Glade Spring
        1871 - White swelling   Parents: D. & E. Tillson

TODD, MALINDA (1y 6m)   WF   Page 22
        27 July 1859 - Flux   Parents: William & A.J. Todd

TOMLINSON, SOPH. (9m 20d)   WF   Page 27
        8 Dec. 1892 - Whooping cough   Parents: L.L. & S.F. Tomlinson

TONCRAY, MARY (82y)   WF   Page 18
        15 July 1858 - Fever   Spouse: Lewis Toncray
        Reported by J.L. Gillenwaters

TOOL, JNO. A. (22y)   WM   Page 13   F
        8 April 1856 - Inflamation Father: Jacob Tool

TRAMEL, MARY F. (1y 6m)   WF   Page 10
        8 Sept. 1856 - Fever   Parents: Harden J. & Frs. Tramel

TRAMEL, SARAH E. (2y 10m)   WF   Page 10
        9 Oct. 1856 - Fever   Parents: Wm. & L.W. Tramel

TRAMEL, SARAH G. (4y 4m 4d)   WF   Page 10
  4 Sept. 1856 - Fever   Parents: Harden J. & Frs. Tramel

TRENT, MARY (81y 7m)   WF   Page 27
  8 Aug. 1892 - Dropsey   Reported by Mrs. Thomas, daughter

TRENT, MATILDA (33y)   WF   Page 12
  27 Feb. 1856 - Consumption   Reported by Andrew Trent, son

TRENT, OLIVER W. (6y 5m)   WM   Page 27
  11 Nov. 1892 - Heart disease Parents: Lewis & Eliz. Trent

TRIGG, JANE (75y)   WF   Page 29   Abingdon Dist.
  19 Aug. 1892 - Fever   Parents: Jno. & Cath Davis
  Reported by A.F. Trigg

TROXELL, CATHERINE (75y)   WF   Page 19
  10 April 1858 - Diareah   Father: Jacob Huffaker
  Reported by Geo. W. Troxell, son   Spouse: D. Troxell

TURNER, LINIE (25y)   WF   Page 28   Kinderhook
  10 Dec. 1892 - Flux   Reported by James Turner

VANCE, DAVID V. (1y 8m)   WM   Page 18
  2 July 1858 - Fever   Parents: James & Mary Vance

VANCE, PEGLANTINE (25y 9m)   WF   Page 16   F
  25 Jan. 1857 - Flux   Parents: Shelton & W. Thompson
    Spouse: Jno. A. Vance

VANDERPOOL, JULIA O. (27y)   WF   Page 23
  18 Jan. 1871 - Consumption

VANDERPOOL, RACHEL (70y)   WF   Page 24   F
  1871 - Consumption   Parents: Alex & Nancy Robinson

VANHUSS, ADAM R. (17y 4m 27d)   WM   Page 8
  7 April 1855 - Drowned   Parents: Christ. & Cath. Vanhuss

VANHUSS, BENJAMIN (3m)   WM   Page 21
  26 Dec. 1859 - Pneumonia   Father: Valentine Vanhuss

VANHUSS, CATHERINE (1y 5m)   WF   Page 14
  10 April 1857 - Scarlet fev. Father: Anthony Vanhuss

VANHUSS, COLSEN C. (4y 4m)   WM   Page 3
  7 Oct. 1854 - Dysentery   Parents: Christoph. & Catharine Vanhuss

VANHUSS, EMELINE (7y 4m)   WF   Page 3
  10 Oct. 1854 - Dysentery   Parents: Christoph. & Catharine Vanhuss

VAWTER, CLARY V. (5m)   WF   Page 24   Glade Spring
  1871   Parents: C.E. & V.F. Vawter

VESTAL, ALLEN (12y)   WM   Page 12
  12 Feb. 1856 - Fl.   Father: John Vestal

VESTAL, JAMES (88y)   WM   Page 8
  23 Aug. 1855 - Old age   Reported by James Lowrey, neighbor

VINEY (7m)   SF   Page 21
  15 April 1859 - Scarlet fev. Master: Geo. W. Alderson

WALDEN, LEWIS J. (35y)   WM   Page 12   F
    20 Aug. 1856 - Pneumonia

WALDEN, MILLY (60y)   WF   Page 7
    14 April 1855 - Palsey   Father: Wm. Hunt
    Reported by Lewis J. Walden, son   Spouse: Lewis Walden

WALDEN, SINAH J. (8y 11m 25d)   WF   Page 7
    7 July 1855 - Inflammation in brain
                                Parents: Lewis J. & Sarah J. Walden

WALLACE, CHARLES H. (4y 3m 20d) WM   Page 6
    11 Oct. 1854 - Flux   Parents: Jno. H. & Martha Wallace
    Reported by JAS. H. Wallace, father

WALLACE, JNO. H. (8y 10m)   WM   Page 6
    21 Aug. 1854 - Flux   Parents: Jno. H. & Martha Wallace
    Reported by JAS. H. Wallace, father

WAMPLER, CATHARINE (29y)   WF   Page 7
    28 Dec. 1855 - Consumption Parents: Thos. & Mary Grogan
                                Spouse: Jno. Wampler

WARREN, BASIL (71y 11m)   WM   Page 9
    26 Dec. 1855 - Old age   Parents: George & E. Warren
    Reported by Henry Roberts, son in law

WARD, CHARLES M. (1m)   WM   Page 23
    4 Jan. 1871 - Not known   Parents: Ota H. & Martha L. Ward
    Born in North Fork Twp.

WARREN, JAMES C. (33y)   WM   Page 6   F
    27 Oct. 1892 - Consumption Parents: Basil & M. Warren
    Reported by W.B. Warren, brother

WARREN, NANCY (52y)   WF   Page 2
    28 Sept. 1853 - Consumption Spouse: Walter Warren

WARREN, SARAH (72y)   WF   Page 28   F   North Fork
    15 April 1892 - La grippe   Reported by Nancy Warren

WARD, SUSANAH (4y 8m)   WF   Page 14
    9 May 1857 - Scarlet fev.   Father: Otah H. Ward
    Reported by Martha Duff, sister

WASHAM, WM. (56y)   WM   Page 24   Saltville
    1871

WATERMAN, E.L. (22y)   WM   Page 22   Sullivan Co.,
    31 Aug. 1859 - Fever   Parents: L.L. & Mary A. Waterman

WATSON, [n.n.]   WF   Page 18
    15 Dec. 1858 - Born dead   Parents: Henry & Jane Watson

WATSON, MARTHA (54y)   WF   Page 3
    30 Sept. 1854 - Consumption Parents: Robt. & Martha Clark
    Born in Scotland   Spouse: James Watson

WATSON, MARTIN (2m)   WF   Page 28   Kinderhook
    30 Dec. 1892 - Flux   Parents: Wm. & Harriet Watson

WATSON, ROBERT (19y)   WM   Page 3
    11 June 1854 - Consumption   Parents: James & Martha Watson

WATSON, ROBERT (64y)   WM   Page 22
    17 June 1859 - Fever   Parents: Jas. & Margaret Watson
    Born in Ireland   Spouse: Jane Watson

WEATHERLEY, HIRAM W. (3m)   WM   Page 3
    7 Sept. 1854 - Dysentery   Parents: Hosea & Ann Weatherley

WEATHERLEY, MARTHA E. (7y)   WF   Page 3
    1 Sept. 1854 - Dysentery   Parents: Hosea M. & Ann Weatherley

WEATHERLY, N.W. (40y)   WF   Page 28   Kinderhook
    15 Aug. 1859 - Brain fev.

WELCH, SALLY (25y)   WF   Page 1
    9 Oct. 1853   Father: Obadiah Neal
    Reported by Eliza Neal   Spouse: Patrick Welch

WELLS, PRIER L. (27y 1m 12d)   WM   Page 8
    9 June 1855 - Neuralgia   Parent: [Armina] Wells
    Born in Smyth Co., Va.

WHEATLY, GEO. A. (6y 3d)   WM   Page 16
    19 Sept. 1857 - Flux   Parents: Wm. & Lucinda Wheatley

WHEELER, SUSAN (22y 6m)   WF   Page 16   F
    10 Nov. 1857 - Consumption   Parents: Alfred & R. Richards
    Reported by Jno. Richards, brother   Spouse: Francis Wheeler

WHICKER, [n.n.]   WF   Page 18
    11 March 1858 - Born dead   Parents: Saml. & E. Whicker

WHICKER, EDWIN C. (3y)   WM   Page 18
    11 Oct. 1858 - Fever   Parents: Saml. & E. Whicker

WHICKER, N.P.M. (37y 5m)   WF   Page 22
    5 Oct. 1859 - Fever   Parents: Fred & Ann Leonard
    Reported by Zach Jordon, neighbor   Spouse: Newell Whicker

WHIT, DAVID K. (1y)   WM   Page 29   North Fork
    12 Nov. 1892 - Not known   Parents: F.H. & Balie Whit

[WHIT], GEORGE (4y)   WM   Page 28   North Fork
    12 Nov. 1892 - Fever   Reported by M.H. Warren

WHIT, SARAH (6y)   WF   Page 29   North Fork
    25 Sept. 1892 - Fever   Parents: F.H. & Polly Whit

WHITE, AMANDA J. (12y)   WF   Page 29   North Fork
    6 Oct. 1892 - Typhoid fev.   Parents: R.E. & Mary White

WHITE, CATHARINE (2y)   WF   Page 9
    15 Sept. 1855 - Flux   Parents: P.H. & E. White

WHITE, ISAAC N. (7y 5m)   WM   Page 18
    5 March 1858 - Flux   Parents: John & Hannah White

WHITE, JULIA (78y)   WF   Page 29   North Fork
    8 Oct. 1892 - Not known

WHITE, MARY   WF   Page 24   Glade Spring
    1871 - Consumption   Parents: Robt. & Mary White

WHITE, MOLLIE (13y)   WF   Page 29   North Fork
    22 Jan. 1892 - Fever   Parents: Robt. & Mary White

WHITE, MOLLIE (13y)   WF   Page 29   North Fork
    8 Oct. 1892 - Fever   Parents: R.E. & Mary White

WHITE, THOMAS (1y 2m)   WM   Page 19
    26 May 1858 - Spasms   Father: Patrick White

WHITE, THURSA A.J. (9m)   WF   Page 18
    7 Aug. 1858 - Flux   Parents: Spencer & E.J. White

WIDENER, [n.n.]   WM   Page 21
    15 June 1859   Father: Elias Widener

WIDENER, AMY C. (7y)   WMF   Page 5   Widener Valle\
    9 Sept. 1854 - Dysentery   Parents: Philip & Winney Widener

WIDENER, ANDREW (11y)   WM   Page 14
    20 Sept. 1857 - Consumption   Father: Joel Widener

WIDENER, ANDW. B. (1y 6m)   WM   Page 5   Widener Valle\
    25 Sept. 1854 - Dysentery   Parents: Philip & Winny Widener

WIDENER, ELIZA (9m)   WF   Page 12
    20 Aug. 1856 - Unknown   Parents: Andrew & Eliza Widener

WIDENER, ELIZABETH (12y)   WF   Page 3
    July 1854 - Dysentery   Parents: James & Martha Widener
    Reported by Peter Mock, neighbor

WIDENER, ELIZABETH (44y)   WF   Page 21   F
    26 Sept. 1859 - Consumption   Spouse: Elijah Widener

WIDENER, EPHRAIM (7y)   WM   Page 3
    6 July 1854 - Dysentery   Parents: Jacob & Sarah Widener

WIDENER, ISAAC (8y)   WM   Page 4
    27 Sept. 1854 - Dysentery   Parents: Wm. S. & Phoebe Widener

WIDENER, JOHN (5y 1m)   WM   Page 4
    4 Oct. 1854 - Dysentery   Parents: Wm. S. & Phoebe Widener

WIDENER, KISIAH (17y)   WF   Page 21   F
    15 Aug. 1859 - Consumption   Father: Jacob R. Widener

WIDENER, MARTH. (7y)   WF   Page 3
    July 1854 - Dysentery   Parents: James & Martha Widener
    Reported by Peter Mock, neighbor

WIDENER, MARY (21y)   WF   Page 14
    1 June 1857 - Inflamation   Father: Samuel Widener
    Reported by Saml. Widener, f. in law

WIDENER, MARY JANE (9y 7m)   WF   Page 5   Widener Valley
    14 Aug. 1854 - Dysentery   Parents: Philip & Winney Widener

WIDENER, MOSES (9y)   WM   Page 5   Widener Valley
    Sept. 1854 - Dysentery   Parents: Elijah & Elizabeth Widener

WIDENER, OBEDIENCE (76y)   WF   Page 5   Widener Valley
    7 Sept. 1854 - Old age   Parents: Thos. & Hannah Owen
    Born in Wilks Co., N.C.   Spouse: Jno. Widener
    Reported by Andw. Widener, son & adm'r

WIDENER, PHOEBE (45y)   WF   Page 4
    4 Oct. 1854 - Dysentery   Parents: Jas. & Polly Snodgrass
                             Spouse: Wm. S. Widener

WIDENER, RICHARD (2y)   WM   Page 5   Widener Valley
    Sept. 1854 - Dysentery   Parents: Elijah & Elizabeth Widener

WIDENER, SUSAN (1y 6m)   WF   Page 1
    1 June 1853   Father: Ryburn Widener

WIDENER, WILLIAM W. (6y 6m)   WM   Page 5   Widener Valley
    Oct. 1854 - Dysentery   Parents: David S. & Nancy Widener

WILEY, CHAS. S. (8m)   WM   Page 7   E. & H. College
    1 July 1855 - Unknown   Parents: Ephn. E. & Elizabeth Wiley
    Born at E. & H. College

WILEY, M.F. (29y)   WM   Page 14   PH   Ash Co., N.C.
    1 Feb. 1857 - Inflamation   Spouse: Mary Wiley
    Reported by J.W. Davis, f. in law

WILLIAM (5y)   SM   Page 7
    Aug. 1855 - Dysentery   Mother: Martha
                             Reported by Saml. Dunn, owner & physician

WILLIAMS, [n.n.] (1d)   WF   Page 29   North Fork
    21 Sept. 1892 - Not known   Parents: B.F. & Jude Williams

WILLIAMS, MARTHA JANE (23y)   WF   Page 7
    12 Aug. 1855 - Dysentery   Parents: Jno. J. & Susan Clark
                             Spouse: David S. Williams

WILLIAMS, WM. (45y)   WM   Page 29   North Fork
    22 Dec. 1892 - Consumption   Reported by wife

WILLIS, JOHN (45y)   WM   Page 9
    20 Dec. 1855 - Killed   Parents: A. & E. Willis
    Reported by James. L. Davis, neighbor

WILLOUGHBY, SUSAN (65y)   WF   Page 18
    18 Aug. 1858 - Flux   Parents: Daniel & Sarah Kaylor
                             Spouse: Wallace Willoughby

WITHERSPOON, [n.n.] (1d)   WM   Page 29   North Fork
    20 Feb. 1892 - Not known   Parents: S.J. & Sarah Witherspoon

WITSEL, BENJ. F. (11d)   WM   Page 10
    23 Sept. 1856 - Unknown   Parents: Jeff & Catherine Wetsel

WILSON, [n.n.] (1d)   WF   Page 9
    5 May 1855 - Cough   Parents: Nathl. D. & E. Wilson

WILSON, DAVID (1y 4m)   WM   Page 1
    July 1853   Parents: John M. & Mary Wilson

WILSON, DOLLY ANN (2y 2m)   WF   Page 4
    Oct. 1854 - Croup   Parents: Andw. J. & Eliz'th Wilson

WILSON, [LEVISEY] (2y)   WF   Page 3
     4 Oct. 1854 - Dysentery   Parents: Jno. B. & Mary Wilson

WILSON, MARTHA (28y)   WF   Page 10
     1 June 1856 - Ulcer   Parents: Jno. & Betty Wood
                                 Spouse: Abel Wilson

WILSON, MICAJAH M. (2y 4m 20d) WF   Page 10
     29 April 1856 - Fever   Parents: A.T. & Ellen Wilson

WOOD, WM.   WM   Page 23   Kinderhook
     12 Sept. 1871   Parents: Dempsy & M. Wood

WOODARD, JAMES (5y)   WM   Page 13
     5 Aug. 1856 - Scarlet fev. Father: Bartley Woodard
     Reported by Bartley WOODWARD, father

WOODARD, JULIA (2y)   WF   Page 13
     5 Aug. 1856 - Scarlet fev. Father: Bartley Woodard
     Reported by Bartley WOODWARD, father

WOOTEN, ELIZABETH (21y)   WF   Page 12
     18 June 1856 - Plurisy   Parents: Jehu & Frs. Wooten
     Born in North Carolina

WORLEY, [n.n.]   WF   Page 6
     Aoril 1854 - Stillborn   Parents: L. & Jemima Worley

WORLEY, AMANDA (35y)   WF   Page 22
     3 Oct. 1859 - Fever   Parents: Jas. & Nancy Buchanan
                                 Spouse: Geo. L. Worley

WORLEY, JOANAH (5y)   WF   Page 28   Kinderhook
     10 Dec. 1892 - Burned to death   Parent: J.K. Worley

WORLEY, JNO. W. (78y)   WM   Page 29   Kinderhook
     12 May 1892 - Perelses   Parents: R.E. & Mary White
     Reported by a friend

WORLEY, MIMA (35y 9m)   WF   Page 22
     15 Feb. 1859 - Fever   Parents: Frank & Elizabeth Moore
                                   Spouse: Leander Worley

WORLEY, NATHAN (31y 25d)   WM   Page 10   F
     27 Feb. 1856 - Consumption Parents: Nat. & Susan Worley

WORLEY, SUSAN (73y 10m)   WF   Page 13
     3 Dec. 1858   Parents: M. & L. Worley
     Reported by Geo. L. Worley, son   Spouse: Nathan Worley

WORSHAM, W.D. (60y)   WM   Page 29   Goodson Dist.
     19 March 1892 - Pneumonia Reported by son

WRIGHT, [n.n.]   WF   Page 14
     24 Oct. 1857 - Still born Father: Jas. H. Wright

WRIGHT, ANDREW (3m)   WM   Page 12
     27 Jan. 1856 - Unknown   Parents: And. & Dorcas Wright
     Reported by Andrew RIGHT, father

WRIGHT, FRS. P. (35y)   WF   Page 14
    24 Oct. 1857 - Consumption   Father: Benjamin Sharp
                               Spouse: Jas. H. Wright

WRIGHT, JOHN J. (3m)   WM   Page 3
    13 July 1854 - Dysentery or flux   Parents: Robt. & Dicey Wright

WRIGHT, OLIVER (62y 8m)   CM   Page 10   F
    7 July 1855 - Stabed   Reported by Jno. J. Scott, neighbor

WRIGHT, REBECCA (9d)   WF   ·Page 23   Kinderhook
    24 Dec. 1871 - Congestion of lungs
                               Parents: R.A. & Rebecca Wright

WYETT, ANDW. E. (7m 7d)   WM   Page 3
    29 July 1854 - Dysentery   Parents: Wm. & Emiline WRIGHT

YANCY, MILTON H. (1y)   WM   Page 19
    8 July 1858   Father: Stephen Yancy

ZIMERMAN, ABRAM C. (4y)   WM   Page 2
    23 April 1853 - Inflammation brain
                               Parents: Benjn. F. & M. Zimerman

ZIMERMAN, B.F. (33y)   WM   Page 6   DO
    11 Nov. 1854 - Fever   Parents: Abram & Mary C. Zimerman
                               Spouse: Martha Zimerman

www.ingramcontent.com/pod-product-compliance
Lightning Source LLC
Chambersburg PA
CBHW080418270326
41929CB00018B/3073